About the Author

Born in Germany, Edgar Rothermich studied music and sound engineering at the prestigious Tonmeister program at the Berlin Institute of Technology (TU) and the University of Arts (UdK) in Berlin where he graduated in 1989 with a Master's Degree. He worked as a composer and music producer in Berlin and moved to Los Angeles in 1991 where he continued his work on numerous projects in the music and film industry ("The Celestine Prophecy", "Outer Limits", "Babylon 5", "What the Bleep Do We Know", "Fuel", and "Big Money Rustlas").

For the past 20 years Edgar has had a successful musical partnership with electronic music pioneer and founding Tangerine Dream member Christopher Franke. Recently in addition to his collaboration with Christopher, Edgar has been working with other artists, as well as on his own projects.

In 2010 he started to release his solo records in the "Why Not …" series with different styles and genres. The current releases are "Why Not Solo Piano", "Why Not Electronica", "Why Not Electronica Again", and "Why Not 90s Electronica". This previously unreleased album was produced in 1991/1992 by Christopher Franke. All albums are available on Amazon and iTunes, including the 2012 release, the re-recording of the Blade Runner Soundtrack.

In addition to composing music, Edgar Rothermich is writing technical manuals with a unique style, focusing on rich graphics and diagrams to explain concepts and functionality of software applications under his popular GEM series (Graphically Enhanced Manuals). His bestselling titles are available as printed books on Amazon, as Multi-Touch iBooks on the iBookstore, and as pdf downloads from his website.
(languages: English, Deutsch, Español, 简体中文)

www.DingDingMusic.com   GEM@DingDingMusic.com

About the Editor

Many thanks to Mike Stine for editing and proofreading my manual www.mikefreelancer.com.

Special Thanks

Special thanks to my beautiful wife Li for her love, support, and understanding during those long hours of working on the books. And not to forget my son, Winston. Waiting for him during soccer practice or Chinese class always gives me extra time to work on a few chapters.

The manual is based on GarageBand X v10.0.2

Book: Print Version 2014-0526

ISBN-13: 978-1494897963

ISBN-10: 1494897962

Copyright © 2014 Edgar Rothermich

All rights reserved

Disclaimer: While every precaution has been taken in the writing of this manual, the author has no liability to any person or entity in respect to any damage or loss alleged to be caused by the instructions in this manual.

About the GEM (Graphically Enhanced Manuals)

UNDERSTAND, not just LEARN

What are Graphically Enhanced Manuals? They're a new type of manual with a visual approach that helps you UNDERSTAND a program, not just LEARN it. No need to read through 500 of pages of dry text explanations. Rich graphics and diagrams help you to get that "aha" effect and make it easy to comprehend difficult concepts. The Graphically Enhanced Manuals help you master a program much faster with a much deeper understanding of concepts, features and workflows in a very intuitive way that is easy to understand.

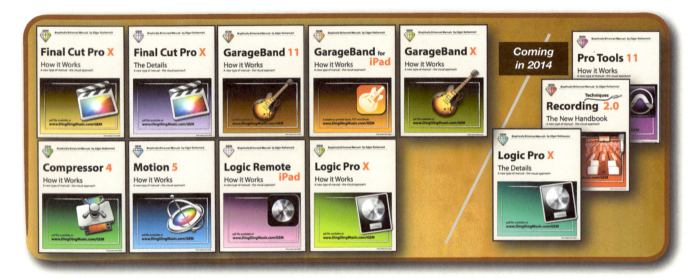

All titles are available in three different formats (languages: English, Deutsch, Español, 简体中文)

.... pdf downloads from my website www.DingDingMusic.com/Manuals

.... interactive multi-touch iBooks on Apple's iBook Store

.... printed books on Amazon.com

For a list of all the available titles and bundles: www.DingDingMusic.com/Manuals
To be notified about new releases and updates, subscribe to subscribe@DingDingMusic.com

About the Formatting

I use a specific color code in my books:

Green colored text indicates keyboard shortcuts or mouse actions. I use the following abbreviations: **sh** (shift key), **ctr** (control key), **opt** (option key), **cmd** (command key). A plus (+) between the keys means that you have to press all those keys at the same time.
sh+opt+K means: Hold the shift and the option key while pressing the K key.
Brown colored text indicates Menu Commands with a greater sign (➤) indicating submenus.
Edit ➤ Source Media ➤ All means "Click on the Edit Menu, scroll down to Source Media and select the submenu All.
Blue arrows indicate what happens if you click on an item or popup menu

Table of Contents

1 - Introduction — 6
- My Approach — 6
- Your Level — 7
- What is GarageBand — 8
- GarageBand - the big picture — 10
- What you will Learn — 13

2 - Prior Knowledge — 14
- OSX Window Elements — 14
- Directories — 18
- Package File — 19
- Traditional Studio — 20
- Tracks vs Channels — 23
- Hardware Setup — 27
- Devices — 31
- MIDI — 38
- Mono - Stereo — 40
- Digital Audio — 42

3 - Getting Started — 44
- Installing GarageBand X — 44
- User Interface — 51
- GarageBand 6.0.5 vs GarageBand 10.0 — 55

4 - The Project — 60
- Basics — 60
- Project Chooser — 64
- File Menu — 67
- Autosave — 72

5 - Tracks Area — 73
- Tracks Area — 73
- Ruler — 80

6 - Control Bar — 82
- View Buttons — 83
- Mode Buttons — 86
- Master Volume — 90
- Control Bar Display (LCD) — 91
- Transport Controls — 95

7 - Tracks — 99
- Type of Tracks — 100
- Create a new Track — 104
- Global Tracks — 108
- Tracks - under the hood — 109
- Track Header — 112

8 - Smart Controls — 119
- A New Concept — 119
- The Interface — 126
- Effects — 136

9 - Library — 138
- Window Pane — 138
- Patch — 139
- Library — 140

10 - Regions — 144
- Types of Regions — 145
- Where do Regions come from? — 148

11 - Recording MIDI — 149
- Checklist — 149
- Recording Procedure — 154
- MIDI Signal Routing — 157

12 - Recording Audio — 158
- Audio Signal Routing — 158
- Checklist — 161
- Recording Procedure — 168

13 - Media Browser — 173
- Basics — 173
- Import Audio — 177
- Import Movies — 181

14 - Apple Loops — 182
- Delicious Canned Food — 182
- Basics — 183
- Types of Loops — 188
- Loop Browser — 192
- Create your own Apple Loops — 198

15 - Editing Regions (in the Workspace) — 199
- Basics — 199
- Region Editing — 202
- Editors Window — 207

16 - Editing MIDI — 209

    MIDI Editing — 209

    Understanding Quantize — 215

17 - The MIDI Editors — 220

    Piano Roll Editor — 220

    Score Editor — 232

18 - Editing Audio — 239

    Basics — 239

    Interface — 243

    Flex Mode — 245

19 - The Audio Editor — 250

    Edit Regions — 250

    Edit Region Content (Pitch) — 256

    Edit Region Content (Time) — 259

20 - The Drummer Editor — 268

    Concept — 268

    Add a Drummer — 270

    Drummer Editor — 271

    Track-based Editing — 273

    Region-based Editing — 274

21 - Mixing — 279

    A different Concept — 279

    Amp Designer & Pedalboard — 282

    Automation — 288

    Tempo & Transposition Tracks — 298

    Master Track — 303

22 - Share — 305

    Final Steps — 306

    Share — 309

23 - Additional Features — 314

    Scoring Movies — 314

    Learn to Play — 317

    Logic Remote — 318

    Shortcuts — 319

Conclusion — 320

1 - Introduction

My Approach

Welcome to my manual for GarageBand X. If you've never read any of my other books and you aren't familiar with my Graphically Enhanced Manuals (GEM) series, let me explain my approach. As I mentioned at the beginning, my motto is:

"UNDERSTAND, not just LEARN"

Other manuals (original documentations or third party books) often provide just a quick way to: "press here and then click there, then that will happen ... now click over there and something else will happen". This will go on for the next couple hundred of pages and all you'll do is memorize lots of steps without understanding the reason for doing them in the first place. Even more problematic is that you are stuck when you try to perform a procedure and the promised outcome doesn't happen. You will have no understanding why it didn't happen and, most importantly, what to do in order to make it happen.

Don't get me wrong, I'll also explain all the necessary procedures, but beyond that, the understanding of the underlying concept so you'll know the reason why you have to click here or there. Teaching you "why" develops a much deeper understanding of the application that later enables you to react to "unexpected" situations based on your knowledge. In the end, you will master the application.

And how do I provide that understanding? The key element is the visual approach, presenting easy to understand diagrams that describe an underlying concept better than five pages of descriptions.

The Visual Approach

Your Level

When writing a book, there is always the question of who is the audience. In the case of an instructional manual, this question is even more important. Here, the question is, who are the readers/students, and especially at what level are they.

GarageBand is a so-called "content-creation" application and as any content creation app (Logic Pro X, Final Cut Pro X, Motion) it is a tool that allows you to create new content. However, there are two sides to the story. In order to learn the application (the tool), you have to be first somewhat familiar with the subject. Without an understanding of the specific field (music production, video production, animation), any manual for those software applications would be hard to comprehend.

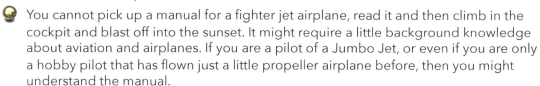

When writing for a high-end application designed for professionals, the author can assume that the target audience is familiar with the material and the field it was created for (music production, video editing, animation, etc.). For example:

- You cannot pick up a manual for a fighter jet airplane, read it and then climb in the cockpit and blast off into the sunset. It might require a little background knowledge about aviation and airplanes. If you are a pilot of a Jumbo Jet, or even if you are only a hobby pilot that has flown just a little propeller airplane before, then you might understand the manual.
- How about picking up a manual to create your first iPhone app. If you have no experience in writing Objective-C or any other computer programming code, you might have a hard time understanding what the manual is talking about if it assumes that you have basic programming skills.

Most applications require you to have a background in the field they cover (i.e. aviation, programming). A manual either assumes that the reader has that necessary knowledge and targets an experienced user, or it has to provide that basic background knowledge along with the teaching of the app if the potential user is a beginner.

In this manual, I teach the tool GarageBand. The field/subject is audio production and everything related to it.

Because GarageBand comes pre-installed with every Mac and is available for free on the Mac App Store, everybody has access to it and could start recording their own songs. However, not everybody might have a prior knowledge in the field of music production and its related topics. For those users, I created the next chapter "Prior Knowledge" that covers a few topics to provide some important background knowledge and understanding about audio production but also some important topics about OSX you might or might not know.

What is GarageBand

GarageBand is a "music and audio application". The longer description from Apple is:

> *The new GarageBand is a whole music creation studio right inside your Mac – complete with keyboard, synths, orchestral and percussion instruments, presets for guitar and voice, an entirely redesigned sound library, and virtual session drummers. A beautiful and intuitive interface makes it easy to learn, play, record, and create great-sounding songs. And you can share your hits worldwide with just a few clicks. It's never been easier to make music like a pro. Even if you've never played a note.*

GarageBand is the type of application that is also referred to as a Digital Audio Workstation (DAW):

- **Digital**: This means that we are working in the digital domain, using a computer. The opposite would be "analog" with analog tape machines, mixing consoles and effect racks, all connected with wires carrying analog signals.
- **Audio**: This word means that we are working in the audio field, dealing with music and sound and not taking pictures or making a movie, although you can add a video to your GarageBand Project to work on the audio aspect (create a soundtrack).
- **Workstation**: This word hints at the "Swiss army knife" aspect of the program. DAWs can usually perform a wide variety of tasks (recording, editing, mixing, mastering). This also means that there is a lot to learn.

The GarageBand App

GarageBand comes pre-installed with every Mac computer and can be downloaded for free from the Mac App Store (requires an Apple ID). The application (880MB) comes with the following content:

Free Content

The initial download of the app includes the following content:
- ☑ 50 Sounds
- ☑ 500 Apple Loops
- ☑ 1 Drummer
- ☑ 2 Basic Lessons (Guitar, Piano)

Additional Content

For a $4.99 in-app purchase, you can expand the content to:
- ☑ 200 Sounds
- ☑ 2000 Apple Loops
- ☑ 18 Drummers
- ☑ 40 Guitar and Piano Basic Lessons

Specifications

Here is a list of the requirements and stuff that works and doesn't work in GarageBand/

- ▶ **System Requirement**
    - OS X v10.9 or later
- ▶ **Project File Compatibility**
    - Open GarageBand for iOS Projects
    - Open GarageBand 6.0.5 Projects
- ▶ **Specs**
    - 960 tick MIDI resolution per beat (quarter note)
    - Sample Rate: 44.1kHz (fixed)
    - Audio file and I/O resolution: 16 or 24 bit
    - Maximum project length: approx. 11 hours
    - 256 Audio Tracks, 256 Software Instruments Tracks, 1 Drummer Track
    - Per Track: 4 AU Audio FX Plugins (64bit AU plugins only !)
- ▶ **Audio Formats**
    - Import AIFF, CAF, WAV, Apple Lossless, MP3 and AAC (except protected AAC files)
    - Record AIFF (16bit or 24bit)
    - Bounce to AIFF, AAC, and MP3
- ▶ **Import**
    - MIDI Files as MIDI Regions
- ▶ **Support for**
    - Core Audio compliant MIDI and audio hardware
    - 64bit Audio Units effect and instrument
- ▶ **Control Surface support via control surface plug-ins**
    - iPad: Logic Remote

What to do with it

And here is a list of things you can do with GarageBand:
- ☑ Record your music with microphones, electric guitars or MIDI keyboards
- ☑ Mix your music and add loop based audio files
- ☑ Print music notations
- ☑ Create Ringtones
- ☑ Use it as a synthesizer instrument (sound module)
- ☑ Use it as a guitar amp with stompboxes to play your electric guitar
- ☑ Create a soundtrack for your video
- ☑ Learn how to play guitar and piano with included lessons

GarageBand - the big picture

As I just pointed out, readers have different kinds of experiences and prior knowledge. If you are using this new version of GarageBand or plan on using it, you might fit into any of the following categories:

- ☐ **A** - I never used any music production software
- ☐ **B** - I used other music production software
- ☑ **C** - I used a previous version of GarageBand before
- ☐ **D** - I use(d) Logic Pro

Regardless which category you fit in, it might help to understand the big picture of GarageBand. You have to know that this is not a single app. GarageBand belongs to an ecosystem of multiple apps. Understanding the relationship to the other related apps and Apple's long term strategy for those apps helps you answer the following question:

- What is the strength of GarageBand?
- What are the limitations of GarageBand (and why)?
- What are the reasons for the dramatic changes in the new version of GarageBand?

Completely New - but better?

Apple released this major upgrade for Garageband in October 2013. This was not only a dramatic new version, it was also "traumatic" for many longtime GarageBand users.

Not only did the user interface change completely, the new version eliminated some of the functions and features that users relied on in the previous GarageBand version (i.e. Podcast creation). This was a major deal breaker and all the powerful features in the new version couldn't "ease the pain".

I cannot bring back the Podcast feature or other previous functionality, but I can help with this book to explain the new features and functionality, the new interface and workflows. If you upgraded from a previous GarageBand version, over time, you might find that the new GarageBand is even better, easier, more powerful and after all, more "logical" (despite some limitations).

I included a separate section in this book where I show the major differences between the old and new GarageBand.

First, let me show you the history of GarageBand and how it fits into the ecosystem of Apple's music production software. This might also explain why Garageband looks and functions the way it is right now.

History

Here is a rough timeline of how we got to the current state of Apple's music apps

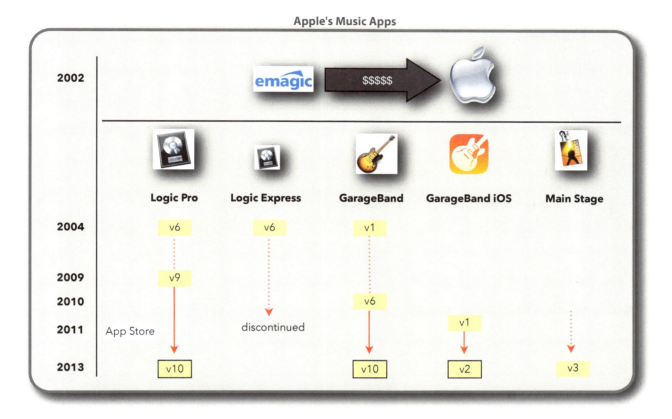

- In 2002, Apple bought the German software company emagic and it seemed that they were interested in their popular audio application "Logic". Although this might be true, it became apparent that Apple also might have had a long term strategy to get emagic's engineers and their know-how to build Apple's entry level music app "GarageBand" which was released as v1 in 2004 together with Logic Pro v6 and a lighter version of Logic Pro called "Logic Express".
- In 2011, after a couple of updates of those apps, came a big shift to how Apple sold their apps. No more installer CDs, every software was now available only as a download from the new Mac App Store.
- In the same year, Logic Express was discontinued. Also, an iOS version of GarageBand was introduced that ran on all the iOS Devices like iPad, iPod Touch and iPhone.
- MainStage, a special music app for live musicians (based on the same code base as Logic) was introduced at that time.
- In 2013, Apple's big picture came into place. Logic Pro got its long overdue upgrade to "Logic Pro X" with a brand new interface. GarageBand too got its long overdue upgrade, also with a brand new interface that is based exactly on Logic Pro X.

Although there were always some "cross-pollination" of features between GarageBand and Logic, they always looked and felt like different apps. Now with the current Logic Pro X and GarageBand X, they are basically the same app with the same user interface and workflows, just different feature sets. You can work yourself up from GarageBand to Logic or switch between the apps and basically continue working in the same app. Logic even has settings that let you disable specific advanced features when you "move up" to Logic. It even adds the wooden side panel to make you feel like home in GarageBand.

Maybe Apple's goal to put GarageBand and Logic on the same code base was the reason why some original GarageBand features got removed. Although, adding those features to Logic instead of removing them from GarageBand might have been a better solution - just saying.

Name Confusion

The previous version of GarageBand was version 6.0.5. It was part of the iLife suite, a collection of apps, before Apple made all their apps available as individual downloads from the App Store. The last version of the iLife suite was "iLife 11" and GarageBand was therefore also referred to as "GarageBand '11".

Now, the new version jumped from v6.0.5 to v10.0.0 when it was released in October 2013. Apple doesn't use any version number in the app name. The app is just called "GarageBand" with the same app icon. This could cause some confusion (if you think you upgraded from GarageBand 11 to GarageBand 10).

The Logic app on the other hand has its version number in the name with the letter X referring to the number 10, "Logic Pro X". That is the reason why I refer to the new GarageBand version as "GarageBand X" to distinguish it from the previous version. The letter X indicates the version number 10 and also reflects the relationship to Logic Pro X, their common code base.

Apple's Music Apps Ecosystem

Here is an overview how all of Apple's music apps "play together":

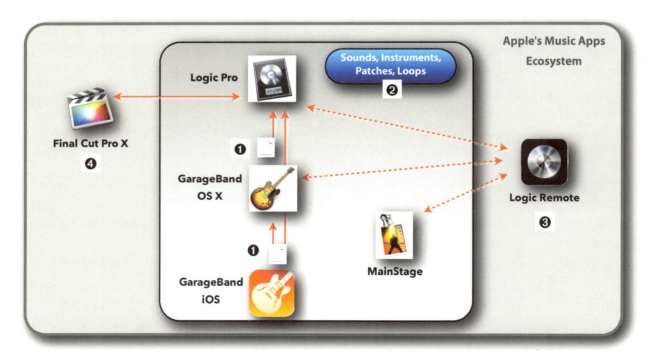

❶ The Project files are upwards compatible from GarageBand iOS to GarageBand X to Logic Pro X. You can start your Project in one app and continue on the next "higher" level.
❷ All the apps share the same pool of Sounds, Instruments, Patches and Apple Loops.
❸ The Logic Remote app on the iPad can control Logic, GarageBand or MainStage.
❹ Final Cut Pro X, Apple's professional video editing software, can import and export its audio files with Logic.

What you will Learn

Here are the topics of my book, the roadmap, and how I will teach GarageBand step by step. I recommend that you go through the book in sequential order because I put a lot of effort into coming up with the right sequence of how and when to explain the specific features and related topics. Of course, if you have some previous knowledge, you can glance over specific sections and skip to the next one.

"GarageBand X - How it Works"

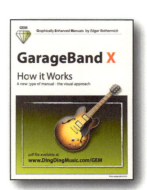

1 - Introduction: This is the current chapter you are reading right now.

2 - Prior Knowledge: Here, you find an extensive introduction to several topics related to music production and OSX workflows.

3 - Getting Started: Here, I show all the steps on how to acquire and install GarageBand with a detailed look at the download procedure, plus, a first look at the user interface,

4 - The Project: Understanding the core of GarageBand, your Project.

5 - Tracks Area: This is the area where you might spend the most time in. So you better get yourself comfortable with the Tracks Area.

6 - Control Bar: The control center where you pull all the strings.

7 - Tracks: You might know what a Track is, but there is so much more to it, so much more to discover, so much exciting stuff.

8 - Smart Controls: This is the place where you create your unique sound for your song. It is not a mixer but a new and unique interface for mixing your Project.

9 - Library: A source of sheer endless sound material for you to try in your mix. Time to explore.

10 - Regions: The building blocks of your song. Another topic that is so much deeper than it looks on the surface.

11 - Recording MIDI: Everything you need to know for recording your MIDI signal.

12 - Recording Audio: Everything you need to know for recording your Audio signal.

13 - Media Browser: A look at your media files on your disk, maybe something you might want to use in your Project.

14 - Apple Loops: The infamous quick-fix to put some basic tracks together in no time.

15 - Editing Regions: Getting your song into shape by moving stuff around. A little nip and tuck here and there that makes your song structure so much better.

16 - Editing MIDI: An introduction into open heart surgery on the MIDI data level.

17 - The MIDI Editors: The many windows into the wonderful world of MIDI Events. Please step in.

18 - Editing Audio: Now the introduction into audio. This time, scheduled for brain surgery.

19 - The Audio Editor: Or also known as "I didn't know, you could do that".

20 - The Drummer Editor: Welcome to the brand new world of the Drummer. Top notch performer at your finger tips.

21 - Mixing: Putting it all together. The wizardry and the potions, the art of making your song sound awesome - if you know how to use the tools.

22 - Share: Is the world ready to listen to your new creation? Find out how you can share it.

23 - Additional Feature: Last but not least, additional features to explore in GarageBand

2 - Prior Knowledge

Next are a few topics that a GarageBand user should be familiar with before starting to use the application. Instead of assuming that you, the reader, have that knowledge, I will discuss these topics briefly. Maybe you are familiar with the topics already or maybe you find some a little bit too advanced. Either way, having that foundation and background information definitely helps you when using GarageBand.

OSX Window Elements

First, let's go over some common user interface elements and conventions in OS X. Stuff you might be using constantly without being aware of.

➡ **Menus**

- **Main Menu**

    These are the main menus, visible on top of the computer screen. They change to whatever app is currently selected. Please note that the Main Menus will be hidden when entering "Full Screen" mode.

- **Shortcut Menu**

    A Shortcut Menu (also called Contextual Menu) is a window element that pops up when you *ctr+click* (same as *right+click*) on an object or a special area of the window. It offers a list of commands that are specific to that object and the current context.

    Some commands might be identical to the ones in the Main Menu.

- **Popup Menu**

    Other menus open up when clicking on a button or little arrows. There are specific terminologies like drop down list, pop-up menus or pop-down menus. I just use the term "popup menus" in my manual.

    Popup menus usually provide a list where you select a specific item. The selected item on the list usually has a checkmark.

➡ Active - Inactive Window

- The **Active Window** is usually the one that has the colored Window Title Buttons. If the window is one of those black panels that doesn't have those buttons, then you will see a white (or blue) frame around it (i.e. the Plugin Window). Switching to a different window turns the buttons gray and the window becomes an Inactive Window.
- The **Inactive Window** has gray Window Title Buttons. Black panels are hard to identify if active or inactive because you have to see if there is a white frame around it or not.

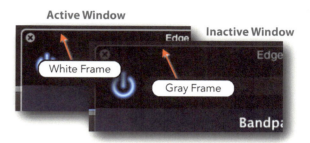

➡ Key Window (key focus)

This is an important concept that Mac users are often not aware of. The question is, when you type on your keyboard, who receives that character or key command. Usually the "recipient" is the selected window, the Active Window. In that case, the selected window is called the "Key Window", or "the window that has key focus". It means that the window "focuses" to accept whatever you type on your keyboard". However, not all keys are directed to the Key Window. Some keys are directed to the app in general (i.e. Key Commands) and some are directed to the OSX (System Key Commands).

In GarageBand, you definitely have to be aware of that concept because you can have different windows open (or active) and you have to know what happens in which window when you type a command or text on your keyboard.

- Usually the Active Window is automatically the Key Window. Look for the indicator, colored buttons ❶ or white frame ❷.
- However, a window can have multiple, independent sections, so-called "Window Panes", which are indicated by a blue frame ❸ when active. In such a case, only the window section with a blue frame has key focus.
- If a text entry box is selected, it also gets a blue frame ❹. This indicates that the text entry box has key focus and has text input priority over the window or window frame of the Active Window.
- Please note that system-wide Key Commands and even GarageBand Key Commands can have priority over any key focus, which means those keys are not used as input for the Key Window. For example, *cmd+space* opens the Spotlight Search or *cmd+,* opens the GarageBand Preferences.

Active Window Indicators (key focus)

➡ Inspector and the Main Window

This is not the title of a spy novel. It is the underlying concept of most content-creation applications. The Inspector is an auxiliary window for displaying and editing the values of a selected object or window.

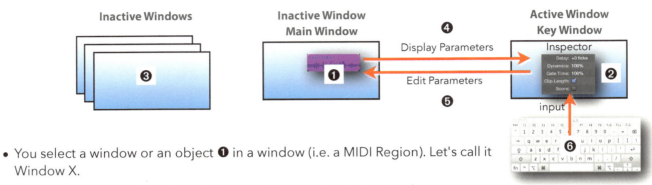

- You select a window or an object ❶ in a window (i.e. a MIDI Region). Let's call it Window X.
- As we just learned, this selected Window X is now the Active Window.
- In order to change some parameters of the selected Window X (or an Object on it), you select the Inspector window ❷.
- Now the Inspector window becomes the Active Window and Window X becomes an Inactive Window.
- However Window X is not just any Inactive Window like maybe three other open windows ❸. Window X is now the "Main Window", the window (prior selected) that is now linked to the Inspector.
- The Inspector displays ❹ the parameter values of the Main Window X and it is also the destination for any value edits ❺ made in the Inspector. Remember, the Inspector is just an auxiliary window that acts as a tool for editing something, in this case, the Main Window.
- Here is the whole picture.
  - ☑ The Inspector is the Active Window ❷ and also the Key Window ❻ which accepts the keyboard input.
  - ☑ Window X ❶ is an Inactive Window but also the Main Window that receives the changes from the Inspector.
  - ☑ Any other open window ❸ is a regular Inactive Window.

💡 Inspectors in GarageBand

GarageBand uses the concept of the Inspector in the Smart Controls and Editors window. In those windows, the left area functions as the Inspector that displays and edits the parameters of the selected object or Region on the right of the window.

➡ Floating Window (Panel)

Floating Windows (also called Panels) are little windows that usually float on top of other windows. They often contain controls to edit selected objects in the Main Window and therefore have to be always visible.

There are two types of panels and GarageBand uses both kinds:
- **App-specific Panels**: These panels are only visible when the app is visible. If you switch to a different app, then those windows disappear. In GarageBand, the Musical Typing Window and the Quick Help are app-specific that disappear when you switch to any other app on your computer.
- **System-wide Panels**: These panels stay visible and are always on top regardless which app is selected. Common examples are the Color Panel and the Font Panel. In GarageBand the Plugin Windows are Panels that stay visible when you switch to a different app.

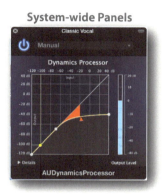

➡ Dialog Windows

A Dialog Window pops up to prompt the user to interact with the given information on the window. The response could be as simple as pressing a button or making some selections. For example, the Save Dialog or the Open Dialog are the most common Dialog Windows. The important characteristic of a Dialog is its mode.

- **App Modal**: In GarageBand, most of the windows are app modal, which means that the app is not responding to any input commands other than the Dialog Window until the Dialog Window closes. The Open Dialog, Save Dialog and Share window all behave that way.
- **Sheet**: Unlike other Dialog Windows that you can be moved around, a Sheet is a special Dialog Window that pulls out from the Window Title Bar. It slides back in when confirming the selection. This is like a special hint that the main window underneath is not responding until you slide the Sheet back in. The New Track Dialog is an example of a Sheet.

Directories

Now, let's review some conventions used to describe the locations of specific files on your drive.

First of all, a "directory" is just another word for "folder".

The location of a folder or file on your drive can be described in the following ways: "Open folder A, inside that folder, open folder B and inside folder B, open folder C, there you find file X". This long string of instructions is usually written as a sequence of all the folder names along the path with a forward slash "/" in between to indicate the "open" command. In this example it would be "*folder A/folder B/folder C/file X*" The important question however is, where do you start the path, or, what is the first folder to open. There are two conventions:

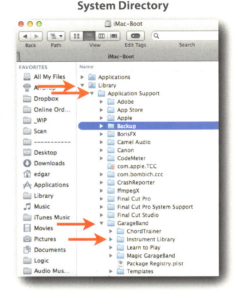

- ▶ **System Directory**: This is also referred to as the "root directory". The path of a file in the System Directory starts at the top level of the boot drive indicated by a forward slash (/) at the beginning of the sequence. The path to the folder "Instrument Library" in this example is written as:

    /Library/Application Support/GarageBand/Instrument Library/

- ▶ **User Directory**: In the root directory of the boot drive is the "Users" folder. That folder contains additional folders, one for each user account with the username as the folder name. This directory contains all the files for that specific user on your computer. Any data you create as a logged in user on your computer will be stored in your User Directory, including your GarageBand data. Although you can write the path to any of that user data, starting from the root directory, most of the time, a short form is used. It starts with the user directory, the folder with your login name in the Users folders. To indicate that a path is referring to a user directory, it starts with a tilde sign (~) in front of the first forward slash (or it starts without a slash at all). The path to the file "My First Project.band" in this example is written as:

    ~/Music/GarageBand/My First Project.band

    or

    Music/GarageBand/My First Project.band

Package File

This is a technology in OSX that, until recently, only advanced users knew about. But now, through its widespread use over recent years, it has become more mainstream on the Mac and users have to start to learn what it is and how to use it. GarageBand also uses it, so let me explain what it is.

> **A Package File is a Folder disguised as a File**

➡ Applications

This concept has always been used for applications in OSX. Every file that needed to run an application is "packaged" into a folder and converted so it looks like a single file on the outside. This has some major advantages.

- An application can be conveniently treated (copy, move, delete) as a single file.
- All the related files are kept together inside the Package File.
- A Package File still can have a single unique extension like a regular file.
- Packaging a folder as a file eliminates the chance that someone will open the folder, delete some files by accident and leave the application corrupted.
- There is a "hidden" command that lets you "open" the Package File. *Ctr+click* on a file in the Finder to open its Shortcut Menu. If it has a "Show Package Contents" item, then it is a Package File and you can select that option to display its content in the Finder like a regular folder.

Even the earlier GarageBand applications in the Applications folder were Package files and you could open them to discover all the files that belong to its app.

➡ Documents

All the advantages of a Package File can also be used for document files. This is especially useful for documents that include "assets", additional content like audio, video and graphics files. This content can be embedded in this folder-like Package File. On the Finder, it still looks like a single file.

Here are a few examples of document files saved from various applications that look like standard files but are actually Package Files. Even the iPhoto Library is a Package File which includes all your photos, thumbnails and photo edits, etc.

Files that are Package Files

The GarageBand Project files are also Package Files. More details about that later in the manual.

Traditional Studio

Here is a short description of the components that are involved in a traditional music production.

Record Music

 Tape Machine

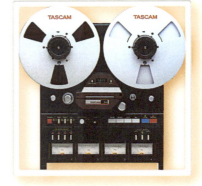

This is the central element in a Recording Studio, the device that you record your music on. Some big studios still have this original type of device, a "Tape Recorder", that thing with the two reels and magnetic tape moving across. Those hardware devices are replaced nowadays by a computer that records your music onto a big hard drive (using a DAW).

Although the mechanics and the functionality of a computer based recording device like GarageBand are quite different, the interface, the terminology and its operation are based on those old Tape Machines.

Transport/Navigation Control

Every type of recording device has to have controls, the so-called Transport Controls or Navigation Controls. With tape-based devices, they let you move the tape to the desired position. Even though there is no tape moved around on a hard drive (or no parts at all with SSD drives), the control buttons look and function the same as in the old days.

 Reader, LCD Display

The essential part in a navigation system is the read out that tells you where you are on the tape. When you want to record the 2nd verse of your song, you have to be sure that you are at the 2nd Verse. Original Tape Machines had a simple time reader (sometimes even mechanical). Nowadays, you have some sort of digital LCD clock. Professional systems use the industry standard called SMPTE time to display time.

 Playhead

A Playhead on an original Tape Machine was a special magnet that picked up the recording in the form of magnetic fields from the tape that rolled by. This Playhead is now represented by a vertical line that represents the position where you play or record your music. That position relates to the number displayed in the LCD Display.

 Tracks

One of the main characteristics of a Tape Recorder is the number of Tracks it can record. A track was originally the horizontal space on the tape where the Playhead reads the recorded information. The wider the tape (1/2 inch, 1 inch, 2 inch) the more separate tracks could fit on that tape. The more tracks a tape recorder provides, the more instruments you can record separately at the same time location. This has the advantage of recording them one after another (overdub) and also feed those separate tracks to separate channels on a mixing board to treat those tracks (instruments) differently. Often you could see the number of available tracks on a machine by the amount of separate Meters on a meter board. Modern DAWs are not restricted by the width of a tape anymore. The number of tracks is determined by the software and often just limited by the capabilities of the computer and the speed of your drive you are recording to.

Mix Music

Recording the music is only half the part in music production. The other part is mixing what has been recorded.

💡 Mixing Console

The second most important element in a recording studio is the mixing console, or mixer. This is the tool you use to mix your recording. Although it is also used for the recording part, its main purpose is to create the final mix of your recorded song.

In modern DAWs, the mixing console is simulated by a visual replica of a mixer so sound engineers feel right at home. But here we are again with the example of the fighter jet plane. If you are not a sound engineer then it doesn't do you any good if the software mixer looks and functions the same as a real life mixing console. You wouldn't know what to do with it in either case.

That's why consumer DAWs like GarageBand try to simplify the part of the user interface that represents the mixing console. GarageBand for example has no Mixer window. You create your sound with a different user interface like the Smart Controls Window, as we will see later.

💡 Channels (Tracks)

The main elements of a mixing console are its Channels, or Channel Strips. These are the identical looking strips with a long fader and all kinds of knobs and buttons. The size of a mixer is usually determined by how many physical channel strips it has (8, 32, 64, …). The signal of each of your recorded Tracks from the recording machine is sent (routed) to their own channel strip so you can treat each instrument differently to achieve the right sound for your song.

GarageBand doesn't have a Mixer and therefore no Channel Strips.

💡 Channel Controls

The available Controls on a Channel Strip determine how you can alter the sound of the instrument that is assigned to it ("runs through that channel"). The main controls are the Fader (change the volume), Pan (change the stereo position left-to-right), Mute (turn it off), Solo (listen only to that instrument), Meter (check the signal level).

In GarageBand those components are placed on the Track Header.

💡 Outboard Effects

The basic step of mixing different Instruments (tracks) to get a great sounding song is to get the balance right. You set the correct volume for each instrument and position them in the stereo field, i.e. make the guitar come out of the left speaker and the keyboard from the right speaker. The singer comes from both speakers and therefore appears to come from the center.

The interesting part of mixing however starts when you add effects to an instrument like delay or distortion. This is where the outboard effects come in. A recording studio usually has a separate rack of effect modules that the engineer could use on specific channel strips.

Nowadays, when using DAWs, all these outboard devices are replicated by Plugins that are little apps that can be added to each Channel Strip (Track). Depending on the available processing power, each Track can load its own Plugin(s) as needed.

GarageBand uses the same concept but with a different workflow (Smart Controls) that is even more efficient and sophisticated.

⚫ Master Channel

While each Channel Strip (Track) affects only the instrument it is assigned to, there is one additional Channel Strip on each Mixing Console and that is the Master Channel. The signals of all the Channels (and their instruments) are added together (routed, summed) and go to that Master Channel. This Master Channel is used to do some last final treatment to the mix, i.e. lower the overall volume or compress the mix to make it sound louder.

GarageBand also has that Master Channel, but it is called the Master Track (and it is hidden by default).

Now and Then

A music production usually involves three stages:

Recording - **Editing** - **Mixing**.

The following illustration shows how these stages have changed over time.

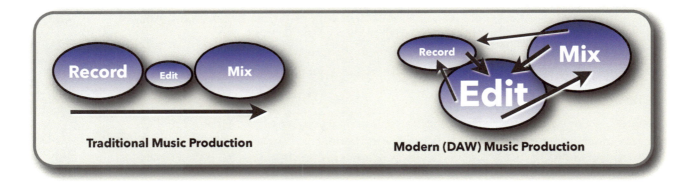

⚫ "Good Old Days"

In a traditional music production, the three stages happened one after another. First, you had your recording session with "real" musicians. Editing of those tape-based recordings was very limited, just the punch in and out procedure and the art of cutting the actual tape with a blade. The multi-track tape was the final material that was then available in stage three, the mixing session.

⚫ "Modern Times"

Nowadays, the roll of real (and *good*) musicians has become less important because a DAW, i.e. GarageBand, allows one to fix and manipulate pretty much everything. Plus, the tools available for mixing have evolved tremendously. In addition, the production process doesn't have to be linear anymore. You can switch back and forth between the different stages of recording, editing and mixing at any time.

Tracks vs Channels

I mentioned earlier that in a conventional recording studio you record the music on Tracks (of the tape machine) and that each Track is connected to Channel Strips of the mixing console.

In GarageBand, the distinction between a Track and a Channel Strip is not that important because GarageBand doesn't have a (visible) Mixer and therefore no Channel Strips. However, it is a good idea to keep this concept in mind because most other DAWs like Logic follow that model. In case you upgrade in the future, you are already familiar with that interface.

Look at the following diagram that compares the two main components in a conventional recording studio. GarageBand, like any other DAW, simulates such a recording studio.

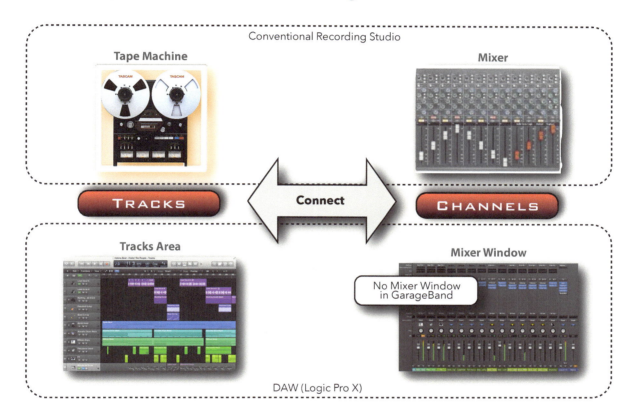

- **Tracks**: The Arrange Window (Tracks Area) is the modern form of a Tape Machine. It has (multiple) **Tracks** were you record the audio signal (and MIDI signal) in digital form as data.
- **Channels**: The Mixer Window is the "software" form of a "hardware" mixer. It has **Channels** (or Channel Strips) where you process the signals (coming from or going to the Tracks). However, GarageBand doesn't have a Mixer window with Channel Strips. Those components are located on the Track Header that function as a mini Channel Strip (plus the controls in the Smart Controls Window).
- **Tracks < > Channels**: In the old days, you used physical cables to connect the Tracks (from the Tape Machine) to Channel Strips (of the Mixing Console) and nowadays (in DAWs) everything is connected via "virtual cables".
- **Terminology**: Now assume you've recorded the vocals on Track 1 and Track 1 is connected to Channel 1 (in either scenario). If you want to lower the level of the vocals in the mix you could say "turn down track 1" or "turn down channel 1" because both terms refer to the same signal, the vocals.

Multi-Track Recording

GarageBand, like any other DAW, lets you do "Multi-Track Recording". I mentioned that term already, but in case you are not familiar with it, here is a brief explanation of that concept.

➡ **"One" Track**

Let's assume you have a band with four musicians. They play together and you record them with one single microphone. On a traditional tape machine, that signal would be recorded on one "Track". Nowadays you would record that signal to one audio file. When playing back that Track (that audio file) on a mixing board, you would need only one Channel Strip with a single fader to control the volume of that single Track before it reaches the speaker.

➡ **"Multiple" (separate) Tracks**

Now assume that you use four microphones and place them in front of each of the four instruments. The signal from each microphone is recorded on its own Track on a tape machine or nowadays, you create four audio files. Instead of recording on a single track, you recorded on "multi-tracks".

And here is the big advantage: When playing back those four individual Tracks (audio files), each one is connected to a separate Channel Strip with its own Fader. That enables you to level each instrument individually (i.e. lower the volume of the drums or raise the volume of the bass). This is the process called "mixing". The output of all four signals (Tracks) is connected (routed) to an additional Channel Strip, the "Master Track", that lets you set the volume of the "mixed" signal before it reaches the speaker.

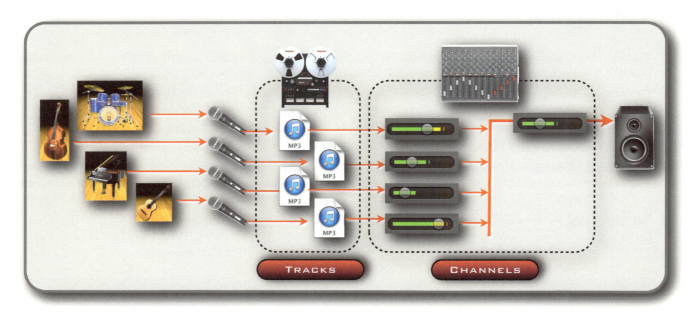

➡ *Overdub*

This is another term used in connection with multi-track recording.

In our previous example, I assumed that all four musicians played at the same time. However, this could be a problem and a limitation of the multi-track recording. For example, if the musicians play in the same room sitting close to each other, then you have to deal with "crosstalk". That means, for example, the microphone that is placed in front of the guitar, would also pick up the signal from the drums. Later in the mix, when you raise the volume on the Channel for the guitar, you would also make the drums louder that were "bleeding" into the guitar mic.

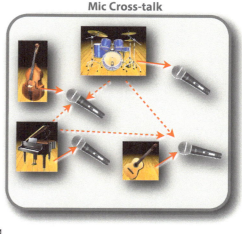

Mic Cross-talk

One remedy of this problem is to isolate the instrument in the recording studio (place them apart with acoustic dividers or a recording booth) to minimize the cross-talk effect. The other solution is to "overdub" instruments. That means each instrument plays by itself and you record them one after another. You overdub a recording on a separate Track to add that recording to your Project in addition to the previously recorded instruments (each one recorded on their own Track). This recording technique is also useful if all the musicians are not available at the same time or if one musician plays all the instruments himself and records them one at a time by overdubbing them on multiple tracks.

You can also overdub on an existing Track to fix (replace) a section of the recorded Track.

Signal Flow

You may have noticed in the last few diagrams that there are a lot of arrows. These arrows indicate the signal flow which is one of the important element you have to pay attention to when working in audio production. GarageBand makes everything easier so you don't have to worry (or know) too much about the signal flow, but knowing a little bit about the "ins and outs" (following the arrows) in GarageBand will help you tremendously whenever you work on your Project.

Think of GarageBand (or any other DAW) as a big black box. You send the signals in (Audio, MIDI) and at the end comes out your final mix, your hit song. Now the question is, what happens inside the box and how much control do you have over it.

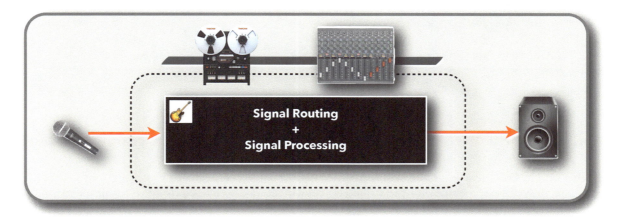

These are the two main elements that happen inside the "black block".

- ▶ **Signal Routing**: This determines where the Audio or MIDI signal is going to along its way from the input to the final output. Does it go straight to the output or does it go through some components that affect the signal.
- ▶ **Signal Processing**: If you want to alter the signal (i.e. make it louder, make it distorted, make it brighter), you have to insert one (or many) of those signal processing components into the signal flow.

➡ Graphical User Interface

So how do you follow the signal flow and see if any (sound altering) components are inserted into the signal flow of any of the Channels? That's what the user interface is for.

GarageBand (like any other DAW) provides a graphical user interface that lets you control everything inside the "black box". As you can see in the following diagram, every element of the user interface represents/controls a part of the signal routing and signal processing that is going on under the hood. The more you are aware of that internal signal routing and processing, the better you understand the effect of all those interface elements and make better use of them (controls, buttons, menus, etc.).

In addition, you can see that specific interface elements belong to a specific task when working on your Project. These are the production steps that I mentioned earlier.

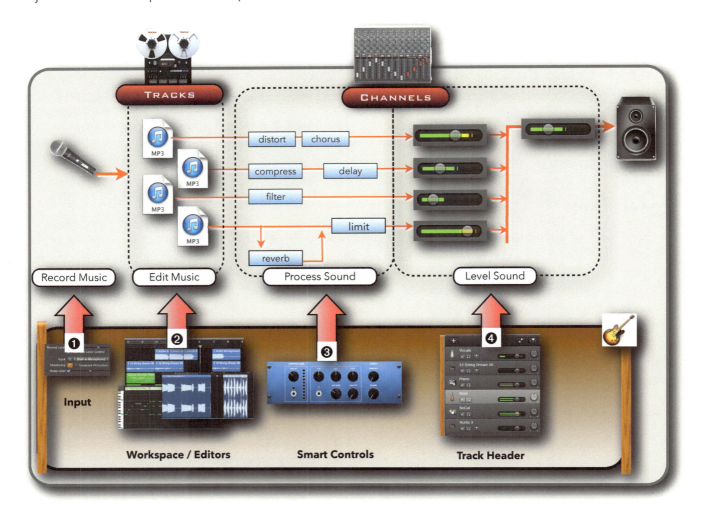

- ▶ **Record the Music ❶**: This is the first step where you determine which input signal to record on which Track.
- ▶ **Edit the Music ❷**: Once you have your music in your Project (recorded or imported), you can edit it on two levels. Edit the Arrangement of the Regions (in the Workspace) and edit the Region Content, what's inside the Region (using the Editor Windows).
- ▶ **Process the Sound ❸**: In this step, you don't edit the music. Instead, you edit the sound of the music by inserting components into your signal flow that process (alter) the sound. This is done in GarageBand in the new Smart Controls Window.
- ▶ **Level the Sound ❹**: In the last step, you set the right balance between all the existing instruments by adjusting the level of each Track a specific instrument is recorded on.

Hardware Setup

Now after that quick glance at a traditional recording studio, let's look at GarageBand which simulates such a recording studio. Before starting with any Project however, you have to be aware of one important aspect.

How to get stuff in and out of GarageBand.

Signal Flow

Connecting devices together is usually not that difficult. For example, you have a guitar that you plug into an amp and the amp connects to the speaker and off you go. If there is no sound, then you check the cables and volume and that's about how complex it gets.

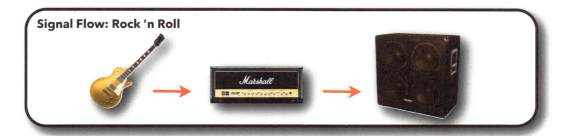

Setting up a DAW is a totally different kind of beast. Look at the following example which is a very simplified (!) diagram of how to get in and out of GarageBand. As you can see, the signal goes through different layers and at every step, something could go wrong. On top of that, each layer, like the hardware or the operating system, contains its own level of complexity.

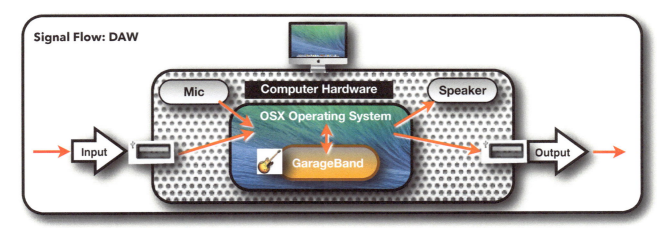

However, this diagram shouldn't scare you. You will find out that it is fairly simple as long you understand the basic components and keep the big picture in mind. Ultimately you'll spend more time making music instead of traveling to Apple's Genius Bar for help.

Before explaining how to get stuff in and out of GarageBand, let's find out what "stuff" that could be.

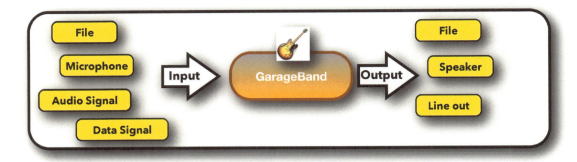

Next is a short explanation of those various Input and Output Sources to get a general overview of the available components.

Input (Source)

The Input determines what the possible sources are for GarageBand. What can you put into ("feed") GarageBand in order to create your Song.

➡ File

This is the case where you don't "record" anything in GarageBand. You don't have to play any instrument but still can use GarageBand to create a song. Instead, you can use pre-recorded material in the form of Apple Loops or any existing audio files (that are supported by GarageBand). So instead of recording, you are importing audio files to create a song.

There is no extra setup needed for this kind of input. As we will see later, GarageBand allows two ways to import those audio files:

- Drag an audio file directly from the Finder onto your GarageBand Project.
- Use a special window in GarageBand (Media Browser and Loop Browser) to conveniently access and import audio files that are available on your hard drive.

➡ Internal Microphone

Most of Apple's computers have a built-in microphone. Although not necessarily the sound quality you want for your song, it provides a quick way to record any acoustic signal into GarageBand. No cables and no hardware hook-up required.

➡ Audio In (Line In)

All of Apple's computers are also equipped with an Audio-In jack, the so-called Line-in. This lets you connect virtually any audio signal directly to your Mac without additional hardware configuration. You can plug an electric piano, an electric guitar or the output of an audio player directly into your Mac and record that signal in GarageBand.

Most Macs are equipped with a mini-jack as the Line Input. The newer laptops have only one jack that functions as a switchable audio input/output (to be selected in the *System Preferences ➤ Sound*).

➡ Audio Interface (audio input)

This type of Input requires an extra piece of hardware, the Audio Interface. It also might require a bit more prep work to set it up. The disadvantage of using the computer's built-in inputs is its average audio quality. Using a separate Audio Interface lets you choose from different models and manufacturers ranging from better quality to the best possible quality (with the highest possible price tag). Besides the quality, those Audio Interfaces often provide more features, i.e. more inputs for recording multiple sources at the same time (multi-track recording).

Many Audio Interfaces require the installation of additional software, so-called Drivers. They tell the Operating System (OS X) on the computer how to communicate with the external hardware device and how to use all those additional features it provides.

Please note that those Audio Interfaces will not be connected to the audio input of the computer. They are connected to the standard computer jacks, mostly USB nowadays. All of your input sources that produce an audio signal (electric guitar, electric piano, microphone, etc.) are now connected to the Audio Interface and GarageBand records those audio input sources through the Audio Interface. There are even USB Microphones that have the audio interface built in so you can connect the mic directly to the USB port of the computer.

➡ MIDI Interface (data input)

I will go into more details about MIDI later. For now, all we have to know is that MIDI is a standard that defines how to send music information as a special Data Signal and not as an Audio Signal.

For example, you can connect the audio output of an electric piano to your speaker system and you will hear the music you are playing, with the sound it produces. If that electric piano has a MIDI-out jack and you would connect that output signal to a speaker system, you would hear just noise. The reason is that the notes you are playing on the keyboard are transferred as a data signal. The data includes a "description" of what you are playing (what note, how loud, etc.). How the music is translated into data is specified by the MIDI standard.

A MIDI keyboard that generates MIDI data can send the signal via a MIDI cable to a device that "understands" the MIDI data. This can be either a sound module that "plays" the music or a computer that can record the MIDI signal and also plays the MIDI signal with its built-in sound modules (like GarageBand).

MIDI was originally connected through a standard 5-pin DIN connector but new devices use the standard USB connection. The good news is that the operating system running on your Mac (OS X) "speaks the MIDI language". You just need to connect your MIDI keyboard to the USB port on your Mac and GarageBand automatically "sees" that keyboard letting you record that MIDI Input Source.

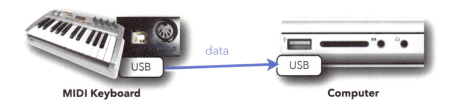

Output (Destination)

The Output in GarageBand determines what the destination is for your song, where you "send" it to.

➡ File

This is most likely the final destination when you export your complete mix of your song as a new audio file that you can play in iTunes, email to your fans or post on the internet.

➡ Internal Speaker

All Apple computers have a built-in speaker, a crappy one but a speaker nonetheless. The advantage of course, no extra hookup of additional hardware devices is needed.

➡ Audio Out (Line out)

All Apple computers have at least one audio output jack. This provides you with two options. You can plug in headphones or connect it to a speaker system.

➡ Audio Interface

Among other advantages, a dedicated Audio Interface for the output delivers a better sound quality than connecting speakers directly to your Mac.

Please note that many of the Audio Interfaces perform a double duty. You use only one (USB) cable to connect the Audio Interface to your computer, but that Audio Interface itself often provides audio connections for the input (connect Microphones and Guitars) and connections for the output (connect it to a speaker system or headphones).

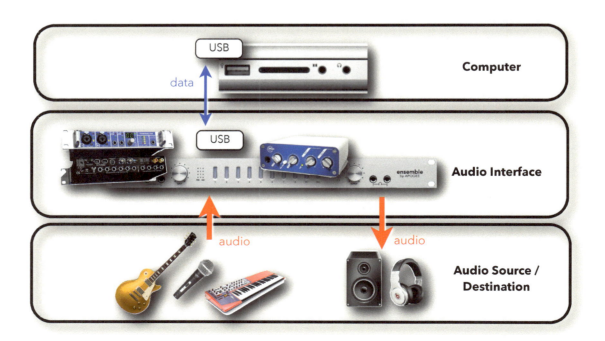

Devices

Working with music production software apps like GarageBand is often referred to as "working inside the box" because most of the components of a traditional recording studio, we just discussed earlier, are provided as software elements in those applications. However, using the built-in microphone on your MacBook might not be the best choice for your vocal session and playing your keyboard parts on a virtual keyboard with your mouse might be somewhat limiting. Under those circumstances, you might be better off to "think outside the box".

In order to use any "external box" with GarageBand (i.e. a microphone, a guitar, a keyboard or any other external controller), you have to connect the Audio Interface or MIDI Interface (also referred to as Devices) to the computer. In addition, your computer and the Device need to "communicate" with each other.

There are three types of Devices

❶ **Audio Devices**: The built-in microphone or the Line-in on your computer are considered internal Audio Devices. For better quality however, an external Audio Interface is recommended to do a better conversion of the audio signal from-and-to the digital domain so it can be used in GarageBand.

❷ **MIDI Devices**: Most MIDI Devices (i.e. MIDI keyboard) send already a digital signal (MIDI signal) and can often be connected directly to the computer.

❸ **Other Devices**: External controllers like the Logic Remote app running on the iPad can be connected to the computer to be used in GarageBand over a WiFi connection.

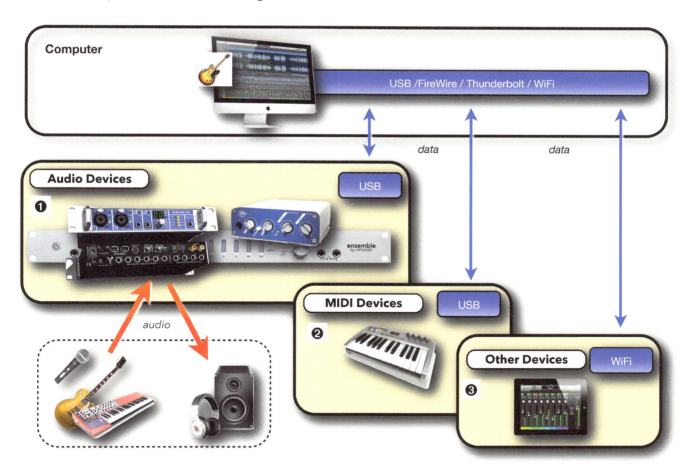

When running into problems using any of those devices in GarageBand, the issue is often not necessary with GarageBand itself. You have to guarantee that the connection and communication between the Device and the computer is working before you can even use it in GarageBand. That's why I discuss a few topics a little bit more in-depth on the next pages to cover some of those OSX basics about Audio and MIDI Devices.

Whatever you are doing on your Mac that involves audio (including GarageBand), involves 4 components. Only one of them, the actual Device, is a hardware component, the other three are software components.

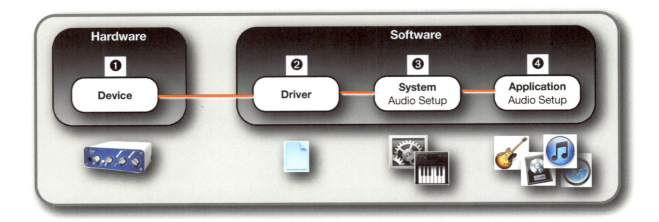

❶ Device

This is the actual physical device in form of the hardware components that your computer software uses. For example, this can be an external Audio Interface that you connect via USB to your computer. Please note that a Device can also be an internal hardware device inside your computer like the built-in microphone or the speaker inside your computer.

❷ Driver

A Driver is a little file on your hard disk that functions as the interpreter between the hardware and the software. It tells your operating system how to communicate with a connected hardware device. Many hardware devices are plug-and-play which means, OSX knows how to communicate with them because the manufacturer who built that device followed basic OSX guidelines ("Core Audio"). Other Audio Devices, however, function in a way that the operating system doesn't know. Those devices require that you install additional software, including a driver that tells OSX how to recognize the device and how to use it. Those Drivers are placed somewhere "under the hood" of your OSX system. Usually, you don't have to deal with them unless they require an update. So keep in mind, whatever Audio Device you want to use with GarageBand, has to have a proper Driver installed. If that piece is missing, then GarageBand won't "see" that device and therefore you cannot use it.

❸ System - Audio Setup

There are two special applications in OSX, the "*System Preferences*" and the "*Audio MIDI Setup*" utility. They provide the user interface to configure the hardware Devices with the help of their Drivers. The two applications let you choose which Device you want to use on your computer (built-in audio, external audio, etc.) and how to use it (control the level, mute, balance, etc.).

❹ Application - Audio Setup

And finally, the application itself. There are two categories of applications that use sound input and/or output.
- Applications that rely on the settings of the System audio settings. Those apps don't have their own configuration window for audio. For example iTunes, Safari and even the Finder that plays the startup chime or alert sounds.
- Applications that provide their own audio settings window. Those apps can talk directly to the Driver (choose, control) without using the System audio setting. GarageBand falls into that category.

➡ Who's controlling What

Here is a diagram with a more in-depth look at the four layers that demonstrates the concept:

- Whatever audio application you are using ❹, has to "reach" the Audio Device ❶ to play or record through it.
- An application can "see" and control the Audio Device only if a proper Driver ❷ is available/installed on your system for that Device.
- Some applications cannot choose or control an Audio Device's Driver directly (iTunes, Safari, Finder, etc.). They rely on the System Audio settings ❸.
- The System Audio settings ❸ can be configured in two applications, the *System Preferences* or the *Audio MIDI Setup* utility. There, you set globally which Driver (Audio Device) will be used for the System and how it is configured. Many audio applications use these system settings.
- Many applications however provide their own audio configuration window where you can choose a Driver directly ❺ instead of using the selection from the System Audio. These are not only audio applications like Logic or GarageBand, other apps like Skype, Quicktime, or VLC also let you choose the Audio Device directly.

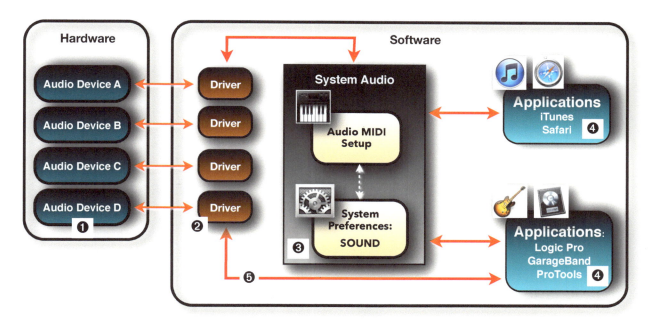

Attention

The red arrow ❺ in the diagram that points to the Drivers could mean two things,

- "choose that Driver (Device)" and also
- "control the Driver's setting".

Most applications just let you choose the Device which is not a problem because multiple applications can play through the same Device. The problem is when two applications both provide Device controls that let you configure the Device. In that case, it is important which app functions as the "master control", potentially disabling (ignoring) the controls of the other app. As we will see later, GarageBand lets you choose ❻ the Device and control ❼ it (set its Input Level).

Now a quick look at the two applications that configure the System Audio and MIDI:

 System Preferences - Sound

Open the System Preferences window from *Apple Menu ➤ System Preferences...* and click on the speaker icon to open the Sound window. This will display the System Sound Preferences window which has three different window views. You switch between them by *clicking* on one of the three tabs at the top:

Please note that these are settings for the System. That means that different computers and operating systems might have slightly different controls. The layout of the window with its sections is similar.

Input

- Select the Input Tab ❶ to switch to the input view.
- The list below will display all the Devices that the System "sees" (connected Audio Device with a proper Driver) ❷. Choose the one you want to use as the Input Device for the System (and all the applications that use the System Audio setting).
- The next section displays the controls for the selected Audio Device ❸. Here, you can set the input volume for that Device. It is like reaching into the Device through its Driver to control its level. The LED meter ❹ gives you a visual feedback to tell you (monitor) if your input level is too low or too high.
- The General Controls section ❺ at the bottom of the window stays the same regardless which window view you've selected.

Output

- Select the Output Tab ❻ to switch to the Output view.
- The list displays all the valid Audio Devices ❼ that have an audio output. Choose the one you want to use.
- The next section again lets you control the selected Device ❽. In this case the left-right balance of your stereo signal.

Sound Effects

This window view gives you a separate control over the system's various Alert sounds, which are all those annoying but helpful sounds that let you know if you clicked something wrong, a task is finished, or just the startup chimes.

Besides selecting your favorite sound, you can choose a separate Output Device. For example, have them routed to the crappy internal speaker while the rest of your System Audio plays through your good speakers connected to your external Audio Device.

Audio MIDI Setup - Audio Devices

The *System Preferences - Sound* window is usually enough for configuring the system audio. However, there is another application that provides more controls. Please keep in mind that both apps have the same functionality in regards to the system audio, they just use a different user interface and different control sets.

The *Audio MIDI Setup* app is stored in the Utilities folder inside your Applications folder
/Applications/Utilities/Audio MIDI Setup

As its name implies, the app performs a double duty. It lets you configure the Audio side and the MIDI side on your system. There is a separate window for each task that can be opened with the menu command
Window ➤ Show/Hide Audio Window - **Window ➤ Show/Hide MIDI Window**

Here is a look at the Audio Devices window.

❶ The sidebar on the left lists all the Audio Devices available on your computer. Please note that this includes not only the hardware Devices. You can also create virtual Audio Devices. Below the name of each device is an indication of how many input and output channels that Device provides.

❷ OSX lets you create two types of virtual Audio Devices. Click on the plus button at the bottom to create them:

- **Aggregate Device**: The OSX system and most audio apps like GarageBand only let you select one Audio Device. An Aggregate Device circumvents that limitation. Here, you can combine two or more hardware Audio Devices into one virtual Device. Choosing that Device in your audio app makes all the inputs and outputs of all those "combined" Devices available.
- **Multi-Output Device**: This is a new feature since OSX 10.8 Mountain Lion. It is similar to the Aggregate Device but uses only the outputs of all the combined devices. This can be very useful in combination with the Airplay feature in OSX that lets you send audio over WiFi to an Apple TV or Airport Base Station. For example, you can set it up to send the output of GarageBand to your local Audio Device in your studio and simultaneously through Airplay to the recording booth or your living room.

❸ Select an Audio Device as the System input and output. In the System Preferences window, you selected the device from each window's list. Here, you have all the Devices displayed in one list. You define them as a system Device in two ways:

 Ctr+click on the Device and choose from the Shortcut Menu.

 Select the Device first and click on the "Gear" icon (Action Menu) ⚙▼ at the bottom. This opens the same Shortcut Menu.

You can choose a Device to be the System sound input, output and also use it as the output for the alerts and sound effects. You can see that the Audio MIDI Setup app and the System Preferences settings are just different user interfaces that configure the same controls. Whatever selection you choose here will change the selection in the System Preferences and vice versa.

❹ The right window pane has two tabs that switch the view between the input and output controls. A tab is grayed out if there are no controls for either the input or output for the selected device.

❺ This section displays the various controls for the Device. Again, think of those controls as "remote controls" that configure a specific Device. This can be either your built-in Devices (speaker, microphone) or an external Device that you hooked up via a USB cable.

Audio MIDI Setup - MIDI Devices

The second window in the Audio MIDI Setup utility lets you configure the MIDI Devices connected to your system. To open this window, the MIDI Studio window, use the menu command
Window ➤ Show MIDI Window.

The basic principles with MIDI Devices are the same as with Audio Devices:

❶ You connect the hardware (the MIDI Device) to your computer via USB.

❷ OSX has to have a software Driver for that MIDI Device installed. Same procedure here. If the manufacturer of your MIDI keyboard follows OSX protocol ("Core MIDI"), then the standard OSX MIDI Driver will work to recognize it. If not, then you need to install its own software Driver (for that MIDI device) so OSX can "see" it.

❸ The system setup for MIDI devices can only be configured in the Audio MIDI Setup utility in its own "MIDI Studio" window (not in the System Preferences). If your MIDI Device doesn't show up here, then you have a Driver or a Hardware issue.

❹ All those MIDI Devices that are displayed in the MIDI Studio window will automatically be available in any application that supports MIDI.

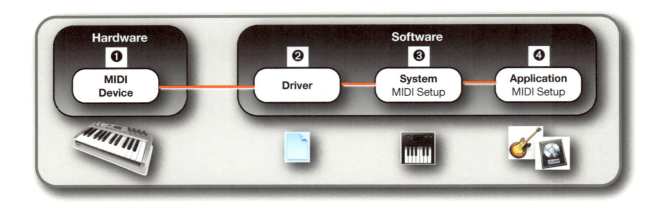

I don't want to go into further details about the MIDI configuration, just a few points:

- The MIDI Studio window displays all the MIDI Devices (you can re-arrange them) plus a customizable toolbar at the top.
- There are two special MIDI Devices listed in addition to your connected Hardware MIDI Devices:
  - **Network**: This lets you configure Devices that send/receive their MIDI information over the network (when working with a multi-computer setup).
  - **IAC Driver**: This device enables you to send MIDI information directly between applications. IAC stands for "Inter Application Communication".
- *Double-click* on any Device icon to open its detailed configuration window.
- You can save and recall different Configurations you made.

Connectors

A wise man once said: "The good thing about a standard is that there are so many of them". This is also true for all the different cables and connectors you might encounter when trying to connect components to use with GarageBand.

Please keep in mind that a specific standard often defines two things

- ☑ The shape of the physical connector
- ☑ The protocol of the signal transfer, where the transfer speed is often the most important aspect.

I differentiate between three types of connections depending on the type of signal they transfer.

➡ Data Signal

● USB (Universal Serial Bus)

This is the most common interface standard used for everything from mice, printers, hard drives and all sorts of external devices to connect to your computer. There are many different shapes of the connector (USB TypeA/B, mini-USB, micro-USB). Also, the protocol has three variations USB-1, USB-2, USB-3. The higher the number, the faster the transfer speed.

● Firewire

This standard was used mainly on Macs and some HD cameras. It is now replaced with the newer Thunderbolt standard. Many Audio Devices used this type of connection. The two protocols were F400 and F800.

● Thunderbolt

This is the new hi-speed connection available on all new Macs, but not many devices are available yet. The connection is so fast that it is even used to connect Video Monitors.

➡ Audio Signal (analog)

● Phone Plug 1/4"

This is the typical connector used for guitar cables or Headphones. It comes as a mono connector (TS, "Tip-Sleeve") or a stereo connector (TRS, "Tip-Ring-Sleeve").

● Phone Plug 1/8"

This is the smaller versions used on computers and hand held devices. It also comes as TR, TRS and even TRRS variations.

● XLR

This is a professional audio connector used to connect Microphones to Audio Devices.

➡ MIDI Signal

● 5-pin Din Connector

This connector was originally used on MIDI Devices but is now widely replaced with the USB connection.

MIDI

Needless to say, if you want to work in GarageBand or any other DAW, you have to know your MIDI. This standard just had its 30th anniversary but it is still relevant and used in every aspect of music making today. Here is just a quick summary of the basics of MIDI.

The MIDI specification describes a "protocol" (a fancy word for a "language") for converting musical information into digital form (as MIDI messages) and transferring the signal between digital instruments. The specs also describe how to physically connect MIDI devices.

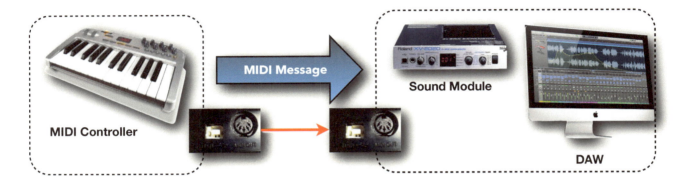

➡ The Concept

The idea behind MIDI was to create an interface standard for digital instruments (**M**usical **I**nstruments **D**igital **I**nterface) so you can connect different devices using that common interface. This allows you to separate the device that generates the musical instruction from the device that generates the sound based on those instructions.

- ☑ **Generate Instructions**: For example, you play on a musical keyboard. What you play (notes) and the way you play (velocity) are translated into "MIDI data" that is transmitted via the MIDI output port.
- ☑ **Generate Sound**: The MIDI data can be sent to an electronic device that can generate sound, based on the MIDI data the device is receiving (incoming MIDI data). The other advantage of MIDI data is that you can store the digital information on a computer (running a DAW software) or further manipulate the MIDI data before sending it to a sound module that can also be part of the DAW, doing everything "inside the box".

➡ The Physical Connection

5-pin DIN

The original MIDI connector was that 5-pin DIN connector but most of the devices nowadays use a standard USB connector. This allows you to connect a MIDI device directly to a computer without the need of a separate box, a MIDI Interface.

➡ The MIDI Interface

Using MIDI requires the proper physical connection (hardware component) but also the proper communication (software component). In order to successfully communicate between Devices (transmit or receive MIDI messages), a Device has to follow (understand) the MIDI protocol (language). On a MIDI keyboard or MIDI sound module that shouldn't be a problem because it is a device that is designed to do exactly that. A computer on the other hand is just a generic machine that can do a thousand things, so you have to make sure to "prepare" it, so it can "do MIDI" too. This is where a "Driver" comes into play. I discussed the function of a Driver already in the previous section.

➡ The MIDI data

Here is the basic structure of the MIDI data.

- The MIDI signal is, like any other digital signal, just a string of 0s and 1s.
- They are organized into **MIDI messages**.
- One MIDI message consists of three data blocks (called bytes), each one with a value from 0 to 127.
- The first byte is called the **Status Byte** which defines what type of MIDI message the next bytes carry: A Channel Message or a System Message.
- Byte two and three are called the **Data Bytes** which carry the actual information of the MIDI message.
- A MIDI message can be assigned a MIDI channel from 1 ...16. These messages are called **Channel Messages**. If you have multiple MIDI sound modules connected to a single controller or have a MIDI sound module that can generate different sounds at the same time (multi-timbral) then you can configure the MIDI devices to send and receive MIDI messages on specific channels.
- A MIDI message without channel information is called a **System Message** that is sent to and received by all connected devices.

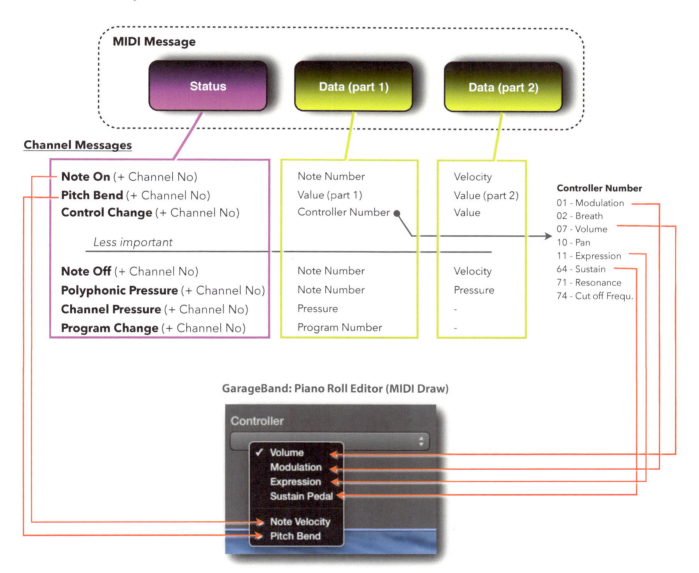

Once you start editing MIDI Regions in GarageBand, you need that basic understanding of MIDI Messages to know what the various commands mean. I will discuss that later in the book.

Mono - Stereo

Mono and Stereo are two terms that can be found everywhere and everybody uses them in audio production. Let me demonstrate what they actually mean.

The most often used phrase is "something is in stereo" or "something is in mono". To explain the meaning, let's first look at another term, "channel". This term is also found everywhere, but I use it in this context in the following way.

> **A Channel represents a transmitted or a recorded Audio Signal**

Here is what I mean by that:

- **One Channel**
    - ▶ You put a microphone in front of one acoustic piano. That microphone picks up that single acoustic signal and transmits it as one electric signal. That one signal represents one channel that is transmitted. You record that one signal onto a file containing that one channel or playing it back on one speaker.
    - ▶ Now you put the one microphone in front of a band. Although you have multiple signals (individual instruments), that one microphone still picks up the combined sound and transmits only one electric signal representing one channel. You can record that one signal (of the band playing) onto a file containing one channel or still play it through one speaker.

- **Two Channels (or Multi-Channel)**
    - ▶ Now you put two microphones in front of the piano. Each microphone picks up its own signal (for example, positioned more to the left or right) and transmits it as its own electric signal. Now you have two signals representing two channels. You can record those two signals onto a file containing these two channels or play it through two speakers.
    - ▶ Now you put the two microphones in front of the band. Same scenario: Each microphone picks up its own signal and transmits it as its own electric signal. The two microphone signals representing the two channels can be recorded onto a file containing these two channels or you play them through two speakers.

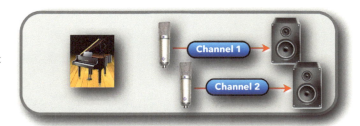

Now let's see how Channels relate to Mono and Stereo.

> **Mono and Stereo describe the relationship between two Channels**

🔶 One Channel

- ▸ **Mono**: If you have only a signal of one single channel (transmitted on a DAW's Track or stored as an audio file), then that is always considered a Mono Signal. There is no relationship to another channel.
  One Channel ➤ Mono

🔶 Two Channels

If you have two channels, then you could have Mono or Stereo

- ▸ **Mono**: If both channels are identical, which means they transmit (or have stored) the exact same signal, then what you hear is still considered a Mono signal (one single source of information coming out of two speakers).
  Channel 1 = Channel 2 ➤ Mono

- ▸ **Stereo**: If both channels are not identical, then what you hear is considered a Stereo signal. Each speaker sending a different signal (the difference can be subtle all the way to completely different).
  Channel 1 ≠ Channel 2 ➤ Stereo

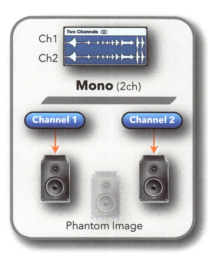
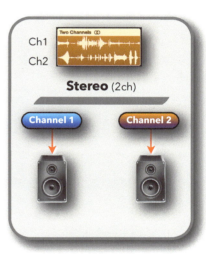

Keep in mind

- If you listen through one speaker, then you always listen to one channel, you listen to Mono.
- If you have two speakers (or headphones), then you have a stereo "setup". That doesn't mean that you hear stereo. Only if the signal from the left and right speaker (left channel - right channel) is different. For example, the guitar comes from the left speaker and the synth sound comes from the right (stereo). If all the instruments come out from both speakers equally, then you "hear them in mono"
- Please note that if both speakers (in a left-right setup) play the same signal, then you hear the signal actually coming from the center even if there is no speaker. This is called a Phantom Image.
- You can see on an audio waveform if it contains one or two channels. You could even see how different the signals are.
- GarageBand displays 1-channel and 2-channel audio signals as a single waveform (simplicity, save space). However, a 2-channel signal is indicated with the stereo icon in the Region Header.

Digital Audio

Here is a brief discussion about "analog audio vs digital audio". Usually, this topic is a book all by itself and another book with all the arguments explaining why analog is better than digital or the other way around.

➡ *What is analog audio?*

Any sound source, whether it's a guitar player, a drummer or even a door slam, creates a vibration that can be described as a waveform. Each of those sound sources vibrates in a specific way ❶ (i.e. the plucked string of the guitar or the cymbal hit by a stick) and by doing so, it moves the air around it ❷ (which adopts the same back and forth movement) until the vibrating air reaches our eardrum ❸ which then vibrates the same way as the original sound source. The result, we "hear" the sound source (this is a very simplified explanation!)

The signal that is transmitted through all the stages, is called an analog signal, a continuous back and forth movement of the specific element (string, metal, air, eardrum) visualized in a waveform.

The diagram below shows this vibrating movement as a simple sine wave ❹ (red).

- ☑ **Amplitude [dB]**: The y-axis (green) on the waveform graph represents the amplitude or intensity of the signal. In other words, how loud is the signal, measured in decibel [dB].
- ☑ **Frequency [Hz]**: The x-axis (blue) on the waveform graph is the time axis, representing the frequency of the signal, measured in Hertz ("how many periodic movements per seconds").

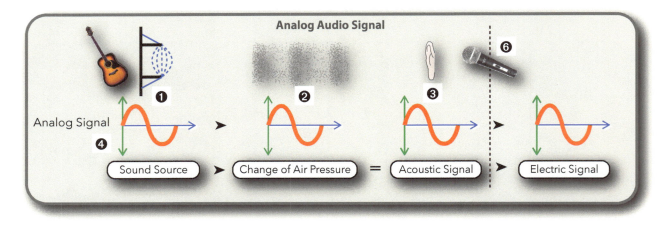

Please note that an analog signal can occur in different forms (acoustic, electric, magnetic, etc.). The signal can also be converted between those forms. What analog signals have in common is a "continuous increase and decrease (i.e. change in air pressure or voltage). This is described by the waveform, which can be a simple "sine wave" or a more complex waveform, the kind you can see in GarageBand on an Audio Region ❺. For example, analog signals can be:

- ⚪ **Acoustic**: This is a mechanical change. The analog signal is transmitted mechanically by moving air molecules, string, cymbal, ear drum and also the membrane of a microphone.
- ⚪ **Electric**: This is a change in voltage. The analog signal is transmitted through an electric cable that represents the signal as a change in voltage.
- ⚪ **Magnetic**: This is a change in magnetic polarization. However, in this form, the analog signal is not transmitted. Instead, the waveform is stored on a magnetic tape of a tape reel.

The diagram above shows a special "tool", the microphone ❻, which transfers an analog signal from an acoustic signal to an electric signal.

➡ What is digital audio?

Digital Audio is the representation of an audio signal in discrete numbers (1, 0) instead of a continuous waveform. A device, called an Analog-Digital Converter (ADC) ❶, converts the analog signal into numbers and a Digital-Analog Converter ❷ (DAC) can reproduce an analog signal from a digital signal.

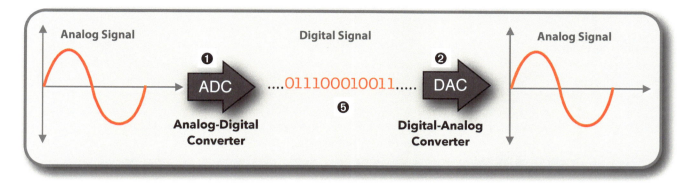

The quality of a digital conversion is based on two parameters. These two parameters describe the two stages of a conversion:

🟡 Sample Rate [kHz] ❸

The first component of a converter takes samples of the analog waveform, like snapshots. These samples must be taken at a very high rate. Based on physics rules, the Sample Rate must be at least twice as high as the highest frequency of the audio signal. The highest frequency a human can hear is about 20kHz (20,000Hz or 20,000 cycles per second). That means that the samples must be taken at least 40,000 times per second. For example, the Sample Rate of an Audio CD is 44,100 Hz or 44.1kHz. The Sample Rate in GarageBand is fixed to 44.1kHz.

🟡 Bit Depth, Resolution [bits] ❹

The second component of a converter now takes each sample and measures its amplitude. However, a converter cannot measure the actual value of a sample. Like on a grid, there are a limited amount of available values and the actual value has to be narrowed to the closest available value on that grid. Of course, the finer the grid (more available values) the smaller the rounding errors.

The available values for a converter are measured in bits (**bi**nary digi**ts**). For example, 65,535 values equal 16bit and 29,360,127 values equal 24bit. And again, the higher the Resolution (also referred to as "bit depth"), the higher the dynamic range with less audible noise at lower signal levels. The default Resolution in GarageBand is 16bit, but you can set it to 24bit in the *Preferences ➤ Advanced*.

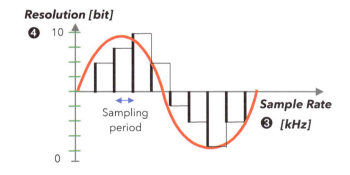

The final Digital Signal is a number sequence ❺ of the values of the consecutive samples. These numbers, representing the audio signal, can now be processed and stored on a computer.

So in general, the higher the Sample Rate and the higher the Bit Depth, the better the conversion process between analog and digital. However, the downside is that this also requires more storage space and more CPU power to process the digital signals.

3 - Getting Started

Installing GarageBand X

As I pointed out in the timeline earlier, since 2011, Apple doesn't sell its software on physical discs anymore. All their apps are now available only through downloads from the various online Apple Stores or from the Apple website.

> **Installing GarageBand v10 does not overwrite GarageBand v6.**
> **It stays in the Application folder but will be moved as GarageBand 6.0.5**
> **into a new folder "GarageBand 6.0.5"**

Please note that there are two different App Stores.

iOS App Store: This store is for all the iOS apps (iPhone, iPad). It can be accessed directly on your iDevice via the App Store app or through iTunes on your Mac.

Mac App Store: This is the store for all the Mac OS X apps. The "App Store" is a separate OSX application that can be accessed from the Main Menu.
Apple Menu ▶ App Store... . This is the place where you get GarageBand.

Like with any other app on the Mac App Store, just enter the name of the app, "GarageBand", in the search field in the upper right corner to bring up the application's detail page.

But before you click the buy button to download the app, there are a few things you have to know and understand about this new download model.

Apple ID - Licensing

Along with the move to the download-only distribution model, Apple also introduced a new licensing model.

- You have to be signed in to an Apple ID to purchase any apps, even the ones that are for free like GarageBand. That means the requirement of getting GarageBand is that you have to have a valid Apple ID. Even for commercial apps, you don't need to have a credit card necessarily attached to an Apple ID to purchase apps with it. You could "fill it up" with gift cards like a charge card.
- Any app that you purchase/download with a specific Apple ID is licensed to that Apple ID. Think of it as your "virtual online license".
- Once you purchased an app with an Apple ID on your machine, you can download that app on other machines (i.e. Laptop) when you are signed in with the same Apple ID on those machines.
- You DON'T have to be signed in to your Apple ID in order to use a purchased app. The Apple ID is only required when purchasing/downloading an app and when updating an app. That means you could download apps to a machine using different Apple IDs. For example an Apple ID to purchase apps for your personal use and a separate Apple ID to purchase apps for business use.
- Not only is this licensing model much more flexible when using apps across multiple computers, it also eliminates the backup of apps. When you have to install a new machine, you just login with your Apple ID and the App Store knows what apps you've purchased in the past and you can download/install them again from the App Store. They are like a "backup in the cloud".

Installation Procedure

You would think that getting GarageBand is as easy as clicking on a "Download" button, waiting for the download to be finished and start using the app. Technically, yes, but there are a few hidden details.

First of all, the *Download/Buy* button can look different depending on various circumstances.

Free — You don't have GarageBand installed on your machine.

Install — You don't have GarageBand installed on your machine. However, you have previously downloaded GarageBand with the Apple ID that you are currently signed in.

Update — You have GarageBand already installed on your machine. However, there is a newer version available on the Mac App Store.

Installed — You have GarageBand already installed on your machine. You are ready to go, just launch the app from your Applications folder.

The little arrow next to the button opens a popup menu that is standard for all apps in the store. It is like a Share button to spread the word about this great app.

Copy Link
Tell a Friend
Share on Twitter
Share to Facebook
Share in Messages

Attention - previous GarageBand user

Please note that the new GarageBand X (v10) app will not overwrite or replace any previous GarageBand app (v6) that you might have in your Applications folder. The Installer will just move the previous app (renamed as "GarageBand 6.0.5) to a new folder named "GarageBand 6.0.5.

These are the different steps how to download GarageBand:

➡ Step 1: "Purchasing" the App

Here is the procedure when you download GarageBand the first time:

- ☑ Click on the "Free" button ❶. It turns into a green "*Install App*" button..
- ☑ Click on the green "*Install App*" button ❷. The Apple ID sign-in sheet will open.
- ☑ Enter your Apple ID and password ❸ (or create a new Apple ID) and click the "*Sign In*" button. Remember, this is the Apple ID the GarageBand app is linked to from now on. You need that Apple ID every time you want to upgrade GarageBand.
- ☑ After successfully signing in with your Apple ID, the button turns into the "*Installing*" button ❹ which indicates exactly that, the GarageBand installation process has started.

➡ Step 2: Downloading the App (986MB)

After initiating the Installation, the actual download process will start. The file size is around 986MB so the download might take a moment depending on how fast your internet connection is. You can follow the download progress in various places:

- In the Mac App Store app ❺ when selecting the "*Purchases*" tab ❻.
- In the Applications folder ❼ (in List view or Icon view).
- In the Dock ❽
- In the Launch Pad ❾.

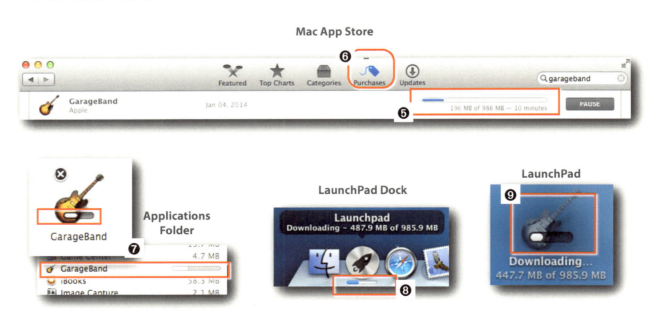

➡ **Step 3: Downloading the Basic Content (2GB)**

When finished downloading, the App Store displays the grayed out "Installed" button ❶.

Please note that so far only the GarageBand app has been installed. The next step would be to launch GarageBand and start making music. However, something else will happen first when you launch GarageBand for the first time.

When you "purchase" GarageBand, you not only get the app for free. Along with it comes the so-called "Basic Content". These are 2GB of essential Apple Loops, Sounds, Lessons, Instruments, and Settings. Later, you can purchase more content with a one time in-app purchase of $4.99.

- ☑ Now launch GarageBand (for the first time) from your Applications folder or the Launchpad. In the Launchpad, the GarageBand app will be surrounded by sparkling stars ❷ to show that it is "excited" to get launched the first time. Now, instead of the app opening up, the download process for the Basic Content will start first by prompting a new window ❸. It displays the download progress ❹ of the 2GB of Basic Content. Again, this might take a moment depending on your download speed.
- ☑ The window has a ❓ button ❺, that opens the Help Center window with the online documentation for GarageBand to read up while you are waiting for the download to finish.
- ☑ When the download is completed (the progress bar is almost at the end), a Dialog Window pops up requesting you to enter the name and password ❻ of your user account. Please note that this has nothing to do with the Apple ID. The 2GB was downloaded to a temporary location on your system drive and has at this time not been installed to the proper location yet.
- ☑ Enter your user name, password and click OK ❺. This authenticates you as the user (with admin privileges) and the system will now install the downloaded files to the System Library folder. That's why it needed the authentication.

3 - Getting Started

➡ Step 4: Installing the Basic Content

Once you hit the OK button in the Dialog Window of the previous step, OSX will copy the downloaded files from the hidden location to the proper location. The progress bar indicates this step with the label "Installing..." ❶. These are the new locations where OSX creates new folders.

> ▸ */Library/Audio/*
>
> This is the Audio folder in the System Library. The installer creates a new "Apple Loops" ❷ folder and puts all the downloaded Apple Loops inside the Apple folder. In addition, it creates the "Impulse Responses" ❸ folder to store the files needed for the "Space Designer", Apple's convolution reverb plugin.
>
> ▸ */Library/Application Support/ GarageBand/*
>
> This is the Application Support folder in the System Library. The installer creates a "GarageBand" ❹ folder that contains specific files for the GarageBand app.
>
> ▸ */Library/Application Support/ Logic/*
>
> The Installer also creates a "Logic" ❺ folder. Why? I explained earlier that GarageBand and Logic Pro share the same code base. Here you can see one of the advantages. Both apps share some of their files. For example, the Drummer, the Instruments and Settings Files are stored in the Logic folder and GarageBand knows to access them there.
>
> ▸ *~/Music/Audio Music Apps/*
>
> This is the Music folder inside your user folder. The Installer creates the "Audio Music Apps" ❻ folder. This is another folder that GarageBand and Logic share. Any user created files (Patches, Presets, Instruments, Templates, etc.), either from Logic or GarageBand, will be stored in this location. The Installer creates only the empty "Sampler Instruments" folder.
>
> ▸ *~/Music/GarageBand/*
>
> The installer also creates the "GarageBand" ❼ folder in the Music directory. This will be the default location when you save GarageBand Projects.

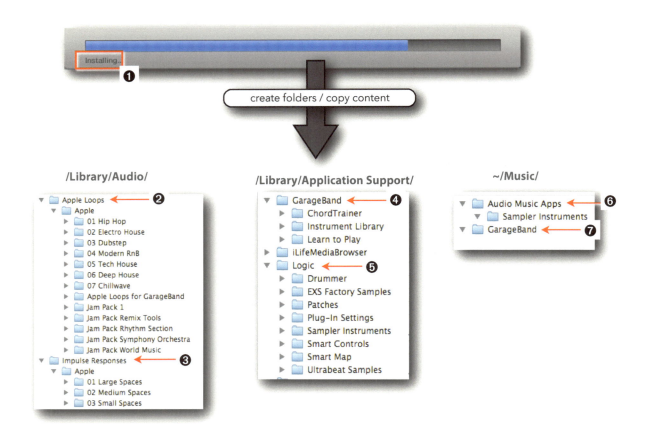

48   3 - Getting Started

➡ Step 5: Launching GarageBand (for the first time)

Once the Installer is finished with the installation process of the Basic Content, three more windows will popup. The "Welcome to GarageBand" ❶ window, the "New in GarageBand" ❷ window and finally the "Project Chooser" ❸ window where you can select a Template to use as your first Project. I will explain that in a minute.

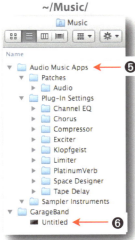

Once GarageBand starts with the first Project ❹, a few more folders are created in the "Audio Music Apps" ❺ folder. In addition, the new Project is named "Untitled" and is automatically saved as the Project File with that name in the "GarageBand" ❻ folder.

More about the Autosave feature later in the book.

3 - Getting Started

➡ Step 6 (optional): Purchase More Sounds

The initial download of the GarageBand app includes 2GB of Basic Content. You can add more content by using the so-called "in-app purchase". That means instead of going to the App Store and look for the product, you can make the purchase (and install) the additional content by clicking on a command directly in GarageBand.

- ☑ *Click* on the Main Menu Command *GarageBand ➤ Purchase more sounds* ❶
- ☑ A Dialog ❷ window opens up with the information to download additional 150 sounds, 1,500 loops, 17 drummers and drum kits, and 38 Basic Lessons. *Click* the Continue Button.
- ☑ The next Dialog ❸ window opens that lets you sign in with your Apple ID.
- ☑ On the final window ❹, *click* the Buy button to start the download and installation process ❺.
- ☑ You can later *click* the command from GarageBand's Main Menu *GarageBand ➤ Restore Purchase* ❻ that opens a window ❼ to download the previously purchased content again (10GB total).
- ☑ Patch names that are dimmed ❽ in the Library indicate that they require sounds or loops that are not installed yet. An Alert Window ❾ pops up when you click on one of those Patches.
- ☑ The Library window in GarageBand will display an icon ❿ in the lower right corner to indicate that there are more sounds available.

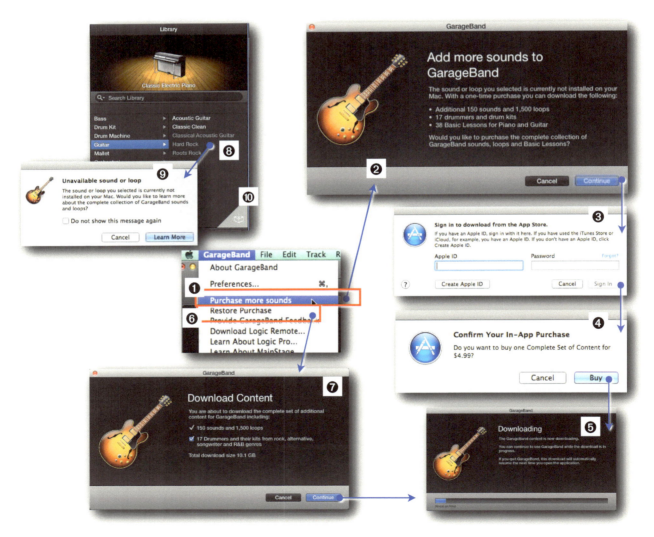

Please note that the GarageBand installer is smart enough to "see" if you have already installed Logic Pro X with all its 50GB of Additional Content or even have the Lessons file from the GarageBand 6.0.5 on your drive. In that case, the Installer will only download the GarageBand app. The "Purchase more sounds" option is then grayed out.

User Interface

As we have just seen, the Project Chooser is the first window that opens up in GarageBand after the installation. I will discuss the details about that window in the next chapter, but first, let's look at the interface elements of the Garageband window.

One major aspect of learning an application is to understand its graphical user interface (GUI) for the simple reason of knowing how things are organized and where to find all the elements. In this section, I will introduce those elements and the functionality of the GarageBand Window in general so you know what it is you are looking at. The discussion about how to use those windows will follow in separate chapters.

Single-Window Interface

GarageBand uses a common interface concept called "single-window". The idea is that instead of opening separate windows for specific tasks (which can easily clutter your screen), almost everything is placed into a single unified window. Your focus always stays on that one window.

This is the basic concept:

- ▸ Working on your GarageBand Project is done in a single unified window - the Garageband Window.
- ▸ The window is divided into sections, called Panes or Window Panes.
- ▸ Some Panes are always visible and some can be shown/hidden as needed.
- ▸ Most Window Panes can be resized by dragging the Divider Line between them.
- ▸ GarageBand still has a few separate windows that open individually and are not part of the Garageband Window.

Here is a look at this single GarageBand Window. It is divided into five Window Panes. The top and center Panes (green frame) are always visible and the left, bottom and right Pane (red frame) can be shown/hidden. The black frame around it represents the single GarageBand Window.

➡ **Resizing the GarageBand Window**

Using any of the following three kinds to resize the GarageBand window will resize the Window Panes inside proportionally. Please note that if the GarageBand window gets too small, then the left Window Pane will close.

🔵 **Manual Resize**

Moving the Mouse Pointer over the edge of the window changes the Mouse Pointer to the Resize Tool. You can *drag* any of the four sides or any of the four corners. Little tip: *Opt +drag* will also resize the opposite side or corner proportionally.

🔵 **Resize Button**

The green Resize Button is one of the three Title Bar Buttons in the left upper corner of a standard window. *Click* on it to resize the GarageBand Window so it uses the whole computer screen. Click on it again to resize it back to its previous size.

🔵 **Full Screen**

Full Screen Mode is a feature that is provided by most single-window apps. The commands for enabling or disabling are standard:

Full Screen Button

▸ **Enter Full Screen**: *Click* on the double arrow in the upper right corner of the GarageBand Window. When switching to Full Screen Mode, the window will take over the whole computer screen. The Main Menu also disappears, but moving the mouse to the top of your screen will temporarily slide out the Main Menu to access the Menu Commands.

▸ **Exit Full Screen**: While in Full Screen Mode, move your mouse to the upper right corner of your screen to *click* on the blue double arrow in the Main Menu (that slides out). Alternatively, click the *Esc* key.

Exit Full Screen

➡ **Resizing the Window Panes**

All the Window Panes can be resized (with the exception of the top Window Pane). You do that by moving the Mouse Pointer over a Divider Line between two Window Panes. The Mouse Pointer changes to a Resize Tool and you can *drag* the divider left/right or up/down. The position of the other Divider Lines are not affected.

52   3 - Getting Started

Window Panes

Now let's have a look at those five Window Panes. This is just a brief overview..

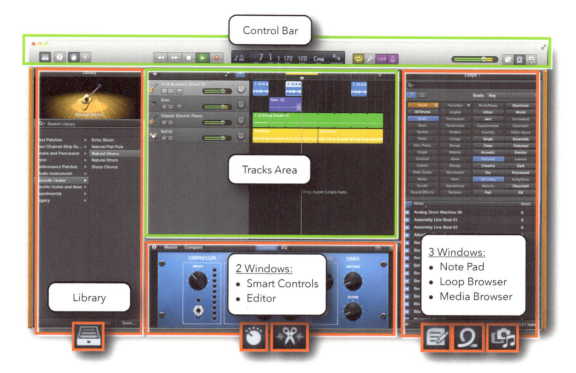

➡ **Top: Control Bar**

The top Window Pane is the Control Bar that is always visible. Its height can't be resized, only the width which follows the width of the Garageband Window.

➡ **Center: Tracks Area**

The center Window Pane is called the Tracks Area. It is also always visible. Its size adjusts to the surrounding Window Panes and their size in relationship to the whole available GarageBand Window.

➡ **Left: Library**

The left Window Pane is the Library Window that can be toggled with the Library Button in the Control Bar.

➡ **Bottom: Smart Controls - Editors**

The bottom Window Pane is a "multipurpose pane" that is used for two different windows:

This button in the Control Bar toggles the Smart Controls Window.

This button in the Control Bar toggles the Editor Windows that can itself be changed between four different Editors.

➡ **Right: Note Pad - Loop Browser - Media Browser**

The right Window Pane is also a "multipurpose pane" that is used for three different windows:

This button in the Control Bar toggles the Note Pad Window.

This button in the Control Bar toggles the Loop Browser Window.

This button in the Control Bar toggles the Media Browser Window.

Individual Windows

Besides the unified GarageBand Window with its Window Panes, GarageBand has only a few windows that open separately:

- **Preferences Window** ❶

    Menu Command *GarageBand ➤ Preferences* or Key Command **cmd+,**

- **Quick Help** ❷

    Menu Command *Help ➤ Quick Help* or click on the QuickHelp Button in the Control Bar

- **Musical Typing** ❸

    Menu Command *Window ➤ Show/Hide Musical Typing* or Key Command **cmd+K**

- **Keyboard** ❹

    Menu Command *Window ➤ Keyboard*

- **Tuner** ❺

    Click on the Tuner Button in the Control Bar (when an Audio Track is selected)

- **Plugin Window** ❻

    Open the Plugin Window from the Audio Units area in the Smart Controls Inspector

- **Fonts** ❼

    Click on the Font Button in the Note Pad Window

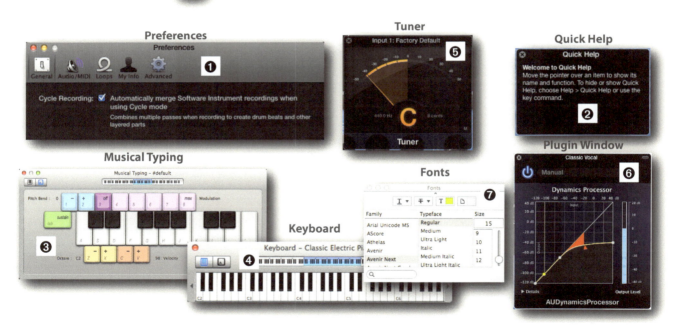

That's about what you will encounter in GarageBand regarding the various windows. It is quite manageable and laid out in an easy and logical way so you will adapt to it very fast. Now we just have to learn how to work with the content of those windows.

In the next section, I will provide a quick comparison about the old user interface in GarageBand 6.0.5 and the new interface in case you used GarageBand before.

GarageBand 6.0.5 vs GarageBand 10.0

If you used GarageBand 6.0.5 and are upgrading to GarageBand X, then instead of learning what is new, you might want to find out first what is different in the new version. The re-learning (or un-learning) of procedures you are used to could be sometimes more difficult than just learning something completely new.
From a GarageBand 6.0.5 user point of view, you might summarize the upgrade the following way:

The Good, the Bad, the Ugly

The Good

Besides all the new features in GarageBand X, there are changes that are just minor, sometimes more cosmetic and arguably an improvement over the previous version.

➡ *Project Chooser*

The concept of the Project Chooser is still the same. Every new Project starts with a Template chosen from the Project Chooser. Some functionality however has changed.

➡ *Create Track*

The Process of creating new Tracks is similar. You click on the Plus Button ⊕, now on top of the Tracks Headers. It also opens the New Track Dialog which looks familiar. However, there are a lot of small details that have changed, including some terminology. More on that in the Tracks chapter.

3 - Getting Started   55

➡ **GarageBand Window**

The main GarageBand Window looks also similar. It has the two (always visible) Window Panes. The Control Bar and the Tracks Area. The obvious difference is that the Control Bar is now on top.

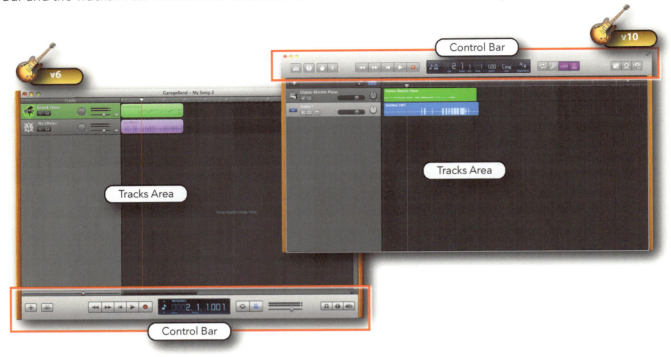

➡ **Control Bar**

Besides being moved to the top, the Control Bar didn't change much. It still has the buttons to toggle the Window Panes, the Transport Buttons and some Mode Buttons for Cycle and Click. The Control Bar Display stayed also at the center. The functionality of the Buttons and the Display has changed slightly.

➡ **Control Bar Display**

The four Display Modes on the Control Bar Display are now consolidated into two Display Modes. One displaying the Musical Time (Bars and Beats) with the Project data and the other one displaying the Absolute Time (SMPTE). The original Chord Mode is now available as a separate Tuner Window.

➡ *Editor*

The Editor Pane can still be opened with the similar looking Editors Button on the Control Bar. Most of the views and functionalities of the various Editor windows are still the same but a lot of detailed changes are there to explore including the new Drummer Editor.

➡ *Loop Browser*

The Loop Browser is almost identical with some minor more cosmetic changes and one major change. The "Podcast Sound View" button is gone. Please note that none of the Apple Loops have been deleted, you still can search for them in the other two views.

➡ *Media Browser*

The Media Browser is also almost the same with one change. The Photos tab has been removed which was useful mainly for the Podcast feature (that also is gone in GarageBand X).

3 - Getting Started   57

➡ **Note Pad**

The difference here is that the separate Notepad window is now part of the right Window Pane that opens with the Note Pad Button  from the Control Bar.

The Bad

Here are some changes that are more substantial. They require a rethinking of previous workflows and therefore might result in some confusion and even frustration among previous GarageBand users.

➡ **Track Info (Browse) ➤ Library**

➡ **Track Info (Edit) ➤ Smart Controls**

GarageBand 6.0.5 displayed the "Track Info" window in the right Window Pane. This window contained the "Browse' tab to manage the Setting Presets for the selected Track and the "Edit" tab to adjust the various components, mostly the Plugins.

Now in GarageBand X, these two tabs now have their own Window Panes. The Browse tab is now the Library Pane on the left, opened with the Library Button. The Edit tab is now the Smart Controls Pane at the bottom (opens in the same Pane as the Editors), and can be toggled with the Smart Controls Button. This Smart Controls Window is based on a completely new and different concept that many existing GarageBand users might find strange and even limited compared to the previous GarageBand version.

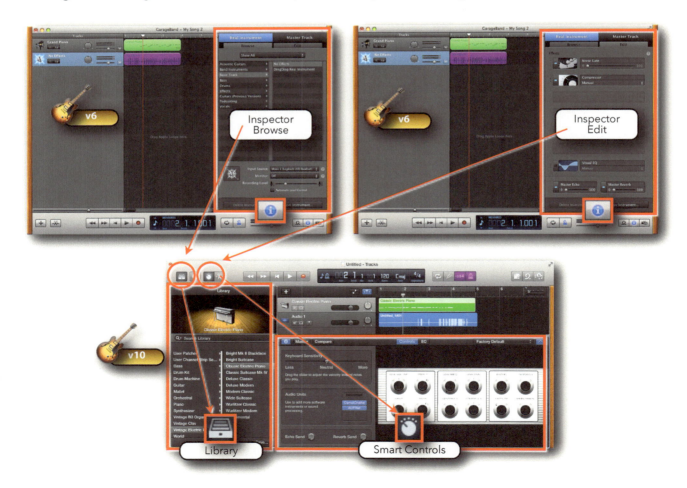

The Ugly

This is the painful part of the GarageBand X upgrade, the features that got removed.

➡ **Podcast Track**

This was the biggest shock of the new GarageBand X. The Podcast Track has been removed completely. This was a feature that was used professionally by many GarageBand users. On top of the anger and frustration came the realization that there is not a real good alternative using another app that would provide such an easy and efficient workflow.

➡ **Movie Track**

Although the Movie Track is still available in GarageBand X, a lot of functionality from Garageband 6.0.5 was removed. No more creation of interactive Chapter Markers. This step has to be performed now with a separate app like Compressor 4.

➡ **Magic GarageBand**

Another feature that was completely removed. Although this was not as crucial where people used it as an integral part of their business like Podcasts. It was still a great way for practicing improvisation or basic playing skills if you don't have your own band at your disposal.

At least you can save the Magic GarageBand songs as GarageBand Projects in the old GarageBand v6.0.5 and open them in GarageBand X.

4 - The Project

After you installed GarageBand and made yourself familiar with the basic user interface, you are now ready to start with your first Project. However, in my manuals I usually start with the discussion about the specific File Management first before I go into the topics of how to create any content with the app. Most books begin right away to show you how to create something cool. That's all exciting and great, but if you don't know yet how to properly save your new creation, then your early experience with an app could be that you lose some of your work that you created with it - not a good experience to begin with.

So let's understand the procedure first how to "safely" save a Project before learning how to create and work on your Project.

Basics

Here are a few basics about File Management in GarageBand.

Project vs Project File

There is one concept, very trivial, but very important nonetheless and you have to be absolutely clear about it. It is the same with most of the so-called content-creation applications.

For example, a word processor: You launch the app and create a new document. For the next few hours, you write ten pages of a short story. You see it right in front of your eyes, on the computer screen, it is right there. However your story is in a very "vulnerable" state because it exists only in the computer memory, the RAM (Random Access Memory). The problem with RAM is that it "loses its memory", in this case your 10 pages, if you turn off the computer, or someone trips over the power cord. To avoid that, you have to do the important step of saving the document as a document file to your computer's hard drive.

The same concept applies to GarageBand. When working in GarageBand, you work on a "GarageBand Project". This is the document, the data that makes up your song and that data exists only in the computer RAM at that moment. You have to save your Project as a Project File to your drive so it is "safe" to turn off your computer. Later, you can "open" that Project File, which loads the data from the file back into the RAM so you can continue to work on the Project.

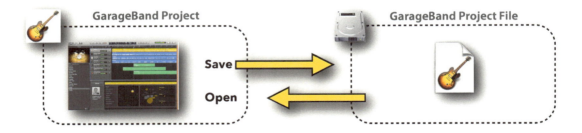

- **Project**

    Your GarageBand Project on the computer screen, currently stored in the computer's RAM

- **Project File**

    Your GarageBand Project, saved to your hard drive as a file, the GarageBand Project File.

Is it Save(d) ?

Once you understand the difference between the Project and the Project File, you realize that both are only "in sync" (representing that same data) under two conditions:
- ☑ You just saved the Project to a Project File and didn't change anything since then
- ☑ You opened a Project File in GarageBand and didn't change anything since then

There are two little indications that tells you if the Project on your screen is different from its saved Project File on the hard drive. These are OSX guidelines that are common in other apps too.

▸ **Red Close Button**: This is one of the three Title Bar Buttons in the upper left corner of the GarageBand Window. If the Project and its Project File are the same, then it shows a solid red button ❶. Once you make a change in GarageBand, then the red button will have a dot inside ❷.

▸ **Proxy Icon**: This is that little file icon ❸ in the middle of the Title Bar, in front of the Window Title (which is the name of current Project plus the name of the window "Tracks"). Once you make the first change in GarageBand after saving to or opening from a GarageBand Project File, then the Proxy Icon will be dimmed ❹. However, this is so subtle that it is hard to see. (Tip: *cmd+click* on the Proxy Icon and a popup menu displays the location of the Project File on your drive).

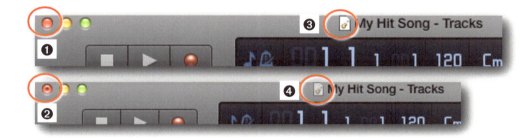

Autosave

Even if the dot in the red button indicates that you have changed something since the last time you saved the Project to the Project File, those changes are not unsaved. GarageBand has a little safety net built in that saves virtually every edit you make after you saved the Project. This way, you don't lose anything, even if you haven't saved your Project. I explain the details at the end of this chapter.

"Untitled" Project

When you start a new Project (and you haven't saved it yet), GarageBand will name it "Untitled" ❺ and saves it automatically as a GarageBand Project File named "Untitled" ❻ to the GarageBand folder inside the user's Music folder.

This extra step has to do with the Autosave feature. You could start a Project and work on it, never save it to a Project File and GarageBand could still "bring it back" after your computer was shut down or crashed. All this time it was saving to this "temporary" Project File. Once you save your Project (with your own name), then that "Untitled" file will disappear from the folder. Please note that you cannot name your Project "Untitled". That name is reserved for apparent reasons.

One Project at a Time

Unlike a word processor where you can have multiple documents open at the same time, GarageBand allows only one Project to be open. Launching the GarageBand app means opening a single GarageBand Project.

File Type

Here is some in-depth information about the GarageBand Project File in case you are interested.

➡ Package File

The GarageBand Project File is a special type of file that is common in OSX. It is called a "Package File" which is basically "**a Folder disguised as a File**". I discussed the details already in chapter 2.

When you "open" the file (***ctr+click*** on it and select "Show Package Contents" ❶ from the Shortcut Menu), you can see all the folders and files that are inside ❷. For example, there is a folder named "Autosave" ❸ that contains all the data when GarageBand auto-saves your edits.

➡ Assets

Assets or "Project Assets" are additional files that "belong" to the Project. These are mainly the audio files you record in your Project but also existing audio files and Apple Loops that you add to your Project. Please note that these files are copied to your Project File and stored in the Media ❹ folder. Keep in mind that your Project File could dramatically increase its size when you record or add a lot of audio files to your Project. They are all "inside" that single "Package File".

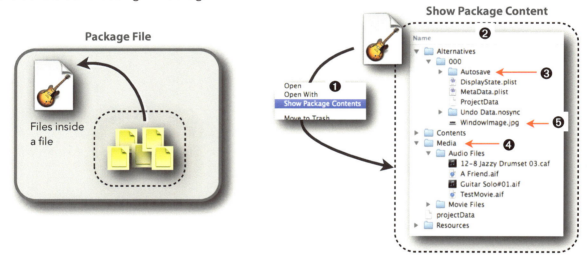

➡ Window Image

Inside the Project File is also a jpg file named "WindowImage.jpg" ❺. This is needed for an OSX feature.

OSX has the option to display a file in the Finder with a generic icon or display a Preview of that file. For example, this enables you to play an audio file or watch a movie directly in the Finder without opening a specific app for that. This feature can be turned on in the Finder Menu ***View ▸ Show View Option ▸ Show icon preview***.

Every time you save your Project, GarageBand takes a screenshot of the GarageBand window and saves it as that jpg file. If the Finder option "Show icon preview" is enabled, then you can see that screenshot ❻ instead of the generic GarageBand icon ❼. If you have to browse through many GarageBands files, then this might be a quick way to "visually" preview them.

➡ File Extension .band

A File Extension is that three (or more) letter code that is automatically attached to a filename, separated by a dot ❶. Usually you don't see the File Extension because it is hidden ❷ in the Finder by default.

You can enable it by unchecking the "Hide extension" checkbox ❸ in the File Info window (open it with the command *cmd+I* for the selected file).

The GarageBand Project Files have the File Extension ".band". Please note that the Projects you save in GarageBand for iPad have the same .band File Extension but they are only upwards compatible.

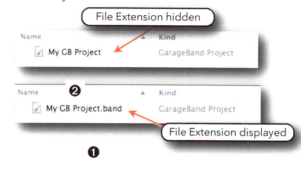

In the File Info window, you can also see the Project's Preview image ❹.

➡ Compatibility

I mentioned already Apple's ecosystem with all its audio applications. Here is a diagram that shows the upward compatibility of the various Project Files saved by each individual app. You only can open a Project File in the next "higher" app but you can't go backwards.

This concept also applies to Project Files that were saved in the GarageBand version 6.0.5. You can open them in the new GarageBand version 10.0 but once a Project is saved in GarageBand 10.0, you cannot open it anymore in GarageBand v6.0.5.

Project File Compatibility

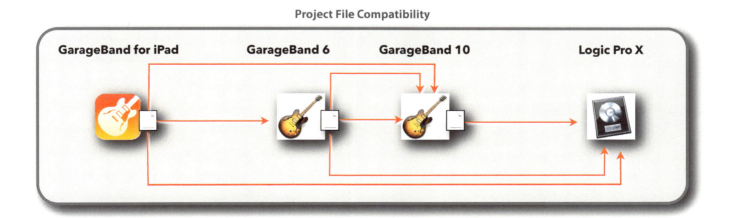

Project Chooser

When you start a new Project in GarageBand, the first window that pops up is the Project Chooser.

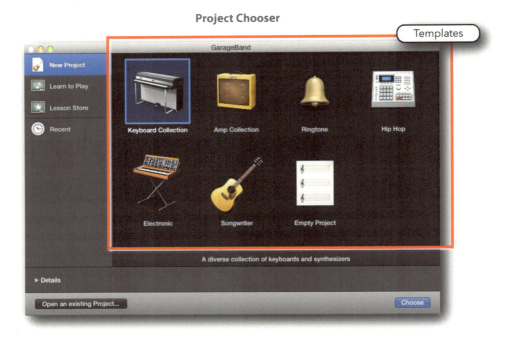

The concept is simple: Instead of starting with a complete blank Project, you have the option to choose from various Templates.

Templates

Templates are just regular GarageBand Projects that were saved with a special configuration of Tracks and Settings (without any Regions). They can be used as a starting point. For example, a Template that already has several keyboard Tracks or a couple of Tracks loaded with guitar amps. The Project Chooser provides seven Templates to choose from. The "Empty Project" is exactly that. This opens a Project that has no Tracks created yet.

The seven Templates are factory Project Files that are embedded in the GarageBand app. There is no option as of GarageBand v10.0.1 to add your own custom Template to the Chooser.

Tip: If you are comfortable hacking into the GarageBand app (it is also a Package File), then you can copy your own Project Files into a specific directory inside the GarageBand app (*GarageBand/Contents/Resources/Project Templates / NewProject/*) and those Project Files will then show up in the Project Chooser as your custom Templates.

🟡 Sidebar ❶

The Sidebar displays items that function like folders (similar to a Finder window). Selecting an item in the Sidebar will display its content in the Browser ❷ section to the right. There are four items in the Sidebar:
- **New Projects ❷**: This displays the seven factory Templates that are stored inside the GarageBand app.
- **Learn To Play ❸**: This is the place that lists all the downloaded lessons and lets you play them.
- **Lesson Store ❹**: This displays the available lessons that you can download for free or as in-app purchases.
- **Recent ❺**: This item displays all the Projects that you recently opened in GarageBand. It displays the same content as the Main Menu *File ➤ Open Recent ➤*

🟡 Browser ❷

The Browser displays the content based on what is selected in the Sidebar. When "New Project" is selected, then all the seven Templates are displayed as icons with an optional description ❻ of the Template. You can *double-click* on an icon (or *click* "Choose") to open a new Project based on that Template. The new Project will have a default length of 32bars.

🟡 Details ❼

The disclosure triangle below the Sidebar lets you show/hide the Details area (New Projects and Recent only). It shows you the main Project Properties ❽. The new Project will open with those settings.

🟡 Toolbar ❾

The Toolbar at the bottom provides the "Choose" button to open the selected Project (or just *double-click* on the icon). *Click* on the "Open an existing Project..." button to bring up the Open Dialog for selecting a Project from your local hard drive or iCloud.

4 - The Project

➡ *Project Properties / Preferences*

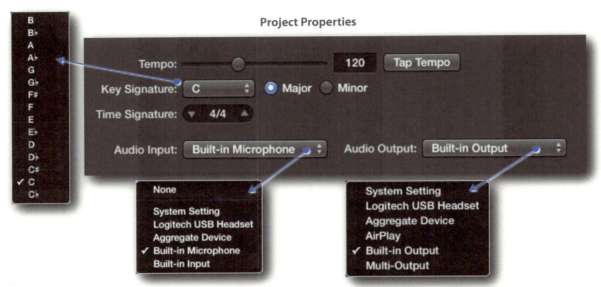

🔘 **Project Properties**

Please note that these settings have a different function:

If you selected New Project ![New Project], then you can set the parameters for the new Project.

If you selected Recent Project ![Recent], then the parameters display the properties of the selected Project.

▶ **Tempo**

You can set the Tempo in three ways:
- *Drag* the Tempo Slider left or right
- *Double-click* on the entry field, enter a numeric value and hit enter.
- *Click* a few times on the "Tap Tempo" button like a drummer counting in. The Tempo will automatically adjust to the tempo you are clicking.

▶ **Key Signature**

Select the key from the popup menu and the Major or Minor scale with the radio button

▶ **Time Signature**

You can change the Time Signature in three ways:
- *Double-click* on the entry field and enter a numeric value (a fraction) and hit enter.
- *Click* on the up or down arrow to increase or decrease the upper number.
- *Drag* individually the first or second number up or down (while dragging, a blue arrow above and below will appear).

🔘 **Project Preferences**

These two settings belong to the GarageBand Preferences and can be changed later in the Preferences window.

▶ **Audio Input / Audio Output**

Click on the buttons to open the popup menu to select any of the available Audio Devices for the audio input and audio output.

File Menu

Before starting with a new Project, let's look at all the commands related to managing Project Files. They are found under the File Menu. Here is a diagram that shows the result of each command.

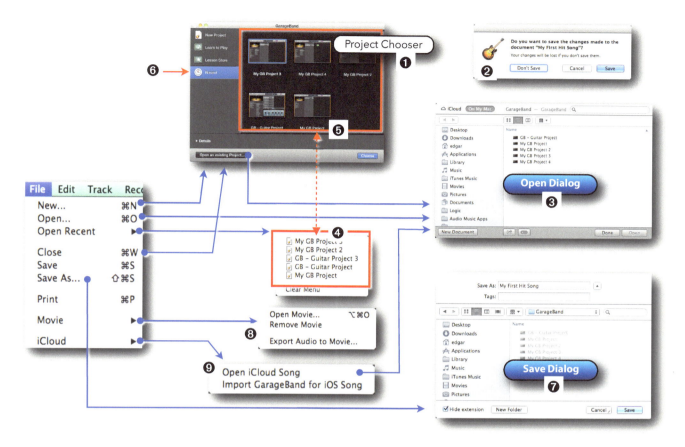

- **New** (*cmd+N*): This command closes the current Project and opens the Project Chooser ❶. A Dialog pops up ❷ first that lets you save unsaved changes.
- **Open** (*cmd+O*): This command opens the Open Dialog ❸ (without closing the current Project yet).
- **Open Recent** ➤: This command opens a submenu ❹ with a list of recently opened Projects plus the "Clear Menu" command to clear this submenu. The submenu lists the same recently opened Projects as the Project Chooser ❺ when selecting "Recent" ❻ from the Sidebar.
- **Close** (*cmd+W*): This command closes the current Project and opens the Project Chooser ❶. A Dialog pops up ❷ first that lets you save unsaved changes.
- **Save** (*cmd+S*): This command saves any changes (since you last saved the Project) to the Project File. If you started with a Template from the Project Chooser, then the Save Dialog ❼ will open first to give your Project a name and save it to the location you determine.
- **Save As...** (*sh+cmd+S*): This command opens the Save Dialog ❼. You save the current Project to a new Project File (choosing a different name and/or different location).
- **Print** (*cmd+P*): This command is only active when you have the Score Editor open. It lets you print out the current Track as a score.
- **Movie**: This command opens a submenu ❽ with commands related to the Movie Track. I cover this feature in a later chapter.
- **iCloud**: This command opens a submenu ❾ with two commands that lets you open GarageBand Projects or GarageBand for iPad Projects that are located in your iCloud storage.

iCloud

In case you are not familiar with iCloud yet, it is Apple's online storage and services solution. When you create an Apple ID, you have access to 5GB of free online storage and various online services that stores their data with your iCloud account. One of the services is that you use the 5GB storage as an alternative to store files from various applications instead of saving them to your local hard drive. This has the advantage that you can access those files from any computer that has internet access (and access to your iCloud account).

➡ Documents and Data

The iCloud Service that lets you save Documents to your iCloud storage is called "Documents and Data".

- Go to the *Apple Menu* ➤ *System Preferences* and select the iCloud icon.
- In the iCloud window ❶ sign in to your account and check "Documents & Data" ❷ in the list.
- *Click* on the Options ❸ button next to it to open a window that shows a list with all apps (only OSX apps) that have files stored on your iCloud storage ❹.
- If you click on the "Manage..." ❺ button, a sheet will slide out with a list ❻ of all apps (OSX and iOS) that have files/data stored on your iCloud storage. You can even delete ❼ files in this window.
- All the files you see in the Manage Storage window are also stored on your local drive. I explain that whole mechanism in more detail in a separate iCloud chapter of my manual "GarageBand for iPad - How it Works".

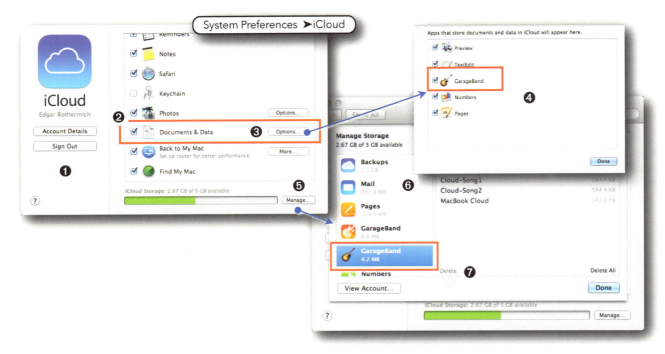

If you want to use the iCloud storage for your GarageBand Project Files, then a Dialog ❽ window will remind you that you have to sign in to iCloud (if you have not) and pops up the Preferences window ❾ with the iCloud login screen.

The option to store files on iCloud instead of on your local drive is also available for other apps. For all those apps, the Open Dialog and the Save Dialog has a few extra features you should make yourself familiar with.

➡ Open Dialog

The Open Dialog has two tabs in the upper left corner. They act like a location selection:

- **iCloud ❶**

    When the "iCloud" tab is selected, the window displays only the GarageBand Project files that are saved to your iCloud storage ❷. Other file types are not relevant at that moment anyway and are hidden from the view.

- **On My Mac ❸**

    When the "On My Mac" tab is selected, the window displays the regular Open Dialog showing your local hard drive ❹, the content of the GarageBand folder in the user's Music folder. You can navigate to any other location using the Sidebar ❺ (or the Key Command *cmd+arrow up*).

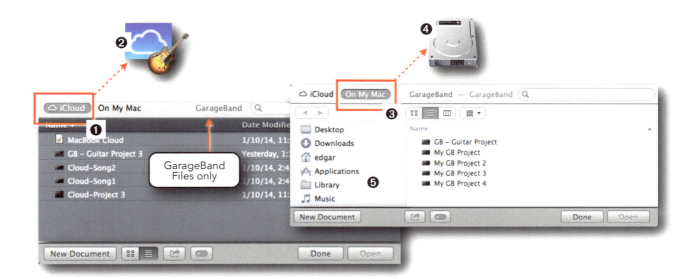

Please note that the Menu Command *File ➤ iCloud ➤ Open iCloud Song* ❻ is actually redundant. Selecting it will open the Open Dialog with the iCloud ❶ tab selected.

This is the same as using the Menu *Command File ➤ Open* and selecting the iCloud tab.

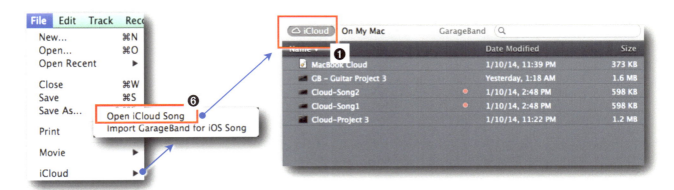

4 - The Project

➡ Save Dialog

The Save Dialog also lets you open both locations. You can save a GarageBand file to your iCloud storage ❶ or to your local hard drive ❷. However, this time, the option is not as clear with tabs like in the Open Dialog.

Now, the window has a popup menu ❸ that lets you select the location "Where" you want to store the GarageBand Project File. When opened, the upper portion of the menu shows the path on your hard drive to the GarageBand folder ❹ and below is just the iCloud icon ❺. There is no further path because files on iCloud cannot be organized in subfolders.

Next to the file name is a disclosure triangle. **Click** on it to toggle the view of the Save Dialog between "minimal" ❻ (with only the popup menu to navigate) and "expanded" ❼ where you have the full Dialog Window with Sidebar and additional controls.

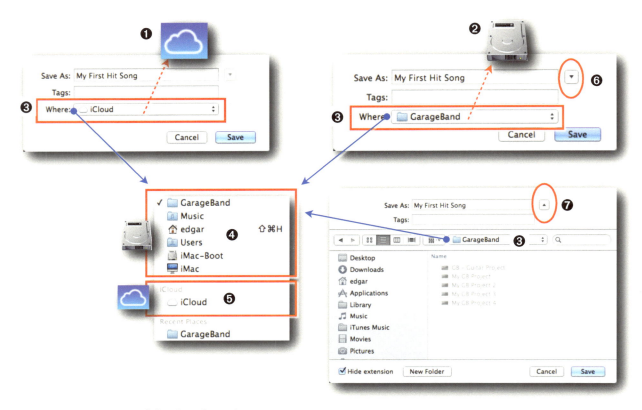

➡ Import GarageBand for iPad Projects

The Menu Command *File ➤ iCloud ➤ Import GarageBand for iOS Song* ❽ also accesses the iCloud storage. But this time, the Dialog Window ❾ displays only the files that are saved from the GarageBand for iPad app. As we have seen earlier, these files are upward compatible and can be opened in GarageBand for OSX (and Logic).

An additional Dialog Window ❿ pops up in case you haven't signed in to your iCloud account yet.

🔘 Launch

Here is a summary of the File Management: There are two scenarios when launching the GarageBand app.

- ❶ GarageBand was open before with a specific Project. In that case GarageBand launches and automatically opens that Project. Hold down the *option* key immediately after launching GarageBand will open it without any Project.
- ❷ Garageband opens the very first time (or can't find the Project it had open before). In that case, GarageBand launches and presents the Project Chooser.

You can also *double-click* on a GarageBand Project File in the Finder (or *drag* the file over the GarageBand icon on the Finder or in the Dock). This will launch GarageBand and open that Project.

🔘 "Untitled" GarageBand Project

Starting with a new Project by choosing a Template from the Project Chooser, will open a Project named "Untitled" ❸. This is a special "temporary" Project that is automatically saved as a Project File "Untitled" ❹ to the GarageBand folder.

- **Save, Save As...**: Both commands have the same function. They open the Save Dialog ❺ to name the Project ❻ and save it to a Project File with that name ❼. This will delete the "Untitled" Project File ❹ from the GarageBand folder.
- **New, Close**: Both commands have the same function. The "Untitled" Project ❸ will be deleted (including the "Untitled" Project File ❹ and the Project Chooser ❷ opens again.
- **Open**: This command opens the Open Dialog ❽ to select an existing Project File on the hard drive or on iCloud.
- **Open Recent**: Select any recently opened Project Files from the submenu ❾.

🔘 GarageBand Project

These are the available commands in GarageBand while a Project (not "Untitled") is open.

- **Save:** This command saves the current Project ❻ to its Project File ❼ (without any Dialog).
- **Save As...**: This command opens the Save Dialog ❺ to give the Project a different name and save it as a new Project File with that name to the selected location.
- **New, Close**: Both have the same function. The current Project will be closed (with a Dialog Window that lets you choose to save the current Project first) and the Project Chooser ❷ opens.
- **Open**: This command opens the Open Dialog ❽ to select an existing Project File on the Hard Drive or on iCloud. Opening a new Project will prompt a Dialog that lets you choose to save the current Project first if there were unsaved changes.
- **Open Recent**: Select any recently opened Project Files from the submenu ❾. Opening a new Project will prompt a Dialog that lets you choose to save the current Project first if there were unsaved changes.

4 - The Project

Autosave

Autosave is a feature that was implemented first in Logic Pro X and works the same in GarageBand, even if it is not specifically mentioned. However, this is not just a simple procedure that saves the Project File based on a specific time interval. Instead, it is a very sophisticated and efficient procedure.

> **GarageBand saves virtually every edit you make - instantly**

Here is an illustration that demonstrates what this means:

- Once you saved your GarageBand Project manually ❶ and continue to make changes in that Project, all those changes are only applied in RAM on your computer. They are not saved to your drive in form of a file. If GarageBand crashes ❷ or someone trips over your power cord, all those changes are gone and your only "fall back" is the last Project you saved ❶. If that was an hour before your crash, then all that hour of work is lost.
- Welcome to GarageBand's Autosave feature. Now, every change you make in your Project ❸ will automatically be saved ❹ to separate files in an Autosave folder inside the Project Package File.
- The Autosave folder contains those files ❺ since you last saved your Project. Every time you save your Project manually, those files will be deleted until you make new changes in your Project. Then the files get created again with the new accumulated changes.

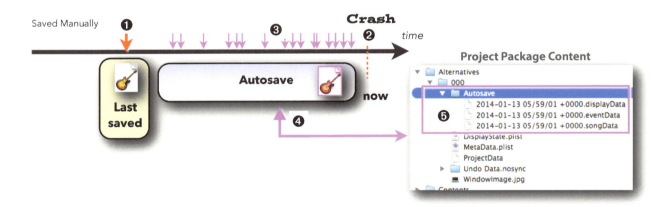

Usually, when you close a Project or quit GarageBand, you would save the Project which automatically empties the Autosave folder. That means whenever you open a Project that has Autosave files in it, GarageBand interprets that as a sign of a previous "sudden interrupted ending" and it brings up an Alert window ❻. It lists the timestamp when the last autosave data was saved and offers you to create a new "Auto-saved" Project ❼. This Project will be the last saved Project ❽ plus all the changes ❾ in the Autosave folder applied to it. "Saved" is the last Project File you saved manually.

5 - Tracks Area

I provided already a basic overview of the GarageBand user interface in an earlier chapter. Now let's explore those windows to get familiar with the look and see what those elements are and what they do.

Tracks Area

The center of the GarageBand Window is the Tracks Area, one of the two Window Panes that is always visible (the other one is the Control Bar). The interface is very clean and simple and similar to other DAWs where it is often called "Arrange Window". After all, here is where you create and arrange your song. If you worked with the previous GarageBand app or any other DAW, then you might be familiar with that window and recognize most of those elements.

One Row - One Track

One of the main elements in the Tracks Area is the similar looking rows. Each one of those rows represents a Track. I discuss everything about Tracks a little bit later in its own chapter. Here is just the introduction of the basic interface.

Each of those Tracks ❶ is divided into two segments. On the left is the Track Header ❷ and on the right is the Track Lane ❸.

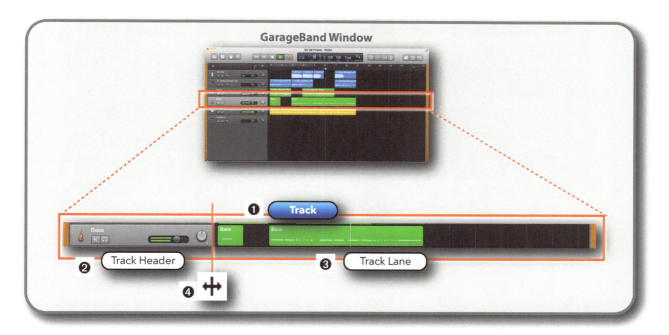

Resizing

- ▶ The height of a row (the Track) is fixed.
- ▶ The width of the Track Header can be changed by *dragging* the Divider Line ❹ between the Track Header and Track Lane.
- ▶ The width of the Track Lane can only be changed by resizing the width of the GarageBand Window itself. As we have already seen, it can also be affected by showing/hiding other Window Panes.
- ▶ Any resizing affects all rows (Tracks) equally.

Four Sections

This was one way to look at the Tracks Area, divide it into the individual rows that represent the Tracks ❶.

However, there are other elements on the Tracks Area. So the other way to look at the Tracks Area is to divide it into four sections. This groups all the Track Headers and all the Track Lanes into a separate section.

❷ **Tracks List**: The area on the left with all the rows of the available Track Headers is called the Track List. It lists all the "Instruments" in your Project that "play" your song.

❸ **Workspace**: The area on the right with all the rows of available Track Lanes is called the Workspace (or Timeline). This is the place where you work on your song. You record, place and arrange your music in the form of Regions, the rectangle objects that are the musical building blocks of your song. These Regions will be played by the "Instrument" defined in the Track Header on the left.

❹ **Ruler**: On top of the Track Lane sits the Ruler. It represents a time reference for the Track Lanes in the Workspace. The Ruler is "attached" to the Workspace and moves horizontally with the Track Lanes when you scroll or zoom that area.

❺ **Menu Bar**: On top of the Track List is an area with three control buttons.

➕ Add aTrack, 🟨 Show/Hide Automation, ▶️ Catch Playhead

Band Analogy

Now that we know the elements on the Tracks Area and the right terminology, let me introduce a model, the "Band Analogy" that I also use in my Logic Pro X manual. It hopefully gives you a better understanding what functions those elements have.

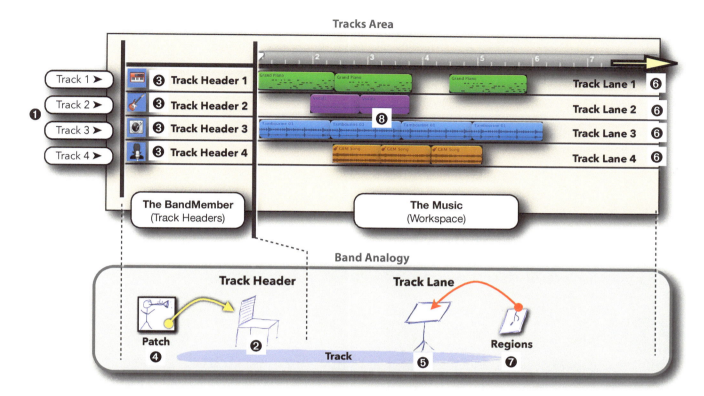

- ▸ **Band**: Think about your GarageBand Project as your composition, your song (or song in the making). However, if you want your song to be played, you need a band. First, you have to determine how many players you need in that band. These players are represented by the Tracks ❶ in your Project. The more players you need, the more Tracks you have to create in your Project.
- ▸ **Chair**: Once you decided that you need, for example, four players for your band, you would prepare four Chairs ❷ for those BandMembers to sit in. Think of those Chairs as the Track Headers ❸.
- ▸ **BandMember (Instrument)**: Now that you've prepared the Chairs, you have to put a BandMember in each of those chairs. This is done by selecting a Patch ❹ from the Library Window (similar to selecting a preset on a synth). When you create a Track in GarageBand, it automatically puts a BandMember (with its instrument) in that Chair. At any time, you can choose a different Patch, like firing the saxophone player and hiring a guitar player instead and put him in that chair. More details about that procedure in the Library chapter.
- ▸ **MusicStand**: Having four BandMembers with their individual Instruments sitting in their Chairs is only half the story. Now you have to tell each BandMember what to play. In real life, you would put a MusicStand ❺ in front of each Player. All those MusicStands in front of the BandMembers are represented by the Track Lanes ❻ "in front" of each Track Header in the Workspace.
- ▸ **SheetMusic**: Now, that each BandMember (Track) has its own MusicStand (Track Lane), You can finally place the SheetMusic ❼ on those individual Music Stands (Track Lanes) that tells each BandMember what to play on their Instrument (Track Header). The SheetMusic is represented by the Regions ❽, the building blocks of your song, your composition.

More Band related issues

This Band Analogy works very well even for other techniques and workflows around the Tracks Area. Here is just a preview of some of the techniques we will learn a little later.

- Create a new Track: Hire a new BandMember
- Delete a Track: Fire a BandMember
- Change the Patch on a Track: Fire the BandMember and hire a different one.
- Adjust the controls on the Track Header: Tell the guitar player to turn up the amp or add reverb to it.
- Move the Region to a different Track Lane: Take the Sheet Music with the melody from the MusicStand of BandMember A and put it on the MusicStand of BandMember B. For example, let the saxophone play the melody instead of the guitar.
- Edit the Regions: Make corrections on the SheetMusic.
- Hit the Play button: Tell the band to start playing at a specific bar.

Think about it

When working in your Project and developing your song, there are three main questions that describe the various procedures and decision making that is going on.

What What to play?

The Regions (SheetMusic) represent the building blocks of your music. They tell the BandMember **what** to play. For example, does the Region contain just plain chords, a melody or the rhythm part?

Who Who is playing it?

By putting the Regions on the Track Lane of a specific Track, you decide **who** is playing those specific instructions.

When When to play it?

Once you determine who is playing what, you have also tell the BandMember **when** to play it. This is determined by where you place the Region on the Track Lane and from where you play back your Project.

▶ **Ruler ❶**: This horizontal strip is linked to the Track Lanes. It gives you the time reference where you place a Region along the Track Lane (i.e. starting at bar 1 or bar 7). The Ruler can display that reference in Musical Time (bars and beats) or in Absolute Time (minutes and seconds).

▶ **Playhead ❷**: This is the white triangle in the Ruler that expands vertically across the Track Lanes. It indicates from what time position the Project is playing back or recording.

I will discuss the Ruler and Playhead a little bit later in more detail.

Tracks Area - the origin of the concept

Here are two examples that show that the concept, used by most DAWs, is not new.

🔸 Example A

If you come from a musical background and are familiar with reading musical notations, look at the following diagram. The Arrange window is nothing other than a representation of a musical score with the same basic elements. The same three questions about What-Who-When also apply to a score.

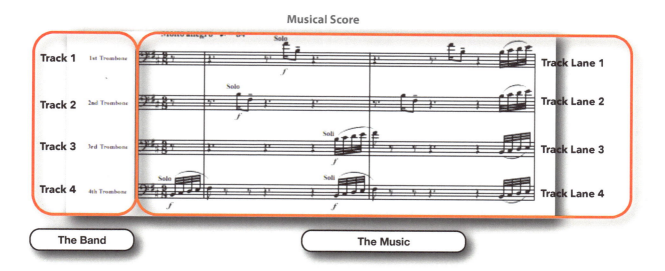

🔸 Example B

If you come from a recording engineer background and are familiar with tape machines, look at the following diagram. The Arrange window is nothing other than a representation of a Tape Machine. The Tracks Area is like the playback/record head that has a specified number of tracks it can record and play back (8, 16, 24, 32). Each Track is used to record and play back one band member (or a section). The Track Lane is the actual magnetic tape where the music is recorded on in electro-magnetic form and the time axis is your tape that is wound up on a reel.

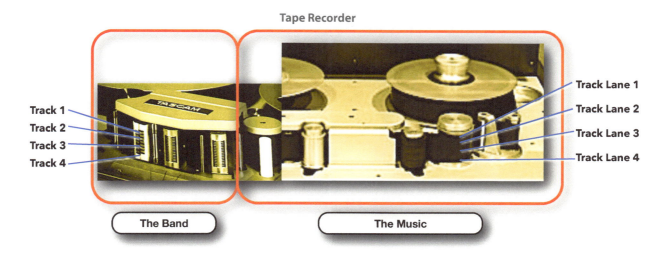

Resize - Zoom - Scroll

Now that we know what the elements in the Tracks Area are and what they represent, let's look at the more "mechanical" aspects of those window elements. The important thing is to know what sections inside the Tracks Area are affected by the following commands: Resize - Zoom - Scroll.

➡ *Resize*

The Tracks Area itself can only be resized by changing the size of the GarageBand Window itself as I showed already in a previous chapter. The exception is when showing or hiding Window Panes that must share the available space with the Tracks Area or when you move the Divider Line between a Window Pane and the Tracks Area.

❶ **Track Header Width**: The Tracks Area itself has a movable Divider Line between the Tracks List and the Workspace. It lets you resize the width of (all) the Track Headers by *dragging* this Divider Line. Of course, this will change the size of the Workspace proportionally because the GarageBand Window itself is not affected and remains the same size.

❷ **GarageBand Window Width**: Moving the left or right border of the GarageBand Window will only increase the width of the Tracks Area. The width of the Track List stays the same.

❸ **GarageBand Window Height**: Moving the upper or lower border of the GarageBand Window will change the height of the available space, to show more or less Tracks (rows). Please note that the height of the individual Track Header and Track Lane is fixed.

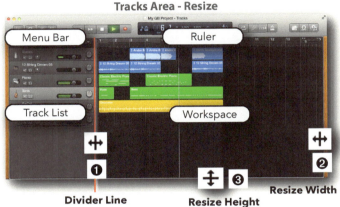

➡ *Zoom*

There is only one section in the Tracks Area that can be zoomed and only in one direction: The Workspace together with the Ruler. You are basically zooming in and out of the Timeline. More on that a little bit later.

Here are the zoom commands.

- Use the Zoom Slider  on the far right of the Ruler ❹.
- *Cmd+LeftArrow* and *Cmd+RightArrow*
- Use the *Pinch* Gesture on a Trackpad
- Use the *Scroll* Gesture on a Trackpad by *opt+dragging* left or right.

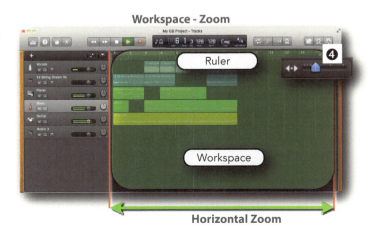

These zoom commands also work in the Editor Window because these are all the windows that show your music referenced against a timeline.

➡ Scroll

The scroll commands are standard as with other windows. However, you have to pay attention to which section in the Tracks Area is scrolled.

🟡 Scroll Commands

You can scroll a window by using the standard commands.
- Use the *Scroll* Gesture on your Track Pad.
- *Drag* the Scroll Bars ❶. In OSX, the Scroll Bars are hidden by default. They only appear when you actually scroll with the Scroll Gesture or mouse movement. This behavior can be changed in the System Preferences.
- Key Command *end* (scroll forward) and *home* (scroll backwards)
- The "Catch Playhead" feature is a horizontal autoscroll function that can be toggled with the Catch Playhead button.

🟡 Scroll areas

The horizontal and vertical scroll affects different sections of the Tracks Area.

▶ **Vertical Scroll ❷**: The Track List and the Workspace move together up or down. The Menu Bar and the Ruler are not affected. They stay fixed on top. Global Tracks are special Tracks (I'll cover them in the Tracks chapter) that can be made visible just below the Ruler. They also are not affected by the scroll movement.

Tracks Area - Vertical Scroll

▶ **Horizontal Scroll ❸**: Only the Ruler together with the Workspace is scrolling left or right. The section with the Track Headers are not affected.

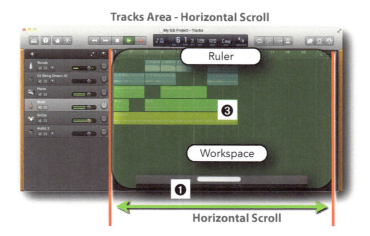

Tracks Area - Horizontal Scroll

Ruler

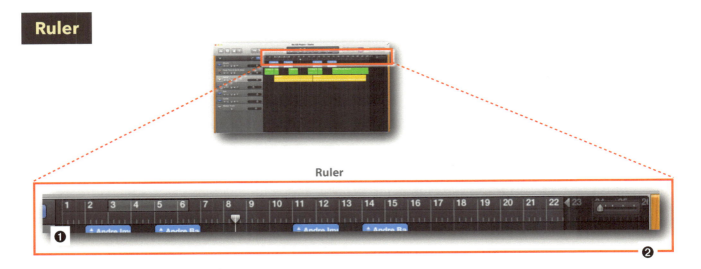

The "Ruler", or "Timeline" as it is sometimes referred to, is a standard component in all DAWs and they function virtually the same.
- ▶ The Ruler ❶ sits on top of the Workspace and as we have seen, it zooms and scrolls horizontally together with the Workspace.
- ▶ The Ruler functions as a timeline reference to place the Regions in the Workspace underneath.
- ▶ The Ruler always starts at bar 1 (which represents the absolute time of 0:00)
- ▶ The more you zoom in, the finer the resolution of the displayed time units on the Ruler for more precise placement of an object.
- ▶ On the far right of the Ruler is the Zoom Slider ❷ for horizontally zooming the Ruler+Workspace. This is an odd placement because it can cover a portion of the Ruler.
- ▶ The Ruler can also be found in the Editor Windows

Time Format

You can choose between two time formats to be displayed as the time reference on the Ruler. You switch between them by selecting one of the two Display Modes in the Control Bar Display. *Click* on the Display Mode Button ❸ on the left of the Control Bar Display to select from the popup menu ❹. The Control Bar Display also switches to that time format.
- ▶ **Musical Time ❺**: This time format displays time in bars and beats (and even finer increments).
- ▶ **Absolute Time ❻**: This time format displays time in standard time of minutes and seconds (and even finer increments).

Ruler Elements

The Ruler has an upper part and a lower part to display various elements.

🔵 Upper Part ❶

The upper part of the Ruler contains three elements.

- ▶ The numbers ❶ display the time reference (musical or absolute)
- ▶ The Cycle Area ❸ is the strip that marks the cycle range and is either gray (disabled) or yellow (enabled). The background of the upper Ruler area outside the Cycle Area also changes depending on the Cycle Mode. I explain the Cycle Mode in the next chapter.
- ▶ The End-of-Project Marker ❹ is the triangle that marks the end of your song. It determines where the playback stops (not the recording!) and also where to end when you export your song (although only one possible scenario. See the Share chapter for details). The space in the Workspace after the End-of-Project Marker is darkened.

🔵 Lower Part ❷

The lower part of the Ruler contains two elements.

- ▶ The division lines ❷ display the time reference. Please note that the amount of division lines (how fine the resolution) depends on the zoom factor. The more you zoom in horizontally, the more division lines are displayed.
- ▶ The Playhead ❺ is displayed as a triangle that moves along the lower part of the Ruler and extends vertically across the Workspace as a white line.
  - 📌 *Click* on the lower part of the Ruler to move the Ruler to that position
  - 📌 *Double-click* on the lower part of the Ruler will start the playback from that position
  - 📌 *Drag* the Playhead along the Ruler to move it to a new position

Grid

The division lines or time units you see on the Ruler represent an invisible grid for the Workspace. Please note that the resolution of the grid (distance between the grid lines) changes depending on the zoom factor.

- ▶ **Snap To Grid**: When this mode is activated (Main Menu *Edit* ➤ *Snap to Grid* or Key Command *cmd +G*) ,then moving or placing any objects in the Workspace (Playhead, Regions, Cycle Area, Automation Control Points) will snap the object to that grid represented by the time units on the Ruler. When zoomed in, the grid gets finer than the displayed units. Objects also snap to any other boundaries of Regions on any Track Lane.
  - • *Ctr+drag*: Disables the Snap to Grid Mode
  - • *Sh+ctr+drag*: Lets you move objects in Tick increments (there are 960 Ticks per quarter note) or Sub-frames.
- ▶ **Alignment Guides**: Many objects have already some alignment guides, long vertical lines that span across the Workspace up to the Ruler, so you can move them with the precise reference of the Ruler. In addition to that, you can activate the extra yellow "Alignment Guides" ❻ that extend over the Ruler ❼ (Main Menu *Edit* ➤ *Alignment Guides* or Key Command *opt+cmd+G*) to appear when the moving objects snap to any boundaries (i.e. Regions ❽), not only time units on the Ruler.

Alignment Guide

6 - Control Bar

The Control Bar on top of the GarageBand Window is always visible. It contains various controls, buttons and displays that are grouped together. They are fixed and cannot be moved or hidden.

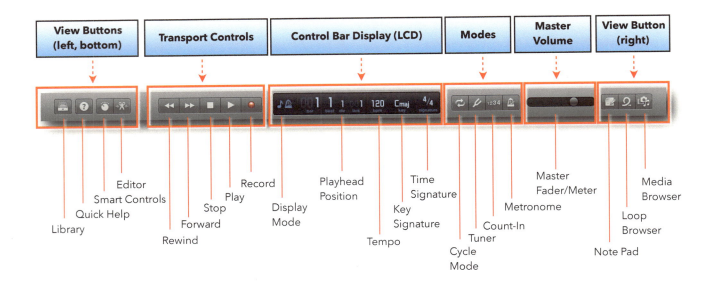

➡ **Hidden Control Bar Buttons**

If you resize the width of the GarageBand Window (and with it the Control Bar), then some Control Bar Buttons will be hidden. This is indicated by the double arrow button ❶ that appears in that case on the Control Bar. **Click** on it to open a popup menu ❷ with the names of the buttons that are hidden. Selecting an item from the menu is the same as clicking the button for that control.

Please note that the Master Volume will not be listed in the popup menu if it is hidden.

This is the view of the Control Bar ❸ when the GarageBand Window is resized to the smallest width.

I will quickly go over the View Buttons first with a short description of the windows that they open. Most of those window are covered later in the manual with their own chapter.

View Buttons

The View Buttons on the Control Bar toggle various Window Panes. The exception is the Quick Help Button that toggles its own floating window.

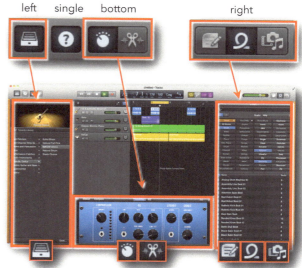

- A button turns dark when that specific window is displayed
- The Window Pane at the bottom can display two different Windows, the Smart Controls Window and the Editors Window. That's why the two buttons are linked. Selecting one button would deselect the other one (if it was selected).
- The Window Pane on the right can display three different Windows, the Note Pad, the Apple Loop Browser and the Media Browser. Same thing here. The three buttons are linked and you can have only one button selected at a time, or none.

Library

The Library Button toggles the Window Pane on the left, displaying the Library Window. It contains all the Patches, configuration presets for your Tracks. See the *Library* chapter for detail.

Double-clicking on the Track Header (on the background, not a control), will also toggle the Library Window.

Quick Help

The Quick Help Button opens a separate floating window that displays a short description of the area in GarageBand where you move the Mouse Pointer over (buttons, controls, etc.). It works like an interactive manual. Using this feature with the Logic Remote for iPad app takes Quick Help to a whole new level.

Smart Controls

The Smart Controls Button toggles the Window Pane at the bottom, displaying the Smart Controls Window. This is technically an Editor Window ("editing the sound" of a Track), displaying the available sound controls for the selected Track. Think of it as GarageBand's Mixer Window with only a single Channel Strip (in the shape of the Smart Controls Window) displaying the sound controls of the Track that is currently selected.

See the *Smart Controls* chapter for detail.

Double-clicking on the Track Icon in the Track Header will also toggle the Smart Controls Window.

 **Editors**

The Editors Button also toggles the Window Pane at the bottom. However, now it displays any of the four Editor Windows ("edit the music"). Which one of the Editor Windows you will see depends on what type of Region (Audio, MIDI, Drummer) is selected in the Track Lane when you click on the Editor Button.
Some windows have additional tabs that let you switch to different Views inside an Editor Window.

➡ Audio Editor

- **Click** on an Audio Region: This switches to the Audio Editor, but only if any of the Editor Windows is already open.
- **Double-Click** on an Audio Region: This switches to the Audio Editor even if the Window Pane was closed or if it was open but displaying a different window.

You can switch the Audio Editor between Track View and Region View with the two tabs on the left.

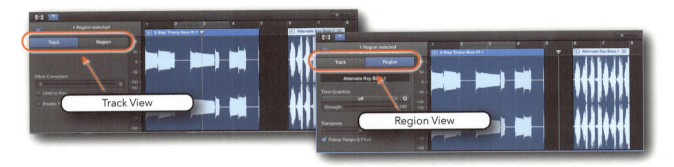

➡ MIDI Editor

- **Click** on a MIDI Region: This switches to the MIDI Editor, but only if any of the Editor Windows are already open.
- **Double-Click** on a MIDI Region: This switches to the MIDI Editor even if the Window Pane was closed or if it was open but displaying a different window.

There are two MIDI Editors, Piano Roll and Score. You can switch between them using the two tabs on the top. In addition, you can switch the MIDI Editor between Region View and Notes View with the two tabs on the left

➡ Drummer Editor

- **Click** on a Drummer Region: This switches to the Drummer Editor, but only if any of the Editor Windows are already open.
- **Double-Click** on a Drummer Region: This toggles the Drummer Editor even if the Window Pane was closed or if it was open but displaying a different window.

Note Pad

The Note Pad Button toggles the Window Pane on the right. It provides a window that lets you enter notes/remarks for your Project in this Text Area. For example, what microphones or setup used during recording, the name of the musicians or any notes for later editing and mixing.

The Fonts Button  opens the system-wide Fonts Panel that even lets you format the text.

Note Pad Window

Apple Loops

Apple Loops

The Apple Loops Button toggles the Window Pane on the right. It displays the Loop Browser that lets you search and preview Apple Loops and drag them onto the Track Lanes to include them in your Project.

See the *Apple Loops* chapter for details.

Media Browser

The Media Browser Button toggles the Window Pane on the right. It displays the Media Browser that lets you search and preview Audio and Movie files that are available on your hard drive in specific folders. You can drag the files from the Browser window directly onto the Track Lanes to include them in your Project.

The two tabs on top switch between Audio View and Movie View.

See the *Media Browser* chapter for details.

6 - Control Bar   85

Mode Buttons

The four Control Bar Buttons next to the Control Bar Display can be toggled on (color) or off (gray).

Cycle Mode

Usually, when you play back your song, it starts at the position where the Playhead is parked and ends at the end of the song (at the End-of-Project Marker) or when you stop the playback manually. When you enable Cycle Mode, the behavior is different:

First of all, when Cycle Mode is enabled, a yellow strip appears at the upper half of the Ruler. This strip is the "Cycle Area" or "Cycle Range". It has an effect on playback and recording.

- **Cycle Mode enabled during Playback**
    - When you start playback, the Playhead jumps to the beginning of the Cycle Area and starts playing from there.
    - Once the Playhead reaches the end of the yellow Cycle Area, it jumps back to the beginning of the Cycle Area and continues to play from there.
    - The playback continues that procedure, repeatedly playing the section marked by the Cycle Area until you stop the playback.

- **Cycle Mode enabled during Recording**
    You also can use Cycle Mode when recording.
    - Now, instead of repeatedly playing the section between the beginning and the end of the Cycle Area, GarageBand continues to record over that section again and again until you stop. I cover the details in the Recording chapter.
    - If the Count-In Mode is also enabled, then the Cycle behavior is slightly different. If the Count-In is set to "1 Bar" or "2 Bars", then GarageBand doesn't start at the beginning of the Cycle Area, it starts playing 1 bar or 2 bars before that and switches to recording at the beginning of the Cycle Area and then repeats the recording over the section of the Cycle Area. There are some details to be aware of that I cover in the Recording chapter.

- **Cycle Mode and Exporting (Sharing)**
    The Cycle Area has one additional function. You can use the Cycle Area to define the range of your Project (from ... to) that you want to export. See the Share chapter for details).

➡ **Commands**

Please note that the following commands work in the Tracks Area but also in the Audio and MIDI Editor Windows.

🔘 **Toggle Cycle Mode on/off**

- 📌 *Click* on the Cycle Button in the Control Bar
- 📌 Key Command **C**
- 📌 *Click* on the Cycle Area. Please note that the Cycle Area is always there in the Ruler, just barely visible ❶.

The area in the upper part of the Ruler left and right of an active Cycle Range is striped to indicate that Cycle Mode is on (in case the Ruler is at a position where the yellow Cycle Area is not visible).

🔘 **Move Cycle Area**

The Mouse Pointer changes to the Hand Tool ❷ when you move it over the yellow Cycle Area. This is a so-called Click Zone, where the Mouse Pointer automatically changes to a different Tool when moving over a specific area. Now *drag* the Cycle Area left or right to move it to a new position without changing its length. Key Command **sh+cmd+comma** and **sh+cmd+period** moves the Cycle Area back or forth by the length of the Cycle Area. A few things to pay attention to:

▸ At the left and right border appear yellow Alignment Guides ❸. These are vertical lines that extend across the Track Lanes area.

▸ A black Help Tag ❹ appears, displaying the start position of the Cycle Area (Cycle Range) and the length of the Cycle Area (which stays the same while moving). Please note that the display reflects the Display Mode of the Control Bar Display. It either displays Musical Time ❺ (bars and beats) or Absolute Time ❻ (SMPTE).

▸ The movement is restricted by the underlying grid when the "Snap to Grid" mode is active. Toggle it with the Menu Command **Edit ➤ Snap To Grid** or with the Key Command **cmd+G**. The underlying grid changes dynamically depending how much you have the Workspace zoomed in or out. *Ctr+drag* overwrites the Snap to Grid Mode and lets you move without snapping to a specific time unit

🔘 **Resize Cycle Area**

The Mouse Pointer changes to the Resize Tool when you move it over the left or right edge of the yellow Cycle Area. Now *drag* the left or right border of the Cycle Area to resize its length. Again, the yellow Alignment Guides and the Help Tag also appear while dragging. The same rules about the time display and Snap To Grid apply.

🔘 **Draw Cycle Area**

You can draw a Cycle Area by *dragging* from left to right (or right to left) on the upper part of the Ruler. The Mouse Pointer keeps the Pointer Tool. Again, the yellow Alignment Guide and the Help Tag appear and the rules about the time display and Snap To Grid apply.

Metronome

A Metronome is a click that will play during playback and recording when Metronome is enabled. A few things to pay attention to:

- You can toggle the Metronome with two commands
    - *Click* on the Metronome Button in the Control Bar
    - Use the Key Command *K* (does not work when the Musical Typing window is open)
- A click sounds on each beat. That means it depends on the Time Signature (and Tempo of course). With a 4/4 Signature, the click will play four quarter notes per measure (bar), with a 3/2 Signature, the click will play three half notes and with a 5/8 Signature, the click will play five eighth notes per measure.
- Each click on the downbeat (the first beat in a bar) has a higher pitch for better orientation.
- You cannot change the sound or the volume of the click.
- The Metronome click will be exported with your song, so don't forget to turn the Metronome off when exporting your song.
- There is a third Metronome status besides on and off which is *"Metronome on only during Count-In when recording"*. This status is indicated with a purple Metronome icon over a gray button.

Count-In

The Count-In is technically a special Metronome function and has only an effect when recording.

Record usually starts at the Playhead Position or the left border of the Cycle Area (when enabled). When Count-In is enabled, the playback starts either one or two bars before that. Please note that GarageBand is already recording during the Count-In although the displayed Audio Region starts after the Count-In.

Toggle the Count-In with the following commands
- *Click* on the Count-In Button in the Control Bar
- Use the Key Command *sh+K*
- Select from the Main Menu *Record ➤ Count-In ➤ 1 Bar/2Bars*. Selecting *None* from the submenu will turn the Count-In off.

Here are the four combinations for the Count-In and Metronome Button:

- off on: Click is playing during Playback and Recording
- on on: Click is playing during Playback and Recording plus the Count-In
- on off: Click is playing only during the Count-In (the Metronome Button looks different!)
- off off: Click is completely off

Tuner

The Tuner Button doesn't toggle a specific mode. It toggles the separate Tuner Window which is one of the few windows that is not part of the single GarageBand Window. It is a resizable floating panel that you can use to check the tuning of your guitar or any other audio source connected to one of GarageBand's audio inputs.

Please note that there is not just one Tuner Window. It is a little bit complex, so make sure you understand the following implementation:

- When working on a GarageBand Project, you have to select a specific Audio Device. It is selected in the GarageBand **Preferences ➤ Audio/MIDI**. Each Audio Device has a specific amount of Input Channels. For example, 4 Input Channels.
- Each of those available Input Channels (1 to 4) has its own Tuner Window in GarageBand.
- The Window Title ❶ of each Tuner Window displays the input the Tuner is "listening to". For example, "Input 1", "Input 2", etc.
- To open a Tuner Window, you are not choosing a specific Input Channel directly. Instead, you open the Tuner window for the selected Audio Track ❷. Now, whatever Input Channel that Audio Track has selected ❸ in the Smart Controls Inspector (I discuss that later in more detail), that Tuner Window will be displayed ❶. For example, if the selected Audio Track is set to Input Channel 2, then clicking on the Tuner Button will open the Tuner Window for "Input 2".

The Tuner Button is not just a button to open a window, it has three states and these states relate to the currently selected Track.

- Button **Dimmed**: If the currently selected Track is not an Audio Track (or has no Audio Input assigned to it), then the button is dimmed.
- Button **Off**: If he currently selected Track is an Audio Track but no Tuner window is open yet for the audio Input Channel of the selected Audio Track.
- Button **On**: The currently selected Track is an Audio Track and a Tuner window is open for the audio Input Channel that is selected for the current Audio Track.

➡ Tuner Display and Parameters

- The Keynote displays the closest Pitch and its deviation in cents ❹. Green color means in-tune ❺, orange means out of tune ❻. The deviation is indicated in cents (100cent is one semitone) ❼
- Drag the Reference Pitch ❽ field up or down to change the Reference Pitch (default 440Hz)
- The Mute ❾ button lets you mute the input signal in case you want to tune just visually without listening to it. Don't forget to un-mute it again!

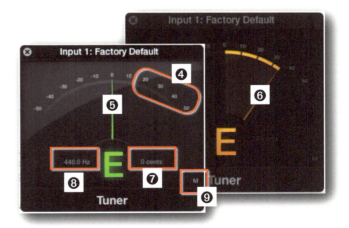

6 - Control Bar

Master Volume

The Master Volume is positioned next to the four Mode buttons.

GarageBand tries to simplify the functionality and workflow of a DAW by eliminating components that might be confusing for the hobby user who might not have the necessary background in understanding the signal flow of a mixing console.

Although this simplification works in many areas, in case of the Master Volume (in conjunction with the Master Track), it still might be confusing. On top of that, the experienced DAW user also might have difficulties understanding the unconventional implementation due to its simplification.

Let me try to explain the Master Volume control in a simplified and advanced way.

● Simplified

The Master Volume on the Control Bar has two elements

- ▸ **Master Volume Meter**: The Stereo Meter displays the overall level of your Project. The Meter is color coded from green to yellow to red. Red means clipping ❶ which could cause distortion of your signal.
- ▸ **Master Volume Slider**: The circle ❷ on top of the meter acts as a slider control that you can drag left (lower the volume) or right (increase the volume).
  - A Help Tag ❸ indicates the position of the slider in Decibel (dB).
  - 0dB means no increase or decrease, a positive value (max +6dB) means increasing the signal level and a negative value means decreasing the signal level.
  - *Opt+click* on the slider to set it to 0dB.

● Advanced

This is the basic signal flow in GarageBand

- ▸ The signals of all Tracks ❹ in the Project are routed to the Master Track ❺ (toggle visibility with *Track ▸ Show/Hide Master Track*).
- ▸ The Master Track ❻ (like an Output Track) has a Volume Slider that controls the output signal. It also lets you add additional processing to the output signal.
- ▸ Before the output signal reaches its final destination (Audio Device or exported file), it passes a gain control. It is controlled by the Master Volume Slider on the Control Bar ❼.
- ▸ Please note that the slider ❻ on the Master Track and the slider ❼ on the Control Bar are two independent volume controls.
- ▸ The signal level that is displayed in both, the slider of the Master Track and the slider on the Control Bar are measuring the same signal. It displays the final output signal ❽ that is sent to the Audio Device or exported to an audio file.

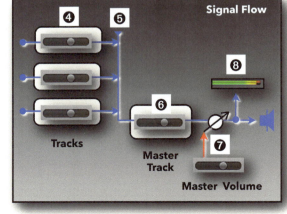

Control Bar Display (LCD)

The Control Bar Display, or short LCD (Liquid Crystal Display), is the center of the Control Bar that is always visible as part of the GarageBand Window. It can display two different types of information.

The left icon ❶ on the LCD functions as a popup button from which you can choose one of the two Display Modes ❷. You can switch between them at any time.

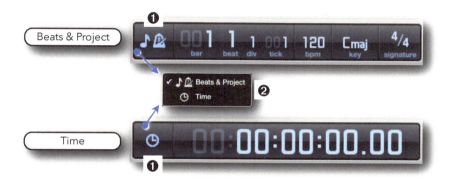

Display Modes

The main purpose of the Display is to show the position of the Playhead ❸. Although you can read the position of the Playhead on the Ruler ❹, the numerical readout on the Display is much more accurate.

Because the Playhead indicates a position along your song, it is therefore a time position. That time can be expressed in two different formats, Musical Time and Absolute Time.

- **Musical Time** ❺: This format expresses the position of the Playhead in your song as bars and beats. For example, the chorus starts at the first beat of bar 23.
- **Absolute Time** ❻: This format expresses the position of the Playhead in your song in standard time units of minute and second. For example, that chorus on bar 23 starts at 44 seconds.

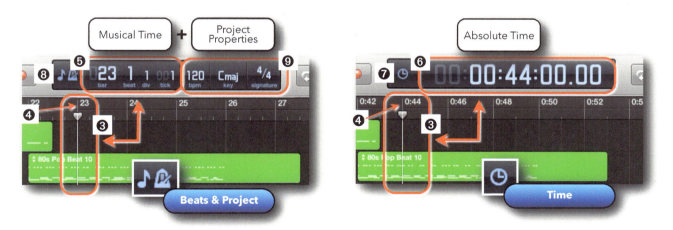

And this is the main difference between the two Display Modes. They determine the displayed time formats on the LCD and on the Ruler.

- **Time** ❼: It displays the Playhead Position in Absolute Time.
- **Beats & Project** ❽: It displays the Playhead Position in Musical Time. In addition, it also displays the three Project Properties ❾: Tempo, Key Signature and Time Signature.

Time Format

The Control Bar Display is not just a read-only display that only shows you the Playhead Position, it is an "active" display that also lets you edit the position right there by changing the numbers. That means you can move the Playhead to a new position by changing the time position on the display. This works in the Musical Time and Absolute Time Display Mode.

You can change the numbers in two ways

 Double-click on the time display to select the whole number and type a new time. A few things to be aware of:
- You type the value from left to right but you can leave out the rightmost digits. For example, typing in "9." will result in "9.1.1.1"
- If you type in a number that is not valid for a specific number value, then GarageBand is smart enough and does the calculation to roll it over to the next higher number value. For example, typing in "3.6" results in "4.2.1.1" because the second number value of "6" is invalid if the Time Signature is 4/4 and therefore has only 4 beats. It calculates the "6beats" as "1bar, 2beats" and the "1bar" gets added to the number "3" that you entered as the Bar value.
- Entering a position that is beyond the End-of-Project Marker will default to that marker position.

 Drag a single number value up or down. Please note that when you drag a number higher than its maximum number value (i.e. 4 beats), then it rolls over (increase the value to the left) and continuous.

➡ *Musical Time*

The standard units for Musical Time are the Bars and Beats. GarageBand uses two more units to divide them even further. Please note that the maximum value of a beat depends on the Time Signature.

- **Bars**: One bar, or one measure, is the musical time unit indicated by bar lines in musical notation.
- **Beats**: Beats are the "musical counts". The Time Signature determines by its lower number what the musical value of one Beat is (half, quarter, eighth) and the upper number determines how many of those Beats are in one Bar (the maximum beat value per bar).
- **Divisions**: A Division is an additional unit that sub-divides a quarter note into four units. That means a Division has the length of a sixteenth note.
- **Ticks**: A Tick is the smallest Musical Time increment in GarageBand. It sub-divides a Division into 240 units. So "1 Division = 1 sixteenth note = 240 Ticks". Please note that the smallest increments that you can position an object on the Track Lane (Playhead, Region, etc.) is based on those Ticks (960/quarter note). This means that the resolution is not based on an absolute time but on a relative time. If you are good in math then you can figure out that at a tempo of 120bpm (beats per minutes) and a resolution of 960Ticks/quarter, the distance between two Ticks is 0.5ms. The faster the tempo the smaller the increments and therefore the higher the resolution.

➡ *Absolute Time*

You can describe an Absolute Time in hours, minutes and seconds. Most DAWs however use a standard form called SMPTE. This is a time format that was standardized by the Society of Motion Picture and Television Engineers (SMPTE) and the European Broadcasting Union (EBU). In addition to the hours, minutes and seconds, it uses frames which divides a second into smaller units. A "Frame Rate" describes how many frames are in one second. GarageBand uses 25fps (frames per second), although there are different Frames Rates in use. A Frame is divided even further into 80 Subframes.

Project Properties

The Display Mode "Bars & Project" displays in addition to the Playhead Position the three Project Properties: Tempo, Key Signature and Time Signature.

Remember, these Properties have to be set at the beginning when you create a new Project with the Project Chooser ❶. Once you are working on the Project, you can change those parameters here in the display. Be aware of the "consequences" when changing the Tempo after you've recorded or imported Audio Regions into your Project.

⚪ Tempo

Although most Projects use a single Tempo value throughout the Song, GarageBand provides the option to create a Tempo Curve in a special Track called "Tempo Track". I discuss that in the Mixing chapter. When you have only one Tempo in your Project, then the LCD displays exactly that Tempo. However, if you use the Tempo Curve, for example, to slow down the tempo at the end of the Song (this is called a "ritardando"), then the LCD displays the Tempo at the current Playhead Position. If you have programmed Tempo changes, then you would see the Tempo display changing accordingly.

▸ Change the Tempo ❷ value (bpm = beats per minutes)
- *Double-click* on the Tempo display and enter a new value
- *Drag* the number up or down
- If you try to change the Tempo in the LCD but have more than one Tempo defined in the Tempo Track, then you will get an Alert window ❸ giving you the option to open the Tempo Track to do the changes there (as of GarageBand v10.0.1, the window says "Tempo List" which is the text for Logic Pro that has a Tempo List).

⚪ Key Signature

Click on the Key Signature to open the popup menu ❹ with the 12 major Keys and 12 minor Keys to choose from.

⚪ Time Signature

Change the upper number (the number of beats in one bar) in two ways:
- *Double-click* on the upper number and enter a new value
- *Drag* the upper number up or down

Click on the lower number (the note value of the beat in a bar) to select any of the seven values from the popup menu ❺.

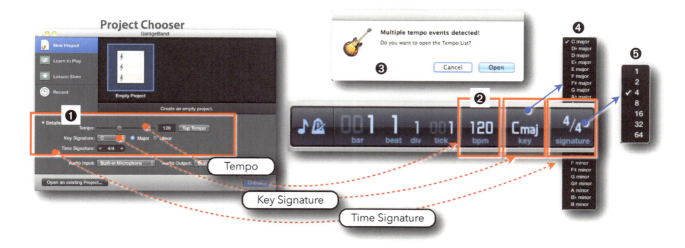

MIDI Indicator

There is one hidden feature in the Control Bar Display, a tiny little dot in the upper right corner.

This dot lights up every time GarageBand receives a MIDI message.

The MIDI message can come from two sources:

▶ **Internal:**

Use the software keyboard in GarageBand (Musical Typing or Keyboard)

▶ **External:**

Use any external MIDI Keyboard connected via USB to your computer or even use the Logic Remote app on your iPad to play MIDI instruments in your GarageBand Project via WiFi.

Chords: The Display can even switch the right side to show any chord you are playing on your MIDI keyboard (only works for USB connected keyboards).

Color Code

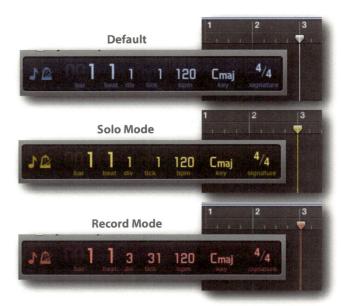

The Control Bar Display can appear in three different colors to indicate a specific status. Please note that the Playhead changes to the same color.

🔵 **Blue**

Blue is the default color of the Control Bar Display. The Playhead is white

🟡 **Yellow**

Whenever a Track or a Region is switched to Solo Mode, the Control Bar Display and the Playhead change to yellow.

🔴 **Red**

Whenever GarageBand switches to Record Mode, the Control Bar Display and the Playhead change to red. If you record while in Solo Mode, then red has priority over yellow.

Transport Controls

The Transport Buttons on the Control Bar are obviously the main Transport Controls. However, there are many more options that let you navigate along the timeline of your Project.

Transport Buttons

The Transport Buttons are similar on every tape machine and DAW. However, the exact functionality is always a little bit different. There are a few details and conditions about the behavior of those Transport Buttons, so read the following pages carefully.

Transport Buttons

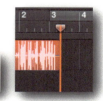

 **Play - Stop**

This button is easy. It toggles between Start and Stop. *Clicking* while the song is in stop mode starts the song and *clicking* while it plays will stops the song.
- Key Command *Space Bar* has the same function as clicking on the Play Button
- *Double-click* on the lower part of the Ruler to toggle play-stop
- Key Command *enter* (on the numeric keyboard) will also start playback. During playback, it has a different function. It will move the Playhead to the position where you started playback and continuous to play back from there.

 **Record**

The Record Button switches into Record Mode and records the input signal (Audio or MIDI) of the selected Track (and other record enabled Tracks) onto a Region on the Track Lane.
There are a few things to consider before using the button.

➡ **What Happens**

A few things happen when GarageBand switches to Record Mode.
- In Record Mode, the Record Button and the Play Button are both enabled (light up) because Record is just a modification of the Play function, the Playhead is moving.
- The LCD turns red to indicate that GarageBand is recording.
- The Playhead also turns red together with the Region that is currently being created (recorded).

➡ **Function of the Button**

To start recording, use any of the two commands:
- *Click* the Record Button
- Use the Key Command *R*

To stop recording, you have to use a different command:
- *Click* on the Play Button or use the Key Command *Space Bar*
- *Click* on the Stop Button or use the Key Command *0* (on the numeric keyboard)

 **Stop ("Back and Forth")**

The Stop Button is a little bit more tricky. It can have three different states and the button displays "what will happen next" when you use the Stop command.

- **Click Stop while the Playhead is moving**

  Whenever the Playhead is moving, the button always displays the Stop Button ■ because when you use the Stop command, the action will be "STOP the playback".

- **Click Stop while the Playhead is not moving**

  The behavior of the Stop command when the Playhead is not moving depends on the Cycle Mode, is it enabled or not:

  ▸ **Cycle Mode Off** ⇄:
  After you've stopped the playback, the button changes to the "Go to the Beginning of the Project" button ⏮. When you use the Stop command now, the Playhead is doing exactly that, jumps to the beginning of the Project at bar 1 and changes to the Stop Button ■. You can further use the Stop command, but it has no effect because the Project has already stopped and the Playhead is at bar 1.

  ▸ **Cycle Mode on** ⇄
  The first step is the same. After you've stopped the playback, the button changes to the "Go to the Beginning of the Project" button ⏮. When you use the Stop command now, the Playhead is doing exactly that, jumps to the beginning of the Project at bar 1. However, the button changes now to the 'Go to the Beginning of the Cycle" button ⏭. Using the Stop command will now jump to the beginning of the Cycle Area and the button changes again to the "Go to the Beginning of the Project" button ⏮. Now, every time you use the Stop command it toggles between these two states.

  📌 The Key Command *0* on the numeric keyboard (if available) has the same function as clicking on the Stop Button.

  📌 The Key Command *return* will always return the Playhead to the beginning of the Project at bar 1. Please note that this works in stop mode but also in playback. In this case it continuous to play, just from the beginning.

⏪ Rewind

The Rewind Button has two functions depending on how you click on it.
- *Click* to move the Playhead back by one bar or to the beginning of the current bar. If you switch the LCD to display Absolute Time, then the steps relate to the absolute time of one bar (which is different for different Tempo settings).
- *Click-drag* left or right to scrub playback in both directions. Scrubbing means, the further you move the mouse in one direction (while pressing down on the button), the faster the rewind or forward speed.
- The Key Command is the *comma* key.

⏩ Forward

The Forward Button has two functions depending on how you click on it.
- *Click* to move the Playhead forward by one bar.
- *Click-drag* left or right to scrub playback in both directions. Scrubbing means, the further you move the mouse in one direction (while pressing down on the button), the faster the rewind or forward speed.
- The Key Command is the *period* key

Playhead and LCD

Although the purpose of the Playhead and the Control Bar Display is mainly to show the current position in your song, you could (and should) use it also as a Transport Control to move the Playhead around.

➡ Playhead

These are the transport commands you can use with the Playhead

- 📌 *Click* in the lower part of the Ruler to move the Playhead to that position
- 📌 *Double-click* in the lower part of the Ruler to start playback from the click position. *Double-click* again to stop playback.
- 📌 *Drag* the Playhead on the Ruler to any new position

➡ LCD

Because the LCD shows the current Playhead Position, you can also use the edit commands to re-position the Playhead.

- 📌 *Double-click* on the time display to select the whole number and type a new time. When you hit enter, the Playhead jumps to that position.
- 📌 *Drag* a single number value up or down. This lets you forward or rewind with different speeds depending on if you slide the bars, the beats or the smaller time values.

Logic Remote app

Using the Logic Remote app on the iPad provides a wide variety of functions and functionality when used with GarageBand. Not only can you use existing functions remotely over Wi-Fi, some functions are only available on that Logic Remote app. This is also the case for the Transport Controls.

Not only can you use the Logic Remote app as a remote for the standard Play, Stop, Record buttons, there are many controls available as Key Commands that are not available in GarageBand itself. Using the Logic Remote app in the Key Command View lets you assign those Key Commands to big Touch Pads on the iPad.

Logic Remote app on the iPad

I wrote a separate comprehensive manual for this amazing app: "Logic Remote - How it Works" It is the only book available that explains all the features.

Apple Remote Control

Apple Remote is a little remote control that comes with the AppleTV and also can be bought separately from Apple for $19. It uses an IR signal (infrared) and can be used on any Mac that has a built-in IR receiver.

Check in your System Profiler under USB ❶ if your Mac has an IR Receiver and make sure that it is not disabled in the **System Preferences ➤ Security & Privacy ➤ General ➤ Advanced** ❷ (or just point the thing at your Mac and see if GarageBand is responding).

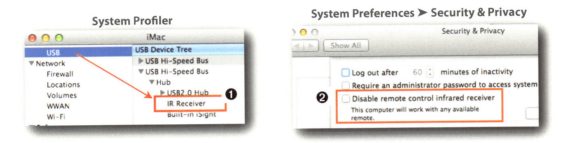

Here are the functions of the Remote Control buttons when used with GarageBand.

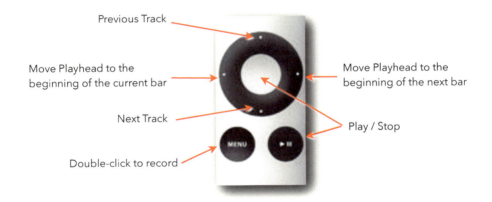

Catch Playhead

This is a special mode that affects the visibility of the Playhead during playback. The three windows, Tracks Area, Audio Editor and Piano Roll have this Catch Playhead button on their Menu Bar where it can be set independently.

When enabled, two things will happen:

- ▶ The Workspace (with the attached Ruler) scrolls automatically during playback so the Playhead stays always visible.
- ▶ Once the Playhead reaches the center of the Workspace, it stays at that position and the Workspace moves underneath the now static Playhead. This function is also called "Scroll in Play"

💡 **Auto-on**

Using the Forward, Rewind, or Stop command will automatically turn the Catch Mode on (in all the three window panes: Tracks Area, Audio Editor, and Piano Roll).

7 - Tracks

By now, we've encountered the term "Track" already many times. In this chapter, we will have a closer look at that term so you fully understand what a Track is and how to work with it.

Let's recap what we've learned so far:
- From a pure layout point of view, a Track is represented by a row in the Tracks Area. Each additional row represents another Track.
- Each row has two segments: The Track Header ❶ which expands into the Track Lane ❷.
- You can think of each Track (each row) as a member of the band that performs your song (remember the Band Analogy).
- So, if we look at the Tracks Area, we have the Track List on the left which lists all the "Band Members" and the Workspace on the right that contains the musical information that each "Band Member" has to play.

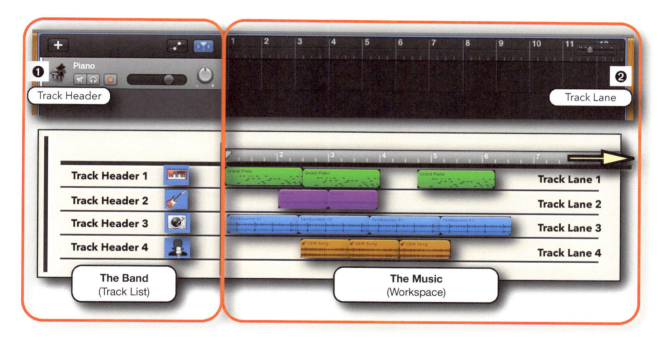

Who's in the Band

As in real life, before you start to play your music, you have to form your band. For that, you ask two basic questions.
- ☑ "How many musicians" - in GarageBand terms that means "how many Tracks".
- ☑ "What kind of musicians" - in GarageBand terms that means "what type of Tracks".

The question about the number of musicians makes sense. You can create a piece of music for a one-man band in the form of a solo pianist (needs only one Track in GarageBand) or for a full Orchestra (needs many Tracks in GarageBand).

The second question about the type of musician or type of Track is not so obvious and that's where we have to look a little deeper.

Type of Tracks

The concept of different types of tracks is very important because it is the foundation for understanding other concepts like Types of Regions. I'll try to explain that simple foundation first and then show how it is implemented in GarageBand.

How to "record" Music

Here are two basic methods of how to record music.

🌀 Method 1: Describe how to Play the Music

This is a traditional form of recording music. You use instructions, most likely in the form of written notes. You write down your song in a commonly understood language, i.e. western music notation. A composer can write down a symphony, and every orchestra can play that piece of music. Or, a musician writes down sheet music or a chord chart and every Jazz Band then can play that tune.

🌀 Method 2: Capture the Sound of Played Music

With the invention of the gramophone in the 20th century, music could be recorded right there when it was performed. You can come up with a great song and instead of writing it down, you would just play it on your instrument and record that performed music. A recording device captures the audio, the sound of the music, from a musician, a band, or an orchestra. Now, instead of describing the music, you capture the audio and store it on a disc or an mp3 file.

But what does that have to do with Tracks? Pretty much everything.

Every DAW on the market has both abilities to record music and there are two different types of Tracks that lets you do that.
- ☑ Record and play a description of music (Method 1) - **MIDI Track**
- ☑ Record and play the sound of performed music (Method 2) - **Audio Track**

MIDI Track

First, we look at a MIDI Track (GarageBand calls this a Software Instrument Track). Let's hold on to the previous analogy that the various Tracks in your Project represent the band members that perform your song.

A "MIDI Track BandMember" would be the one that can read music. This would be Method 1 of capturing music in some form of description. Think of it this way. You come to the rehearsal and hand out your SheetMusic to your fellow BandMember. However, in a DAW, you cannot feed the computer your sheet music. You must use a different form of "music description". The common language of describing music in a DAW is MIDI.

I briefly explained MIDI in the beginning of the book. The MIDI standard defines how to translate (convert) music into computer language (a series of zeros and ones). For example, when you play the notes "c-e-g" on a MIDI keyboard, it will translate the information about those notes and how you played them into the MIDI language which then can be transmitted over a cable from the keyboard to the computer that hosts the DAW. The DAW on the other side "speaks" the MIDI language and understands that specific description of music. It can store the notes (record them) and also play them, which means sending the notes "c-e-g" to a sound module (a Software Instrument, part of the DAW) and you will hear the music "c-e-g".

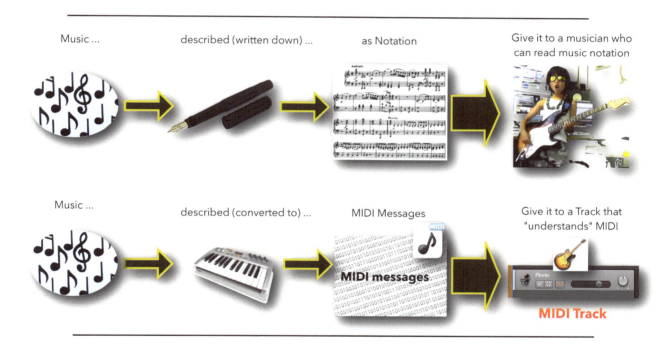

So the important thing is that on a MIDI Track, the DAW records and stores music as a description in the form of a specific music language called MIDI. There are two advantages to recording music as MIDI.

- ☑ **Change the music**

    At any time, you can edit your music. The DAW presents the stored MIDI information in various graphical forms that you can read and understand (even in standard musical notation). This is like taking your sheet music to the rehearsal and there make some corrections in your score.

- ☑ **Change the performer**

    The same way as you can take the SheetMusic from the guitar player during rehearsal and give it to the sax player (because it sounds better), you can assign different sound modules to your stored MIDI information. This provides a great deal of flexibility when it comes to arranging your song.

Audio Track

Besides the MIDI Track, the other type of Track is the "Audio Track". This would be Method 2 of capturing music. As I explained, this represents a sound recording which is quite different from a MIDI recording.

Back to the rehearsal room. All the musicians in our band are like MIDI Tracks that can read or understand "described" music. So who would represent the Audio Track? How about the DJ. Many bands now also have a DJ that scratches some records (let's not get into the discussion of whether a DJ is considered a musician and spinning records is considered playing an instrument). In our model, the DJ is a perfect representation of the Audio Track. He doesn't have to read music in order to play it on his instrument (turntable). Instead, you would hand him a recorded piece of music in the form of a CD or an audio file. This is basically what happens on an Audio Track. There you place an existing audio file or you record a new audio file from a sound source in form of an acoustic signal (microphone) or an electric signal (electric guitar, synth). The Audio Track can then play back that audio recording as part of your song.

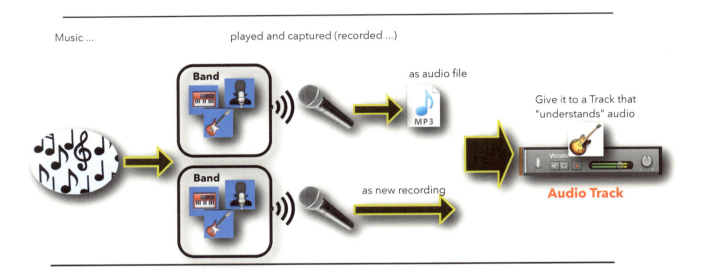

The main advantage you can see from the table below is that MIDI Tracks provide the most flexibility when it comes to editing (changing) anything while you are working on your song. For example, when you record a melody as an audio file from a guitar player, you cannot change the melody or go ahead and change it to the sax player later. However, technology advanced tremendously over the years and there are now tools available that let you change many parameters of an otherwise fixed audio file (tempo, pitch, timing). Some of those tools are available in GarageBand and I will cover them later in the book.

The main advantage of an audio recording is that you capture the performance of a musician with all the nuances of his instrument. Also recording vocals doesn't work well with MIDI instruments (yet!).

	MIDI Track	Audio Track
Band Member Analogy	guitarist, pianist, drummer	DJ
Records what	Music description (MIDI)	Music performance
Change music content	Freely editable	Very limited
Change instrument	Any available electronic instruments	Not possible
Change Song Parameters	Not a problem	very limited
Performance	Restricted to electronic instruments	Record any live instrument

Drummer Track

This is a new type of Track that introduces a different kind of how to "record" music.
- ▸ Audio Track: Music as a **recording**
- ▸ MIDI Track: Music as a **description**
- ▸ Drummer Track: Music as an **instruction**

Apple sells this new feature as if you would have a real drummer play with your Song: "Adding a virtual Drummer to your Project". Although the end result sounds amazingly realistic that you could think that a real drummer is playing, this magic however is just based on some sophisticated technology. To understand the concept behind it helps you get the best results out of this feature.

Think about it.

If you compose a piece for a Jazz Big Band, you would write down the exact notes to be played by the brass and woodwind section. You describe each single note by writing it down. For the drummer however, you wouldn't write down each single note he has to play on each drum kit piece. Instead, you would write down, to play simple patterns, play busy patterns, when to play fills, when to use Toms instead of cymbals, etc. These are more broad instructions, where different drummers would interpret those instructions differently. With a horn arrangement, you want each player to play the exact notes regardless who and when the notes get played.

This is the basic difference between a MIDI Track and a Drummer Track:
- **MIDI Track**: On a MIDI Track, you create (record) specific notes (contained in MIDI Regions) and those notes are played back exactly the same every time. If you want to change the music, you have to change those notes.
- **Drummer Track**: On a Drummer Track, you create (modify) basic instructions (contained in Drummer Regions) and those instructions are sent to a Drum Pattern Generator (the invisible engine on the Drummer Track). That generator creates a drum pattern based on the instructions and sends that as MIDI messages to a MIDI Drum Kit (with professionally recorded drum samples) that is loaded on the Drummer Track which "plays" those notes.

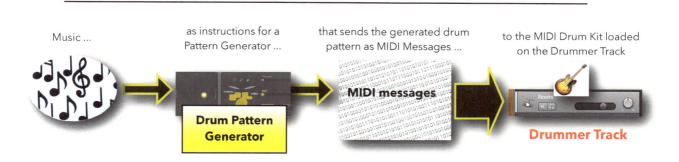

Who are these Drummers?

Apple talks about these different (virtual) Drummers that you can use in GarageBand. What makes them different are the components of that underlying technology that make that magic happen. Different Drummers load different sets of instruction (playing styles) and different drum samples (i.e. a Pop drum kit, a Heavy Metal drum kit, etc.).

Create a new Track

Now let's check GarageBand to see where we can find those three Track types:

MIDI Track - Audio Track - Drummer Track.

Empty Project

Before we can create a Track, we have to create (open) a Project first. We learned already in the Project chapter that you have to select a Project Template when you want to create a new Project. Any of those Project Templates opens with preconfigured Tracks in their Project. The exception is the "Empty Project" Template. This Template opens a Project that has no Tracks created yet. Three things will happen when you select that Template.

- ☑ A New GarageBand Project "Untitled" is created.
- ☑ The GarageBand Window for that Project opens.
- ☑ The "New Track Dialog" window opens immediately in the GarageBand Window. This is a Sheet that slides out below the GarageBand Window Title and forces you to create a Track first before you can do anything else.

This New Track Dialog is the place where we select the Track Type we want to create in our Project.

104   7 - Tracks

New Track Dialog

The New Track Dialog lets you create a new Track. This is the procedure of "adding a new BandMember" to your Project if you follow my Band Analogy. You can open this window with the following commands:

- Select the "Empty Project" Template from the Project Chooser.
- **Click** on the Plus ➕ button in the Menu Bar on top of the Track List.
- Use the Menu Command *Track ➤ New Track*
- Use the Key Command **opt+cmd+N**

➡ **Select a Track**

The window shows four icons. You create a new Track by simply choosing one of the icons. You can do that in two ways:

- **Click** on an icon (the instrument icon gets a spotlight when you click on it) and then **click** on the Create button (or hit **return**).
- You also can just **double-click** on an icon.

MIDI Track: Selecting the keyboard icon will create a MIDI Track. Please note that GarageBand calls this a "Software Instrument Track". I prefer the term "MIDI Track" because it better describes the type of music (type of Regions) you record on such a Track.

Audio Track: Both, the microphone and guitar icon, create an Audio Track. The only difference is that each icon loads a different Patch (a Track configuration) when the Track is created. The guitar icon loads a Patch that has the amp and stompboxes loaded. Audio Regions recorded on a Guitar Audio Track are purple instead of blue.

Drummer Track: Selecting the drum set icon will create a Drummer Track. Please note that a Project can have only one Drummer Track. If you have already one in your Tracks Area, then the drums icon will be grayed out and can't be selected.

➡ Details Area

Below the four icons is the Details area that can be toggled with the disclosure triangle ❶. It provides some settings and controls to pre-configure the new Track. Please note that not all settings are available to all icons (Track Types) when selected.

- ☑ **Input** (Audio Track only) ❷: This button opens a popup menu ❸ listing all the available input channels (as mono ⬤ and stereo ⊚⊚ channels) of the current Audio Device. Here you can select the audio input for the newly created Audio Track.

- ☑ **Input Monitoring** (Audio Track only): This checkbox ❹ with the long text "*I want to hear my instrument as I play and record*" enables the Input Monitoring 🟫 button ❺ on the newly created Track. More on that a little later.

- ☑ **Input Device** (Audio Track only): The text ❻ includes the name of the currently selected Input Device "*My instrument is connected with [name of the Input Device]*". The arrow next to it ⓞ is a button that opens the *Preferences ➤ Audio/MIDI* window ❽ in case you want to change the selected Audio Device.

- ☑ **Output Device**: The text ❼ includes the name of the currently selected Output Device "*I hear sound from [name of the Output Device]*". The arrow next to it ⓞ is a button that opens the *Preferences ➤ Audio/MIDI* window ❽ in case you want to change the selected Audio Device.

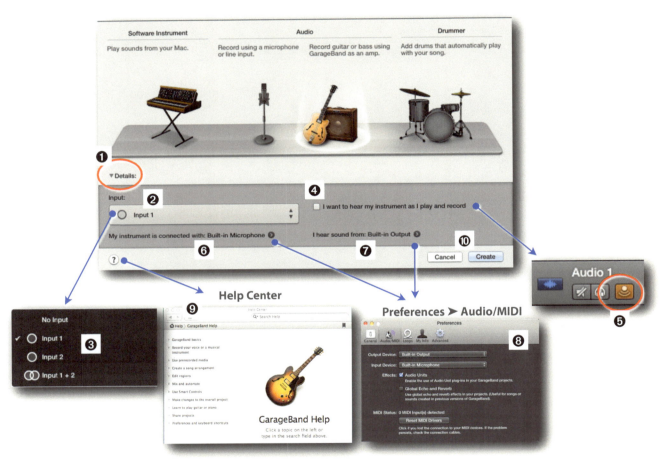

➡ Control Buttons

The control bar at the bottom of the New Track Dialog contains three buttons.

- ☑ **Help Center**: The Question Mark at the bottom of the Details area opens the Help Center ❾ for GarageBand (which can also be opened by the Main Menu *Help ➤ GarageBand Help*).

- ☑ **Cancel / Create**: The Create Button ❿ creates a new Track based on the selected icon and the settings in the Details area. The Cancel Button closes the Dialog without creating a Track.

➡ **Create a Track**

Once you hit the Create Button in the New Track Dialog (or *double-click* on one of the four icons), the following things will happen.

- ☑ The New Track Dialog closes.
- ☑ A new Track will be created in the Tracks Area below the Track that was selected when you opened the New Track Dialog.
- ☑ The newly created Track will be one of the three Track Types (MIDI Track, Audio Track or Drummer Track), depending which icon you selected.
- ☑ A Patch will be loaded onto the Track. This is like a basic configuration. Each Track Type has its default configuration. I discuss that further in the Library chapter.
- ☑ Only the Drummer Track will automatically have Drummer Regions already placed on the Track Lane.

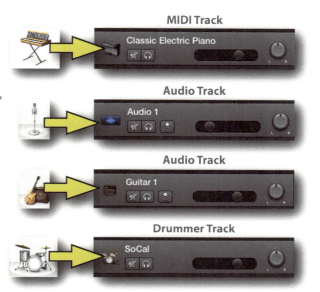

- ▸ **MIDI Track**: The new Track will have the Patch "Classic Electric Piano" loaded. That name is also used as the Track Name.
- ▸ **Audio Track (microphone)**: The new Track will not have a specific Patch loaded. The Track Name will be "Audio 1" where the number increases with each new Track.
- ▸ **Audio Track (guitar)**: The new Track will have the Patch "Brit and Clean" loaded. The Track Name will be "Guitar 1" where the number increases with each new Track.
- ▸ **Drummer Track**: The new Track will have the Patch "SoCal" loaded. That name is also used as the Track Name.

Track Commands

Besides the New Track command, there are a few more commands that let you manage Tracks.

- 🔵 **New Track... ❶**

  This is the command that opens the New Track Dialog.

- 🔵 **New Audio/MIDI/Drummer Track ❷**

  Ctr+click on the Track Header to open its Shortcut Menu that contains three commands that let you create an Audio, MIDI or Drummer Track directly without going to the New Track Dialog. They are also available as individual Key Commands *opt+cmd+A* (Audio Track) and *opt+cmd+S* (MIDI Track).

- 🔵 **New Track With Duplicate Settings ❸**

  This command creates a new Track below the currently selected Track with the same settings (loaded plugins, volume, pan, etc.). This command is not available for a Drummer Track (because there could be only one Drummer Track in the Project).
  -  Available from the Main Menu and as Key Command *cmd+D*

- 🔵 **Delete Track ❹**

  This command deletes the currently selected Track.
  -  Available from the Main Menu, Shortcut Menu and as Key Command *cmd+delete* or just *delete* if no Region is currently selected. An error message warns you if there are Regions on the Track.

7 - Tracks   107

Global Tracks

The three Track Types we just discussed, MIDI Track, Audio Track and Drummer, are the Main Tracks that contain your music, your music in the form of Regions that are placed on the Track Lanes of each Track. However, there are other types of Tracks in GarageBand, "special purpose Tracks". They are more advanced features that I will explain in detail later in the book. Here is just a quick introduction.

- All those Tracks are hidden by default.
- The Tracks can be toggled by using their individual "Show/Hide" command in the Main Menu ❶ or the Shortcut Menu ❷ when *ctr +clicking* on the Track Header of any of the (visible) Tracks or individual Key Commands.
- There is only one of each Track.
- The first four Tracks are the so-called "Global Tracks" that appear between the Ruler and the Main Tracks in your Project.
- The Global Tracks are also divided into the Track Header to the left and the Track Lane to the right. Their Track Lanes zoom and scroll only horizontally with the Main Tracks. They are not affected by the vertical scrolling and stay always visible with the Ruler.
- Technically, the Master Track doesn't belong to the Global Track. It has a different function that I will explain later.
- The Master Track is always placed as the last Track on the bottom of the Track List.
- Although the Master Track looks like any other Track and scrolls vertically and horizontally with them, you cannot place any Regions on its Track Lane.

➡ **Arrangement Track** ❸

The Arrangement Track lets you create Arrangement Markers to structure your song visually. The Markers enable you to quickly swap and replace sections in your song.

➡ **Movie Track** ❹

The Movie Track displays the imported video file as thumbnail pictures along the timeline for quick orientation when scoring to picture.

➡ **Transposition Track** ❺

The Transposition Track lets you mark sections that you want to transpose. All the MIDI Regions and the Audio Regions that have "Follow Tempo & Pitch" enabled will be transposed. No need to edit each individual Region.

➡ **Tempo Track** ❻

The Tempo Track lets you create a Tempo curve in case you need Tempo changes (multiple Tempos) in your song.

➡ **Master Track** ❼

The Master Track is placed at the end of the Track List and controls the sound of your overall song by adjusting its level and adding effects.

Tracks - under the hood

So far, you should have a basic understanding about the Tracks in GarageBand. Now, I want to give you a little peek under the hood of a Track. Remember, in the Prior Knowledge chapter at the beginning of the book I compared GarageBand to a "black box" where a lot of signal routing and signal processing is going on. The only way to control those components is via the various interface elements in GarageBand.

In this, a little bit more advanced, topic, I will open the black box to show what a Track looks like in regards to the signal flow. You still can use GarageBand without that knowledge but I recommend wrapping your head around it for a better understanding how GarageBand works and also why it works that way.

As I mentioned already, recording and mixing are the two main tasks in a music production. In a traditional studio, they are represented by two hardware components, the Tape Machine and the Mixing Console. I also mentioned that most DAWs emulate those hardware components in digital form.

So where in GarageBand do we find their equivalent? The answer is, they are merged together on the GarageBand Track that we just discussed in this chapter.

Signal Flow

Here is a look at the simplified version of a Track's signal flow. It shows the main components the signal is passing through from the input to the output. I marked the section that functions as the Tape Machine and the Mixing Console.

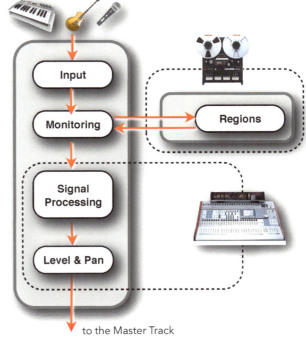

- ▸ **Input**: This component selects the input signal that "enters" the Track and will be recorded as Regions on that Track.
- ▸ **Regions**: The incoming signal will be recorded as (MIDI or Audio) Regions on that Track. When played back, the information on those Regions will be sent back and continues the signal flow through the Track.
- ▸ **Monitoring**: The Monitoring component is like a traffic cop. It decides the flow of the signal, which signal goes where.
- ▸ **Signal Processing**: Both, the Input signal and the signal that is played back as a Region, will reach (if they pass the Monitoring component) the Signal Processing unit. This is where Plugins can be inserted into the signal flow to alter the sound of the signal.
- ▸ **Level & Pan**: The last stage is the Level & Pan unit. This is the component that lets you set the final volume and the position on the left-right stereo field.
- ▸ The output of each Track is sent to the Master Track, where the output signals from all Tracks are combined (mixed) together.

Here is the same (under the hood) signal flow diagram of a Track. This time I added the interface elements in GarageBand that control those components.

There are only three elements, but you have to pay attention which interface element in GarageBand controls which Track component.

- **Track Lane ❶**

    Each Track in your current Project has its own Track Lane. This is where the Regions are recorded on and played back from. The Track Lanes are the direct equivalent of the traditional multi-track Tape Machine.

- **Smart Controls ❷**

    This is the new interface element in GarageBand. Please note that it controls two components.
    - The input settings for each Track are configured in the Smart Controls Window, in the Smart Controls Inspector to be specific.
    - The main task of the Smart Controls Window is to apply any signal processing on that Track. I'll get into those details in the next chapter.

- **Track Header ❸**

    The Track Header contains various controls that affect two components along the signal flow.
    - The Volume Slider sets the final level of the signal and the Pan Knob sets the relative level between the left and right channel of the stereo output signal. The Mute Button and Solo Button also belong to the level controls. Muting a Track is the same as turning the volume down all the way. Soloing a Track is like muting any other Track.
    - The Record Enable Button and the Input Monitoring Button belong to the Monitoring component because they determine which signal is sent where.

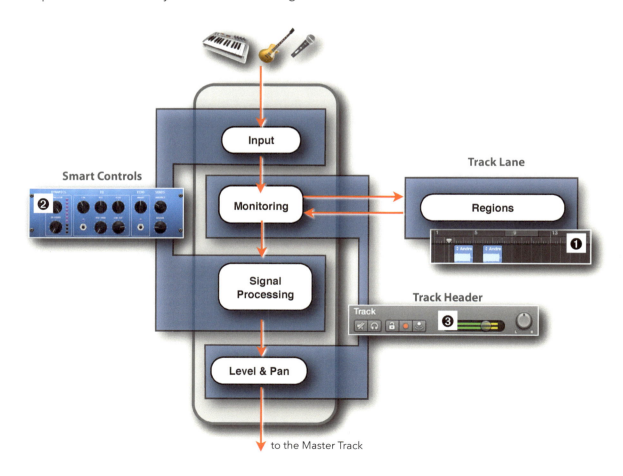

110   7 - Tracks

Signal Flow: Track to Master Track

Here is a different view of the signal flow diagram of a Track including the Master Track.

Again, we have the three main elements of the user interface that belong to each Track.

❶ **Track Lane**: The Track Lane is the component where you record your music on as Audio or MIDI Regions (Drummer Regions are different. They are not recorded, they are placed on the Track Lane).

❷ **Smart Controls**: Please note that the Smart Controls are components that are part of each Track. However the user interface element that lets you control those components is not visible on the Track. Each Track in the GarageBand's Tracks Area contains the Track Header and Track Lane, but not the Smart Controls. They are displayed as an Inspector window like the Audio and MIDI Editor. That means there is only one Window element (Smart Controls Window) and that window (if visible) displays only the controls of whatever Track is currently selected.

❸ **Track Header**: The Track Headers in the Track List look like mini Channel Strips with a Volume Fader, Pan Knob and other buttons that I'll discuss in the next section.

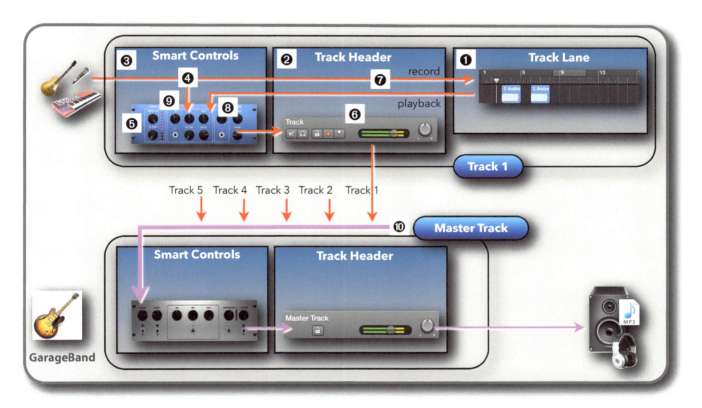

A few important aspects:

▸ The selection of the input signal ❹ of an Audio Track is also part of the Smart Controls Window.

▸ The Audio or MIDI signal you are recording on the Track Lane ❶ is the "dry" input signal. All the effects available in the Smart Controls Window ❺ and even the Volume Fader ❻ on the Track Header do not affect the signal you are recording ❼. Only the signal you are playing back ❽ or playing "through" ❾ the Track.

▸ That means that there are two signals entering the Smart Controls component: The **Input Signal** ❹ (that is recorded on the Track Lane ❼ and also plays through the Track ❾) and the **Playback Signal** ❽ that comes from the Regions on the Track Lane when you play back your song.

▸ The output signals from each Track in your Project are sent (routed) to the Master Track ❿. It has its own Smart Controls that let you add effects to the final mix before it gets sent to the speakers or mixed to a new audio file.

Track Header

Now let's look at the various components on the Track Header.

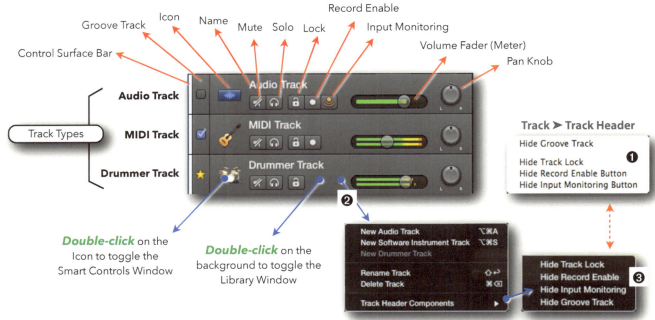

➡ Configure

Configuring the Track Header means to decide which components are visible on the Track Header. You can do this in two ways.

- Main Menu *Track* ➤ *Track Header* ➤ opens a submenu ❶ where you can toggle the visibility of four of the components.
- *Ctr+click* on the Track Header background ❷ (on a component) to select from its *Shortcut Menu* ➤ *Track Header Components* ➤ . The submenu ❸ has the same menu items.

➡ Resize

The height of the Track Header is fixed, but you can resize its width by *dragging* the Divider Line ❹ between the Track Header and the Track Lane. When you make it too small, then first the Pan Knob and then the Volume Slider disappears. Instead, a small LED ❺ appears that functions as a Level indicator.

➡ Automation

One of the three buttons in the Menu Bar on top of the Track List is the Show/Hide Automation button ❻. If you show the Automation controls, then two more components will be displayed in the Track Header. The Track Automation button ❼ for that Track and the popup menu ❽ to select which Automation parameter to display in the Automation Lane.

➡ Reorder

You can Move Tracks up and down the list by *dragging* the Track Header vertically (one at a time).

Control Surface Bar

The Control Surface Bar indicates which Track is controlled by an external Control Surface (i.e. the iPad running the Logic Remote app).
- ▸ The bars are only visible if you are connected to an external Control Surface.

 **Groove Track**

This is a feature that lets you quantize Tracks not based on a fixed grid (8th, 16th, etc.) but choose an existing Track in your Project and use its "feel" (the way it is played) as the basis for quantizing other Tracks to play "tight" together with the reference track. More on the topic about Quantize later. Here is how to enable Groove Track.

- ▸ Move the Mouse Pointer over the left edge of the Track Header of the Track that you want to use as a reference Track. A yellow star ⭐ appears on the Track Header (make sure you have this component enabled). *Click* on it to make it the reference track.
- ▸ The Track Header now adds a new Groove Track column to all Track Headers.
- ▸ Select a checkbox ☑ on any Track to quantize that track based on the reference track (the one with the star).
- ▸ Leave the box unchecked ☐ to keep the Track un-quantized or use the regular quantization command.
- ▸ To turn Groove Track off, *click* on the star of the reference Track and the Groove Track column disappears.

 Track Icon

You can assign an Icon to a Track to better visualize what kind of Track it is or what you are recording on it.

The Track Icon is also displayed on top of the Library Window.

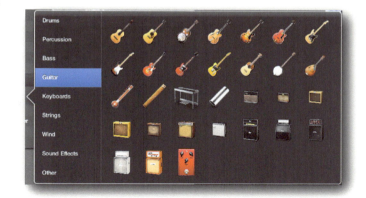

Change the Track Icon by selecting a new icon from the Icon popup window. Open the window with:
- *Ctrl+click* on the icon in the Track Header

Please note that the Track Icon is stored with a Patch (see the Library chapter for the discussion about the Patch). This is the default icon that you see on the Track Header. You can choose a different Icon, however, when you load a new Patch on that Track, your manually selected icon will be overwritten by the icon stored with the new Patch.

Additional Functionality:
- *Double-click* on the Track Icon to open the Smart Controls Window. If no Smart Controls have been assigned yet, then the Library Window will open instead.

 **Mute**

The Mute Button turns off the Track in case you want to silence it to listen to your song without it.

Two things to be aware of:
- Any signal processing on the Plugins of that Track is still active so there is no delay when you un-mute the Track again. Think of it as a guitar player that plays his solo running through all his effect boards. The "Mute " button would not stop him from playing, you would just unplug his speaker cable so you cannot hear what he is playing.
- The Mute Button is automatically activated when you press the solo button on any other Track(s).

Here are the various commands. The Mute Button turns blue when active .

- *Click* on the Mute Button to toggle between muted and un-muted.
- *Cmd+click* on a Mute Button to toggle all Tracks (all on or all off). This is convenient when you want to "un-mute" the buttons on multiple Tracks.
- *Click-hold* on a Mute Button and *drag* up or down across the previous or next Track Headers to switch their buttons to the same status.
- Key Command *M* will toggle the selected Track.
- Key Command *ctr+opt+cmd+M* will un-mute all Tracks.
- Selecting Solo on a Track will also Mute any other (non soloed) Track. In that case, the Mute button on those Tracks is blinking (with a slightly different type of button).
- The Regions on the muted Track turn gray.

Muted Track: Gray Regions

 **Solo**

Activating a Solo Button on any Track will mute any other Track in your Project that is not soloed. Their Mute Button will blink blue to indicate the "forced" Mute mode. This is a helpful feature if you want to listen to only a single Track or few Tracks in isolation.

The Control Bar Display and the Playhead will also turn yellow to indicate that Solo mode is on. Regions of a soloed Track that is selected have a yellow Header. If the soloed Track is not selected, then the Regions will have a thin yellow Frame around it.

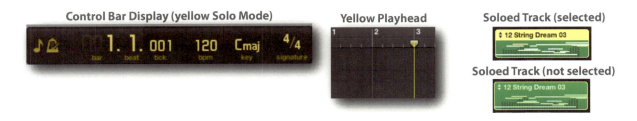

Here are the various commands. The Solo Button turns yellow when active :

- *Click* on the Solo Button to toggle solo mode.
- *Opt+click* on an active Solo Button turns all Solo Buttons off.
- *Opt+click* on an inactive Solo Button turns that Solo Button on and all other active Solo Buttons off.
- *Click-hold* on a Solo Button and *drag* up or down across the previous or next Track Headers to switch their buttons to the same status.
- The Key Command *S* will toggle the selected Track.
- Key Command *ctr+opt+cmd+S* will un-solo all Tracks.

 **Lock (Freeze)**

When a Track is "locked", you can't edit it or add Regions to it, or even record on it (the Record Enable Button disappears). The Volume and Pan control on the Track still can be used.

Please note that this is actually a "Freeze" function. After you enabled the Lock Button on a Track and start playing your song, you will see a progress bar that indicates that the Track(s) you just locked are now mixed down as audio files. This audio file (one file per Track) is temporarily saved inside the Project File (and deleted when you unlock that Track). GarageBand will play now that mixed-down audio file of that Track instead of the visible Regions and all the Track's Plugins. This could save you some CPU power when you are working on a big Project with lots of Plugins.

- 📌 *Click* on a button to toggle between locked  and unlocked 🔓.
- 📌 *Click+drag* across the buttons of multiple Tracks to turn them all on or off.

 **Record Enable**

The Record Enable Button has to be enabled before you can record on a Track. Although this sounds like a simple on-off procedure, there are some details about this button that can be a little bit confusing at times.

First of all, the button reacts slightly different for the three Track Types.

- 💡 **Drummer Track**

    The behavior for the Drummer Track is easy because it doesn't have a Record Enable Button. You can't record on a Drummer Track, you just create Drummer Regions manually and edit them with the Drummer Editor.

- 💡 **MIDI Track**

    ▸ Single Track Recording (automatically enable): A MIDI Track automatically switches the Record Enabled Button on whenever you select a Track. That's why that important button is hidden by default. You don't need it when recording a single MIDI Track. There is an exception:

    ▸ Multi-Track Recording (manually enable): You can manually activate the Record Enable Button on multiple MIDI Tracks. The effect is that the incoming MIDI signal (from the external MIDI Keyboard or the Musical Typing window) will play all those Tracks that are record enabled. This can be used for "layering" multiple Tracks (all the enabled Tracks play the same notes). Please note that the new MIDI Region is only created on the selected Track (maybe it is a bug in 10.0.1 that the Region isn't created on all record enabled Tracks).

    When you select a MIDI Track for the first time, the button changes to "gray button with red dot" 🔘. This indicates that the Track is now record enabled but that the Software Instrument is still in a "sleep mode" and has to be awakened. When you play the first note on your keyboard, the note sounds a little late (you just woke it up) and the button changes to "red button with gray dot" 🔴. That means the Software Instrument is ready to play.

- 💡 **Audio Track**

    ▸ Single Track Recording (automatically enable): Same as with MIDI Tracks, you can record on an Audio Track just by selecting it and hit record without making the Record Enable button visible and enabling it (using the Record Enable Button has at least one advantage that you can monitor the input level on the Volume Meter). If the Record Enable Button is visible, then it switches from ⬜ to 🔴 when you select an Audio Track. *Click* on the button to "enable" the Track and the button starts blinking red 🔴). The button stays on 🔴 once you start recording.

    ▸ Multi-Track Recording (manually enable): You can activate the Record Enable Button on multiple Audio Tracks if you want to record those Tracks at the same time. Please note that all enabled Audio Tracks have to be set to different audio input channels on the Audio Device.

 **Input Monitoring**

Input Monitoring is only available on Audio Tracks, not MIDI or Drummer Tracks.

To understand its functionality, you might have a look again at the GarageBand signal flow diagram I introduced earlier. Here is a modified version that demonstrates the Input Monitoring function.

- ▸ In the Smart Controls Window of the Audio Track, you select the input source ❶, which audio channels of the connected Audio Device you are about to record.
- ▸ That input signal goes straight to the Track Lane ❷ where it will be recorded as Audio Regions. Let me repeat again, it will be recorded as it is. The Volume Fader and any of the Smart Controls effects have no influence on the recorded signal. While you are recording, you will not hear that audio signal.
- ▸ When you play back ❸ your recording, the Audio Region(s) from the Track Lane will be sent through the Fader, Pan and all the effects you have setup in the Smart Controls Window.
- ▸ This configuration might be ok when you record any audio source through a microphone (vocals, acoustic guitar, piano, trumpet, etc.). The musician hears himself and might not want to hear his own signal "going" through the Track. However, your vocalist might want to hear himself with some reverb (that you added on the Track) or if you record an electric guitar using all those cool amp simulations, then the player must hear himself "through" the Audio Track. And this is where the Input Monitoring Button comes in.
- ▸ The Input Monitoring Button ❹ acts like a switch that can send the input signal directly to the Track (Fader, Pan, Effects), in addition to the Track Lane. Now the guitar player can hear his signal right away, regardless if GarageBand is in stop, play or record mode. Same thing with the vocalist. He can hear himself with that nice reverb you added to his Track.
- ▸ There is one drawback with this feature. If you record a microphone and you have Input Monitoring enabled, then the signal (from the vocalist) enters the mic, travels through the Track and plays back through the speaker. If the mic and the speaker are in the same room, then the signal from the speaker can reach the mic ❺, travels through the Audio Track again and creates a looped signal that gets louder and louder. This is called an acoustic Feedback. In that case, you want to turn off the Input Monitoring, turn down the volume or use headphones. GarageBand has an additional remedy called 'Feedback Protection" that I explain in the Smart Controls chapter.

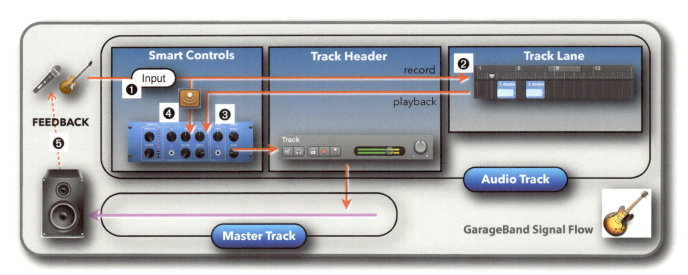

The Input Monitoring Button can have three stages

Input Monitoring is off. Input signal goes only to the Track Lane ❷.

Input Monitoring is on, but the Audio Track is not selected. In that case, you have to activate the Record Enable Button too if you want to hear the input signal ❹.

Input Monitoring is on ❹ and the Audio Track is selected.

 **Volume Fader (Meter)**

The horizontal Volume Fader integrates two functions:

🔸 **Volume Fader**

The round puck ❶ acts as a Fader knob that you slide left and right.
- The Fader doesn't have any scales but when you move or click the Fader, a Help Tag ❷ appears, displaying the position of the Volume Fader between its lowest position (-∞dB, same as muted) and highest position (+6dB).
- *Opt+click* on the Fader control to reset the Fader to the 0dB position. 0dB, also called "Unity Gain", is the position, where the Fader neither raises nor lowers the signal level on the Track.
- *Double-click* on the Fader to enter a value numerically.
- The Volume Fader will be hidden if you resize the width of the Track Header too much to the left.

🔸 **Volume Meter**

The Fader also functions as a Volume Meter.
- The Meter automatically displays a Mono ❸ (one channel) or Stereo ❹ Meter (two channels)
- The Meter is color coded to indicate the level ranging from green (low to medium), to yellow (high) to red (too high).
- The highest segment of the LED always stays on for a second (Peak Hold ❺) to better follow the meter when it is rapidly changing.
- If the Track Header is not wide enough and the Fader is hidden, then a single LED ❻ will be displayed instead. The LED indicates the level with three colors ❼.

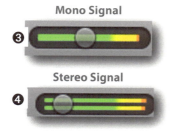

 Pan Knob

The rotary knob lets you place the signal in the stereo panorama between left and right. Technically the function is the same but the outcome sounds different when using the knob on a mono or stereo signal.

▶ **Mono Signal**: The signal can be placed so it comes out only from the left speaker (L position, -64), out of both speakers (C position, 0) or only from the right speaker (R position, +63). Or you can place the knob anywhere in between.

▶ **Stereo Signal**: Turning the knob to the left will gradually lower the level of the right channel of the stereo signal and turning the knob to the right will gradually lower the level of the left channel of the stereo signal.

- *Opt+click* on the knob to reset it to the center position.
- When controlling the knob, a black HelpTag appears that displays the position of the knob ❽ while you are adjusting it.

 **Automation**

The Automation in GarageBand involves two Automation buttons (two steps). Unfortunately the two types of buttons look almost the same so make sure you know which one is which.
- ▶ **Show/Hide Automation on all Tracks**: This is the button ❶ on the Tracks Menu Bar (above the Track List). If enabled (yellow), it will display the Automation Controls on all Track Headers.
- ▶ **Enable Automation on specific Tracks (Track Automation)**: This is the button ❷ on each individual Track Header that is only visible if Show Automation ❶ is activated. The button on the Track Header, if off, functions as an Automation bypass button for that Track.
- ▶ **Automation Parameter**: When the Show Automation is activated in the Menu Bar, the Tracks will not only display the Track Automation Button but also a button ❸ to open a popup menu ❹ for the Automation Parameter. These are all the parameters that can be automated on the Track. Selecting a Parameter will display the Automation Curve of that Parameter on the Automation Lane (part of the Track Lanes).

More about Automation in the Automation chapter.

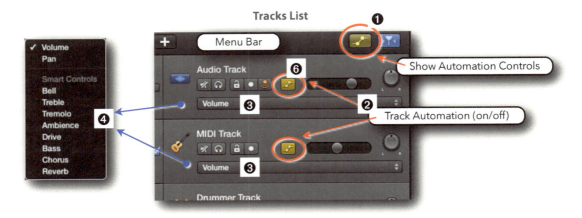

Track Name

The Track Name follows a specific priority.
- ▶ A new Track gets either a generic Name (Audio 1, Audio 2, Guitar 1, Guitar 2, etc.) or it gets the name of the loaded Patch.
- ▶ Loading a different Patch will rename the Track with the new Patch Name.
- ▶ You give the selected Track your own name with the following commands.
  - *Double-click* the name, enter a new name and hit return
  - Use the Key Command **sh+return**, enter a new name and hit return
  - Main Menu *Track ➤ Rename Track*, enter a new name
  - *Ctr+click* on the Track Header to open the *Shortcut Menu ➤ Rename Track*, enter a new name
- ▶ Once you gave the Track your own name, it will not be overwritten with any newly loaded Patch.
- ▶ Deleting the custom name (select and hit delete) will return to the default behavior and takes over the currently loaded Patch Name.

Hotspots

Double-clicking on the background of the Track Header will toggle the Library Window, displaying the currently loaded Patch of that Track (you double clicked on).

Also, remember that *double-clicking* on the Track Icon toggles the Smart Controls Window.

8 - Smart Controls

Usually, the discussion about mixing, the use of Plugins and all the sound treatment would come a little later in the book, after the topic of how to record your song. However, I though I would get into that earlier, because GarageBand X introduced such a new and different concept about Plugins and sound mixing that created a lot of confusion and misunderstanding about what you can do and what you can no longer do in GarageBand - or more importantly, what you have to do differently now.

A New Concept

- ▶ **Yes**: GarageBand targets the casual audio producer who wants to create songs without learning all the details about sound engineering and mixing. Based on that objective, the app leaves out a lot of elements and workflows usually found in other DAWs but still manages to get similar results. Apple just "simplified" the workflows to provide an easy to use product.
- ▶ **But**: The flip side however is that many users who are familiar with DAWs and even users who are familiar with the previous GarageBand version 6.0.5 find themselves somehow lost with this new approach - what is going on, where is my stuff?

Because the casual user might not want to know "why" GarageBand works the way it does, Apple doesn't include much explanation in the GarageBand documentation about the new architecture and functionality that goes on under the hood.

To fill that void, I will discuss the Smart Controls and the Library in this chapter not just from a user point of view (how do the controls and the interface work) but will explain the important aspect how GarageBand is providing that functionality. This discussion might be a little bit advanced for some readers and could be too much information for some, but I think it is valuable in understanding the new and different concept in GarageBand X when it comes to using the tools on your Tracks to create the best sound for your mix.

As the first step of "demystifying" the Smart Controls Window, I want to start with a brief introduction about Plugins.

Plugins

A Plugin in general is a little application that is added to "a bigger application" to extend its functionality. In our case, that "bigger app" is GarageBand (or any other DAW) and the Plugins are the little "add-ons" that are loaded (manually or automatically) into GarageBand to provide additional functionality. This additional functionality is mainly for processing your audio signal but also your MIDI signal in your Project.

➡ Formats

A Plugin has to have a specific format in order to be used in an application. "*The good thing about a format is that there are so many of them*" and Plugins are no exception. Different DAWs support only specific Plugin formats. This is similar to operating systems like OSX, Linux or Windows. Not all computer hardware can run every operating system.

GarageBand (and also Logic Pro) supports only two Plugin formats:

- **Logic Format**: Logic Pro X provides a wide variety of high quality Plugins that come pre-installed with Logic. The good news is that GarageBand not only supports those Plugins, they are also included in GarageBand. From the moment you add a Track to your Project, you are using those professional Logic Plugins without noticing it. I'll get to that in a moment.
- **AU Format**: This is an open standard for Audio Plugins that was developed by Apple. Most third-party Plugin developers release their Plugins in the AU format (Audio Unit) so they can be used in GarageBand or any other DAW. These third-party AU Plugins have to be installed separately. Please note that Apple has their own selection of AU Plugins that come preinstalled on your Mac.

This difference between these two Plugin formats is very important in order to understand what GarageBand is doing.

➡ Purpose

You can differentiate between two types of Plugins based on their purpose.

🔘 Effect Plugins (process)

These types of Plugins are "plugged in" (or inserted) into the signal flow of an audio signal but also a MIDI signal.

- **Audio FX**: Audio FX Plugins are like the little guitar stompboxes. You send the audio signal in and at its output comes out the processed audio signal, altered with whatever the Plugin allows you to do to it.
- **MIDI FX**: The Arpeggiator is an example of a MIDI FX Plugin. The incoming MIDI signal will be processed based on the parameter set in the Arpeggiator.

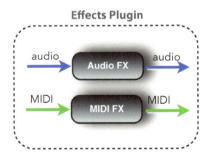

🔘 Instrument Plugins (generate)

These types of Plugins are like MIDI sound modules. Their input is a MIDI signal (coming from your MIDI keyboard or from the MIDI Regions) and the output is an audio signal. The Plugin itself generates the audio signal based on various sound settings (piano, organ, strings, etc.).

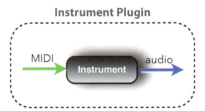

New Rules

Here is a summary of the new rules that apply now in GarageBand regarding Plugins on your Track.

➡ *Simple Rules*

These are the basic.

> **GarageBand still uses Logic Plugins but they are hidden and can only be adjusted via Smart Controls**

- ☑ You cannot load Logic Plugins directly onto your Track anymore.
- ☑ Instead, you load Patches onto a Track ❶.
- ☑ Patches load a complete set of Plugins, including their settings (and other signal routing).
- ☑ The Logic Plugins that are loaded onto a Track by a Patch are hidden ❷.
- ☑ You don't know what specific Plugins are loaded by a Patch only guess by the available Screen Controls.
- ☑ You cannot access/control individual Parameters of those loaded Plugins ❸.
- ☑ Instead, each Patch comes with a pre-configured Smart Controls Layout ❹.
- ☑ The Smart Controls Layout provides Screen Controls that are mapped ❺ to one or multiple parameters of the loaded (hidden) Plugins in a user friendly way.
- ☑ If the Smart Controls don't provide the signal processing you need for a specific Track, then you have to load a different Patch from the Library Window that (hopefully) includes the Effect Plugins you need or load additional AU Plugins (see next page).
- ☑ The Smart Controls Window functions as an Inspector Window. That means, it displays the Screen Controls of only one Track at a time, the currently selected Track ❼.

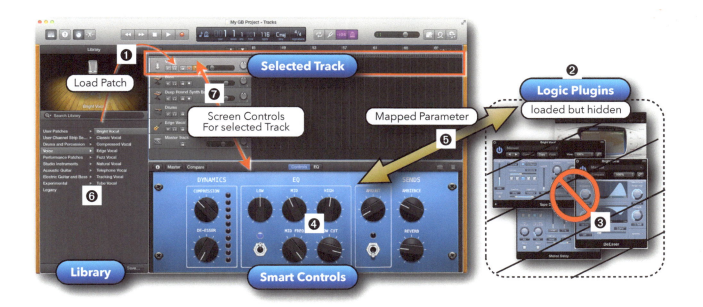

8 - Smart Controls

➡ **Advanced Rules**

Besides those limitations, there are some additional functions.

> You can still load AU Plugins onto your Track

- ☑ Each Track has the option to add up to four Audio FX Plugins in the AU Format ❶.
- ☑ A MIDI Track (and Drummer Track) has also the option to replace the (hidden) Logic Software Instrument with an AU Software Instrument ❷.
- ☑ The windows of those AU Plugins can be opened and you have access to their user interface with all their available parameters ❸.
- ☑ A Dialog Window ❹ gives you the option to use the AU Plugins in addition (Keep) or instead (Bypass) of the currently loaded and hidden Logic Plugins. An AU Instrument Plugin will of course replace the existing Logic Instrument. GarageBand might map the existing Screen Controls to some of the Parameters of the newly added AU Plugins.
- ☑ You can save the state of the current Track as your own User Patch ❺ including all Plugins (Logic Format and AU Format) and signal routing.
- ☑ The Smart Controls Layout can be switched to display the Channel EQ ❻, the only Logic Plugin that allows full access to all its Parameters (besides the Amp Designer and the Pedalboard).
- ☑ Patches are compatible between GarageBand, Logic and MainStage (with some restrictions).
- ☑ Factory Patches only include Logic Plugins.

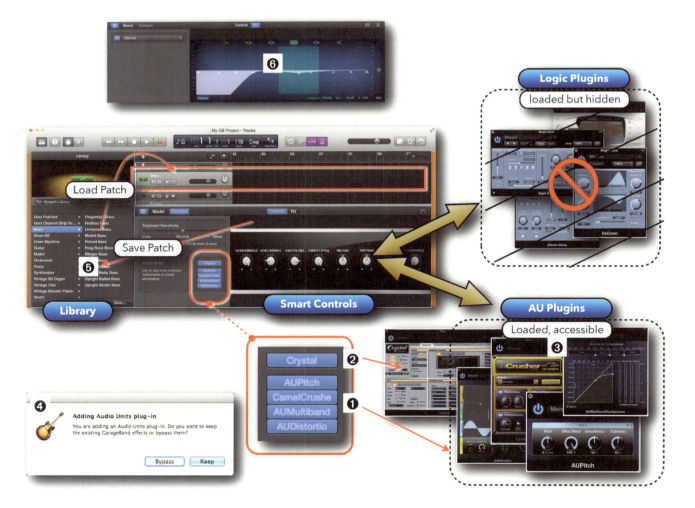

Comparison: GarageBand 6 - GarageBand X

Here is a look at how these new rules transform the user interface from the old to the new GarageBand. The Track Info Pane in GarageBand 6 had two tabs. They switched between the Browse and the Edit View.

- ▶ The Browse View ❶ is now the Library Window ❷ in GarageBand X for browsing Patches.
- ▶ The Edit View ❸ is now the Smart Controls Window ❹ in GarageBand X, the biggest change.
- ▶ The function of the Track Header ❺ itself with the Fader, Pan and other controls is pretty much the same.
- ▶ The option to manually load any Plugins ❻ into the available slots is now restricted to only 4 AU Plugins ❼. There is no direct access to load the Logic/GarageBand Plugins anymore.
- ▶ Editing the Plugin Parameters is now consolidated into one Smart Controls Layout ❽ with a simplified (limited) choice of Screen Controls. Only the loaded AU Plugins in GarageBand X can still be accessed using their own Plugin Window. Please note that the area for the AU Plugins ❼ is hidden by default and has to be enabled in the *Preferences ➤ Audio/MIDI* window.
- ▶ The Master Echo and Master Reverb controls ❾ are still available in GarageBand X ❿ but mainly for compatibility reasons when using legacy Projects or GarageBand for iOS. The two controls are now hidden by default and have to be enabled in the *Preferences ➤ Audio/MIDI* window. You also cannot change the Parameters of those Master Effects anymore and they are not saved with a Patch.

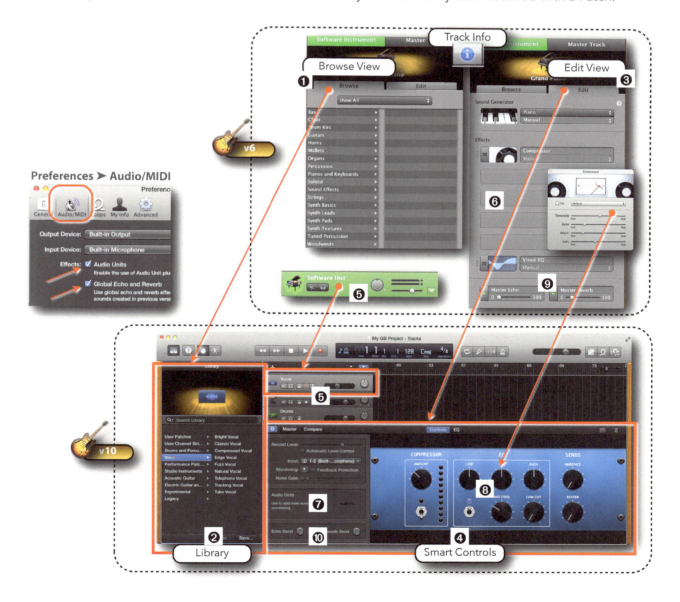

8 - Smart Controls

Comparison: Logic X - GarageBand X

And here is another look. How does the new GarageBand concept compare to Logic (or any other DAW)?

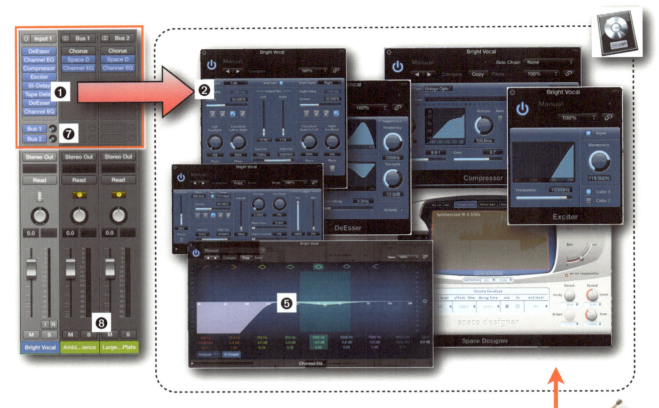

This is a screenshot of Logic Pro X and GarageBand X where both have the same Patch "Bright Vocal" loaded.

▶ You can see that the Patch includes 8 Audio FX ❶ (all Logic Plugins). Every Plugin can be opened in its own window ❷ with access to every Parameter.

▶ GarageBand in comparison provides only one Smart Controls Window ❸ with a few Screen Controls. However, the Track has still the same 8 Plugins loaded. They are just hidden and instead, the Screen Controls ❹ now let you access the main Parameters. Please note that one control might adjust multiple Plugin Parameters (of different Plugins) with some sophisticated mapping configuration that would not be possible when controlling single Parameters in a Plugin Window. That's why Logic also uses those powerful Smart Controls.

▶ One exception is the Channel EQ Plugin ❺. The Smart Controls Window can switch its view to display the full Channel EQ Plugin Window with access to all its Parameters. ❻

▶ As you can see, the Bright Voice Patch contains also two Aux Sends ❼ routed to two additional Aux Channel Strips ❽. GarageBand doesn't have Channel Strips and especially not Aux Channel Strips, or does it? The functionality is actually there in GarageBand under the hood, just not accessible for the user. Most likely, there are some Screen Controls ❾ that adjust the Aux Sends (Ambience, Reverb).

As you can see, the new interface concept in GarageBand is only a self imposed restriction about the access (in favor of simplicity) but not a limitation of the underlying components that deliver the same sound quality as Logic. That's also the reason why Patches are mostly compatible with Logic. It is like you are driving a Ferrari that is restricted to go only up to 50mph. You are driving slow, but still, it is a Ferrari.

New Signal Flow

Here is the signal flow of a GarageBand Track again with the focus on the Smart Controls and Plugins

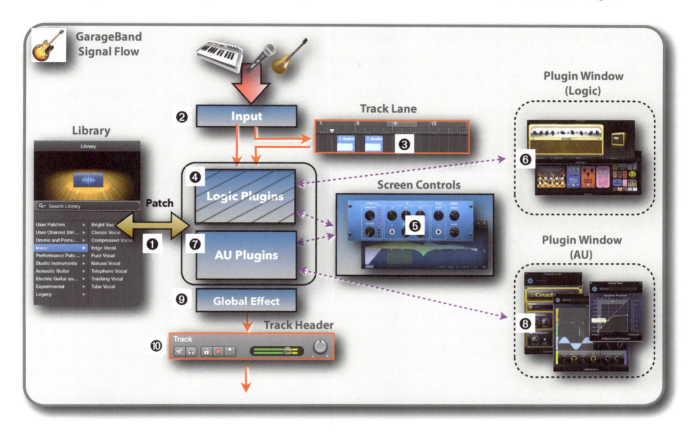

- ▶ When you create a new Track, a Patch ❶ is automatically loaded onto the Track. This is a configuration with a pre-selection of Plugins and a specific signal flow on that Track.
- ▶ Remember, the first component on a Track is the Input Selection ❷. This is where you configure the input source, input gain, etc. This Input Component is part of the Smart Controls Window.
- ▶ From the Input Component, the signal goes to the Track Lane ❸ where it is recorded as Regions and played back when GarageBand is playing. In addition, the signal goes directly to the Logic Plugins Component ❹. As I explained already, those Logic Plugins are hidden and you can't manage them, i.e. remove existing ones, add new ones.
- ▶ The Smart Controls Window provides the user interface with Screen Controls ❺ to control the Parameter of the "invisible" Logic Plugins. The only exception is the EQ, the Amp and Pedalboard Plugin that allows you to open its Plugin Window separately.
- ▶ After the Logic Plugins Components, the signal enters the AU Plugins Component ❼. Here you can manually load up to 4 AU Plugins, that you can control by opening their individual Plugin Windows ❽. Depending on the configuration, GarageBand can also map Parameters of the AU Plugin to the Screen Controls ❺.
- ▶ After the AU Plugin Component, the signal goes to the Global Effects Components ❾. They are not part of the new signal flow concept and should not be used except when needed for older Projects.
- ▶ At the end, the signal reaches the Track Header ❿, where you can set the Level, the Pan (in addition to the Mute and Solo function).
- ▶ The Library Window ❶ lets you save any changes you made in the Smart Controls as a new Patch. Please note that the Patch only includes the Plugin settings (Logic Plugin and AU Plugin) plus any signal routing (which is not visible in GarageBand). What's not saved with the Patch are the Global Effects, Fader and Pan knob position and input configuration.

The Interface

That was a lot of information so far and it might need some time and playing around to digest.
Now, let's have a closer look at the interface to learn how to use Smart Controls.

First, we have to open the Smart Controls Window. Again, the window displays the sound controls for only one Track at the time, the currently selected Track. You can have the window open and select a different Track in the Tracks List to make changes for that Track, and so on. Please note that the Smart Controls Window opens in the lower Window Pane, the same space as the Editor Windows, so you can view either or, but not both at the same time.

Toggle the Smart Controls Window with any of the following commands.
- Main Menu *View* ➤ *Show/Hide Smart Controls*
- Key Command *B*
- *Click* on the Smart Controls Button in the Control Bar
- *Double-click* on the Track Icon

The Interface for the Smart Controls Window is very clean and easy to use. It has three sections.

- **Menu Bar ❶**

    This strip on top of the window has only a few control elements; on the left, in the center, and on the right. Please note that they change depending on what type of Track is selected (Audio, MIDI, Drummer).

- **Layout ❷**

    This is the main section that can switch between two different layouts, the Screen Controls and the EQ.

- **Inspector ❸**

    This area can be toggled with a *click* on the i-Button in the Menu Bar to show/hide the Smart Controls Inspector. It provides additional controls and settings for the selected Track. Make sure that the Window Pane for the Smart Controls is high enough to display all the elements (especially when working on a smaller laptop screen).

Menu Bar

The Menu Bar has the control elements on the left, in the center, and on the right. Please note that some controls change depending on what type of Track is selected (Audio, MIDI, Drummer).

Smart Control Menu Bar

Left Controls   Center Controls   Right Controls

➡ **Left**

There are three buttons on the left.

▶ The Inspector Button toggles the left Pane of the Smart Controls Window, to show/hide the Smart Controls Inspector.

▶ The Smart Controls Window always displays the Screen Controls of the selected Track. This button toggles that layout and switches the layout to display the controls of the Master Track instead. Please note that the Master Track is hidden from the Tracks Area by default so this button lets you quickly toggle between the Smart Controls for the selected Track and the Master Track without making the Master Track visible and selecting it in the Track List first.

▶ The Compare Button functions as an Undo-Redo toggle when you use the controls to compare the edit you just did: Before (gray) - after (blue).

➡ **Center**

The center of the Menu Bar has two buttons that switch the layout of the Smart Controls Window.

▶ *Click* on the Controls Button ❶ to switch the layout to display the Screen Controls ❷ of the currently selected Track.
- If the selected Track is the Master Track, then this button changes to the Output Button ❸. When selected, the layout will display the Screen Controls ❹ that affect the Plugins loaded on the Master Track.

▶ *Click* on the the EQ Button ❺ to switch the layout to display the Channel EQ Plugin ❻ of the selected Track, a Logic Plugin that is always available on a Track. This is one of the exceptions where you have access to all the controls of a loaded Logic Plugin. Please note that when the Master Track is selected, *clicking* on the EQ Button ❼ will display the EQ Plugin ❽ for the Master Track to adjust the frequency of the final mix.

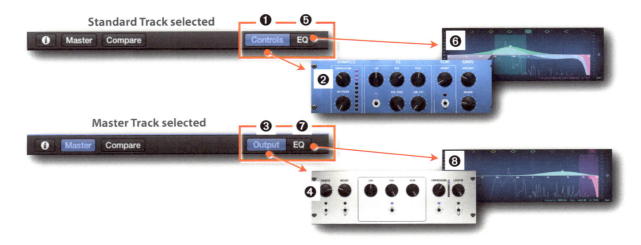

8 - Smart Controls   127

➡ **Right**

Here is an overview how the buttons on the right side of the Menu Bar change depending on what type of Track is selected.

🔘 MIDI Track

The Arpeggiator Button indicates that the Logic MIDI FX Plugin is loaded as part of the Patch.

When you click on the button, the Plugin gets turned on and an additional popup menu appears that lets you choose from presets and do further configurations for the Arpeggiator.

🔘 Drummer Track

The right side of the Menu Bar is empty when a Drummer Track is selected. No additional buttons there.

🔘 Audio Track

When an Audio Track is selected, then the right side displays two additional buttons. This indicates the status of two Audio FX Plugins (Logic Format), the Amp Designer and the Pedalboard.

- Dimmed: The Plugins are not loaded. Most likely a non-guitar Patch.
- Gray: The Plugins are loaded. Most likely, the current Patch is a guitar Patch. ***Clicking*** on the buttons will open the Plugin Windows.
- Blue: The Plugins are loaded and the Plugin Window is opened. This is one of the exceptions in GarageBand (besides the EQ) where you have access to the Parameters of a loaded Logic Plugin.

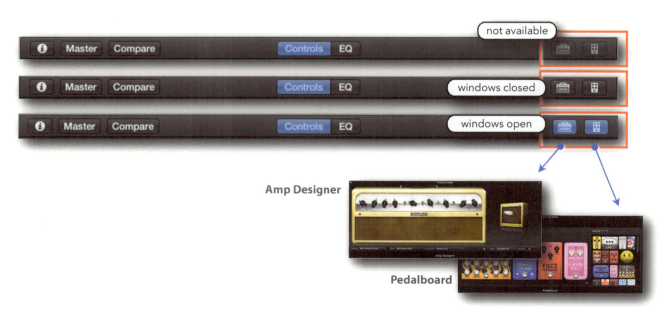

Master Track

When the Smart Controls display the Master Track by selecting the Master Track in the Tracks Area or just by clicking on the Master Button [Master] in the Smart Controls Menu Bar (regardless which Track is selected), then no further buttons are displayed on the right side. However, the Controls Button in the center turns into the Output Button [Output] to indicate that the displayed Screen Controls are mapped to Plugins on the Master Output Track.

Layout

This is the main section of the Smart Controls Window that can switch between two different views: Screen Controls View ([Controls] or [Output]) or the Equalizer View [EQ].

The Layout is stored with the Patch and cannot be changed manually in GarageBand. It includes two things: First, the actual mapping (what Screen Control is controlling what Plugin Parameter) and a specific graphics layout (skins) to indicate the purpose of the controls.

Priority

Some Patches have many Plugins with a lot of Parameters but there are only a few Screen Controls available to control all those Parameters. Therefore, GarageBand has a built-in a priority to choose which of the available Plugin Parameters are mapped to the available Screen Controls. The priority is mainly based on the type of Track.

MIDI / Drummer Track

- ▸ **MIDI/Drummer Track**: The Screen Controls are mapped to the loaded Software Instrument and the graphics indicate what type of instrument that could be (piano, organ, clavinet, strings, etc.).
- ▸ **Audio Track (with Amp Plugin)**: The Screen Controls are mapped to the Amp Plugin and the graphics indicate what type of amp it is.
- ▸ **Audio Track (without Amp Plugin)**: The Screen Controls are mapped to the Audio FX plugins and the graphics use just a generic blue skin or a silver skin (for the Master Track).

Audio Track (with Amp)

Audio Track (without Amp)

Smart Controls Inspector

The third area in the Smart Controls Window is the Smart Controls Inspector. *Click* on the Inspector Button ❶ in the Menu Bar to show/hide that Inspector. It provides additional controls and settings for the selected Track. Make sure that the Window Pane for the Smart Controls is big enough (height) to display all the elements (especially when working on a smaller laptop screen).

The Inspector has three sections.

- ▶ **Input Configuration** ❷: This area is more important for Audio Tracks with several input controls ❸. The MIDI and Drummer Track provide only a single slider ❹ that sets the Keyboard Sensitivity. This is the range of the generated velocity value depending on how hard you strike a key on your external MIDI Keyboard.
- ▶ **Audio Unit Configuration** ❺: This area lets you select the four AU FX Plugins ❻. MIDI and Drummer Tracks have an additional Plugin slot to select an AU Software Instrument Plugin ❼. You have to select the checkbox for this Audio Units section in the GarageBand *Preferences* ➤ *Audio/MIDI* ❽ to be displayed.
- ▶ **Master Effects** ❾: This area is hidden by default and also has to be selected with a checkbox in the GarageBand *Preferences* ➤ *Audio/MIDI* ❿ to be visible in the Inspector. These two knobs are only available for compatibility reasons with older GarageBand Projects and GarageBand for iPad Projects. They shouldn't be used for new Projects. They are not included when saving the Smart Controls as a new Patch.

➡ *Audio Input Configuration*

Remember the Signal Flow Diagram of a Track that I showed in the previous chapter. You could see that the Smart Controls contains two components.

- **Input**: The Input component contains all the configurations necessary for recording, mainly audio recording. These are controls found in the Smart Controls Inspector. They are not as cool looking like the Smart Controls but at least as important.
- **Signal Processing**: The main component is the Signal Processing with all the Plugins used for mixing that is available in those colorful layouts.

So keep that in mind that the Smart Controls Window is not only there for mixing your Project but also for preparing the proper input configuration when recording audio signals in your Project.

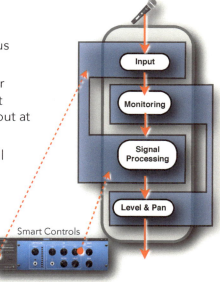

Here are the six Controls found in the Smart Controls Inspector when an Audio Track is selected.

Audio Input Configuration

🔸 Input ❶

The Input selection should be the first control because this is where you select the source that you are about to record.

▸ Before doing any configurations in this area, you have to select the Audio Device that you want to use with GarageBand. This is done in the *Preferences ➤ Audio/MIDI*. Please refer to the discussion about the Audio Devices in the "Prior Knowledge" chapter at the beginning of the book.

▸ Once you have selected the Audio Device, the popup menu in the Smart Controls Inspector lists all the input options for that Audio Device.

- First, you have to select if you want to use a mono input ❷ (one channel ⓞ) or a stereo input ❸ (two channels ⓦ). **Click** on the circle button to toggle between the two. Please refer also to the discussion about mono vs. stereo in the Prior Knowledge chapter.

- The mono/stereo selection determines how the available input channels are presented in the popup menu. Here is an example where the selected Audio Device (with the name "Aggregate Device") has four audio input channels. When mono ⓞ is selected ❷, then the menu will list all four channels ❹ individually (1, 2, 3, 4). This way you can connect four microphones to GarageBand via your Audio Device. When stereo ⓦ is selected ❸, then all four channels are grouped as two stereo channels ❺ (1-2 and 3-4). Choose this option when your audio source you want to record is in stereo.

Mono Channel   **Stereo Channel**

🔸 Record Level ❻

Once you select the input source, you have to set the proper Record Level.

This is a very important: The Record Level slider in GarageBand's Smart Controls Window is actually a "remote control". I discussed that functionality in the Prior Knowledge chapter about Drivers for specific Audio Devices. This slider ❼ in GarageBand controls the input level of the Audio Device through its Driver. This is the same functionality when setting the level in the System Preferences ❽ or the Audio MIDI Setup utility ❾. If you have all windows open, then you see that one slider moves the sliders in the other windows too.

Please note that some Audio Devices won't allow that. In that case, the Record Level slider is inactive and you have to set the Record Level on the Audio Device itself.

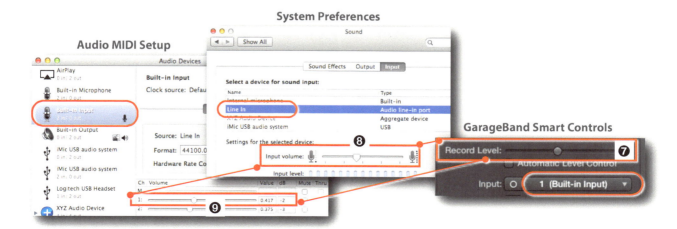

🌀 Automatic Level Control ❶

If the "Automatic Level Control" is checked (not available for all Audio Interfaces), then GarageBand will automatically lower the Record Level to prevent Feedback and it raises the level if it is too low.

🌀 Monitoring ❷

The Monitoring Button in the Smart Controls Inspector is the same button as the Input Monitoring Button 🟠 on the Track Header ❸. It sends the input signal directly through the Track ❹ in addition to sending it to the Track Lane ❺ for recording the signal as Audio Regions. With this button on, you will always hear the input signal.

If Monitoring is off, then the input signal will be recorded, but you will hear it only when the recorded signal is played back from the Track Lane.

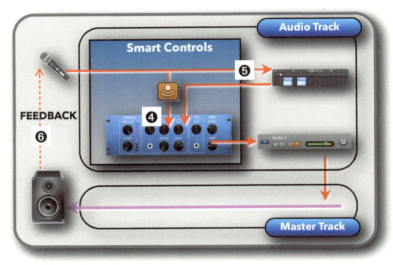

GarageBand knows when you have the internal microphone and the internal speaker selected. This is a potential problem for Feedback ❻. In this case, when you try to enable Monitoring, a Dialog Window ❼ pops up reminding you of that problem. A button lets you open the GarageBand Preferences window to choose a different Audio Device.

🌀 Feedback Protection ❽

If you check this option, GarageBand will automatically turn the Monitoring ❷ off when a Feedback occurs. It pops up a Dialog Window ❾ with three options.

- Monitoring off: Turns it off
- Monitoring on: Keeps everything as it is
- No Feedback Protection: Turns the checkbox off ❽ and leaves Input Monitoring on ❷.

🌀 Noise Gate ❿

A Noise Gate is an audio effects unit that automatically turns the input signal off if it is below a specific level. A slider lets you set that threshold when to "open and close the gate". This is a common effect used with electric guitars that often have a low level hum. Adjusting the slider lets you block that low level hum signal but "opens the gate" when the guitarist plays and the input signal is higher.

Adjust the threshold (Noise Gate Slider) carefully so it doesn't chop off some of the "wanted signal" (i.e. ring out of a sustained note).

> **Attention**

Here is a little detail you have to be aware of about the six controls for the Audio Input Configuration we just discussed. They "belong" to different entities. Here is what that means.

▶ **Track Related**

You know by now that the Screen Controls and even the selection for the AU Plugins that you see in the Smart Controls Window "belong" to the currently selected Track. Selecting a different Track switches the Smart Controls Window to display the controls for that Track. Three of the six Input Configuration controls behave exactly like that. They are Track-related. Each Track can set these controls individually.

- Monitoring
- Feedback Protection
- Noise Gate

▶ **Input Device Related**

The other three controls are not Track related, they are properties of the selected Input Source of the Audio Device. Changing the settings for the Record Level and Automatic Level Controls on one Track will change those controls in every Track that has the same Input Source selected.

- Input Selection
- Record Level
- Automatic Level Control

➡ *Audio Units*

💡 **Enabling Audio Units**

Before adding any AU Plugins to a Track you have to enable the Audio Units in the *Preferences ➤ Audio/MIDI* by selecting the checkbox ❶. This will add the Audio Units area ❷ in the Smart Controls Inspector.

Please note that when you try to uncheck the Effects again, you will get a Dialog Window ❸. You have to remove all AU Plugins from any Track before you can deselect the checkbox again.

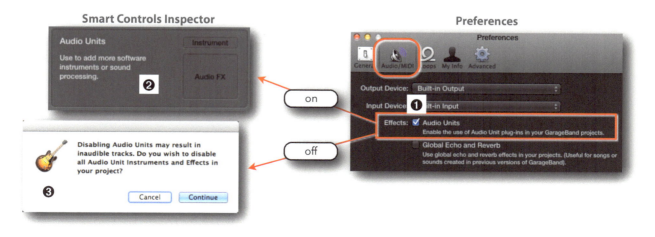

8 - Smart Controls

Adding AU Plugins

The Audio Units area has two fields.
- ▸ **Audio FX Plugin ❶**: Audio Tracks, MIDI Tracks, Drummer Tracks and even the Master Track display a square which represents four slots where you can load AU Audio FX Plugins.
- ▸ **Software Instrument Plugin ❷**: MIDI Tracks have one additional slot above that square to load an AU Software Instrument Plugin.

When you try to load the first AU Plugin, a Dialog Window ❸ gives you the option to Keep or Bypass any existing Logic Plugins that were installed with the current Patch.

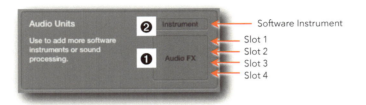

Plugin Button

The Plugin Buttons are multi purpose buttons. Their function changes depending on your Mouse Pointer position:
- ▸ When you move the Mouse Pointer over an empty slot, that slot turns dark ❹ and shows the double arrow to indicate that this opens a popup menu when clicked on. The Audio Units submenu displays all the available AU Plugins that are installed on your computer grouped by manufacturer. Even if you haven't' installed any AU Plugins yet, there are already 20 AU Plugins that are pre-installed on your computer under the Apple submenu ❺.
- ▸ Once you've selected a Plugin from the menu, the button turns blue ❻ and displays the name of the Plugin you just loaded into that slot.
- ▸ When you move the Mouse Pointer over the button, it changes to a different appearance with three Click Zones ❼.
    - **On/Off ❽**: *Click* on this button to toggle the Plugin on and off.
    - **Toggle Plugin Window ❾**: *Click* on this button to open/close the Plugin Window.
    - **Open Plugin Menu ❿**: *Click* on this button to open the popup menu with the Effect Plugins to load a different Plugin for that slot or remove it ("No Plug-in").

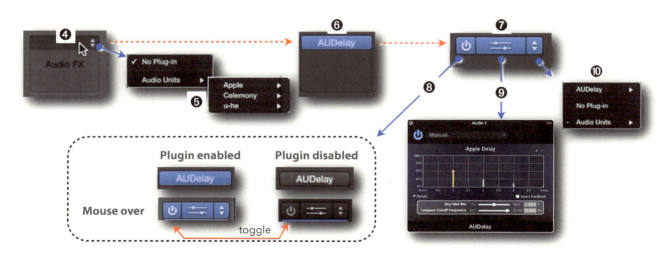

Move/Copy/Swap between Slots

Please note that the order of the Plugins from top to bottom is very important. The output of Plugin in slot 1 connects to the input of Plugin in slot 2 and so on. For example, adding distortion to a reverb'ed signal or adding reverb to a distorted signal can change the sound of the final signal. That's why it is important that you have the option to easily move Plugins around.

- ▶ **Move**: *Drag* the button to an empty slot. A ghost button is attached to the Mouse Pointer and the target slot will get a white frame when you move over it.
- ▶ **Copy**: *Opt+drag* the button to an empty slot. A ghost button is attached to the Mouse Pointer and the target slot will get a white frame when you move over it.
- ▶ **Swap**: *Drag* the button over another button. A ghost button is attached to the Mouse Pointer and the target slot will get a white frame when you move over it. When you release the mouse, both Plugins swap their slot position.

move

copy

swap

Remove Plugins

Remove a Plugin by selecting "No Plug-in" from the popup menu.

An Instrument Plugin can't be removed, only replaced with another AU Plugin. Its menu doesn't have the "No Plug-in" option.

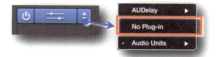

➡ Master Effects

The two knobs "Echo Send" and "Reverb Send" ❶ are "leftovers" from the previous GarageBand v6.0.5 architecture. The controls are only there to be compatible with older Projects. The area is hidden in the Smart Controls Inspector when opening a new GarageBand Project and they have to be enabled with the checkbox in the **Preference ➤ Audio/MIDI** ❷. You only can control the amount of the effect but you cannot change the effect itself anymore in GarageBand X.

Opening a legacy Project ❸ from GarageBand v6.0.5 will automatically select the checkbox ❷ and makes them visible. Deselecting the checkbox will prompt a Dialog Window ❹, letting you know that you'll bypass the effects when they are hidden.

Effects

The following four effects are the only Logic Plugins that you can control directly in GarageBand.

Equalizer

Every Track in GarageBand, including the Master Track, has an Equalizer Plugin (EQ). This is a type of Audio FX Plugin that is arguably the most used and maybe misused or misunderstood signal processing unit. It is beyond the scope of this book to explain how to use it, and more importantly, how not to use it. Only two tips:

- ☑ Read up and learn more about this important "sound shaping" device.
- ☑ Only use it together with your most important studio gear - **your ears**.

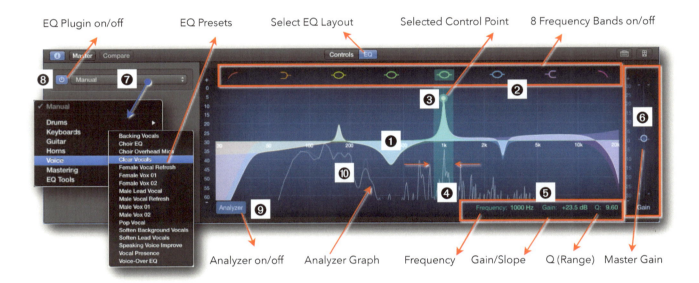

- ▸ The EQ displays a graph that indicates the level change (y-axis, in dB) of a specific frequency range (x-axis, in Hz) as shaded areas ❶.
- ▸ The EQ has eight frequency bands that you can control individually. Click on the colored symbol ❷ to toggle the band on/off. The icons indicate the type of band: Filter, Shelf and Bell-curved.
- ▸ Adjust each frequency band graphically by dragging its Control Point ❸ up/down (change its gain) or left/right (change its frequency). *Click* on the frequency band to activate (highlight) it first and make the Control Point visible. A colored shaded area ❹ marks the frequency range that is affected by that band.
- ▸ Adjust the selected frequency band numerically by *dragging* the number value ❺ of the Frequency, Gain/Slope or Q/Octave (the shape of the affected frequency band) up and down or *double-click* the number and enter a value. The graphic display updates accordingly.
- ▸ Adjust the overall Gain ❻ of the EQ Plugin. This effect will also be visible in the graphic display.
- ▸ If the EQ is selected in the Smart Controls, then its Inspector on the left changes to display a popup menu with EQ Presets ❼ for a wide variety of situations.
- ▸ Next to the Preset menu is the on/off Button ❽ for the EQ. This is useful for A/B comparison.
- ▸ Click on the Analyzer Button ❾ to toggle the Analyzer graph ❿. This is a frequency curve that appears in the graph which shows the level of the frequencies of its input signal in real time. This can help you to spot frequencies that are to high (i.e. a resonance or a boom), or to low (i.e. not bright enough in the high frequency range). Be aware that this feature uses a lot of processing power!

Amps & Pedalboards

I will explain the Amp and Pedalboard Plugin in the Mixing chapter. Here is just a quick introduction.

If a Patch contains the Logic Plugin "Amp Designer" and/or "Pedalboard" and that Patch is loaded onto an Audio Track, then the following will happen:

- ▸ The Smart Controls Window ❶ shows the two gray icons ❷ on the right side of its Menu Bar.
- ▸ *Click* on an icon to open the separate Plugin Window that gives you access to all the Parameters of that Amp Designer Plugin ❸ or the Pedalboard Plugin ❹. An icon turns blue if its Plugin Window is open.
- ▸ Although you can edit each Parameter in the Plugin Window, the Smart Controls Window (with the graphics of an amp) provides a layout with its Screen Controls mapped to important Parameters of both, the Amp Designer ❺ and the Pedalboard Plugin ❻.

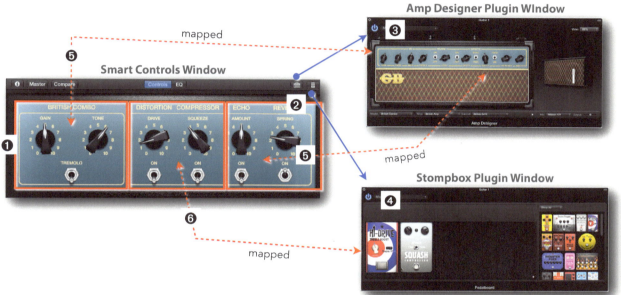

Arpeggiator

The Arpeggiator is also a Plugin, but this one is not an Audio FX Plugin, it is a MIDI FX Plugin. That means it processes a MIDI signal not an Audio signal. In the signal flow, it is located right before the input of the Software Instrument Plugin.

The MIDI signal coming from the MIDI keyboard or from the MIDI Region will be processed before it enters the Software Instrument. Any chord of two or more notes will be played in sequence. The parameters let you determine the order and the range how it plays these notes.

What does it do:

- ▸ The Arpeggiator Plugin is part of most Patches with Software Instrument Plugins that are used on MIDI Tracks.
- ▸ The right side of the Smart Control's Menu Bar displays the Arpeggiator Button ❼.
- ▸ *Click* on the Button to toggle the Plugin on ❽ and off ❼.
- ▸ When enabled, the Button turns blue ❽ and a popup menu ❾ appears.
- ▸ The Menu contains a wide variety of Presets ❿ and controls to configure the Arpeggiator.

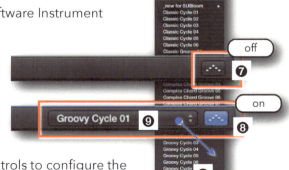

9 - Library

Window Pane

I mentioned the Library and the Patches already so often; let's finally have a closer look at it.

The Library Window can be shown or hidden as a Window Pane on the left side of the GarageBand Window.

There is a wide variety of controls that open and close the Library window. Choose the ones that suit your workflow:

➡ ***Toggle Show/Hide***

- ***Click*** on the Library button in the Control Bar
- Main Menu ***View ➤ Show/Hide Library***
- Key Command ***Y***
- ***Double-click*** on the background of a Track Header

➡ ***Show or Hide***

- ***Double-click*** on the Library Header ❶ to close the Library.
- ***Double-click*** on the Divider Line ❷ or *drag* it all the way to the left to close the Library.
- ***Drag*** the left edge of the GarageBand Window ❸ (on the edge of the wood panel) to the right to open the Library. The Mouse Pointer changes to the Resize Tool.

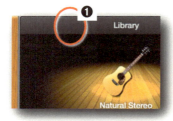  

Patch

Before explaining what the Library is, we have to first know what a Patch is.

> **A Patch is like a Preset.**
> **It contains all the elements of a Track that are responsible for its "SOUND"**

What are the elements that affect the sound on a Track? These are all the components in the Track's signal flow that alter the signal. For example:

- ▶ **Software Instrument Plugin**: For MIDI Tracks, selecting a Piano Instrument or a String Instrument affects how the MIDI Regions on that Track "sound".
- ▶ **Audio FX Plugins**: The selection of EQ, Distortion or Reverb Plugins all affect how your MIDI or Audio Region "sound" on a specific Track.
- ▶ **MIDI FX Plugin**: Even the Arpeggiator affects the "sound" by changing the incoming MIDI data.

All that information (what Plugins are used, what values were their Parameters set, etc.) is then saved to disk as a special file. This is the work that Apple did already. They had professional sound engineers that created different settings for all purposes and saved them as Patch files.

The Library acts as a browser that can display all those Patch files, nicely organized by categories (Keyboard, Strings, Drums, etc.), like organizing files (Patches) in folders (Categories).

When loading such a Patch file onto a Track, then all those settings are applied to that Track and the Track "sounds" exactly like the Track that was saved as a Patch file. Now, when you play your guitar on a Track that has one of those Guitar Patches loaded, it is like having a professional engineer creating your sound in GarageBand.

What's included in a Patch file:

Included

- ☑ **Plugins**: This includes the name of the Plugins and the settings of all their Parameters.
- ☑ **Routing Information**: Aux Sends and Aux Channel Strips do not exist in GarageBand, at least on the surface. Patches however do include such routing information. GarageBand processes that, it just hides it from the user and is only adjustable through Smart Controls.
- ☑ **Others**: The Smart Controls layout and the mapping of the Controls to the Plugin Parameters and even the Track Icon.

Not Included

- ☐ **Volume & Pan**: The values of these two controls are not included in a Patch.
- ☐ **NO MUSIC CONTENT**: A Patch never contains any music data in the form of MIDI or Audio Regions.

Library

Here is the summary about the function of the Library Window.

- ▸ The Library is a browser window that displays all the available Patch files on your drive organized by Categories and Sub-categories.
- ▸ The functionality of the Library Window is almost like an Inspector window. Selecting a Track in the Track List will display the Patch in the Library that was loaded onto that Track.
- ▸ There are different types of Patches for different Track Types (Audio Track, MIDI Track, etc.).
- ▸ When you *click* on a Patch, it will be immediately loaded into the currently selected Track (you can use the Undo command if you clicked it by accident).
- ▸ Selecting a different Track will switch the content of the Library Window to display the Patch that was loaded into that Track. Please note that it will not be indicated if you have made changes to the Track (loaded new Plugins, changed the Smart Controls) since you loaded a Patch.

➡ Patch Icon

Each Patch has an Icon stored along with all the data. This Patch Icon is displayed on top of the Library Window for the selected Patch in the Library. This Icon becomes the Track Icon when you load the Patch onto a Track.

By the way, you can remove the Patch Icon area in the Library Window by dragging its Divider Line all the way up (and dragging the Divider Line down to show it again).

Interface

🔘 Search

Click the Search Field ❶ to search for a Patch by name. Once you enter the first character into the search field, the Column View changes to a List View. The functionality is technically a Filter and not a Search command. The more characters you enter into the search field, the smaller the list gets because more items get filtered out that don't match the entered text string.

- ▸ The first column in the list displays the items that match the search string and the second column lists the date when the item was saved.
- ▸ You can **click** on the header to change the sorting order (ascending, descending) and even move the columns.
- ▸ When you move the Mouse Pointer over an item, a yellow Help Tag ❼ appears with the path name to the file.

🔘 Navigate

The Library is displayed in column view with a maximum of three columns. You might have to resize the Library Window by dragging its right border (Divider Line) to display all three columns.

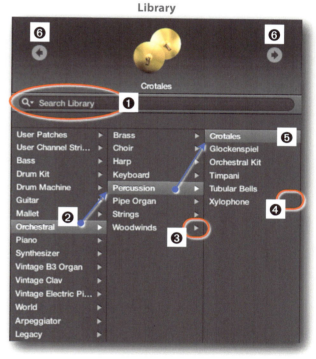

Click on a folder ❷ (representing a category with a triangle) to display its content in the next column. If it contains more folders, then click on those. If the item in the column is a Patch ❺, **click** on it to load it. **Scroll** the columns up and down if the list contains more Patches.

🔘 Load a Patch

Click on a Patch ❺ (the one without a triangle ▶ on the right ❹).

🔘 Step Through Patches

Once you selected a Patch in the list, you can **click** the left and right arrows ❻ next to the Patch icon to load the next or previous Patch in the list. The arrows only appear when you move the Mouse Pointer over that area.

Alternatively, you can use the *up arrow* key and *down arrow* key on the keyboard. The keys can also be used to navigate through the list and columns (left, right, up, down).

🔘 Always active

Be careful when navigating (*clicking*) in the column view.

- ▸ Folder (Category): A name in a column with a triangle ▶ on the right ❸ is a folder. **Click** on it to select it and display its content in the next column to the right.
- ▸ Patch: A name without a triangle ❹ is a Patch. **Click** on it to load that Patch into the currently selected Track. This has a potential danger when navigating through the columns. You could click on an item to look inside because you think it is a folder. However, if you realized that it was not a folder but a Patch, then you have just overwritten your settings of the current Track because clicking on any Patch will immediately load that Patch. Use the Undo command.

🔘 Current Patch

Opening the Library will display (highlight) the Patch ❺ that was loaded into the current Track.

Resize Columns

The Library can display a maximum of three columns. When the folder hierarchy is "deeper" than 3 levels or you resize the Library window to show only two or one column, then you get a slightly different interface behavior.

Single Columns Library

- If you ***click*** on a folder, the display scrolls to the next column to show the content of the folder. Use the arrow keys on your keyboard to navigate left or right.
- The area just below the search field now lists the path to the currently displayed item in the list. You can click on the file path to switch to the browse view with this item selected.

File Management

The bottom of the Library window has two buttons to manage the Library.

Save...: Save the current Track Setting (the state of the current Track) as a new Patch.

Delete: This command deletes the currently selected Patch from your disk. Only User Patches can be deleted, not the Factory Patches. You can also delete the Patch file directly in the Finder location.

The Library Window lists the Patches grouped by their location where they are stored on your hard drive. Besides Patches, the Library lists also a different file type called "Channel Strip Settings" a legacy settings file (.cst) that is now obsolete with the Patch files. You can still load those settings but they don't contain any Smart Controls assignments.

- **❶ User Patches**

    This folder contains all the Patches (.patch) that you saved yourself. The folder is only visible once you've saved your first Patch. The "Save..." command at the bottom of the Library Window lets you save your own Patches. Please note that this lists also Patches that you created in Logic.

- **❷ User Channel Strip Settings**

    This folder contains all the Channel Strip Settings (.cst) that you saved yourself. This folder too is only visible when you have saved at least one Channel Strip Setting yourself.

- **❸ "Patches"**

    The next folders are the categories containing all the new Factory Patches (.patch). Please note that these are actually Logic Patches saved in a Logic folder.

- **❹ Legacy**

    The folder "Legacy" at the end of the list contains all the factory Channel Strip Settings from earlier GarageBand (and Logic) versions.

Track-specific Patches

The Library window is not a "static" window that displays some fixed content. What you see depends on the currently selected Track. I already explained the different Track Types in the Tracks chapter. Similarly, there are different types of Patches.

In GarageBand

- GarageBand supports three types of Patches (Logic supports a few more).
- These types of Patches can only be loaded into a specific type of Track.
  - **Instrument Patch ❶**: MIDI Track ❹ and Drummer Track ❺
  - **Audio Patch ❷**: Audio Track ❻
  - **Master Patch ❸**: Master Track ❼
- Selecting a Track in the Track Header automatically changes the content of the Library Window to display only the appropriate Patches.

In the Finder

- The Patches for each Patch type are stored on your drive in separate folders inside the Patches folder.
- The Patches that come pre-installed with GarageBand are stored in the system directory ❽ */Library/Application Support/Logic/Patches/*. Patches are shared with Logic, that's why they are located in the Logic folder.
- The Patches you save yourself are stored in the user directory ❾ *~/Music/Audio Music Apps/Patches/*. You can manage those files on the Finder level (copy, move, delete, etc.) as long as you don't mix different Patch types (move between folders).

Logic Remote

The Logic Remote app on the iPad provides a great interface to use the Library with an external device to free up space on your computer screen for other GarageBand windows.

9 - Library

10 - Regions

We learned so far the concept about Tracks in GarageBand (and DAWs in general). They represent the BandMembers in our Band Analogy. Now, it is time we give them something to play, the **Regions**. Here is the simple concept.

The Regions are the building blocks of your song, similar to a score or lead sheet that has the music content written on it. You hand them out to each musician in a band or orchestra so they know what to play. The same way you put the score for each musician on his or her music stand, you put the Regions for each Track on its Track Lane. This way you determine what Regions are played by which Track.

What is a Region

The basic concept and use of Regions is pretty much the same with all the DAWs. These are the basics:
- ▶ A Region is represented by a rectangle on the Track's Track Lane.
- ▶ You can think of the Region as a container that holds the information (music) for the Track, telling it what to play.
- ▶ Another model is to think of a Region as a music score with one long single piece of paper, reading the notes from left to right.
- ▶ The length of the Region defines the length of the "musical instruction" for the Track.
- ▶ The beginning of a Region doesn't necessarily mean that the Track starts to play right away. If the instruction says "pause for two bars" then you won't hear anything in the first two bars from the musician either.
- ▶ In the previous chapter, I also compared the Track Lane to the tape of a tape recorder. Recording a guitar solo at 1 minute into the song would be the same as recording the guitar solo at 1 minute on the Track Lane in the form of an Audio Region. The advantage with a DAW however, is that you can move that Region later to any place in the song with a graphical user interface, something that isn't possible with tape based recording.
- ▶ The "musical instruction" for a Track can be one long Region or many shorter Regions that are placed on the Track Lane only at the position where the Track has to play something. This way, you get a visual representation of your arrangement where you can quickly see what Track is playing and when.
- ▶ The Regions are also color coded which provides an additional indication what kind of Regions are placed (and play) at what part of the song. The different colors hint at different purposes of the Region.
- ▶ The most important thing however is to understand that there are three fundamentally different types of Regions in GarageBand.

Types of Regions

We already learned in the Tracks chapter that there are three main types of Tracks: MIDI Tracks, Audio Tracks and the Drummer Track (the Master Track is a special type of Track that doesn't "contain" music). The same distinction exists for Regions. There are MIDI Regions, Audio Regions and Drummer Regions.

Although they look and behave similarly in a lot of ways, there are some fundamental differences that need to be understood.

Region Types

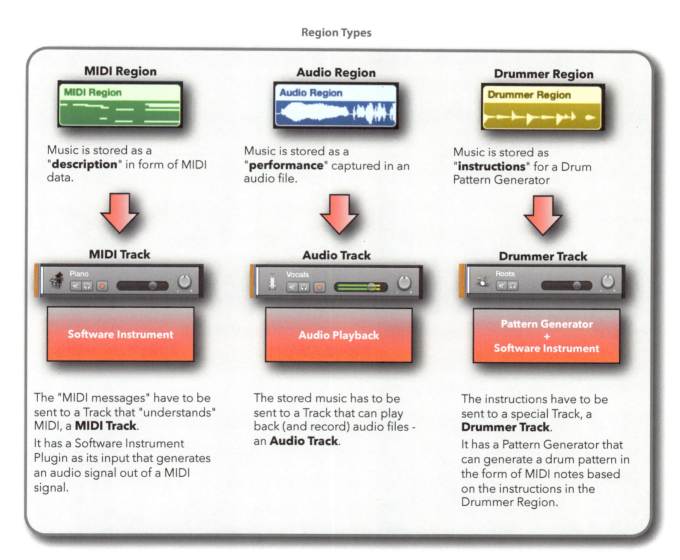

Musicians - DJs - Drummers

I already explained the main differences of the three Tracks Types in the Tracks chapter. Here is a summary of those diagrams when adding the three Region Types into the picture.

➡ **MIDI Regions on a MIDI Track (Musicians)**

Giving the musicians in your Band the SheetMusic they can read

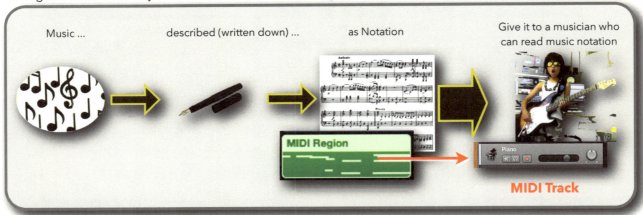

➡ **Audio Regions on an Audio Track (DJs)**

Giving the DJ in your Band the pre-recorded music (CDs, mp3) to spin

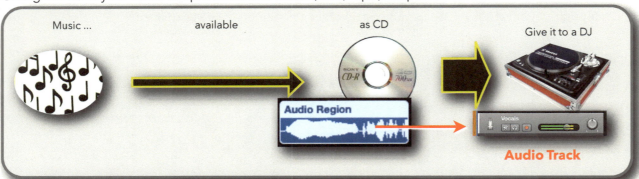

➡ **Drummer Region on a Drummer Track**

Giving the Drummer in your Band instructions how to play (soft, simple, busy, lots of fills, ...)

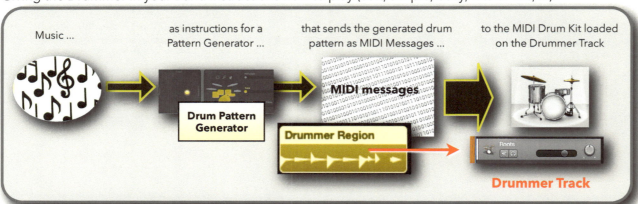

What's in a Region

When you look at a Region, it appears that you can see the data that is stored inside (Region Content). However, there is something special with the Audio Region you have to be aware of.

💡 MIDI Region

On a MIDI Region, you see horizontal lines or dots. These are the MIDI Events, the music description that is stored inside (as a rough indication). Using any of the MIDI Editors lets you "open" the MIDI Region and display it in different forms for precise editing. This data inside the Region, which needs very little storage space, is stored with your Project File.

💡 Drummer Region

The Drummer Region looks almost like a waveform. However, these are special indications that shows you the resulting drum pattern based on the instruction you configured. I discuss that in detail in the Drummer chapter. This data inside the Region needs also very little storage space and is stored with your Project File.

💡 Audio Region (+ Audio File)

Now, let's look at the Audio Region. It is fundamentally different from a MIDI Region. The MIDI Region contains the actual musical instructions similar to the notation you give to, for example, the guitar player. As for an Audio Region, think of it as instructions for "how to play music from a CD" (i.e. play track 2 from 2:15 to 3:45).

For example, you have to give the DJ two things; the actual CD ❶ and the instruction ❷ on how to play it and from where to where. The Audio Region ❸ represents these instructions for the Audio File ❹. However without the CD, the DJ cannot do anything with those instructions. In GarageBand, this would be the same scenario when you have an Audio Region (the instructions) visible on the Track Lane but you cannot "play" the Audio Region because the Audio File is missing. So the Audio Region ❸ contains the play instructions and the information about what Audio File to apply those instructions to (the link ❺ between Audio Region and Audio File).

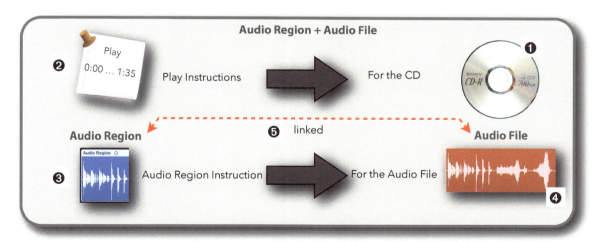

This is the important part: When you look at an Audio Region in GarageBand, you don't look at the actual Audio File (the "pre-recorded music"), you look at the instructions about what to do with the Audio File. The waveform that you see on the Audio Region lets you believe you are looking at the Audio File but it is just a "look-up" for the actual Audio File, which helps you edit (position) the instructions.

The data for a MIDI Region (play instructions) and the data for the Audio Region ❷ (play instructions) are stored with the Project and are not accessible as separate files. The Audio Files ❹, on the other hand, are stored as separate files, so-called "Project Assets". They are stored, "embedded", in the Project File as part of a "Package File".

Where do Regions come from?

We are well equipped by now with all the information and knowledge about GarageBand but haven't recorded a single thing yet. We know that we record our music as Regions so the final question is, how do we record/create those Regions for our song.

There are three ways to create Regions in GarageBand and not all three are available for all three Region types. Here is a quick overview:

🎵 Record

This is the traditional way. You have a musician playing his instrument and you record what he is playing.

- ☑ MIDI Region: With MIDI, you don't record an audio signal. Instead, you record the MIDI signal that is generated from a MIDI device, i.e. MIDI Keyboard.
- ☑ Audio Region: Here you connect a microphone or the output of an electric instrument (electric guitar or hardware synth) to your computer (or Audio Device) and GarageBand records the audio signal into an Audio Region.
- ☐ Drummer Region: Drummer Regions cannot be recorded. They only can be created manually in GarageBand.

🎵 Create

Instead of recording a signal "live" where GarageBand creates the Regions containing that recording, you can create Regions manually and "enter" the music by hand like writing it down on a piece of paper.

- ☑ MIDI Region: You can use the MIDI Editors to manually enter MIDI Events (Piano Roll Editor) or musical notes (Score Editor). **Cmd+click** on the Track Lane of a MIDI Track (Mouse Pointer changes to the Pencil Tool ✏️) to create an empty 1-bar MIDI Region.
- ☐ Audio Region: Audio Regions cannot be created manually only recorded or imported.
- ☑ Drummer Region: This is the only method of creating a Drummer Region in GarageBand. You have to manually create/edit those instructions for the Drum Pattern Generator using the Drummer Editor.

🎵 Import

This is the easiest way to create a song. Here you rely on existing recordings that you import into your Project. These are not complete songs but little building blocks. For example, a drum groove, a bass, a rhythm guitar pattern, or a solo guitar lick. All you have to do is find the right bits and pieces and put them together in GarageBand. Although this method is somewhat limited, it doesn't require any instrument playing skills.

- ☑ MIDI Region: **Drag** any MIDI File onto a MIDI Track and GarageBand creates a MIDI Region for that.
- ☑ Audio Region: **Drag** any Audio File onto an Audio Track and GarageBand creates an Audio Region for that. GarageBand provides a more elegant procedure that I explain in the Apple Loops chapter and Media Browser chapter.
- ☐ Drummer Region: Only Logic provides the feature that lets you import (and export) Drummer Presets that you can import into a Drummer Region.

11 - Recording MIDI

So let's finally look at the recording procedure starting with MIDI recording. Unfortunately, it is not as simple as just hitting the record button. There are many steps involved (and the understanding of those steps), so the best practice is to start with a quick checklist to make sure everything is setup and functions correctly.

Checklist

- ❶ Connect an external MIDI Keyboard or use the software Keyboard "Musical Typing" (*cmd+K*).
- ❷ Check the MIDI Indicator to see if the MIDI signal "arrives" in GarageBand.
- ❸ Select a Track or create a new Track to record your MIDI signal.
- ❹ Place the Playhead at the position you want to start recording.
- ❺ Optional: Setup the Metronome and Count-In configuration.
- ❻ Configure the Record Settings.
- ❼ Hit record.

MIDI Source

I covered the topic of the MIDI Input in the Hardware chapter and explained how to select an external MIDI Keyboard. However, you don't need an external MIDI Keyboard to record a MIDI signal in GarageBand. You have actually three input options:

➡ External MIDI Keyboard

Use an external MIDI Keyboard (or any other MIDI controller) that is connected to your computer directly to its USB port, or via a MIDI port from a MIDI interface that is then connect to USB. Using the Logic Remote app lets you also use the iPad as a wireless MIDI controller.

- MIDI Keyboard (MIDI port to USB)
- MIDI Keyboard (USB)
- iPad (WiFi)

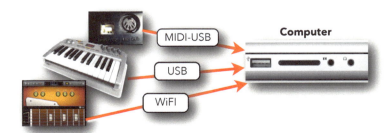

➡ **Onscreen Keyboard (mouse)**

You also can use your Mouse Pointer to play (click) on a virtual Keyboard in GarageBand. This is very limited but gives you the option to quickly input some MIDI notes for those occasions when you don't have an external MIDI Keyboard available. The following commands will open that separate Keyboard window.

 Main Menu Command **Window ➤ Show/Hide Keyboard**
 Key Command **cmd+K**. Once the window is open, you also can use the two buttons on that window to switch between the Keyboard window and the Musical Typing window.

➡ **Computer Keyboard**

Instead of using your Mouse Pointer and clicking on a virtual keyboard, you can also type on your computer keyboard to enter MIDI notes. This method gives you a few more options. GarageBand calls this method "Musical Typing" and you can open the window with any of the following commands:

 Main Menu Command **Window ➤ Show/Hide Musical Typing**
 Key Command **cmd+K**. Once the window is open, you also can use the two buttons on that window to switch between the Keyboard window and the Musical Typing window.

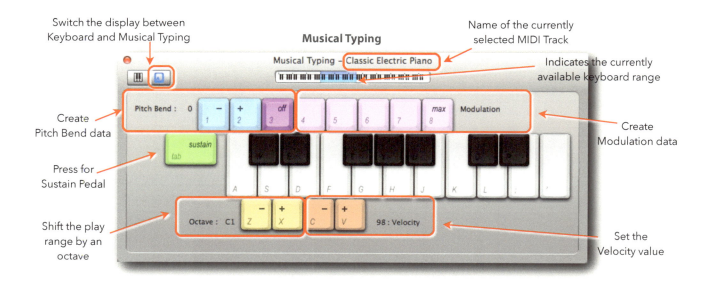

150 11 - Recording MIDI

MIDI Indicator

Preferences ➤ Audio/MIDI

The first reaction when playing a MIDI controller and you don't hear a sound is to look at the MIDI Indicator LED in the upper right corner of the Control Bar Display. When you play a note on your controller, which sends a MIDI message, and you don't see the LED indicating the incoming MIDI message, then ... no MIDI message is coming into GarageBand.

Please refer to the earlier chapter in this book about the Hardware Setup. There I show how to use the Audio MIDI Setup utility and explain the role of a proper Driver for your MIDI devices.

Also, check the *Preferences ➤ Audio/MIDI* to see if GarageBand recognizes any external MIDI Input Device. If you connect a new external MIDI Keyboard while GarageBands is running, *click* the "Reset MIDI Drivers" button if the Device doesn't show up automatically.

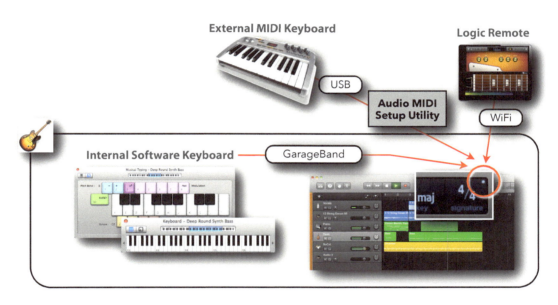

Track Selection

You can record MIDI only on a MIDI Track. Therefore, you have to select (or create) a MIDI Track first (the one you want to record on).

▶ **Single Track Recording**: GarageBand records the incoming MIDI signal on the currently selected MIDI Track. There is no need to record-enable ("arm") the Track first.

▶ **Multi-Track Recording**: You can also record on multiple Tracks at the same time, i.e. when creating synth layer (multiple Tracks with different synth sounds playing in unison). *Click* the Record Enable Button on each Track Header you want to record on. You have to make the button visible on the Track Header first with any of these commands:

 Main Menu
 Track ➤ Track Header ➤ Show/Hide Record Enable Button

 Shortcut Menu on the Track Header
 Track Header Components ➤ Show/Hide Record Enable

Playhead Position

Before you start recording, you have to position the Playhead so GarageBand knows where along the timeline to start the recording. However, there are two factors that overwrite the current Playhead Position and have GarageBand start at a different position. The Cycle Mode and the Count-in Mode.

Please keep in mind that when you start recording a MIDI signal, GarageBand switches to Record Mode but it does not create a new MIDI Region until it receives a MIDI signal from your MIDI Device.

 Cycle off - Count-in off
GarageBand starts recording at the current Playhead Position.

 Cycle off / Count-in **on**
GarageBand starts one bar or two bars (depending on the Count-in setting) prior to the current Playhead Position.

Cycle **on** / Count-in off
GarageBand starts recording at the beginning of the yellow Cycle Area regardless of the current Playhead Position.

 Cycle **on** / Count-in **on**
GarageBand starts one bar or two bars (depending on the Count-in setting) prior to the beginning of the yellow Cycle Area regardless of the current Playhead Position.

Metronome & Count-in

I already covered the Metronome (Click) and the Count-In earlier in the book. Here is just the summary.

Toggle the Metronome with any of the two commands
- *Click* on the Metronome Button in the Control Bar
- Use the Key Command **K** (does not work when the Musical Typing window is open)

Toggle the Count-In with any of the following commands
- *Click* on the Count-In Button in the Control Bar
- Use the Key Command **sh+K**
- Select from the Main Menu *Record* ➤ *Count-In* ➤ *1 Bar/2Bars*. Selecting **None** from the submenu will turn the Count-In off.

off on: Click is playing during Playback and Recording
on on: Click is playing during Playback and Recording plus the Count-in
on off: Click is playing only during the Count-In (the Metronome Button looks different!)
off off: Click is completely off

Record Settings

There are two settings that affect the MIDI Recording:

 Cycle Mode

The Cycle Mode is very useful during playback to repeat a section over and over again. However, it also can be used for recording. Therefore, you have to make sure if Cycle Mode is enabled or not before you start the recording.

Off: The recording starts at the Playhead Position (minus the Count-in) and stops when you hit the Stop command. Recording does not stop automatically at the end of your Project determined by the End-of-Project Marker. GarageBand automatically extends the length of your Project to accommodate your new ongoing recording.

On: As we've just learned, having Cycle Mode active when recording starts the recording at the beginning of the Cycle Area (minus the Count-in). When the Playhead reaches the end of the Cycle Area, it jumps back to the beginning of the Cycle Area while continuing to record. What happens to the recorded MIDI signal of each pass depends on the next setting.

 Join vs Take

There is one checkbox hidden away in the Preferences Window that completely changes the behavior when recording on a MIDI Track. The labeling of the checkbox "Cycle Recording" and its explanation is misleading regarding its effect. See the next page for more details.

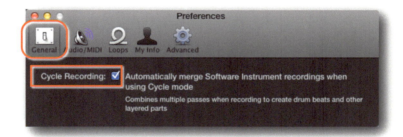

Finally: Record MIDI

Now the final step after running down the checklist is to start the recording.

You can use the following commands. The Play Button and the Record Button both light up.

- **Click** the Record Button on the Control Bar.
- Use the Key Command **R**

You can stop the recording

- **Click** on the Play Button or Stop Button on the Control Bar.
- Use the Key Command **space bar** or **0** on the numeric keyboard.

Recording Procedure

To find out what exactly happens when you record a MIDI signal in GarageBand, you have to differentiate between two scenarios.

- **Non-Overlapping Recording**: This is the basic recording. You just record one new take on the Track Lane where there are no other Regions yet or no other Region at the position where you are about to record.
- **Overlapping Recording**: In this case, the new recording overlaps with an existing recording (MIDI Region). The existing recording could be another Region on the Track Lane or you are recording over a section again (and again) using the Cycle Mode.

➡ Non-Overlapping Recording

Here is the simple procedure for recording a single section on a Track Lane:

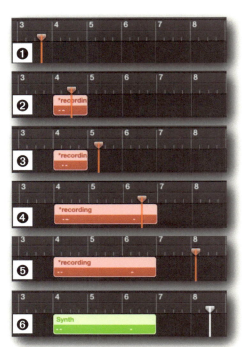

❶ I started the recording at Bar 3. The Playhead turns red and moves ahead. Please note that there is no new Region created as long as I don't send any MIDI signal.

❷ At the moment I play my first note, GarageBand creates a red Region that is one bar long in whatever bar I played the note. The Region name is "*recording" to indicate that it is a "Region in the making'. As you can see, even though the Playhead is not at bar 5 yet, the Region length is already rounded to the end of the current bar.

❸ If the recording continues, but I didn't play any new notes in the following bar 5, then the currently created (red) Region ended.

❹ Now if I play another note somewhere in bar 6, GarageBand extends the current red Region to the end of that bar I'm playing in. You can actually see the MIDI Events as little dots and lines on the Region as you record them.

❺ This is now the same behavior as in step 3. If you don't play any more notes in the next bar(s) then the red Region won't extend.

❻ At the moment you stop recording, the red "*recording" Region turns into a standard (green) MIDI Region. The Playhead turns white again and the new Region is automatically selected.

➡ Overlapping Recording

The new recording can overlap with previously recorded Regions in two ways:

❼ There is an existing Region on the Track Lane that you are about to "record over".

❽ You use Cycle Mode during recording and therefore record over your previous passes.

❼ **Existing Region**

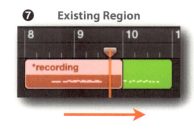

❽ **Cycle Mode**

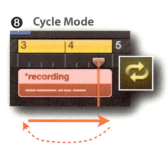

Recording Modes when Overlapping

GarageBand has two different recording modes that determine what happens when you record over an existing MIDI Region (overlapping). The implementation is highly confusing. Instead of using a radio button that lets you switch between the two modes, there is a checkbox in the Preferences window with a questionable label and a text that doesn't explain the correct behavior.

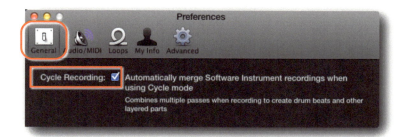

The actual two recording modes are **Join** and **Take Folder**

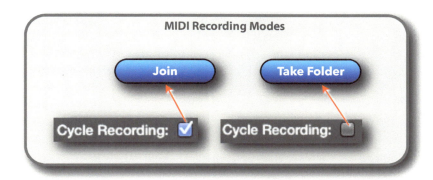

➡ **Join (Merge)** <img inline>

In Join Mode (checkbox is checked), the newly recorded Region(s) and the existing Region(s) are merged together in a single Region containing all their MIDI Events, the existing ones and the newly recorded ones.

Here is an example that shows that the Join Recording Mode can be used with or without Cycle Mode.

- ▶ **Cycle Mode on** 🔁: This is especially useful when you want to add new notes with each pass. For example, play the bass drum first, then the snare, then the HiHat, etc.
- ▶ **Cycle Mode off** 🔁: You can use this Recording Mode when you just want to add another layer or notes to an existing Region in a single pass. You can start anywhere on the existing Region and whatever you play "on top" of the existing Region will be added to it (overdub). If the new overlapping recording starts earlier or extends beyond the existing Region, then the Region will be extended to include all the new recorded MIDI Events before or after its original border.

➡ **Take Folder**

Take Folder Mode (checkbox is unchecked) behaves completely different when a new recording overlaps with an existing recording:

> When you start recording then
>> • If Cycle Mode is off ↻, then a new Region will be created in the background for the new recording
>> • If Cycle Mode is on ↻, then a new Region will be created in the background for each pass.
> When you stop recording, a new Region that is actually a special type of Region, a so-called "Take Folder" Region will be created and placed on the Track Lane. It can be identified as a Take Folder by having a number button in the upper left corner of the Region.
> This special Take Folder contains all the individual MIDI Regions created for each "Take", or each pass you recorded over.

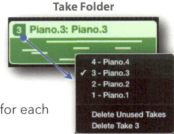

This Recording Mode is often used in music production where you want to keep your options open for later. You don't have to decide during the recording which take is the best one to keep. You can keep multiple recordings of the same section to decide later (during editing or mixing) which take is the best. For example, record multiple versions of a synth solo or record different versions of a rhythm pattern.

Here are the commands how to manage those Takes.

💡 Manage Takes

Click on the Number on the Take Folder Region to open a popup menu with three commands:

- **Select Take**: The top portion of the menu lists all the MIDI Regions that are stored in this Take Folder. Select any Take (a specific MIDI Region) to make it the active MIDI Region. The number on the Take Folder displays the Take number of the currently selected Region. The Take Folder updates its appearance to show the MIDI Events (lines) on the Region.
- **Delete Unused Takes**: This deletes all the Takes except the currently selected Take (if you chose the best Take and don't need the other ones anymore). The Take Folder Region on the Track Lane will then be replaced by that standard MIDI Region.
- **Delete Take**: This command removes the currently selected Region from the Take Folder. For example, a really bad Take that you know you definitely don't need any more.

No Replace Mode

There is no Replace Mode (overwrite) in GarageBand when recording MIDI. When recording over existing MIDI Events (Regions), the new Events will be either added to the existing ones (Join) or a new Region will be added to the existing one(s) as part of a Take Folder.

MIDI Signal Routing

I already discussed the signal routing in the Smart Controls chapter. Here is just a reminder what happens to the MIDI signal when you record it on a MIDI Track.

▸ The MIDI signal from your input source ❶ goes to two destinations.
▸ It will be recorded as MIDI Regions on the Track Lane ❷.
▸ In addition, it travels directly ❸ (thru) to the input of the Software Instrument Plugin ❹ that is loaded on that MIDI Track. The Software Instrument Plugin acts as the BandMember that "plays" your music.
▸ Please note that the Instrument Plugin receives a MIDI signal (green) and outputs an audio signal (blue) ❺. The question about "what is it playing" is determined by the incoming MIDI messages and the question about "how does it sound" is determined by the loaded Patch that includes a specific Software Instrument ❹.

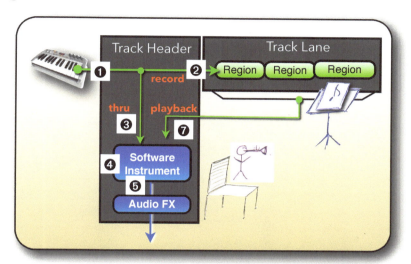

▸ The parameters of the Instrument Plugin plus any other audio signal processing controls are available as Screen Controls in the Smart Controls Window ❻.
▸ The Software Instrument Plugin receives a second MIDI input signal and these are the MIDI messages from the recorded MIDI Region (SheetMusic) on the Track Lane (MusicStand) when you play back ❼ your Song (tell the BandMember to play it).

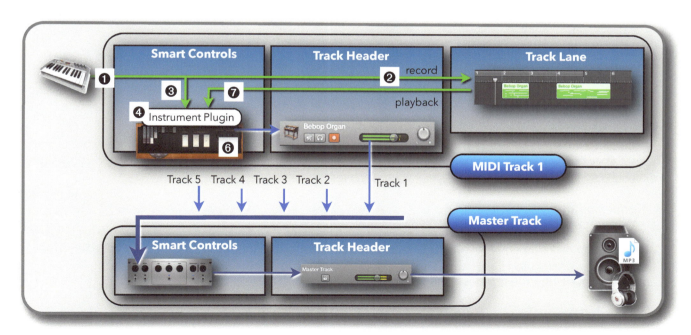

I hope you can see on the diagram that whatever you record as MIDI Regions ❷ are the instructions that represent your music. The MIDI Regions contain no information about the sound. It is the Patch with the included Software Instrument ❹ and other Audio Effects that determine how the music "sounds".

12 - Recording Audio

Audio Signal Routing

Although the recording procedure for audio signals is somewhat similar to MIDI signals, there are fundamental differences that you have to be aware of. This time, let's start with the Audio Signal Routing.

The Hookup

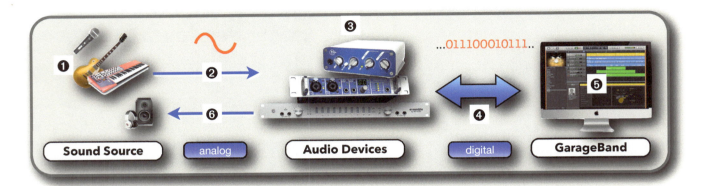

Sound Source

At the beginning, there is the sound source ❶, the audio signal that you want to record. That signal can be an acoustic signal (i.e. voice, acoustic instrument, speaker cabinet) that needs to be transferred into an electric signal with the help of a microphone. Other sound sources like synthesizers or electric guitars already produce an electric signal.

Analog Audio

The electric signals from microphones and electronic instruments are audio signals in analog form ❷. Logic, however, is a piece of software that needs the audio signal in digital form ❹. Please refer to the Prior Knowledge chapter about analog vs digital.

Audio Devices

Audio Devices ❸ are basically converter boxes. They convert an incoming analog signal ❷ into a digital signal ❹ via an Analog-to-Digital Converter (ADC) and an incoming digital signal ❹ into an analog signal ❻ via a Digital-Analog Converter (DAC).

Digital Audio

The Audio Device is connected to the computer via a digital cable ❹ (USB, Firewire, Thunderbolt). Please note that you can also connect an analog signal to the computer (Line-in, or talk into the microphone). In that case, the analog-to-digital conversion is performed inside the computer and that specific Audio Device is called "Built-In Input" or "Built-In Microphone".

GarageBand

In GarageBand ❺, you have to choose the Audio Device to which the Sound Source you want to record is connected to. Of course, you're also selecting the Audio Device that your speakers ❻ are connected to in order to send the audio signal back for monitoring purposes.

The Setup

Once you have all the components connected, you have to make sure that they are properly setup in order to start your audio recording in GarageBand.

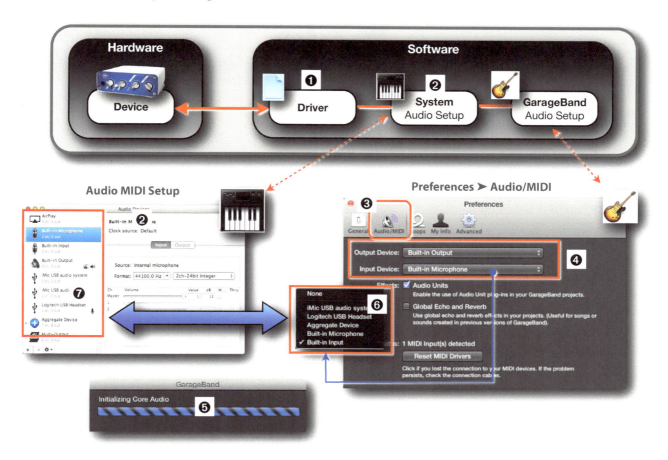

▸ The first step of your setup is to make sure that your system (OSX) can "communicate" with your Audio Device. That communication is established through a "Driver" ❶, a little interpreter file. Many Audio Devices are plug-and-play by using the OSX Driver (based on Core Audio). Other Audio Devices might need the installation of a special Driver (that has to be up-to-date).

▸ Once OSX can "see" your Audio Device through the Driver, it will be displayed in the utilities app "Audio MIDI Setup" ❷. You can check there to see if it is recognized.

▸ The next step is to tell GarageBand which of the available Audio Devices you want to use for audio input and output. This is done in the *Preferences ➤ Audio/MIDI* window ❸.

▸ You can choose two separate Devices ❹, one to receive the audio from (Input Device) and one to send the audio to (Output Device). The changes will apply automatically indicated by a brief Progress ❺ window.

▸ Both popup menus ❻ list all the Audio Devices that are available in the Audio MIDI Setup window ❼. You can choose "None" for the input but you always have to select an Audio Device for the Output.

Remote Control - forced 44.1kHz

Please note that by selecting a specific Audio Device in GarageBand, you are not only determining where GarageBand is sending and receiving its audio signal, but you are also remote controlling the Audio Device. You are switching the Sample Rate on the Audio Device to 44.1kHz. This is very important to realize if you are using that Audio Device with other apps on your Mac which might be negatively affected by that switch.

The Routing

Now, let's look at how the audio signal is routed through GarageBand. In this context, I like to point out one key element.

When working in GarageBand (or any other DAW), you are dealing with two types of fundamentally different signals, Audio Signals and MIDI Signals. This almost seems too trivial to make a big deal out of, but I like to make it a big deal. Whatever you are doing in GarageBand while working on your music, you have to be aware of the differences between working (recording, editing, manipulating, looking at, ..) on a MIDI signal or an Audio Signal.

➡ *Audio Recording vs. MIDI Recording*

The recording procedure looks similar when recording a MIDI Signal or an Audio Signal on a Track. It creates a Region on the Track Lane. However, look at the simplified diagram below to see how the audio recording is different from the MIDI recording.

- ▸ **Recording on a <u>MIDI Track</u>**: The incoming signal is a MIDI signal (green) ❶ and that is recorded as a green MIDI Region on the Track Lane ❷. The MIDI signal itself feeds the Software Instrument ❸ Plugin which then creates an audio signal (blue). The rest of the signal flow ❹ now behaves like an Audio Track.
- ▸ **Recording on an <u>Audio Track</u>**: The incoming signal is an Audio signal (blue) ❺. This is the signal from the available input selected in the Smart Control Inspector ❻. And here is the big difference. The selected signal will now be recorded onto the Track Lane as a blue Audio Region ❼.

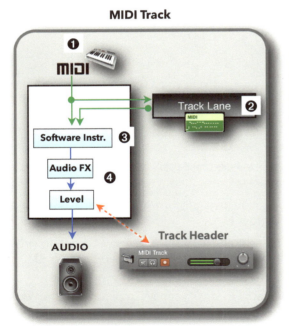
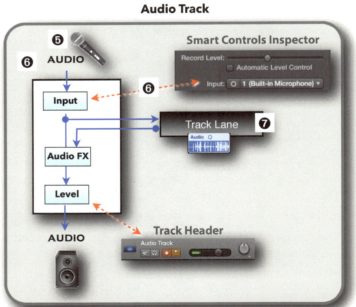

Please note that in both Tracks, the signal, MIDI or Audio, is recorded directly onto the Track Lane. Any signal processing (Audio FX, Level, Pan) does not affect the recorded signal. It is located after the MIDI Region or Audio Region is played back from the Track Lane.

Checklist

So now we are GarageBand Audio experts and know where and how the Audio signal is routed to. Let's finally record something with audio.

Checklist

And again, same as our airplane pilot before taking off, we have to run down the checklist before hitting the Record Button. The checklist for audio recording is a little bit longer than that for MIDI recording.

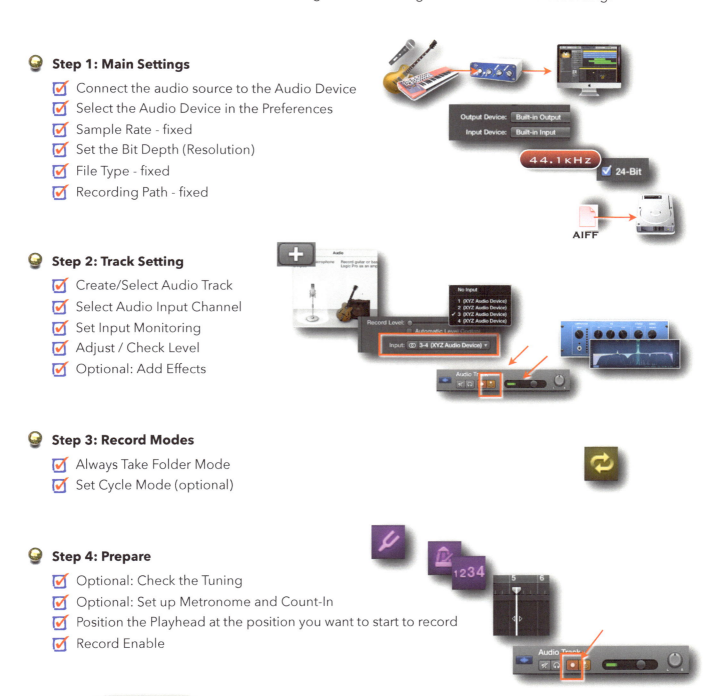

- **Step 1: Main Settings**
  - ☑ Connect the audio source to the Audio Device
  - ☑ Select the Audio Device in the Preferences
  - ☑ Sample Rate - fixed
  - ☑ Set the Bit Depth (Resolution)
  - ☑ File Type - fixed
  - ☑ Recording Path - fixed

- **Step 2: Track Setting**
  - ☑ Create/Select Audio Track
  - ☑ Select Audio Input Channel
  - ☑ Set Input Monitoring
  - ☑ Adjust / Check Level
  - ☑ Optional: Add Effects

- **Step 3: Record Modes**
  - ☑ Always Take Folder Mode
  - ☑ Set Cycle Mode (optional)

- **Step 4: Prepare**
  - ☑ Optional: Check the Tuning
  - ☑ Optional: Set up Metronome and Count-In
  - ☑ Position the Playhead at the position you want to start to record
  - ☑ Record Enable

RECORD

Now, let's go through each step.

Step 1: Main Settings

The following settings include all the basic preparations to record audio in your Project.

➡ Connect the audio source to the Audio Device

I already covered that step in the previous section. It involves the physical connection of the Audio Device to your Mac and making sure the proper Driver is installed so OSX can "see" it.

➡ Select the Audio Device in the Preferences

In this step, you tell GarageBand which one of the available Audio Devices to use by selecting it from the popup menu in the *Preferences ➤ Audio/MIDI*.

➡ Sample Rate (fixed)

The Sample Rate setting might be arguably the most important audio setting in a DAW. Usually 44.1kHz is used for CD Projects, while 48kHz is used for film scoring. Higher Sample Rates result in a better audio quality but it also increases the audio file size and puts a higher burden on your computer's CPU. Luckily (or unfortunately) we don't have to worry about that setting because it is fixed in GarageBand. It is always 44.1kHz.

I already pointed out in the previous section that the Sample Rate on a DAW is like a "remote control" setting for your selected Audio Device. It sets this main quality parameter of the Analog-to-Digital conversion (ADC) in your Audio Device. Whenever you select an Audio Device in the GarageBand Preferences, you switch that Audio Device to 44.1kHz Sample Rate.

➡ Set the Bit Depth

The Bit Depth (Resolution) setting is not as critical because you can mix and match audio files with different Bit Depth in your Project. You set the Bit Depth in *Preferences ➤ Advanced* by checking the 24-Bit checkbox for "Audio Recording Resolution". If it is unchecked, GarageBand will record audio files in 16bit Resolution.

Although 24bit results in slightly bigger files size, it is recommended for better audio quality (higher dynamic range).

➡ Audio File Type (fixed)

GarageBand always records audio files in the uncompressed aif file format.

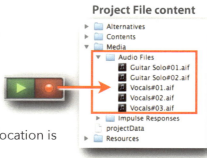

➡ Audio Recording Path (fixed)

GarageBand stores the recorded audio files inside its Project File. Remember, the Project File is a Package File type (a folder disguised as a file) that contains other files inside, including the recorded audio files. The location is *"ProjectFile"/Media/Audio Files/*.

Step 2: Track Setting

The following settings are related to the Track you are recording on.

➡ Create/Select Audio Track

Select the Track you want to record on, or create a new Track. I described the different ways of creating Tracks in the Tracks chapter.

➡ Select the Audio Input

Before you record any audio, you have to select the input channel. Don't confuse that with the Audio Device.

- ☑ **Audio Device**: We did the first step already by selecting the Audio Device, the Hardware that functions as the Analog-to-Digital Converter (ADC). That is in Step 1.
- ☑ **Input Channel**: After that, you have to choose which input channel on the selected Audio Device you want to use. Many Audio Devices have multiple input channels. For example, if you have connected your guitar or the mic to input 3 on your Audio Device, then you have to select input channel 3 in GarageBand to direct (route) that input signal to the selected Track.

▸ Select the Track ❶ you want to record on and open the Smart Controls Window ❷. It displays all the controls for the selected Track.

▸ Open the Inspector pane on the Smart Controls Window by clicking on the i-Button.

▸ The Smart Controls Inspector ❸ contains all the Audio Input controls for the selected Track including the Audio Input Button ❹.

▸ The Input Button has two clickable section.
  - The area on the right ❺ displays the name of the currently selected Input Channel. *Clicking* on this button will open a popup menu ❻ where you select from all the available Input Channels. However, what inputs are shown depends on the left side of the button.
  - *Click* on the icon on the left side of the button to toggle between the channel configurations: Select mono ❼ input signals and the popup menu displays all the individual ❽ input channels. Select stereo ❾ input signals and the popup menu displays the input channels as stereo pairs ❿.

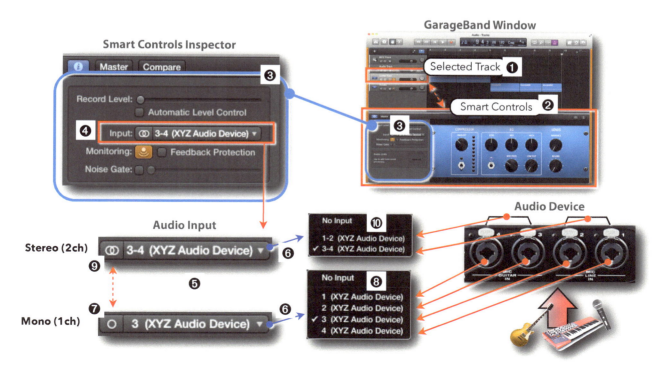

12 - Recording Audio

➡ **Set Input Monitoring**

Input Monitoring is only available on Audio Tracks. Only those Tracks have the Input Monitoring Button ![] to toggle Input Monitoring on ![] and off ![].

But what is Input Monitoring? Remember the signal flow at the input.
  ❶ The signal from the Input runs straight through the channel strip
  ❷ The signal from the Input runs to the Track Lane so it can be recorded as a Region
  ❸ The Track Lane feeds a signal back (these are the recorded Regions) into the Track

This Input Monitoring Button represents an on/off switch for the signal ❶ that runs directly from the input to the Track. Whenever you select an input signal (a mic, an electric guitar, a synthesizer, etc.) you have to turn this button on (Monitor on) so you can hear (monitor) the input. It only affects the monitoring of the input signal, not the signal that goes to the Track Lane for recording.

Feedback

I already discussed the Feedback phenomena in the Smart Controls chapter. It happens when the sound signal, coming from the (turned up) loud speaker ❹, is picked up by the microphone ❺, gets amplified, blasting through the speaker again and the microphone picks it up again and runs through the amplifier again, and so on. The result is a loud high pitched tone.

To avoid such a feedback, you could lower the speaker volume, use headphones, or turn the Monitor Switch ❻ off ![] to interrupt the loop. In order to record your singing from the microphone (or recording of an acoustic instrument) you don't have to hear yourself amplified through the speakers anyway. The signal only has to reach the Track Lane ❼, to record your part. Playing back the recorded parts from the Track Lane through the speakers is ok because that signal is not coming from the microphone directly.

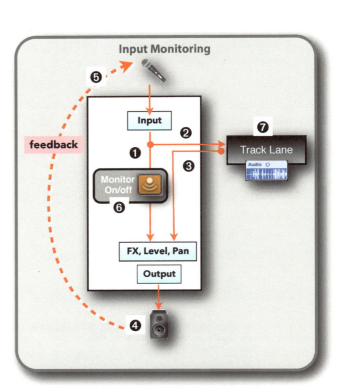

New Track Dialog

On the New Track Dialog Sheet where you select what type of Track you want to create, there is a special checkbox labeled "*I want to hear my instrument as I play and record*". This is another way to say "turn Input Monitoring on ![]".

This checkbox is auto-selected when you choose a "Guitar" Audio Track but it is deselected when you click on the "Microphone" Audio Track. The reason is that a microphone input can cause "Feedback".

➡ Adjust / Check Level

Once you select the Audio Input ❶, i.e. the microphone that is connected to the Audio Device ❷, you have to set the proper audio level. The input level is something that you don't have to worry about with a MIDI signal. It is just a data stream that is either there or not there. With an audio signal on the other hand, it is very important to set the level not too low (possible audible noise) or too high (possible audible distortion).

If you remember the Prior Knowledge chapter about digital audio, then you know that the Audio Device is a box that converts the analog signal of a microphone (or an electric guitar) into a digital signal that is sent to GarageBand ❸ (GarageBand is a software that can only process an audio signal in digital form).

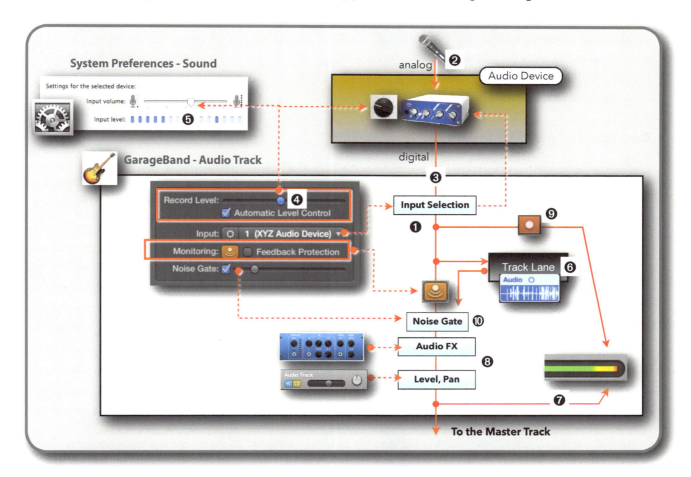

▶ **Record Level Adjustment**: The Record Level Slider ❹ in the Smart Controls Inspector is a "remote control" that adjusts the level of the selected input channel on the Audio Device (the analog signal before it gets converted into a digital signal). Although the slider is part of the Audio Track in GarageBand, it actually controls the signal outside of GarageBand, even outside the computer. This is the same slider as in the System Preference Sound ❺ window (or the Audio MIDI Setup app). For some Audio Devices, this functionality is disabled and you have to set the level on the Audio Device itself. The signal level you adjust with this slider is the level that is recorded on the Track Lane ❻. As you can see in the signal flow diagram, the Volume Meter ❼ on the Track Header has no effect on the recorded signal because it is located "later" at the output of the Audio Track.

▶ **Record Level Meter**: You can visually monitor the level of the audio signal you are about to record by using the Volume Meter on the Audio Device itself (if it has one) or the Meter in the System Preferences - Sound ❺. The Volume Meter on the Track Header ❼ doesn't seem to be suitable to be used to accurately display the input level because it is measuring the output level of the Audio Track after the Audio FX ❽ and the Volume Slider (which all change the audio signal). However, there is one hidden feature. If you activate the Record Enable ❾ Button on a Track, then the Meter measures the signal at the input, right before it is recorded on the Track Lane. The Noise Gate ❿ is part of the playback effects and doesn't affect the signal you are about to record.

💡 Automatic Level Control

Sometimes, setting the proper Recording Level is difficult if the audio level from the source you are recording is fluctuating too much over a wide range. For these occasions there is one feature that helps you with that problem. Below the Record Level Slider in the Smart Controls Inspector is a checkbox called "Automatic Level Control" and it does exactly that. GarageBand is paying attention to the input signal and if it is getting to low, it automatically raises the Record Level Slider. If the incoming signal is getting too hot, it will lower the slider.

This feature might not be supported with all Audio Devices. Also, for mission critical recording, it might be better to disable the feature to avoid unexpected level changes. It is better to teach the singer to increase the distance from the microphone when switching from whispering into "hysterical screaming mode".

➡ Add Effect

You can use all the different effects in the Smart Controls Window and add additional AU Plugins already during the recording procedure. You don't have to wait until the final mix. Just remember that all that signal processing will not be recorded on the Track Lane. It is only good for treating the signal the way you would do it later in the final mix (kind of a pre-mix) and also give the performer you are recording (vocalist, guitarist, etc.) a good sound for his performance by adding reverb or effects to make them feel more comfortable while performing.

💡 Keep your options open

There is one special aspect regarding the topic of "after"-effects, and that is recording guitars.

Usually, you have the guitarist play through his amp ❶ and the signal coming from the speaker is then the sound source that you record with a microphone ❷. You are recording the "processed" signal ❸ as it is. Once it is recorded, it is impossible to reduce the amount of distortion, play back the guitar clean or change the sound to a different amp.

However, if you record the guitar directly into GarageBand ❹ without the amp, you end up recording that clean guitar signal on the Track Lane ❺. Now you can use the Amp Designer Plugin (that is part of the loaded Patch or you load a Patch that includes the Amp Designer Plugin) to select the sound you want. Your guitar player will hear the processed sound (through the Input Monitoring ❻) while he is playing/recording. Later in the mix, you will have all your options open to change the sound (amp, cabinet, stompboxes) by selecting different Plugin settings or Patches ❼.

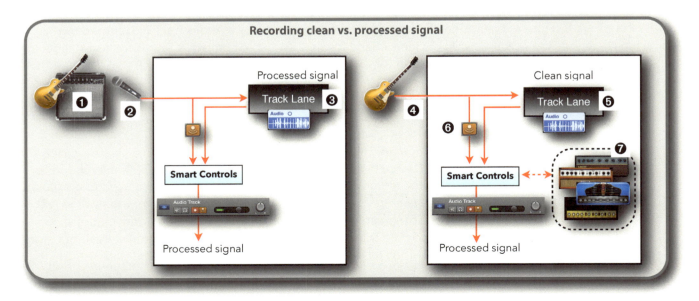

Step 3: Record Modes

Unlike with MIDI Recording, GarageBand always creates a Take Folder when recording audio over an existing Audio Region. Therefore, the recording behavior is always the same and no prior Record Mode has to be set.

 That means when recording audio while Cycle Mode is enabled, every pass will become a single Audio Region contained in the Take Folder.

Step 4: Prepare

These are the last settings before you actually start recording.

➡ **Optional: Check the Tuning**

If you are recording a guitar or any other acoustic instrument, you have the option to check its tuning before you hit record. **Click** on the Tuner Button on the Control Bar to toggle the Tuner Window for the selected input channel of the current Audio Device. I explained that feature already in the *Control Bar* chapter.

➡ **Optional: Set up Metronome and Count-In**

I explained already the details about the Metronome and the Count-in the previous chapter. Please note that GarageBand is already recording your audio signal during the Count-in (resize the Audio Region later).

➡ **Position the Playhead at the position you want to start to record**

And again, the most important information before you hit the Record Button is to tell GarageBand from where you want to record by positioning the Playhead. Same exception here:

- The enabled Count-in ![1234] starts the recording 1 bar or 2 bars prior depending on the setting.
- The enabled Cycle Mode ![cycle] ignores the Playhead Position and GarageBand starts at the beginning of the yellow Cycle Area (minus the Count-in, if enabled).

➡ **Record Enable**

Technically, you don't need the Record Enable Button (it is hidden by default) to record on a single Track. Just select the Audio Track and it is ready to be recorded on. If the Record Enable Button is visible, then it switches from ● to ● when you select an Audio Track. **Click** on the button to "enable" the Track ("the Track is armed") and the button starts blinking red ●. The button stays on ● once you start recording.

You can record multiple Audio Tracks at the same time but they have to be assigned to different Input Channels on the current Audio Device. If you've enabled more than one Track assigned to the same Input Channel, then only the first Track (on top) will record that signal. Please note that you also can enable both Audio Tracks and MIDI Tracks and record them at the same time.

Finally: Record Audio

The commands to start recording audio are the same as recording MIDI. Now let's look in the next section at the details of what's happening when recording audio.

Recording Procedure

What is actually happening

Now that we are ready to hit that magic Record button, it is important to understand what is actually happening when recording audio. Ignoring those little details could lead to some confusion, or even worse, to serious frustration due to the loss of audio recordings. So let me try to lay it out step by step.

➡ What we see

Similar to the MIDI recording procedure, three main things will happen when GarageBand switches into Record Mode on an Audio Track:

- ☑ The Record Button and the Play Button are both enabled (light up).
- ☑ The Control Bar Display turns red to indicate that GarageBand is in Record Mode.
- ☑ The Playhead also turns red together with the Region that is currently created (recorded) in front of your eyes.

However, there are a few things on the "outside" that are different when compared to MIDI recording.

- ▸ The red Region that is created as the Playhead moves across doesn't have the name "*recording" displayed in the Region. OK, that was minor.
- ▸ The start and end of the recorded Region <u>will not be rounded</u> to the nearest bar. When recording audio, the Region starts and ends exactly where you start and stop the recording (please keep the Cycle Mode and Count-In setting in mind).
- ▸ The Audio Region is created during the recording regardless of the audio signal or the absence of a signal (recording silence). Remember that a MIDI Region is only created if the Track receives a MIDI signal during recording.
- ▸ The red Region displays the waveform of the incoming audio signal while it is recording. GarageBand has to calculate the waveform so it is displayed with a little lag.

MIDI Recording

Audio Recording

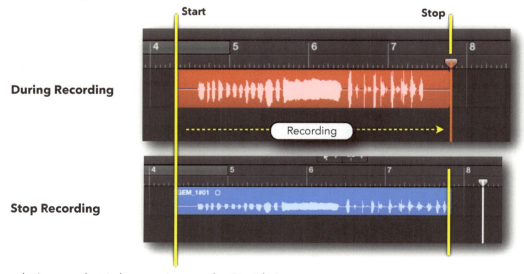

Now let's see what is happening on the "inside".

168   12 - Recording Audio

➡ *What we don't see*

I explained already in the *Regions* chapter the important difference between an Audio Region and an Audio File (please review it). The following diagram now shows the process of recording audio that will hopefully help you understand the relationship between them. Think about two places:

The **Track Lane** is the place that contains the Audio Region, the play instruction for the Audio File.

The **Hard Drive** is the place that contains the actual Audio File.

Record (during recording)

When you record audio on an Audio Track ❶, GarageBand creates a new Audio File and saves it to the Hard Drive ❷.

Stop (after recording)

Once you stop recording, two things will happen:
- ☑ The new Audio File ❸ will be placed in the current Project File ❹ inside the Media/Audio File folder
- ☑ A new Audio Region ❺ will be created based on the Audio File ❸ and will be placed onto the Track Lane replacing the red "recording in process" Region ❶

- ▸ The displayed waveform on the Audio Region might give you the wrong impression that the Audio Region contains the actual audio data. Again, this is not the case. It is just a lookup from the Audio File for better editing of the Audio Region.
- ▸ Instead of the audio data, the Audio Region only contains the following information:
    - ☑ **What** is the referred (linked) Audio File
    - ☑ **Where** to start and stop playing the Audio File
- ▸ All the edits on the Audio Regions are "non-destructive" (they don't edit the Audio File directly). Everything is just an offset, a description of "how" to play back the Audio File.
- ▸ You can make multiple copies ❻ of the same Audio Region on the same Track or different Tracks. All those Regions then refer ❼ to the same Audio File ❸. Editing one of the Audio Regions will change the "play instruction" for that specific Audio Region

Take Folder

We learned the functionality of a Take Folder already in the MIDI Recording chapter. This is the special recording mode when you record over an existing Region. For MIDI recording, the Take Folder functionality is one of two recording modes. When recording audio, the Take Folder is the only recording mode when recording over an existing Audio Region.

The Take Folder, being the default record mode for recording audio, has an advantage. You don't have to worry about overwriting (deleting) any existing Audio Regions when recording. For example, you record just another version over an existing guitar solo and decide later which one you want to use in the mix. Or, use the Cycle Mode and let him play a few versions in a row (and let GarageBand record all of them).

Create New Take Folder

A new Take Folder is created under two circumstances:
- ☑ You record over an existing Audio Region.
- ☑ You record over an empty section in Cycle Mode ⟲. Each cycle pass records (overlaps) over the previous pass (take).

When you stop recording, a new Take Folder Region will be created and placed on the Track Lane. This special Take Folder contains all the individual Audio Regions created for each "Take" (each pass you recorded over). The Header shows:

❶ The number of the selected Take. This is an active menu button
❷ The name of the Take Folder, inherited from the Audio Track ("Lead Vocals:")
❸ The name of the active Audio Region ("Take 4")

Add to existing Take Folder

You also can record over an existing Take Folder. The newly recorded Regions will then be added as additional Takes to the Take Folder. You can do that by manually recording over the Take Folder (add one Take), or use the Cycle Mode (add multiple Takes).

Manage Takes

Click on the Number on the Take Folder Region to open a popup menu with three commands.

- **Select Take**: The top portion of the menu lists all the Audio Regions that are stored in this Take Folder. The first number displays how many Takes are in the Folder followed by the name of the Audio Region. Please note that the Audio Regions inside a Take Folder get a generic name "Take n" (n is the consecutive number of each pass). Select any Take (a specific Audio Region) to make it the active Audio Region. The Take Folder Region on the Track Lane updates its appearance to show the waveform of the currently selected Audio Region.
- **Delete Unused Takes**: This deletes all the Takes except the currently selected Take (if you chose the best Take and don't need the other ones anymore). The Take Folder on the Track Lane will then be replaced by that selected Audio Region.
- **Delete Take**: This command removes the currently selected Region from the Take Folder. For example, a really bad Take that you know you definitely don't need any more. Please note what happens in the popup menu after you deleted some Takes. The first number row still displays the number of Takes in the Folder ❹ (1, 2, 3, 4) but the (deleted) "Take 1" and "Take 4" are now missing ❺.

Management of Audio Files/Regions

It is important to know about the relationship (link) between Audio Files and Audio Regions or even the existence of the Audio Files (stored somewhere on your drive). However, GarageBand keeps it simple and transparent and doesn't bother you with those details. In GarageBand, you are dealing only with the Audio Regions on the Track Lane. The management of the Audio File is automatically handled by GarageBand in the background. When it comes to editing Regions on the Track Lane, you only have to keep in mind that those Audio Regions are play instructions for a specific Audio File it is linked to. Also, multiple Audio Regions (with different "play instructions") can be linked to the same Audio File.

The following section is a little bit more advanced. Please continue to read if you are curious and want to understand what is going on "behind the scene" of Audio Regions and Audio Files.

➡ *Naming*

Here are the rules about the naming conventions when recording audio in GarageBand.
- A newly recorded Audio File will automatically be named based on the following conditions:
    - If the Audio Track hasn't been renamed yet ❶: "**ProjectName_TrackNumber#nn**". The first part of the Audio File name is the Project Name ❻. Please note that when you create new Audio Tracks in GarageBand, they are named "Audio" followed by an incrementing number (Audio 1 ❸, Audio 2, Audio 3 ❹, etc.). This is the Track Number that is included in the Audio File name. The two digit number after the pound sign (#nn) is the incremental number of each newly created Audio File ❺ on the same Audio Track.
    - If the Audio Track has been renamed ❷: "**TrackName#nn**". The Audio File name now includes the Track Name ❼ (custom name) followed by the pound sign and the two digit incremental number. For example ❽, "Solo Guitar#01", "Solo Guitar#02", etc.
- The linked Audio Region for that new Audio File that is created on the Track Lane gets the same name as the Audio File it is referring to.

➡ *Renaming*

It is highly recommended to rename the Audio Regions on the Track Lane to give them a more meaningful name in the context of your Project.
- You can rename the Audio Region with the following commands. This also works for Take Folder Regions.
    - Use the Key Command *sh+N* on a selected Region
    - Use the Shortcut Menu on a Region *Rename Region*
- Please note that renaming the Audio Region will not rename its linked Audio File.

➡ Naming/Renaming Take Folder Region

Please note the special naming convention for Take Folder Regions. Remember, Take Folder Regions are just containers without any link to an Audio File. Only the Audio Regions inside a Take Folder Region have the individual link to their referenced Audio File.

A Take Folder Region will be named based on the following conditions:

- Recording in Cycle Mode: In this case, the created Take Folder Region will inherit the Track Name. Any other Take Folder Region that you create on the same Track Lane will have the same name (no incremental numbers). Therefore, it is a good idea to rename Take Folder Regions.
- Recording over an existing Audio Region: The newly created Take Folder Region will be named after the Region you are recording over.

➡ Copy Regions

- When you copy an Audio Region (*opt+drag*), you just create new "Play Instructions" for the same Audio File ❶. The new Region inherits the same name of the Region you are copying followed by an incremental decimal number (Solo Guitar#02.1 ❷, Solo Guitar#02.2 ❸, etc.).
- You could rename the copied Region but be aware that once you do that, there is no indication to what Audio File it is referring to.
- Copying a Take Folder Region (yes, you can also copy Take Folders) will not add a decimal number to the copy. In this case, it might be a good idea to rename it right away.

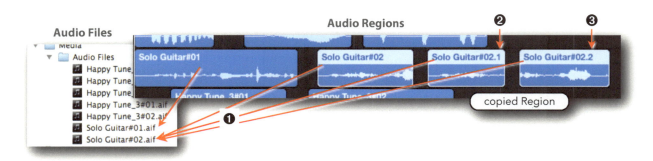

➡ Delete an Audio Region

- Deleting an Audio Region on the Track Lane will move its linked Audio File from the embedded Project File to the Trash Bin.
- The Undo command (*cmd+Z*) doesn't work properly in this case. It will not place the Audio Region back on the Track Lane. However, it will move the Audio File from the Trash Bin back to its original location, "inside" the Project File (*"ProjectFile"/Media/Audio Files/*). This doesn't make much sense because the Audio File is now an orphan file that is not linked to any Audio Region in your Project. The next Save command however takes care of that (see next step).
- Whenever you save your Project, GarageBand will delete any orphan Audio Files inside the Project File that are not linked to any Audio Region in your Project. This functionality guarantees that you don't have any orphan (old, unused) Audio Files stored in your Project File that are increasing the file size unnecessarily.
- If you have multiple Audio Regions that are linked to the same Audio File, then deleting an Audio Region will not delete the Audio File until it is the last Audio Region linking to that Audio File.
- As we will see in the Edit chapter, when moving a Region over another Region that completely "covers" the existing Region, then that Region will be deleted. This could mean that this action will also delete the Audio File it is referring to.

13 - Media Browser

Basics

Interface

GarageBand Window

The Media Browser Window can be shown or hidden as a Window Pane on the right side of the GarageBand Window.

There is a wide variety of commands that open and close the window. Choose the ones that suit your workflow:

➡ **Toggle Show/Hide**

- **Click** on the Media Browser ⊞ button ❶ in the Control Bar (drag the GarageBand Window wide enough to make the button visible)
- Main Menu **View ➤ Show/Hide Media Browser**
- Key Command **F**

➡ **Show or Hide**

- **Double-click** on the Media Browser Header ❷ to hide the Window Pane
- **Double-click** on the Divider Line ❸ or **drag** it all the way to the right to hide the Window Pane
- **Drag** the right side of the GarageBand Window ❹ (on the edge of the wood panel) to the left to open the Media Browser. This only works when the Media Browser was last visible in the Window Pane. The Mouse Pointer changes to the Resize Tool.

Import

Now that we know how to open the Media Browser Window, the next question would be - what do we need it for.

In the previous chapter we learned how to record new audio files in our GarageBand Project. Sometimes however you have already existing audio files on your hard drive that you want to use in your Project. For that you have to import them into your GarageBand Project. Please note that imported Audio Files create orange Audio Regions

There are three ways to do that.

➡ Drag-and-Drop

You can drag any audio file (or movie file and even a MIDI file) directly from an open Finder window ❶ onto a Track Lane ❷ of your GarageBand Window. This is an easy procedure with only one downside. You have to know where on your drive you stored the audio files and then have to navigate to that place or different places by opening and closing various Finder windows.

➡ Open File Dialog

Cmd+click on an empty Track Lane of an Audio Track. The Mouse Pointer temporarily changes to the Pencil Tool and an "Open File" Dialog pops up where you can navigate to the audio file that you want to import at the clicked position. You can even audition a file first by clicking on the Play button.

➡ Media Browser

The Media Browser on the other hand provides a more convenient way to import audio files (or movie files) into your GarageBand Project.

- ☑ Think of the Media Browser Window as a special Finder window.
- ☑ GarageBand searches your drive ❸ and only displays relevant files in the Media Browser Window ❹, either audio files or movie files.
- ☑ The Media Browser displays subfolders that group the files by their location or application that created those files. This can help you narrow down the search for specific audio files.
- ☑ Any file displayed in the Media Browser can easily be dragged from the Media Browser Window ❹ onto a Track Lane ❷ of the GarageBand Window.

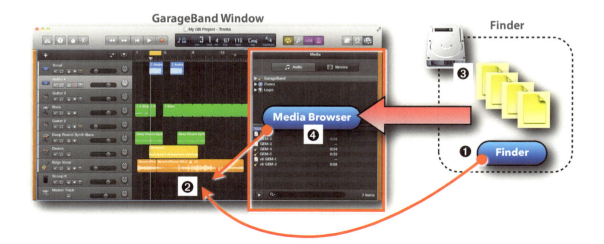

Next, let's have a closer look at the interface elements in the Media Browser Window.

Media Browser Window

The Media Browser Window is divided into the following areas:

● **View Buttons**

At the top of the window are the two View Buttons ❶ that switch the view so you can browse for audio files or movie files. You can no longer search for graphics files like in GarageBand v6. Those media files were used mainly for the Podcast feature that is not available anymore in GarageBand X.

 Audio Tab

Movies Tab

● **Browser**

The Browser area ❷ displays folder-like items that you select first. Use the disclosure triangle to open a "folder" and display its enclosed files or subfolders. The content of the selected item in the Browser is then displayed in the Results List below. Please note that GarageBand performs a "live search", so if you select an item with a lot of content (i.e. a huge iTunes library), then you might get a spinning beach ball for a moment while GarageBand collects all the files to display in the Results List.

● **Divider Line**

Dragging the Divider Line ❸ lets you resize the Browser area and the Results List area proportionally while keeping the Media Browser Window the same size.

● **Results List**

The Results List ❹ area displays the content of the selected item in the Browser area above. You can restrict the list of the displayed items with a search term in the search field ❻ below.

The list has three columns (Name, Time, Artist) that you can reorder by dragging left or right. *Click* on the Header to change the sort order of that column from ascending ▲ to descending ▼.

Media Browser

● **Control Bar**

The Control Bar at the bottom of the Media Browser has three elements.

▶ **Play Button**: *Click* the Play Button ❺ to toggle the playback of the selected item in the Results List. You also can use the Key Command *space bar* if the Media Browser has Key Focus. The file icon changes to a speaker icon .

▶ **Search Field**: Enter a search term in the search field ❻ to limit the displayed items in the Results List to only those files that match that text string. *Click* on the magnifying glass icon to open a popup menu ❼. This lets you apply the search to the file "Name" or the embedded "Artist" or "Album" keyword in the files. The X button clears the search term.

▶ **Found Items**: The number on the right ❽ displays the total amount of displayed files in the Results List.

The Media Browser Concept

 The Media Browser looks fairly simple so far. It just displays some audio or movie files and you drag them over to your Project. However, there is much more to it. Media Browser is one of those cool features that Apple implements but then forgets to tell anybody. There is no detailed explanation about it in the GarageBand documentation.

The Media Browser concept was introduced with the suite of iLife applications (GarageBand, iMovie, iPhoto, iWeb, iDVD). The idea was to have a common browser window in those apps that displays specific types of media files (audio, movie, graphics) instead of navigating through individual Finder windows. This is the concept I explained at the beginning of this chapter. A procedure that is convenient when importing existing media files into one of those apps. This concept got adopted in the Pages and Numbers app and even pro apps like Logic Pro and Final Cut Pro. They all share this common Media Browser Button that opens the Media Browser Window with a similar interface across all those apps.

➡ *App-related Media Files*

When you search in the Finder for media files, you are limited to how the audio files were organized, in which folders and subfolders. Therefore you have to navigate through the folder structure to look for files (unless you use the OSX Spotlight search).

The advantage of the Media Browser is that it displays media files based on the following criteria:

- **Content-creation App**

    GarageBand, Logic, iMovie and Final Cut Pro are so-called content-creation apps. They create Projects, i.e. a GarageBand Project or Logic Project. When any of those icons is displayed in the Browser area then you have media files related to those Projects on your drive and the Media Browser window displays them conveniently without you having to know where those files are stored. Please note, if you don't have Logic Projects or a Final Cut Pro Project on your drive, then the Media Browser won't display those items.

- **Content-management App**

    iTunes and iPhoto belong to the so-called content-management apps. They don't create new files (audio or graphics) they just manage them in their Library. The Media Browser will display all the files that are in those Libraries. However, the Media Browser lists only the relevant files. For example, when selecting iTunes in the Audio tab ❶, then it displays only the audio files in your iTunes Library and selecting iTunes in the Movies tab ❷, then it displays only the movie files in your iTunes Library. The same filtering happens with the iPhoto Library. When iPhoto ❸ is selected in the Movies tab, then you will see only the movies in your iPhoto Library and not the thousands of pictures you might have. Also, opening the disclosure triangle reveals the same structure you have in your iTunes or iPhoto Library. For example, you can search for audio files in a specific iTunes Playlist.

- **Folder Content**

    There is one item in the Browser's Movies tab that is not an app and that is the Movies ❹ item. It displays the content of the user's Movies folder that you can navigate through.

Import Audio

With that basic understanding of the Media Browser concept, let's use the Media Browser Window to import some audio files. For that, you first have to **click** on the Audio tab to switch to the Audio view.

Preview File

To understand what you see in this window, you have to know about another mechanism of the app-wide Media Browser concept, the Preview File.

➡ GarageBand v6

If you used GarageBand v6, then you might remember the Dialog Window that popped up when saving a GarageBand Project. It asked you to save an "iLife Preview". This exported a mixdown of your current Project to an audio file (Output.aif) and saved it to a special folder inside the GarageBand Project file (which was also a Package File). Any app that supports the Media Browser functionality could "look inside" that GarageBand Project File to see if that Preview file existed, play it and even copy it.

➡ GarageBand X

GarageBand X doesn't use that "export Preview File during save" functionality anymore. However, you still can create that special Preview File, this time with the dedicated command in the Main Menu **Share ➤ Media Browser ...** . This command will create the Output.aif file and saves it to the current Project File, embedded inside the Package File structure **"ProjectName"/Alternatives/000/Previews/Output.aif**. If you look closely, you also will see an Output folder containing an Alias of that Output.aif file. This might be for compatibility reasons.

I will discuss the various export/share features later in the Share chapter, but in this context it already makes sense why the command is called "Share to Media Browser". You share the audio file to the "Media Browser ecosystem" so every app that supports that mechanism has access to that file. Please note that GarageBand can have only one file in this Previews folder. That's why every time you use this command, you are overwriting the previous Output.aif file.

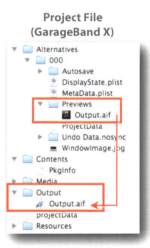

Project File
(GarageBand X)

➡ Logic Pro X

Logic Pro also has the same **Share ➤ Media Browser** ... command. It saves the current Project (or a selection of it) to that Previews folder inside the Projects File. However, there are two major differences. Logic gives you a Dialog Window where you can name the file (other than "Output") with additional format configurations and second, you can save as many Preview Files as you want.

The reason I explain that Logic feature in this GarageBand manual is that you can make sense out of what you might see in the Media Browser window in GarageBand.

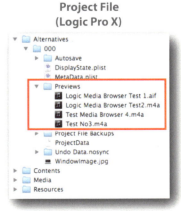

Project File
(Logic Pro X)

Display Preview File

The previous page might be a little bit too much in-depth information for some users but without the understanding of this Media Browser concept and its Preview File it would be hard to understand (or to explain) what you see in the Media Browser window.

GarageBand

Here is what you see in the Media Browser for GarageBand Projects

- Selecting the GarageBand item ❶ in the Browser area will display in the Results List all the GarageBand Project Files that are currently located in the dedicated GarageBand folder (*~/Music/GarageBand/*)
- Opening the GarageBand item with the disclosure triangle will display that GarageBand folder ❷. Selecting the GarageBand item or the GarageBand folder has the same effect. It displays in the Results List the GarageBand Project Files in that folder.
- And here is the important detail. The Results List uses two different icons for displaying GarageBand Project Files.

 GarageBand Project without Preview File ❸
This GarageBand Project has no embedded Preview File. The value in the Time column is empty ❹. This Project cannot be dragged onto the Track Lane of your Project. You will get an Alert window if you try to do that ❺. Pay attention to the message. The "iLife preview" is that Output.aif file it is locking for in the embedded Previews folder of the GarageBand Project file.

 GarageBand Project with Preview File
This GarageBand Project has a Preview File. **Dragging** this icon to the Track Lane will use that Preview File as the imported audio file. Please note that these Projects have a time value in the Result List. It is the length of the audio file (not necessarily the Project).

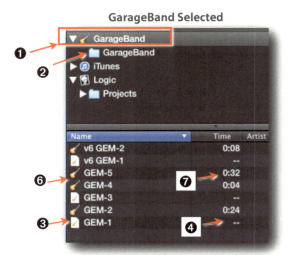

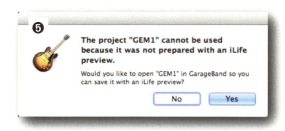

Logic

The functionality for Logic Projects that are displayed in the Media Browser is a little bit different.

- ▸ Inside the Logic item ❶ is a folder ❷ named Projects.
- ▸ Opening this Projects folder with the disclosure triangle will display all the Logic Projects ❸.
- ▸ The main difference with Logic Projects is that the Media Browser displays all the Logic Projects, stored anywhere on your drive, not only the ones inside the Logic folder.
- ▸ The Results List displays two different states:
  - Select the Logic item or the "Projects" folder: The Results List displays all ❹ the Preview Files of all available Logic Projects on your drive.
  - Select a single Project inside the Project folder: The Results List displays all the Preview Files of that specific Logic Project ❺. The Results List will be empty ❻ if the selected Project File has no Preview File embedded.

Logic Selected

iTunes

Selecting the iTunes item in the Browser Area is much easier. This has nothing to do with Preview Files.

- ▸ Selecting the iTunes item or the Music item ❼ inside will display in the Results List all the audio files ❽ of your iTunes Library.
- ▸ Selecting any other enclosed item, folder or Playlist ❾ will display only the audio files for that selection.

iTunes Selected

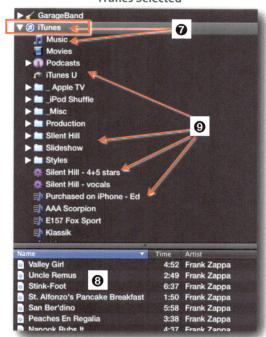

Folder

There can be one additional item in the Media Browser. When we add folders to the Media Browser by *dragging* them onto the Media Browser, then GarageBand creates the "Folders" item and any folder (or alias) you drag onto the Media Browser will be listed inside that Folders regardless of their actual location on your drive.

User Folders

Please note that when you delete (or move or rename) the folder on your drive, GarageBand won't find it and you have to delete the item manually from the Media Browser window.

13 - Media Browser

Import

Once the Results List displays the available audio files, you can preview them first before dragging them onto your Project.

➡ **Preview Audio**

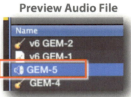
Preview Audio File

There are three commands to preview an audio file. The file icon changes to a speaker icon 🔊 while playing.

- Select an item and *click* on the Play ▶ Button to toggle Play and Stop ⏸
- Select an item and use the Key Command *space bar*. The Media Browser needs to have Key Focus (it has to be selected, indicated by the blue frame around it)
- *Double-click* on an item to play. You have to use the other commands to stop playback.

➡ **Import**

Importing any audio file from the Results List to your current Project is as simple as *dragging* it onto a Track Lane. Here are a few details:

- The files in the list represent audio files and can only be *dragged* onto the Track Lane of an Audio Track.
- *Dragging* a file onto a MIDI Track or Drummer Track will change the Mouse Pointer 🚫❶ and display a warning message that "This is not an Audio Track".
- You can *drag* a file below the last Track Lane in your Workspace and GarageBand will create a new Audio Track first.
- When you *click-hold* the file, a "ghost icon" ❷ appears with the Mouse Pointer displaying what type of audio file you are about to copy over (aiff, mp3, MPEG).
- When you continue to move it over to the Workspace, the following things will happen:
  - ☑ The Mouse Pointer gets a green plus ➕ sign ❸ to indicate that you are copying a file.
  - ☑ A ghost region ❹ appears on the Track Lane to indicate the position of your Mouse Pointer.
  - ☑ A white crosshair ❺ helps you position the Region.
  - ☑ A black Help Tag ❻ indicates the bar position of your Mouse Pointer. You can only place it on the beginning of a bar.
- Once you release the mouse, the audio file will be placed on that Track Lane as an orange Audio Region ❼. The orange color indicates an imported (non Apple Loop) Audio File.
- The Track Name ❽ inherits the name of the audio file if it hasn't been manually named yet.

180   13 - Media Browser

Import Movies

To import Movie files from the Media Browser window, *click* on the Movies tab to switch to the Movies view first.

You can import one movie file per GarageBand Project to score music to it. There are multiple ways to import a Movie.

- *Drag* a movie file from the Media Browser onto your Project
- *Drag* a movie file directly from a Finder window onto your Project
- Use the Main Menu command *File ➤ Movie ➤ Open Movie* or the Key Command *opt+cmd+O* to open a movie file from an Open Dialog Window

Media Browser - Movies

➡ **Browse area**

The app icons represent all the apps that have movie files on your drive. If you don't have a specific app or it doesn't contain movie files, then it will not be displayed in the Browse area.

The Movies folder ❶ lets you navigate through the user's Movies folder to search for files.

➡ **Results List**

The Results List displays all the movie files ❷ based on what you selected in the Browse area, plus the search term in the search field ❸.

➡ **Preview Movie**

You can use the same preview commands:

- Select an item and *click* on the Play ▶ Button ❹ to toggle Play and Stop ⏸.
- Select an item and use the Key Command *space bar*. The Media Browser needs to have Key Focus (it has to be selected, indicated by the blue frame ❺ around it).
- *Double-click* on an item to play. You have to use the other commands to stop playback).
- When you start playing a movie file, the Results List area changes to display a Quicktime Window ❻. Now you can use all those controls ❼ in the Quicktime window too. Volume, Pause, Playhead, Frame forward-backwards.

Movie Preview (in QuickTime Window)

➡ **Import Movie**

To import a movie, just *drag* the movie file from the Result List (or the QuickTime window) onto the Workspace of your Project ❽ and the movie file will be placed on the Movie Track.

More details about using the Movie Track later in the Additional Features chapter.

14 - Apple Loops

Delicious Canned Food

We know by now all the details about how to do our own Audio and MIDI recording, so let's learn how we can build a GarageBand song **without** all that knowledge - *Welcome to the Wonderful World of Apple Loops*.

But seriously, there is no reason to look down on Apple Loops as "canned music", something that is often used by non-musicians to "compose" a song without a clue about music in the first place. First of all, the root of the word "to compose" is from the Latin word "componere" which loosely translated means "putting stuff together". So let's learn how to "compose" a Song by putting stuff (in our case Apple Loops) together.

One of the reasons Apple Loops are so popular is that they are so easy to use.
- ❶ Open the Loop Browser in the GarageBand Window
- ❷ Search for Apple Loops with the built-in search engine
- ❸ *Drag* the Loops you like from the Browser directly onto the Track Lanes

Now, GarageBand creates Regions out of those Loops and you can edit them pretty much the same way as any other Region. Add a few more Apple Loops and your Song is done in no time - almost.

And that would be the end of this Apple Loops chapter. Unless …

… you realize that the Apple Loops feature is not just a toy for "non-musicians". Those Loops can truly add value to your Project. Maybe you need one Loop to quickly supplement your Project, or you discovered that you can use Loops as source material which you process and alter into a different shape and form, therefore making it a unique element in your composition.

Besides, there is some amazing technology behind Apple Loops that is worthwhile to learn and use to your advantage when composing a great Song.

Basics

The first question would be, what are Apple Loops. The simple answer is, "special" audio files.

> **Apple Loops are "special" audio files**

The reason these audio files are special is because they contain <u>additional data</u> that enables them to be used in your Project <u>in a way</u> that would not be possible with a standard audio file.

That raises two questions:
- ▶ "**What way**" is that and, consequently, what might you want to use those audio files for?
- ▶ "**What data**" is necessary to make that happen?

➡ How You Want to use Apple Loops

Let's look at it from a different angle. Instead of first showing you the features of Apple Loops, I'll give you two examples that demonstrate the limitations of standard audio files. Then we'll see how those "special" audio files, called Apple Loops, could lift that limitation. Here are three requirements for external audio files if you want to use them in your Project:
- ☑ #1 Contain Music
- ☑ #2 Easy to Loop
- ☑ #3 Work in your Project

🟡 About #1: Audio Files contain Music

Usually, when you create a new song, you record your own music. That means you or other musicians play their instruments and you record the performance in GarageBand, which creates the Audio Regions or MIDI Regions. However, you have a problem if you need a rhythm guitar part in your song but you don't play the guitar, or you need a live drummer but you don't have a recording booth to record those drums.

With the wide spread popularity of DAWs, companies recognized that need and provided a new type of product.

> **Audio Files with pre-recorded music**

However, these were not your typical audio files that contain pre-recorded music like mp3 files from your favorite artist that you buy on iTunes. The new music files were meant to be used as building blocks in your song and therefore contain mostly single instruments playing repeatable musical patterns that you can use in your song. For example, an audio file of a great live drummer playing a basic groove on a great sounding drum set, recorded with expensive equipment. Or a strumming guitar pattern played by a top studio musician on his $3,000 Martin guitar through a $2,000 microphone, ... you get the idea.

You can buy those little "audio files" (or even better, they come free with GarageBand) and lay them into your Project, mix them with your other tracks and you've got yourself a great sounding song with just a few clicks.
By the way, those audio files are licensed for this purpose and therefore legal to use in your song (read the fine print for details).

💡 About #2: Audio Files must be easy to loop

All those audio files, used as building blocks, have something in common. They are usually short, maybe only one or two bars, but often not longer than 8-32 bars. Most of them are generic musical patterns or phrases that can be repeated. For example, a live drummer would repeat the same one bar groove throughout the eight bars of a verse (and later in the second and third verse again). Same procedure with a live guitar player that you record. The strumming might be the same one bar pattern throughout an 8 bar verse.

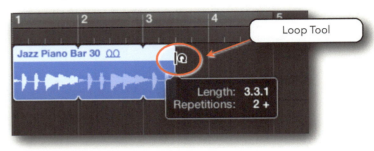

In GarageBand, you would only need the audio file of that one bar which is represented by a one bar Audio Region. You then just copy that Region eight times. But instead of repeating the same Region by copying it manually, you would use the more efficient Loop Tool by *dragging* the upper corner of the Region to the right and GarageBand creates those repetitions automatically, or use the Key Command *L*.

However, that only works if the audio file has been properly trimmed ("truncated"). Otherwise the music will not line up.

Audio Files must be properly truncated

Here is an example of the same recording of a two-bar drum pattern.
- Sample ❶ shows the original Audio File with silence at the beginning and end of the recording.
- The audio file in example ❷ has been trimmed so the file starts exactly at the first signal (downbeat) and ends exactly at the end of the second bar.

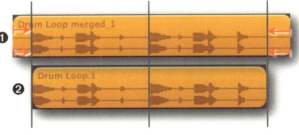

If you would place the un-trimmed audio file on bar one of your Project ❸ and loop it, the drum beat wouldn't line up at the first bar (due to the silence at the beginning) and the repeated Regions would never line up to the following beats of your song either.

However, if you place the properly trimmed audio file on bar one ❹, the drum beat will perfectly start at bar one and each repetition lines up perfectly every two bars. That file is "easy to loop". You just place it at any bar in your song and loop it, no prior Region trimming required.

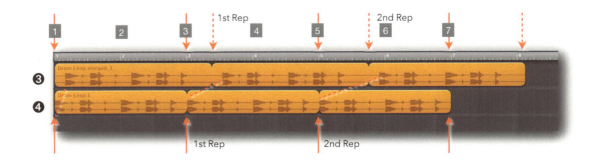

184   14 - Apple Loops

💡 About #3: Audio Files must work in your Project

So the first two requirements we just discussed can easily be done with standard audio files, no need for a "special" audio file. So let's stick with our example and import the perfectly trimmed and "ready to loop" audio file and import it into a different Project.
What just happened?

The drum groove still lines up perfectly on the first bar but now it is getting out of sync. Every two bars, the start of the repeated Region is further away from the bar it is supposed to be. We ignored one fundamental parameter of music. The Tempo. Taking a perfectly trimmed audio file and using it in a Project, only works if the music in that audio file was performed at the same tempo as the tempo of your Project. In the previous example, we were lucky that the drum beat was recorded at 120bpm and imported into our Project with a tempo set to 120bpm, perfect match. In this example, the same 120bpm audio file was imported into a Project with a tempo of 110bpm. The result, the drummer "plays too fast".

▶ **Match Tempo**: This is one of the first "special features" of an Apple Loop. Regardless of its originally recorded tempo, Apple Loops can match (adapt to) the tempo of any Project. In our example, that would mean that the audio file would slow down the drum groove to play in the 110bpm tempo. But not only that, it has to slow down the tempo without changing its original pitch. And that is not necessarily an easy task.

> **Audio Files must match the Project Tempo**

But wait, what about the other example with the strumming guitar player. Even if the Apple Loop is able to match the different tempo, there is another important parameter in music that could be a problem. What if the guitar pattern was recorded in C and you import that audio file into a Project that is set to a different key like E?

▶ **Match Key**: To make a long story short, another requirement for the special audio file called Apple Loop is the ability to match the key of the recorded audio file to the key of the Project. In other words, GarageBand must be able to transpose the audio file. This time it must make the change without affecting the tempo of the audio file.

> **Audio Files must match the Project Key**

Match Tempo - Match Key

So these are the two most important features to make an audio file work in your Project without the restriction of tempo and key. An Apple Loop provides those features, making it a "special" audio file that allows GarageBand to perform a Tempo Match and a Key Match.

Apple Loops - What's inside

➡ Audio File

The main content in an Apple Loop is the audio data. After all, it is still an audio file that looks like a regular audio file with a standard audio file extension (.aif, .caf) and it can be played by any audio application, even iTunes. They just ignore the additional information.

➡ Loop Type

The first additional data besides the audio data is a flag that is set to *"Loop"* or *"One-shot"*. It tells Logic whether or not it should apply the Tempo and Key Matching to that audio file.

So far we've discussed only musical patterns that are suitable for looping. However, there is also use for audio files with musical (or non musical) content that is not based on a rhythmical pattern. Long drones, atmospheric synth pads or short hits and stings. Even sound effects and spoken words are available as Apple Loops. They make use of the other Apple Loop feature, Keywords. See below.

- ☑ **Loop** is used for musical patterns and is expressed by its duration in **beats**
- ☑ **One-shot** is used for non-pattern based audio files and is expressed by its duration in **min:sec**

➡ Match Tempo

Waveform with a grid of Transient Markers

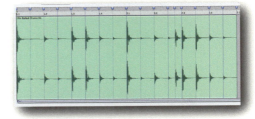

Match Tempo requires two components. First, it needs to know the original tempo the audio file was recorded in. Secondly, the audio file has to be marked with so-called "Transient Markers". This is the same technology we find in the Audio Editor when enabling quantization for Audio Regions. Those Transient Markers act as a grid that is "glued" on top of the audio waveform. When you slow down an audio waveform, the grid gets stretched and when you speed up an audio waveform you squeeze the grid and the waveform with it.

➡ Match Key

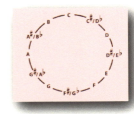

Match Key also relies on Transient Markers, plus, it needs the information of the key the audio file was recorded in. Now, the process is the opposite of Tempo Match. This time GarageBand transposes the audio file based on the difference between the key embedded in the audio file and the Project Key. Since the required pitch shift speeds up the audio file, it applies a reverse tempo change (with the help of the Transient Markers) to compensate it. Now the audio file plays back in the Project's own tempo.

➡ Keywords

This is another important type of data. Apple Loops provide a set of Keywords (aka Metadata, Tags) that function similarly to the tags that you use in iTunes. There you add Artist, Album, Genre, etc. as keywords to your audio files and later can search for those keywords in your huge iTunes Library.

Apple Loops provide the following keywords that can be added to each audio file:

- ☑ **Genre**: Jazz, Blues, Urban, World, etc.
- ☑ **Instrument Description**: This is a two part field, i.e. "Bass - Electric Bass" or "Bass - Acoustic Bass", etc.
- ☑ **Mood Description**: This category allows you to select 8 mutually exclusive descriptions: Acoustic-Electric, Relaxed-Intense, etc. but also a more practical description like Part-Fill or Single-Ensemble.
- ☑ **Scale**: The Key information in the Tempo Match only provides the root note without determining whether the musical pattern is playing in a major or minor key. The Scale tag provides this additional information.

Here are the available values of the four category fields that an Apple Loop can be tagged with. These are the same fields that you can search for later in the Loop Browser when you're looking for a specific Apple Loop.

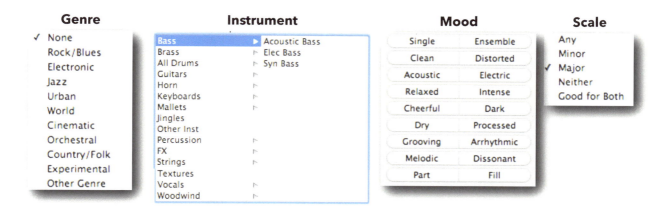

As we will see, you can make any audio file into an Apple Loop by just using its tagging feature. If you have a huge selection of audio files, adding those tags lets you use the Loop Browser later as a powerful search engine without using any of the Tempo and Key Matching feature.

➡ MIDI Region + Channel Strip Settings

This is another interesting type of content that can be part of the Apple Loop.

Apple Loops are available for all different types of styles, genres, instruments and patterns. Many of them are recorded with live instruments but the audio file could also be based, for example, on the pattern of a synth bass played on a MIDI keyboard. Think about that recording process. Someone could use Logic (GarageBand's big brother), load a synth bass Instrument, tweak the sound, load a couple of plugins to fatten up the sound even more, record a 2 bar MIDI Region and bounce (export) that as a two bar audio file for an Apple Loop library.

Apple Loops says, *"wait a minute, what if along with that audio file, I let you store the MIDI Region* ❶, *the setting of the sound generator* ❷ *plus all the names of the used plugins with their settings* ❸ *and the left-right pan* ❹ *that you just used".* And that is exactly what happens. With such an Apple Loop, you would have the option to use the audio file on an Audio Track or drag it onto a MIDI Track and GarageBand would load the exact Software Instrument and all its plugins with the exact settings that were used when the Apple Loop was created and put the MIDI Region (the notes that were played) on that Track.

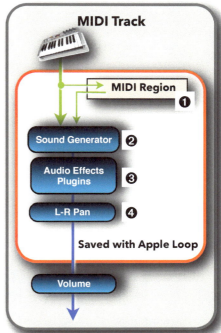

This has the advantage that you not only can change individual MIDI notes but also tweak the sound or load a completely different Software Instrument to play the pattern. Besides that, the musical pattern is performed "live" with a Software Instrument so Tempo and Key Matching are not required. This eliminates the following problem:

 I haven't pointed out that the process of Matching Tempo and Key has some limitations. Depending on the source material and the amount of tempo change and transposition, this could produce some sonic artifacts that could degrade the sound quality quite a bit.

This last category of 'what is inside an Apple Loop', the MIDI content, is very important. So far I haven't mentioned that there are two types of Apple Loops. One kind has MIDI content and the other one doesn't.

Types of Loops

There are **two** types of Apple Loops and some confusion about their differences.

If you followed the previous section about the added content in an Apple Loop, then the distinction between those two Apple Loop types will be easy to understand, especially if you separate the various content into two groups:

The **Music Data** (content data) and the **Data about the Music** (metadata)

And here are the two types of Apple Loops:

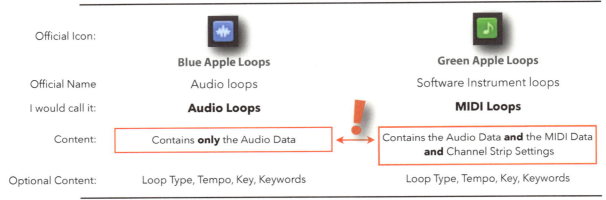

And here is what happens in GarageBand when you drag an Apple Loop from the Loop Browser onto your Project.

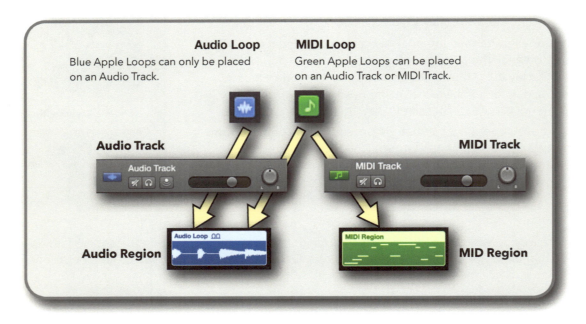

Adding Audio Loops

Let's look at the Audio Loop first and see what happens when you drag one of those from the Loop Browser into your Project - onto the Track Lane to be specific.

Blue Apple Loops can only be dragged onto an Audio Track. If you try to drag an Audio Loop onto the Track Lane of a MIDI Track, the following will happen:

- The Mouse Pointer changes from the plus sign ⊕ to a crossed-out circle ⊘.
- The Track Lane turns dark and displays the following message: *"Not an Audio Track (drag green Apple Loops here)"*.

😀 Drag the Loop

When you drag the Audio Loop from the Loop Browser to a proper Audio Track, the following will happen:
- ▸ The Mouse Pointer ❶ will have an added green plus sign ⊕ to indicate that you add something to the Track Lane.
- ▸ A Ghost Region ❷ of the dragged Loop will be attached to that Pointer Tool displaying the name of the Loop you are about to add.
- ▸ A white crosshair guide ❸ helps you position the Loop.
- ▸ A black Help Tag ❹ displays the bar position of the Mouse Pointer. You can place the Loop only at the beginning of a bar. Later, you can drag it to any position.

😀 Place the Loop

At the moment you release the mouse and drop the Apple Loop on the Track Lane, the following things will happen:
- ▸ On your hard drive, the Audio File (Apple Loop) will be copied to your Project File ❶ inside the Media Folder, inside the Audio Files folder. Remember, your Project File is a Package File type that stores the media files inside the actual Project File.
- ▸ An Audio Region with the full length of the audio file will be created that is referenced ❷ to the copied Audio File "inside" the Project File.
- ▸ That Audio Region will be placed on the Track's Track Lane ❸ at the position where you dropped it.
- ▸ The Track will also be named after the Audio Loop ❹ (only if the Track hasn't been renamed yet).

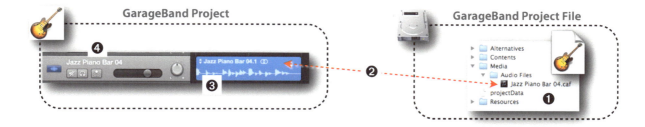

New Track

If you drag an Audio Loop to the empty space below the last Track Lane, then GarageBand automatically creates a new Audio Track first and places the Audio Region on it.

Loop Family

Loop Family Popup Menu

If an Apple Loop belongs to a group of Loops with variations (displayed as the same Apple Loop name with sequential numbers), then the Region on the Track Lane will have a double arrow icon ⇳ that opens the Loop Family popup menu. Select a Loop from that group to replace the current one without going back to the Loop Browser.

Adding MIDI Loops

Here are the procedures and rules regarding the Green Apple Loops ("MIDI Loops"):
Green Apple Loops can be dragged on Audio Tracks or MIDI Tracks (with completely different outcome).

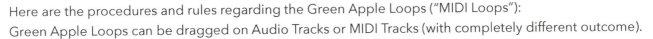

Drag the Loop

The dragging procedure is the same as for Blue Apple Loops, regardless if you drag the Green Loop on an Audio Track or MIDI Track.

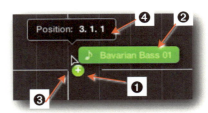

- ▸ The Mouse Pointer ❶ will have an added green plus sign ➕ to indicate that you add something.
- ▸ A Ghost Region ❷ of the Loop will be attached to that Tool displaying the name of the Loop you are about to add.
- ▸ A white crosshair guide ❸ helps you position the Loop.
- ▸ A black Help Tag ❹ displays the bar position of the Mouse Pointer. You can place the Loop only at the beginning of a bar. Later you can drag it to any position.

Place the Loop ➤ Audio Track

When dragging the Green Apple Loop over the Track Lane of an Audio Track, then the Ghost Region attached to the Mouse Pointer still displays the Green Apple Loop ❷. However, once you release the mouse, the following will happen:

- ▸ GarageBand takes only the Audio File data from the Apple Loop (plus the necessary metadata) and pretends that it is a Blue Apple Loop.
- ▸ All the actions that take place are exactly like the ones if it would have been a Blue Apple Loop:
  - The Audio File is copied to the Project File and referenced to the new Audio Region.
  - The Audio Region is placed on the Track Lane as an Apple Loop Audio Region.
  - The Audio Track will be named after the Apple Loop (if it hasn't been renamed yet).

🍏 Place the Loop ➤ MIDI Track

When dragging the Green Apple Loop over the Track Lane of a MIDI Track, something completely different will happen.
- ▸ First of all, the actual Audio File in the Apple Loop will be ignored.
- ▸ The MIDI data from the Apple Loop will be placed as a MIDI Region on the Track Lane, named after the Apple Loop.
- ▸ What happens to the Channel Strip Settings embedded in the Green Apple Loop depends on the following condition:
  - Current MIDI Track has no other Regions on its Track Lane yet: In this case, the Channel Strip Settings (Smart Controls) embedded in the Green Apple Loop will be loaded onto the Track, overwriting any existing configuration. Also, the Track Name will be overwritten.
  - Current MIDI Track has already other Regions on its Track Lane: In this case, the MIDI Track keeps its original settings and they will not be overwritten by the Green Apple Loop.

🍏 Place the Loop ➤ "empty" Track

When you drag a Green Apple Loop to the empty space below the Track Lanes, then Logic creates a new MIDI Track with the stored Channel Strip Settings information and places the MIDI Region on that Track.

Comparison

Here is a screenshot of the result after dragging the same Green Apple Loop (Bavarian Bass 01) ❶ on a MIDI Track and also on an Audio Track.

Two things I want to point out:

- The MIDI Track extracts the MIDI Region ❷ and the Audio Track extracts the Audio File (Audio Region ❸).
- The MIDI Track extracts the Channel Strip Settings (Smart Controls) of the Apple Loop ❹. The Smart Controls of the Audio Track ❺ doesn't change.
- The naming of the Tracks is different. The Audio Track gets the Apple Loop name (Bavarian Bass 01) ❻ while the MIDI Track inherits the Channel Strip Settings name (Muted Electric Brass) ❼.

Apple Loops - Region Editing

An Audio Region created from an Apple Loop (Blue or Green) behaves differently in your Project.

MIDI Regions that were created from Green Apple Loops however have no indication that they originated from Apple Loops. They look and behave exactly like other MIDI Regions.

Loop Browser

Let's summarize what we've learned so far about Apple Loops:
- ☑ Apple Loops contain musical patterns and phrases that are ready to use
- ☑ That music is stored as an audio file
- ☑ Sometimes the music is also available as MIDI data including sound settings
- ☑ The audio file can adapt to the current Tempo of the Project (Tempo Matching)
- ☑ The audio file can play in the current Key of the Project (Key Matching)
- ☑ Apple Loops contain keywords that make them easily searchable

The last feature, the search of Apple Loops, is done in the Loop Browser. It is the window pane that slides out on the right side of the GarageBand Window.

Toggle the Loop Browser with any of the following commands:
- Main Menu *View* ➤ *Show/Hide Apple Loops*
- Key Command *O*
- Click the Loop Browser 🔁 button on the Control Bar (if visible)
- Close the Loop browser by *clicking* on the window header ❶ or the Divider Line ❷ or *dragging* the Divider Line all the way to the right.

Window Elements

Here is an overview of the various interface elements on the Loop Browser.

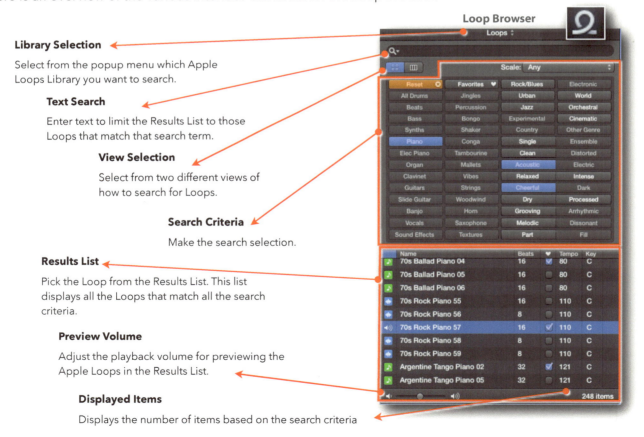

Library Selection

Select from the popup menu which Apple Loops Library you want to search.

Text Search

Enter text to limit the Results List to those Loops that match that search term.

View Selection

Select from two different views of how to search for Loops.

Search Criteria

Make the search selection.

Results List

Pick the Loop from the Results List. This list displays all the Loops that match all the search criteria.

Preview Volume

Adjust the playback volume for previewing the Apple Loops in the Results List.

Displayed Items

Displays the number of items based on the search criteria

➡ Library Selection

The Header of the Loop Browser is actually a popup button ❶. To understand what items are listed in this menu, let me explain how the Apple Loops are organized (which is different from the earlier GarageBand).

- 🔘 In order for GarageBand to find any Apple Loops and display them in the Loop Browser, they have to be in either of two specific folders on your hard drive (unless they are referenced at their original location).
    - System Directory: **/Library/Audio/Apple Loops/Apple/** ❷
      This is the location where Apple stores all the Apple Loops that are installed by an application (Logic Pro, GarageBand, Final Cut Pro) or by a software package (Jam Packs).
    - User Directory: **~/Library/Audio/Apple Loops/User Loops/** ❸
      This is the location where all the Apple Loops are stored that are created by the user (i.e. by dragging a Region onto the Loop Browser).
- 🔘 GarageBand creates the database "LoopsDatabaseV08.db" (located in **~/Music/Audio Music Apps/**) where it stores all the information about the Loops on your drive. This procedure is called **Indexing**. Every time you install new Loops or add a new Loop, GarageBand will update that database. You also can manually update the database with the command "Reindex All Loops ❹". Please note that GarageBand doesn't use the old scheme of "Apple Loops Index" files anymore.
- 🔘 The Loop Browser is technically a user interface for that database. It displays all the Loops that are indexed in that database. Searching for a Loop in the Loop Browser is basically a search in that database file.

Here is what is listed in the Library Selection Menu ❶:

- ▶ **Loops ❺**: Select this item to display in the Loop Browser all the Loops indexed in the database.
- ▶ **My Loops ❻**: This selection displays only the Loops in the "SingleFiles" folder. This is the default location for all the Apple Loops you create in GarageBand (or Logic Pro).
- ▶ **Factory Loops ❼**: This section lists all the Factory Loops Libraries that are installed on your drive.
- ▶ **User Loops ❽**: In the Finder you can manually create folders inside the "User Loops" directory and place Apple Loops in there. After you manually *Reindex All Loops*, those folders will be listed in the section at the bottom of the popup menu.
- ▶ **Reindex All Loops**: This is the command to start updating the database. GarageBand displays a progress bar ❾ and you have to wait until it is finished indexing (could take a minute or two depending on the amount of Loops you have).
- ▶ You can also drag an Apple Loop file or an entire Folder with Apple Loops from the Finder onto the Loop Browser. In this case, a Dialog Window ❿ pops up where you can choose to move those files to the User directory ❸ or just reference them at their current location.

➡ **Button View - Column View**

You can choose between two different views to select the Keywords in the Loop Browser by clicking on their button: Button View - Column View.

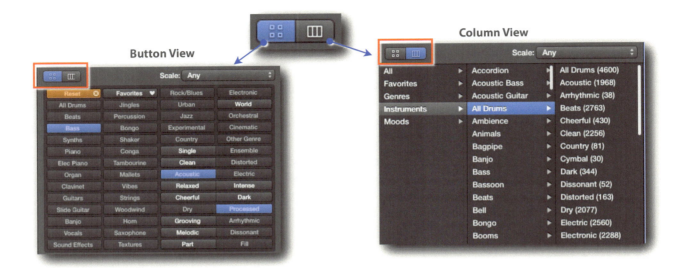

➡ **Search Criteria**

Before you use the Loop Browser to search for any Apple Loops, you have to be aware of how the search works so you understand what kind of search results or "hits" you will get.

Technically, you are applying a filter when performing a search in the Loop Browser. You are starting with all the available Loops on your computer and with each additional criteria, you filter out all the Loops that don't match that criteria.

For example:
- ☑ Filter 1 - search only the "My Loops" Library
- ☑ Filter 2 - only Loops that are marked "Major Scale" in the Scale field
- ☑ Filter 3 - only Loops in the Genre "Blues"
- ☑ Filter 4 - only Loops with Instrument Description "Acoustic Bass"
- ☑ Filter 5 - only the Loops that have "great" in the file name

The Loop Browser will show you (filter out) only those Apple Loops that meet "ALL" the selected criteria. In this case that would be: *"Show me all the Apple Loops with Acoustic Bass in the Blues genre from the My Loops Library that are marked as played in the Major scale and have the word "great" in their name."*

The Loop Browser performs this as an "instant search" which means changing any criteria will instantly update the search results in the window section below. And if you remember the previous page, this is the procedure:

❶ In the upper section of the Loop Browser you create the search query
❷ The Loop Browser sends that query to the "*LoopsDatabaseV08.db*" database file
❸ The results from the database file (matching Apple Loops) are displayed in the lower section of the Loop Browser, the Results List

These are the available areas that let you apply search criteria to narrow down the result to the Apple Loops that match those criteria:

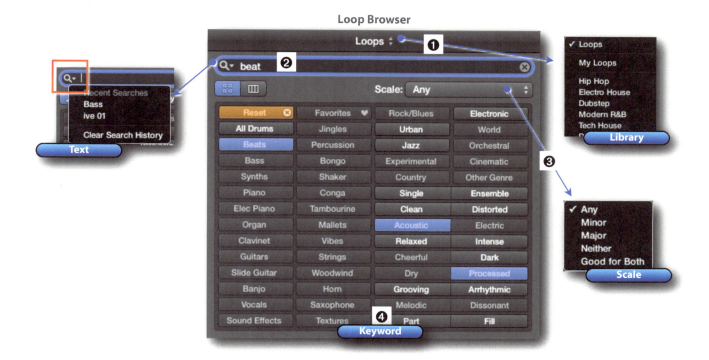

❶ Library

As I've shown you before, this is the first step where you select which Library you are searching. You can select either all ("Loops") or one of the Libraries. However, you cannot apply the search to a group of Libraries.

❷ Text

Type any text into the Search Field to search for that search term in the Apple Loop name.
- You cannot use any of the Boolean search techniques (and, or), just straight text. However, each text string, separated by a space, is matched individually against each word in the name of an Apple Loop. For example, typing "ive 01" matches every name that has in two words of its name the characters "**ive**" and "**01**". "Locomot**ive** Beat **01**", "Provoca**tive** 00**10**", Reflect**ive** Bass **01**", R**ive**r Sax **01**".
- *Click* on the Magnifying Glass to bring up a popup menu with the *Recent Searches*. The command "*Clear Search History*" lets you clear that list.
- The X Button at the end of the Search Field clears the Search Field.

❸ Scale

The Scale popup menu lets you narrow down the search to find a musical pattern played in the major or minor key (or any, neither, or good for both). Please note that this is not based on an analysis of the audio file. Instead, it is just a label entered by the creator of the Apple Loop so this search result is only as accurate as the original entry in the Apple Loop. This is also true for the other keywords.

❹ Keywords

There are three types of Keywords (Genre - Instrument - Mood) and as we have seen already, there are two different Views available (Button View and Column View) to make a selection that matches Apple Loops containing those Keywords.

Keyword Views

Column View

In the Column View, you make one selection based on the available columns.

- ▸ **Column ❶**: Lets you search in "All" categories, or just in the Favorites, Genres, Instruments or Moods category.
- ▸ **Column ❷**: This column shows you all the available subcategories of the category you selected in column 1.
- ▸ **Column ❸**: This column shows you the available sub-category of the selected sub-category in column 2. The number in the parenthesis tells you how many Apple Loops are found in that specific category. *Click* on an item in that column to display those Loops in the Results List section below.

Please note that selecting an item in a column will determine what is displayed in the column to the right but it also becomes the current selection for what is displayed in the Results List.

Button View

The Button View provides a 4x14 matrix of selectable buttons. You can resize it to 4x1 by sliding up the Divider Line.

- ▸ Each button represents a specific Keyword with the exception of the Reset ❹ button and the Favorites ❺ button
- ▸ **Status**: A button can have three states: ❻ Blue=Selected, ❼ WhiteFont=Selectable, ❽ GrayFont=NonSelectable.
- ▸ **Select**: Any selection made with the one of the other search criteria (library, text, scale) determines which keyword is selectable. This way the buttons are kind of "intelligent". Only the buttons that provide a potential hit will be highlighted. For example, if you selected "Urban", "Synth" and "Distorted" and none of the Apple Loops that meet those criteria have a keyword "Relaxed", then that button will be grayed out.
  Click on a button to include that Keyword in the search. More buttons will be dimmed (*more Loops got eliminated from the Results List*).
- ▸ **De-Select**: *Click* on a blue button to de-select it or *click* the Reset ❹ button to deselect all buttons.
- ▸ **Move** a Keyword button by simply dragging the button to a new slot and it will swap its position with the button you moved it over to.
- ▸ **Reassign** a button by *ctr+clicking* on it. This will open a popup menu ❾ to assign a Genre or Instrument Keyword to it. Mood buttons cannot be reassigned. You can reset the button view to its default layout by clicking the Reset button in the *Preferences ▸ Loops ▸ Keyword Layout*
- ▸ **Favorites**: Selecting this button ❺ limits the search to only the Apple Loops that you flagged with the "Favorites" checkbox in the Loop Browser's Results List.

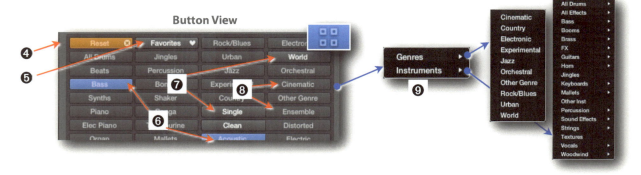

Results List

The Results List displays all the hits, all the Apple Loops that meet your search criteria.

It is a list view with six columns

- ▶ **Loop Type**: The first column displays the icon for the Loop so you know right away if it is a Blue 〰️ or Green 🎵 Apple Loop. You can preview a Loop by *clicking* on the icon or on this row. This toggles the preview on/off and changes the Loop icon to a speaker icon 🔊 when playing ❶.
- ▶ **Name**: This lists the name of the Apple Loop. The Loops are listed in alphabetical order and you can change the sort order with the little triangle button on the header.
- ▶ **Beats/Length**: This column can display one of two values, depending on the type of Apple Loop. If it is a "Loop" type Apple Loop, then the field will display the number of beats ❷ of that Loop. If it is a "One-shot" type Apple Loop, then the field will display the length of that Apple Loop in min:sec ❸.
- ▶ **Tempo**: This lists the original Tempo the Apple Loop was recorded in. If the Loop is a "One-shot" type, then that field is empty ❹.
- ▶ **Key**: This column lists the original Key the Apple Loop was recorded in. If the field is empty ❹, then it is either a non-pitched loop (drums) or a One-shot type loop.
- ▶ **Favorites** ♥: You can mark any Loop in the Results List as a "Favorite" ❺ by clicking on the checkbox. As you've seen in the search criteria sections, this lets you later limit your search to only your Favorite Apple Loops. Please note that this tag is not stored with the Apple Loop. It is part of the *LoopsDatabaseV08.db* file that stores all the metadata information of the indexed Apple Loops.

You can re-arrange the columns by dragging them around, resize them and change the sorting order by *clicking* on the Columns Header. Resize the entire list by dragging the Divider Line ❻ up (making the Keyword area smaller) or make the GarageBand Window bigger.

The items number ❽ in the lower right corner displays how many Apple Loops are currently displayed in the Results List.

➡ Loops Preferences

The Preferences window has a special Loops section ❾ where you can set if you want to view the Tempo and Key column in the Results List. You can also restrict the search results only to the Loops within two semitones of the Project's Key.

➡ Preview

There are three parameters that affect the Preview of an Apple Loop in the Results List. Please note that when the song is playing while previewing an Apple Loop, the Loop will play in sync (starts on the downbeat).

- ▶ **Tempo**: The previewed Apple Loop always follows the current Tempo of your Project (even tempo changes).
- ▶ **Key**: The previewed Apple Loop will always play in the Project's Key (if the Apple Loops has Key Match data).
- ▶ **Volume**: The previewed Apple Loop will always play back with the level set with the Volume Slider ❼. *Opt+click* on the volume slider will reset it to -6dB.

Create your own Apple Loops

These are the easy steps for creating your own Apple Loops right from within GarageBand.

- **Select a Region**
  - You can only select a single Region. If you have more than one Region, then use the Join command to merge them first.
  - An Audio Region will create a Blue Apple Loop and a MIDI Region will create a Green Apple Loop.
  - A Region has to be trimmed to exactly one bar (or multiple bars) length to create a "Loop" type Apple Loop. Otherwise, GarageBand will create a "One-shot" type Apple Loop.

- **Command**
  - *Drag* the Region from the Track Lane over the Loop Browser

- **Settings Window**
  - **Name ❶**: Enter a name for your Apple Loop ❶.
  - **Type ❷**: This is the important flag that tells GarageBand how to treat the Apple Loop when you use it in a Project:
    - Loop: The newly created Apple Loop will store the Key and Tempo information of the current Project plus the Transient Marker Grid. Later, when you add that Apple Loop to any Project, GarageBand will perform the Tempo Matching and Key Matching.
    - One-Shot: No Key or Tempo information will be stored with this type of Apple Loop. GarageBand will use the Loop in any Project without any Tempo and Key Matching.

    If a Loop is not properly trimmed before, then the se ection automatically defaults to "One-shot" and is grayed out so you can't overwrite it.
  - **Keywords**: The next four sections let you assign the Keywords to the Apple Loop. The Loop Browser can later search for those keywords.
    - Scale ❸: Select from the popup menu.
    - Genre ❹: Select from the popup menu.
    - Instrument Description ❺: Select the category from the first column and a sub-category from the second column if available.
    - Mood ❻: *Click* on up to eight mood buttons. They come in pairs and are mutually exclusive.

- **Create**

When you click the Create button, the Apple Loop will be created and placed in the following location on your hard drive: *~/Library/Audio/Apple Loops/User Loops/SingleFiles/*

The new Apple Loop will automatically be indexed and can be immediately searched for in the Loop Browser.

15 - Editing Regions (in the Workspace)

Basics

Region - Region Content

We already talked a lot about Regions throughout the manual and I assume that everybody who is working with DAWs is familiar with Regions. However, before editing anything in your Project, you have to be aware of the important difference between the Region and the Region Content.

- ▸ **Region**: The Region, regardless of the Region Type (MIDI, Audio, Drummer) is just a container for your music. For example, the recording of an instrument on a specific Track can be in one long Region (big container), or it can be broken up into multiple shorter Regions (smaller containers). The actual data (your music) is what's inside the Region. That is the Region Content. Regions are edited in the Workspace on the Track Lane of each Track. Whenever you edit a Region there, you have to know if and how it affects the content inside (your music).
- ▸ **Region Content**: This is your actual music, as data, "embedded" inside a Region. To edit the Region Content, you have to "open" a Region in any of the Editors that display the content.

Objects

The process of editing means that "you edit an object", something that you click on or select first to apply a command to. When you are in the Workspace, then those Objects are the Regions. However, you have to be aware that there are three types of Regions (Audio ❶, MIDI ❷, Drummer ❸). The result of an editing command might look the same on the outside but it can have different results on the Region Content inside.

Although you can see the Region Content on the Region ❹, you cannot edit it there (with some exceptions). It's like a store front window. To edit the Region Content, you have to ("step inside") look at it in its own Editor Window ❺. When opened, you can click on those Objects ❻ to edit them. But as we will see in the next chapter, the Region Content (the objects inside) and the procedure to edit that content is quite different.

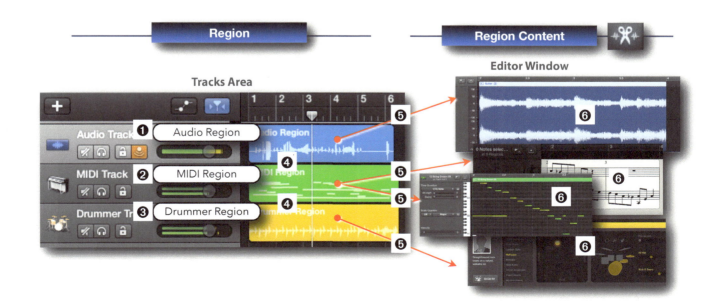

Region editing in the Workspace is basically the same for all the different Regions. There are only a few exceptions that I will point out later.

Editing Restrictions

Before you learn how to edit something, you have to know what you can not edit. There are a few restrictions.

➡ *Track Lock*

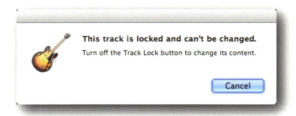

The Track *Lock Mode* locks down a whole Track if it is enabled on the Track Header (the button is hidden by default). It is like a master "hands off" sign. You cannot record on it, you cannot move Regions to it and any Regions on it can't be edited. You also cannot edit any content inside.

If you try to edit anything on that Track, an Alert Window will pop up.

➡ *Prohibited*

Another restriction is imposed by the different Track Types and Region Types. For example, when you try to move a MIDI Region to an Audio Track or an Audio Region to a MIDI Track, the Mouse Pointer changes to the "prohibit" sign ⊘ to indicate that this operation is not allowed.

Editing Target

Before you apply any of the editing commands, you have to tell the computer what Region you want to edit by selecting it. This procedure is common to virtually all software applications: Any edit command applies only to the selected object(s).

Here are the basic commands for selecting Regions:

- *Click* on one Region to select a single Region. Selected Regions have a highlighted Header.
- *Sh+click* on multiple Regions in a sequence to select them all. This also works for selecting multiple Regions on different Tracks. *Click* again to deselect individual Regions from that group.
- *Drag* an area around Regions ("lasso around them") to select them all.
- Select All Regions with the Key Command *cmd+A* or Menu Command *Edit ➤ Select All*
- *Click* on the Track Header to select all the Regions on that Track. *Click* on the background of a Workspace to deselect all Regions.

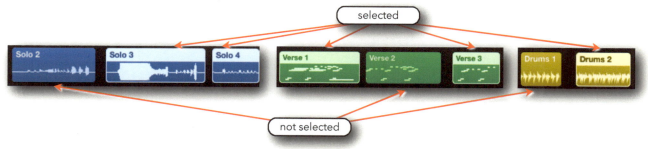

Any edit you apply can be undone with the Undo command. You can apply this command multiple times to undo the last few edits in a sequence or use the "Redo" command to "redo the undo":

- Undo/Redo Menu Command *Edit ➤ Undo* or *Edit ➤ Redo*
- Undo Key Command *cmd+Z* or Redo Key Command *sh+cmd+Z*

Editing Assistance

Here are a few of the features that can "assist" you when editing objects:

➡ Zoom

Zoom Slider

Before applying any edits, you have to make sure to properly zoom in or out. Zoom in enough that you make the precise edit and zoom out enough to see the Objects that are affected by the edit. There are two commands:

- **Drag** the Zoom Slider (at the right end of the Ruler) left or right
- Use the **Pinch** Gesture on the Track Pad
- **Opt+scroll** horizontally

➡ Crosshair (white)

Crosshair

When you move any Region(s) on the Track Lane, a white crosshair, centered at the lower left corner of the Region, will move with the Region to help you position it. Especially the vertical line that extends all the way up to the Ruler, lets you align the Region to a specific Ruler position.

➡ Alignment Guides (yellow)

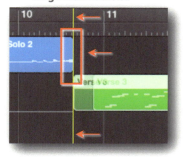
Alignment Guides

In addition to the white crosshair, GarageBand can display a yellow vertical line, called the "Alignment Guides" when a moving Region (or an Automation Control Point) aligns with the border of another object. This can be the beginning but also the end of a Region. The Alignment Guide extends all the way through the Ruler for optimal Timeline positioning.

Toggle the Alignment Guide with the following commands

- Main Menu Command **Edit ➤ Alignment Guides** (only visible when Tracks Area has Key Focus)
- Key Command **opt+cmd+G**

➡ Snap to Grid

Snap to Grid is a useful feature that lets you position an object perfectly aligned to the time grid or another object. The main purpose is to snap objects to a specific time division of the Timeline grid (i.e beginning of the bar or a beat). In addition, it is also used to snap to the Alignment Guides, the Playhead or Cycle Area. Please note that the time grid (an object is snapping to) depends on the zoom factor. And you also can temporarily disable the snap feature by holding down the **control** key when moving objects. **Sh+ctr+drag** will snap the movement to the finest time grid, Ticks or Sub-frames (depending on the Control Bar Display).

Toggle the Snap feature with the following command (Editor Windows have Snap enabled by default):

- Main Menu Command **Edit ➤ Snap to Grid** (only visible when Tracks Area has Key Focus)
- Key Command **cmd+G**

➡ Help Tags

A black Help Tag will pop up during many edit procedures to provide additional information about the movement along the timeline.

  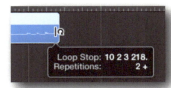

15 - Editing Regions (in the Workspace)

Region Editing

Now let's go over some commands for editing Regions in the Workspace. The main task with these commands is for the procedure called "arranging". Mainly, you copy, paste, move, repeat, trim Regions or groups of Regions to develop your Song.

Edit the Region as it is

The following are commands that treat the whole Region without changing its content.

➡ Name

You can rename the selected Audio Region(s) with the following commands (this also works for Take Folder Regions).
- Key Command **sh+N**
- Shortcut Menu on a Region **Rename Region**

The command highlights the name field so you can enter a new name and hit **return**.

There is a nice hidden procedure for naming a sequence of multiple Regions. For example, selecting five Regions (even across different Tracks) and entering "Piano 1" in the field, will name all the Regions in sequence "Piano 1". "Piano 2", "Piano 3", etc. You can even enter a different number ("Piano 25") and the Regions will be numbered through starting with that number ("Piano 25", Piano 26", etc).

➡ Create (Pencil Tool)

This is a command to create a new Region at the click position on the Track Lane. Holding down the **command key** while the mouse is positioned over a Track Lane, will change the Pointer Tool to the Pencil Tool.

You know by now that a MIDI Track, an Audio Track and a Drummer Track are completely different. Therefore, the result on **cmd+clicking** on one of those Track Lanes will produce a different Region:
- MIDI Track: A new, empty, 1-bar MIDI Region is created.
- Drummer Region: A new 8-bar Drummer Region will be created with the Default Drummer Preset.
- Audio: An Open Dialog popups up that lets you navigate to an Audio File on your drive. The selected Audio File will be copied into the Project File and its linked Audio Region is placed on the Track Lane.

➡ Delete

You can delete a selected Region(s) with the following commands:
- Key Command **delete**
- Main Menu Command **Edit ➤ Delete** or **Edit ➤ Cut**
- Main Menu Command **Edit ➤ Delete and Move** deletes that Region(s) and moves any existing Region at a later position on that Track Lane to the left. How far they are moved to the left is determined by the length of the deleted Region(s).

While MIDI Regions and Drummer Regions get removed right away, an Audio Region requires special attention when it comes to deleting.
- If there are other Audio Regions referring to the same Audio File, then only the "to be deleted" Audio Region will be deleted but not the Audio File it is referring to.
- If the Audio Region is the last Region referring to a specific Audio File, then this action will also delete the Audio File on your drive.

➡ **Move**

Move Region procedure

The basic move command functions as expected. You *drag* the Object(s) with the Mouse Pointer (it changes to the Hand Tool to the new position. A Ghost Region(s) will indicate the new position along with the Help Tag. It displays the target position, the distance from the original position plus the number of the Track you are currently hovering over.

- When you move a group of Regions, then the new Position is indicating the left Region border of the Region you are clicking on and not the first Region of the group.
- When you want to move (or copy) a Region to a different Track but at the same start time, then you can use the *sh+drag* command which will snap the target position to the same start position.
- The Position value on the Help Tag turns yellow to indicate when you are moving (back) over the original position.

➡ **Copy**

There are two standard commands for copying Regions:

- *Opt+drag* the Region(s) to the new position.
- Use the Copy-Paste command either from the Edit Menu (*Edit ➤ Copy* and *Edit ➤ Paste*) or use the Key Commands *cmd+C* and *cmd+V*. The Region(s) will be placed at the Playhead Position of the currently selected Track. Existing Regions will be overwritten! You can use this method to copy/past Regions between Projects:
Copy Region(s) ➤ Close Project A ➤ Open Project B ➤ Paste Region(s).

The Pointer Tool will have the added green plus icon during the copy procedure. And of course, Regions can only be copied to the same Track Type (MIDI or Audio). The same overwrite rules apply.

➡ **Loop**

To "loop" a Region is the process of repeating a Region for a specific amount of times. You could accomplish that by copying the Region multiple times and place them one after another. The Loop command does exactly that, just in a more elegant way.

Move the Mouse Pointer over the right upper corner of the Region you want to loop. This is a Click Zone, which means, the Pointer Tool changes to a different Tool when moved over that zone. In this case the Pointer Tool changes to the Loop Tool. *Dragging* the Region with the Loop Tool to the right will lengthen the looped section. This way you tell GarageBand up to what position on the timeline it should repeat the Region. This is the position where you release the mouse. The result looks like many Regions aligned in a sequence, but this is actually just one Region (plus its repetitions, not a resize command). A looped sequence doesn't have a separation line ❶ between the Regions (just a nudge) and also no name ❷.

How to use the Loop Tool

- *Drag* the right border of the Region with the Loop Tool ❸ to extend the range to any position. A Help Tag ❹ displays the end point of the Region (Length) and the number of repetitions.
- *Dragging* the right border with the Loop Tool all the way to the left will turn the Loop off ❺ (no repetitions).
- Use the Key Command *L* to toggle the Loop on or off.

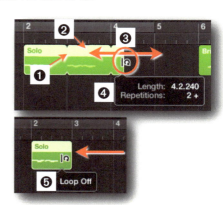

Please note that if you change the length of the original Region (the first segment in the sequence), the section that repeats and the numbers of its repetitions (amount of Regions) changes to maintain the end position of the sequence.

Change the Region

The following commands will change the current Region as it is.

➡ Resize (Trim Tool, Junction Tool)

The Trim Tool is also part of the Click Zone. It will automatically appear when you move the Mouse Pointer over the lower left or right border of a Region. A Help Tag displays the start position and length when trimming the left border and the length and the length change when trimming the right border.

Please pay attention when trimming different types of Regions:

- <u>MIDI Region</u>: You can freely extend and shorten the left and right border. Shortening a section that contains MIDI Events will "ignore" those enclosed MIDI Events during playback. They will not be deleted. Whenever you extend the section of the Region again, then the MIDI Events will still be there (unless you've joined the trimmed Region with another Region).
- <u>Drummer Region</u>: Resizing the Drummer Region will affect the drum pattern (i.e. drum fill at the end of a Region).
- <u>Audio Region</u>: You can extend the borders of an Audio Region only as long as the Audio File is itself. Moving the Mouse Pointer between the Header of two adjacent Regions, lets you trim the right border (of the Region to the left) and the left border (of the the Region to the right) together with the Junction Tool.

➡ Split

This command splits all the selected Regions at the Playhead Position into two Regions, even across multiple Tracks. Splitting an existing Region is useful when you want to move or copy only a portion of a Region or want to edit only a section of it (i.e. for individual quantize rules). Please note that Notes in a MIDI Region that extend beyond a split point will be shortened so they end at the split point.

The commands are:

- Main Menu Command **Edit ▶ Split Regions at Playhead**
- Key Command **cmd+T**

➡ Join

The Join command is the opposite of the Split command. It merges all the selected Regions together.

This command can only be applied to selected Regions on a single Track. Select one or multiple Regions (with or without gaps in between) and use any of the commands.

- Menu Command **Edit ▶ Join Regions**
- Key Command **cmd+J**

Joined Audio Regions = New Audio File

Please note that you cannot join Audio Regions the same way as MIDI or Drummer Regions. An Audio Region contains the play instructions for its linked Audio File. When you join two or more Audio Files, GarageBand first performs a mixdown of those Audio Regions which creates a new Audio File. The new Audio Region for that Audio File will be the new "Joined Audio Region".

When you try to join two Audio Files, you'll get prompted with a Dialog Window with the option to Create the new Audio File.

Arrangement Track

The Arrangement Track is one of the four Global Tracks that are hidden by default. Toggle it with the Menu Command **Track ➤ Show/Hide Arrangement Track** or Key Command **sh+cmd+A**. Instead of moving, copying, and trimming individual Regions, this feature provides commands that let you do that more efficiently.

Let's assume the Project you are working on is based more on a song-like structure than a music cue of a film score. Typically, a song has various sections (i.e. Intro, Verse, Bride, Chorus, Solo, etc.) and some of those sections often repeat throughout the song. When you start your song with some basic Tracks or even if you are close to finishing, you might want to experiment to find the best structure for that song ("repeat the Verse three times instead of two times", "move the Solo after the second Chorus instead of the first Chorus"). In order to do that, you have to do some major editing by moving around big amounts of Regions, cutting and splicing and hoping that stuff doesn't get messed up along the way. This is where Arrangement Markers come in.

> ▸ First, you create Markers along the Arrangement Track Lane that should represent the various sections of your song, like the Intro, Verse, Chorus, etc.
> ▸ Now, instead of moving individual Regions around, you move the Arrangement Markers and only the Regions (or portions of Regions) that fall inside that sections of the Arrangement Marker will be moved. No need to cut up Regions, select them and move them to other Regions to make space or fill up gaps.

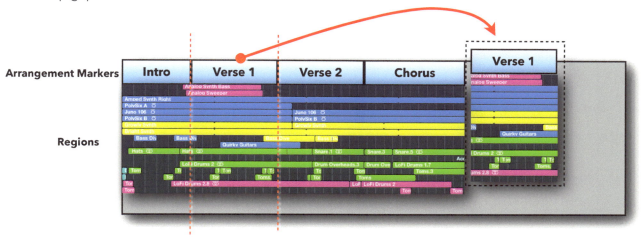

Before you work with those Arrangement Markers, make sure that you fully understand the two steps involved:

> Commands to **manage** the Markers
> Commands to **use** the Markers

Once you've created a Marker, all the Regions that fall inside the Marker's range are tied to that Marker. Consequently, you have to be absolutely sure which commands let you manage Markers (build your structure) and which commands let you use the Markers (play around with your song structure). By doing so you affect all the Regions "underneath."

➡ Manage Arrangement Markers

These are the commands that affect only the Markers and not the Regions underneath them.

- ◯ **Create New:** There are two ways to create Arrangement Markers
    - *Click* on the Plus button 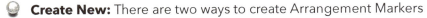 in the Header of the Arrangement Track. This creates a new eight bar long Marker starting at the beginning of the Project (if it is the first Arrangement Marker) or at the end of the last existing Arrangement Marker.
    - *Cmd+click* on the Arrangement Track Lane. This creates a four bar Marker named "Marker n"
- ◯ **Insert** a Marker by *cmd+clicking* on that position. The Pointer Tool changes to the Pencil Tool.
- ◯ **Resize** the Marker by *dragging* the end ❶ of the last Marker or the edge ❷ between two Markers. A black Help Tag appears while dragging to show the Marker length ❸ or the moving position ❹.
- ◯ **Rename** a Marker by *clicking* on its name ❺. This opens a popup menu ❻ with five common names to choose from. You can also select "Rename..." from the popup menu to open the entry box for entering your own name.

➡ Remove

There is no specific command for removing an Arrangement Marker, but you can merge two Markers by dragging the right edge of a Marker all the way to the left so it covers the Marker on the left.

➡ Using Arrangement Markers

These are the commands for the Arrangement Markers that affect all the Regions underneath them.

- ◯ **Move Arrangement Marker (and data underneath it)**

    Drag a Marker to move every Region, Marker and Automation Control Points with it with the exception of Protected Tracks ("Track Locked"). The target position can be either the end of the last Marker or the position between two Markers (insert). Existing Markers are moved to the right to make space and any gap from the source Marker will close up.

- ◯ **Copy Arrangement Marker (and data underneath it)**

    Opt+drag the Marker to the new position. The target position can be either the end of the last Marker or the position between two Markers (insert). Existing Markers are moved to the right to make space.

- ◯ **Replace Arrangement Marker (and data underneath it)**

    Cmd+Drag Marker A over Marker B. Marker B will be replaced with Marker A and the gap of the original position of Marker A will be closed.

- ◯ **Delete Arrangement Marker**

    This is a two step procedure:
    - Select the Marker and hit the *delete* key: This will delete the Regions underneath the Marker.
    - Hit the *delete* key again: This will delete the Marker and moves all the Regions underneath to close the gap.

Editors Window

All the editing commands in this chapter showed you how to edit your music on the Region level". Next, we are "stepping inside" a Region and editing the Region Content.

 Although there are three different types of Regions (MIDI, Audio, Drummer) with completely different kinds of "content", they all share the same window to edit their Region Content. This Window is the Editors Window, the bottom Window Pane in the GarageBand Window

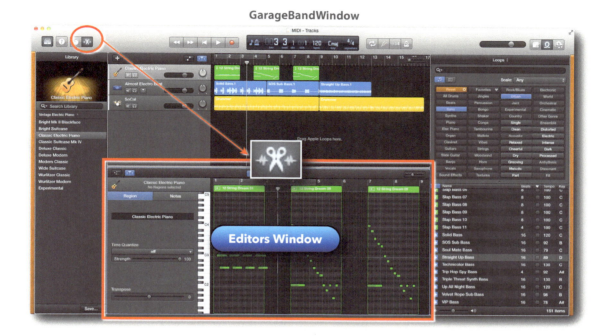

There is a wide variety of controls that open and close the Editors Window. Which of the Editors will be displayed in the Window Pane depends on what Region is currently selected.

Choose the command that suits your workflow:

➡ **Toggle Show/Hide**

- *Click* the Editors Button on the Control Bar. The button turns dark when the Editor Window is open.
- Main Menu Command *View ➤ Show/Hide Editor*
- Key Command *E*
- *Double-click* on a Region in the Track Lane directly to toggle the Editor pane
- Once the Editor is open, you just click on any Region in the Workspace to switch the view of the Editor Window to display the Track the selected Region belongs to

➡ **Hide**

- *Double-click* on the Divider Line between the Editors Window and Tracks Area
- *Drag* the Divider Line all the way to the bottom to close the Editors Window
- *Click* on the blue Piano Roll or Score Button in the Menu Bar (whatever is active)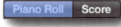

15 - Editing Regions (in the Workspace)

Interface Concept

As we know by now, the Tracks Area ❶ lists all your Tracks in two sections, the Track List ❷ with the individual Track Headers on the left that extend to their Track Lanes in the Workspace ❸. On top of the Timeline Area is the Time Ruler ❹ which is tied to the Workspace. Here is what happens when you open the Editors Window:

- Opening the Editors Window ❻ will shrink the height of the Tracks Area (they share the same space in the GarageBand Window). You can resize both areas proportionally with the Divider Line in between.
- The Editor Window acts like an Inspector window. Remember, the concept of an Inspector window is to display/edit content depending on the selection made in another window. Here, the content of the Editors Window depends on what Track/Region is selected in the Tracks Area ❻.
- The Editor Window displays the selected Track ❺ with more detailed information and functionality which allows you to edit the content of the Regions on that Track.
- The Editor Window is also divided into two sections. On the left is the Inspector ❼ which provides specific controls for editing the Regions. To the right is the Display Area with the Track Lane ❽ which is tied to its own Time Ruler above ❾.
- The Track Lane in the Editor pane displays the same Regions that you can see on the selected Track in the Tracks Area. It just provides you with an alternate view of the Track's Regions that allows you to edit the content of those Regions.

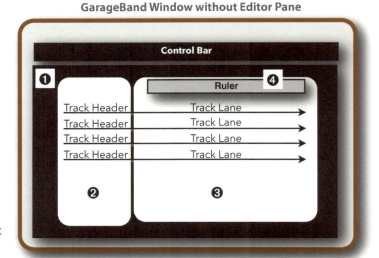

➡ 1 Window - 4 Editors

The Editors Window switches between four different interfaces depending on which type of Region is selected in the Tracks Area (MIDI, Audio and Drummer). For MIDI Regions, you can choose between two different Editors. They all share this Window Pane with the Smart Controls Window.

16 - Editing MIDI

MIDI Editing

The procedure of editing MIDI data is similar in most DAWs. If you have any experience with that, then you just have to find out if GarageBand follows those common editing conventions (that you expect) or if it has some special procedures you have to be aware of (learn first). I'll start with the basics about MIDI Editing in this chapter in case this is your first DAW.

Three Stages of MIDI

Please note that we talk about the MIDI data (your music in the form of MIDI) and how to edit that data. In other words, we talk about the **MUSIC** (what to play) and not about the **SOUND** (who is playing it). The latter belongs to the topic I covered already, choosing different Patches and adding Audio FX on that Track.

When you use MIDI in your Project, you have to be aware of three stages.

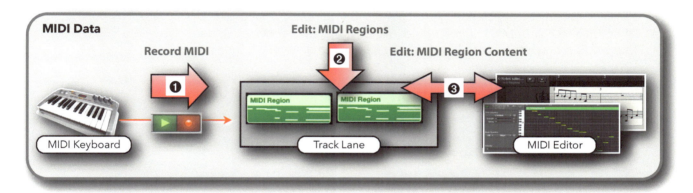

- **Record MIDI ❶**
  This is the first stage where you "generate" the MIDI data by playing on a MIDI keyboard. The MIDI keyboard translates "the music" (your keystrokes) to MIDI data. That data is sent to GarageBand where you record that data on a MIDI Track as a MIDI Region. That MIDI Region functions as a container that holds the MIDI data you recorded. Every new recording creates a new container, a new MIDI Region.

- **Edit MIDI Region ❷**
  All the MIDI Regions you've recorded are placed on the Track Lanes in GarageBand where you can edit them. That's what we just learned in the previous chapter. Moving the "containers" around, making them bigger or smaller without "touching" the data inside.

- **Edit MIDI Region Content ❸**
  The third stage is for those occasions when you want to change (edit) the data inside the MIDI Region. For that you need access to it. This access to the Region Content is provided by a MIDI Editor and GarageBand provides even two of those, the Piano Roll Editor and the Score Editor.

What is a MIDI Editor

Let's assume you played a nice synth solo on your MIDI keyboard that you recorded in GarageBand. You can see the MIDI Region in GarageBand on the Track Lane of that MIDI Track you recorded on. Here again is the difference between editing the Region and editing the Region Content.

- ▶ **Editing Region**: If you just want to edit the Region as a whole, you can move it around. For example, move that synth solo part after the second chorus instead of having it play after the first chorus. You can even shorten the solo. However, what if you played a wrong note? Region editing doesn't help you there. You need access to the Region Content.
- ▶ **Editing Region Content**: A MIDI Editor gives you access to the content of a Region so you can edit your music, the way you recorded it. For example, fix that wrong note C# to a C.

In order to do any edit, the MIDI Editor has to provide two things:
- ☑ Let you <u>View</u> the Data
- ☑ Let you <u>Edit</u> the Data

➡ *View the Data*

If the MIDI Editor would just show the MIDI data inside a Region, it would look something like that ❶:

- **Raw Data ❶**: When you played your synth solo on your MIDI keyboard, it translated your playing into MIDI Events that were sent as digital data to GarageBand. That digital data is what is stored in a Region and if your MIDI Editor would just let you view that raw MIDI data, you might find it difficult to locate that one wrong note (C#) that you wanted to correct.

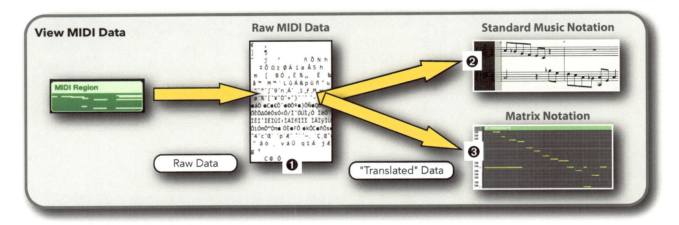

So the MIDI Editor has to do one extra step. It has to take that raw data and translate it to a form that you can understand. Because there are different forms of how to write down and view music, there are also different types of MIDI Editors that each use a specific form of displaying the MIDI data stored in a Region:

- **Standard Music Notation ❷**: This is the traditional form of notation for western music. Note symbols placed on music staffs. In GarageBand, this is what the **Score Editor** does.
- **Matrix Notation ❸**: This is a concept that is used in old mechanical player pianos. Notes as horizontal bars on a Matrix where the placement along the vertical axis determines the pitch of a note and the placement along the horizontal axis determines the timing information. In GarageBand, this is what the **Piano Roll Editor** does.

Time-Stamped MIDI Messages

So, whatever you see in the Piano Roll Editor or the Score Editor, is a translation of the recorded MIDI data. Although these editors are "user friendly" and don't require too much technical (MIDI) background knowledge in order to use them, it helps if you know a little bit more about what is going on under the hood. Here is a diagram that shows the procedure of recording a single note in GarageBand.

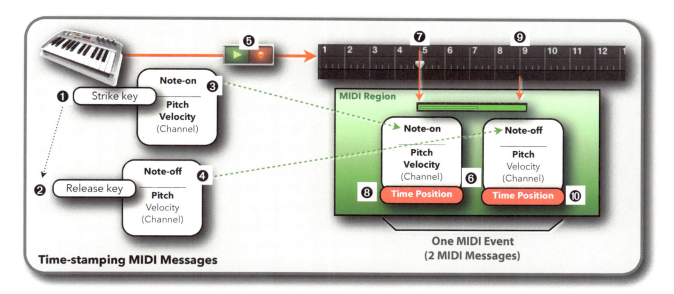

- ▸ If you think about it, playing a single note on your MIDI keyboard actually involves two actions:
    - Strike the key ❶
    - Release the key ❷
- ▸ The same "two-in-one" concept applies to MIDI. When the keyboard translates that action into MIDI, it sends two MIDI Messages.
    - Strike the key ➤ **Note-on message** ❸
    - Release the key ➤ **Note-off message** ❹
- ▸ Each message contains three pieces of information:
    - The **Pitch**: This is the most important and easy to understand information; what key.
    - The **Velocity**: This is a measurement how hard you hit the key; a value between 0-127.
    - The MIDI Channel: Each note message can be set to a channel from 1-16. This information is not relevant in GarageBand but we will see it later in one of the Editors so now you know its origin.
- ▸ When you send these two MIDI Messages to a MIDI sound module (i.a. a synth), you would hear that one note based on its pitch and velocity. When you record ❺ these two MIDI Messages in GarageBand, a MIDI Region will be created and these two MIDI Messages will be stored in that Region.
- ▸ When recording MIDI Messages in GarageBand, another important thing happens. GarageBand adds a fourth information to each recorded MIDI Message and that is its **Time Position** ❻.
- ▸ When you start recording ❺ in GarageBand, the Playhead moves along the timeline in the Ruler. Now when GarageBand receives an incoming MIDI Message (you pressed down the key), it looks up the time at that moment ❼ and adds that "time stamp" information to the MIDI Message ❽ when it stores it in the Region. This is the Time Position of that MIDI Message.
- ▸ When you release the key on your keyboard, it sends the Note-off message to GarageBand which looks up the time at that moment ❾ and stores that "time stamp" information ❿ with the that MIDI Message.
- ▸ So it needs two MIDI Messages to define one MIDI Event, a single note. Next, we will learn how the Editors use those stored MIDI Messages to visualize that note so you can see it and edit it.

Visualize Timing

Here is how the two MIDI Editors display the timing of notes based on the stored MIDI data.

 MIDI

Now we know that there are two separate MIDI Messages stored in the MIDI Region for each note. Only the time-stamp information (Time Position) is needed to visualize the timing aspect of the note.

 Piano Roll Editor

The Piano Roll Editor displays a matrix. Its vertical lines represent a time grid based on Musical Time. That means Bars and Beats (and Division and Ticks). Which grid lines you see depends on the zoom factor. Regardless which lines you see, the smallest time unit in GarageBand is one Tick. One quarter note is divided into 960 segments, Ticks. Think of 960 Divider Lines between two beat lines. That is the highest resolution in GarageBand, the native time grid. Each MIDI Message has to be placed on (rounded to) one of those Tick lines. Even if you can't see those fine Tick lines, the Control Bar Display shows the exact time value based on the four number values (bar, beat, division, tick). Any time stamp information that is stored with a recorded MIDI Message contains such a time value as its Time Position.

Now, when GarageBand visualizes a note in the Piano Roll Editor, it displays the note as a horizontal bar. The beginning of the bar indicates the time stamp of the Note-on Message and the end of that bar is at the time stamp of the Note-off Message. That means you can see against the Ruler where each note starts and stops. Also, as a nice visual reference, the longer the horizontal bar, the longer the duration of a note.

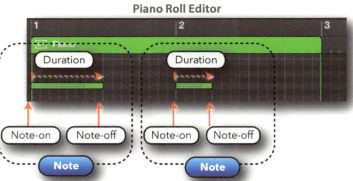

 Score Editor

The Score Editor uses western music notion with a staff as its time axis that is divided into bars with vertical lines. The Ruler on top again functions as a reference for the timeline. The visualization of the MIDI Messages is fairly simple. The time stamp of a Note-on message is used to place the note symbol on that position in the staff (1st bar, 2nd bar, etc.). The notation however doesn't use length as a reference of the note duration. Instead, each note length has a different symbol (that you learn in music class)  . The absence of a note produces a rest.

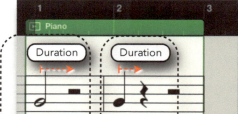

Absolute Time

The time base in GarageBand is always the native time grid referenced to the Musical Time of bars and beats even if you change the Ruler to display Absolute Time.

Visualize Pitch

MIDI

The Pitch is one of the four pieces of information stored in a MIDI Message of each note. That pitch information will be visualized in the Editors in the following way.

Piano Roll Editor

As we have just seen, the horizontal axis of the matrix represents the timing. Now the vertical axis is used for the pitch information. On the left side of the Matrix is a vertical keyboard that functions as a pitch reference. Based on the pitch information in the MIDI Message, the Piano Roll Editor places the bar that represents the note along the vertical axis.

Score Editor

The Score Editor uses the pitch information from the MIDI Message and places the note symbol on the 5-line staff. The note's vertical position on that staff and the clef sign at the beginning determine its pitch.

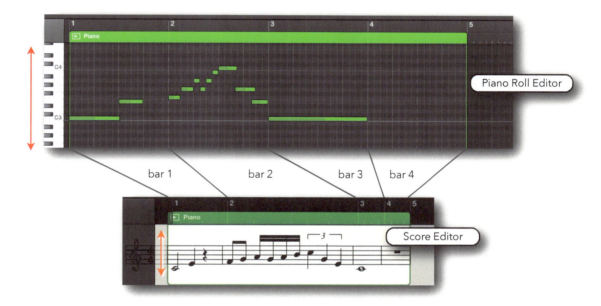

Visualize Velocity

MIDI

The Velocity is one of the four pieces of information stored in a MIDI Message of each note.

Piano Roll Editor

If you look closely, you can see a line inside each note bar. This line represents the Velocity of that note. The length of that line in relation to the length of the bar represents the Velocity value.

Score Editor

The Score Editor cannot display the Velocity information stored in a MIDI Message.

Other MIDI Messages

Most of the data that is stored in a MIDI Region are all the notes you played on your keyboard when you recorded your performance. However, there are other types of data that can be generated on a MIDI Controller and stored along with the notes in a MIDI Region. These MIDI Messages are often referred to as Controller because they control how the notes are affected by other parameters.

All those various controller data are also time-stamped when recorded in a MIDI Region in GarageBand. Those recorded MIDI Messages are displayed as individual Control Points that create an Automation Curve. That data can be displayed in the Piano Roll Editor in an optional lane below the notes in the so-called MIDI Draw Area.

Please note that the sound module (MIDI Software Instrument) that receives the MIDI signal has to have a Patch selected that can respond to those controller data.

➡ Pitch Bend

Many MIDI Keyboards have a special controller called a Pitch Bend Wheel on the left side of the Keyboard. This wheel can be moved up or down to generate Pitch Bend data that slides the pitch of the current note up or down. This is the typical Portamento effect.

➡ Modulation (CC#1)

A second wheel often found on MIDI Keyboards is the so-called "Mod Wheel". It modulates the pitch of a note up and down in a periodical movement also known as a Vibrato effect. This type of data belongs to the "Continuous Controller" data (CC). There are 128 available Continuous Controller in the MIDI specifications. The Modulation data is CC#1.

➡ Volume (CC#7)

Volume Controller data, also one of the Continuous Controller (number 7), can control the volume of a MIDI Software Instrument. This is in addition to the Volume Slider on the Track Header.

➡ Expression (CC#11)

The Expression Controller data (Continuous Controller No11) is sometimes used in Patches to also control the Volume.

➡ Sustain (CC#64)

The Sustain Controller has the same effect as the sustain pedal on a piano. It uses only two values, on or off. When on, it ignores all Note-off commands and lets all the notes ring out (sustain) until you send a Sustain off message.

This is the only controller data that is also displayed in the Score Editor as the standard Pedal on sign and Pedal off sign.

Understanding Quantize

Quantize might be one of the most important and often used features during editing. Everybody uses it and everybody seems to know how to use it. You play a MIDI Track with not-so-perfect timing, then you click the magic Quantize button and the timing is perfect. It's that simple. Or maybe there is a little more to it.

Let me reveal four insights about Quantization that you might or might not know (advanced topic!).

Insight 1: Quantization adds a Time Position Offset

To understand this statement, you have to be familiar with the following concept.

> GarageBand stores two time positions with each MIDI Note:
> The **Original Position** and the **Playback Position**

🔵 Original Position

The Original Position of a MIDI Note in a MIDI Region is defined by any of the three circumstances:
- **Record**: You record a new MIDI note at a specific position, its Original Position.
- **Create**: You create a new MIDI note at a specific position, its Original Position.
- **Move**: You move an existing MIDI note by manually dragging it to a new position, its new Original Position.

By default, this Original Position is also the Playback Position, the position the MIDI note is played back when the Playhead moves across during playback. So far so good. But now something could happen:

🔵 Offset (Quantize)

GarageBand can automatically move a MIDI note from its Original Position to a different time position. It does that when we use the Quantize Command to apply a Quantize value to a note. That Quantize Command, based on its instructions and other circumstances (which I'll get to in a moment), tells GarageBand to apply a time offset to the Original Position value (i.e. 19Ticks earlier, 420Ticks later). That means, the Playback Position is now different from the Original Position of the MIDI note, GarageBand moved the MIDI Note.

🔵 Playback Position

So, whenever we look at a MIDI note to see what its Playback Position is, know that it is determined by two factors, its Original Position + the Position Offset. Only if the Position Offset is zero, then the Playback Position is the same as the Original Position.

Time Position of a MIDI Note

➡ Timing Grid

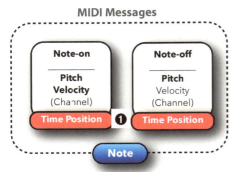

Remember, I explained earlier that a MIDI Note Message carries three pieces of information (Pitch, Velocity, Channel) and when recording that MIDI Message, GarageBand will add a forth one to it, its Time Position ❶ along the timeline in your Project. This Time Position determines where on GarageBand's Native Time Grid (bar-beat-division-tick) that note is located.

➡ Native Grid vs Quantize Grid

- The Original Position of a Note is its placement on GarageBand's Native Time Grid, on one of the 960 grid lines per beat. For example, the value in the Control Bar Display shows you at which position (which grid line) the Playhead is currently parked at (bar-beat-division-tick) ❷.
- To Quantize a note means to use a different grid, a special Quantize Grid. That tells GarageBand to move the Note now to the nearest of the available grid lines of the selected Quantize Grid.
- GarageBand offers 33 different Quantize Grids ❸ that you select from the Quantize Menu.

Here is an example that shows one bar of the Ruler ❹ and what happens when you apply different quantize values (different Quantize Grids) to a note.

- The green gridlines represent GarageBand's Native Time Grid which is 960 lines (ticks) per beat or 3840 lines per bar (if it is a 4/4 time signature). Selecting "off" ❺ from the Quantize Menu always places the note(s) back to their original Position based on the Native Grid.
- The blue lines represent the various Quantize Grids ❻. The lower number in the fraction indicates how many grid lines there are in one bar. For example, 1/16 means 16 available grid lines to move the note to. So the smallest note value can be a 16th note.
- The red dot indicates a recorded note. You can see the different position the quantize command moves that note depending what Quantize Grid is selected.

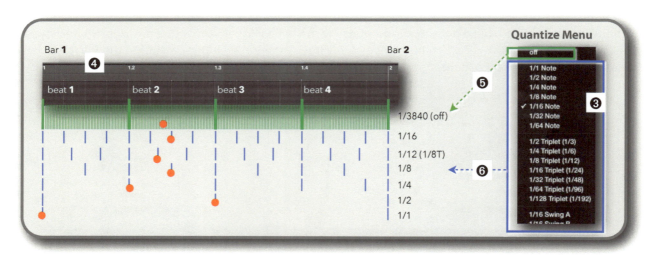

Insight 2: Quantize is a Command not a Parameter

Once we understand the concept of "Original Position + Position Offset = Playback Position," there is another important fact.

> A Quantize Value is a **Command** and not a **Parameter**

What does that mean?

Look at the following screenshot of the Piano Roll Editor. There is one note selected ❶ and the Inspector on the left ❷ displays its parameters, or does it?

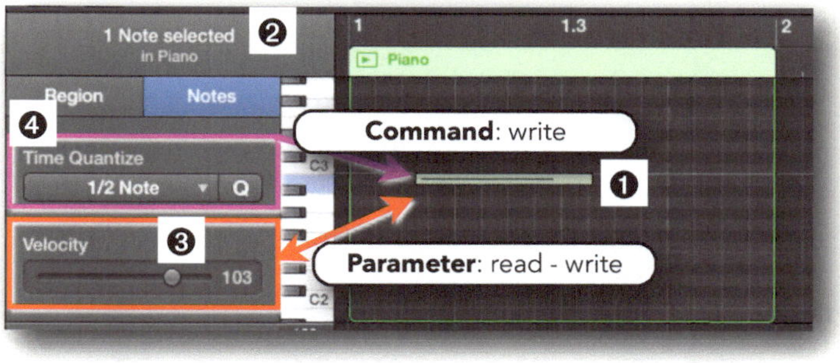

▶ **Velocity Parameter**: The Velocity Slider displays a value of 103 ❸. This is the Parameter value that is stored with the MIDI note. Any time we select a note, the slider will display (read) the velocity parameter value that is stored with the note. Changing that value on the slider will change (write) that new Velocity value.

▶ **Time Quantize Command**: Now let's look at the other "Parameter", the Quantize value. It looks like the note was quantized to a 1/2 note grid ❹. But that is NOT the case. The Quantize value in the Inspector does not display how the selected note <u>was quantized</u>. Instead, it shows, with what quantization value the selected note <u>will be quantized</u> when we use the Quantize Command.

What about when applying a Quantize to a Region?

A Region behaves differently than a Note regarding the Quantize feature. That's why there are two tabs in the MIDI Editors.

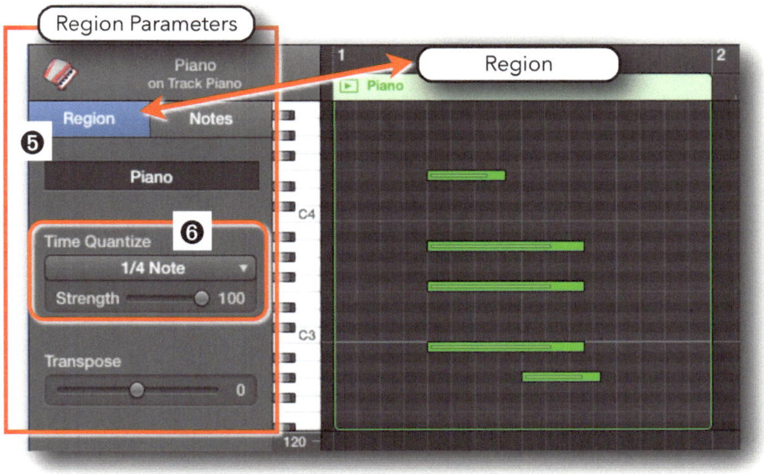

- Notes Tab selected ❷: In this view, you apply a quantize value as a command as I just explained. The applied Quantize value will not be stored with the note.

- Region Tab selected ❺: Whenever you apply a Quantize value to a Region, it actually stores that value as a "Region Parameter" with that MIDI Region. When you switch between Regions, the Quantize Button ❻ in the Inspector displays that Region Parameter and changes its value if a Region has a different Quantize value stored than the previously selected Region.

Although the Quantize value is stored with the Region (and can be considered a Parameter) it is not necessarily the value that **all** the MIDI notes inside the Region are quantized. To better understand this, let's reveal the next insight.

Insight 3: Quantization can be applied on two Levels

In the following diagram, I try to illustrate the complete picture how the Quantize feature is implemented in GarageBand. The most important aspect is that the Quantize command can be applied on two different levels and each one overwrites the other one.

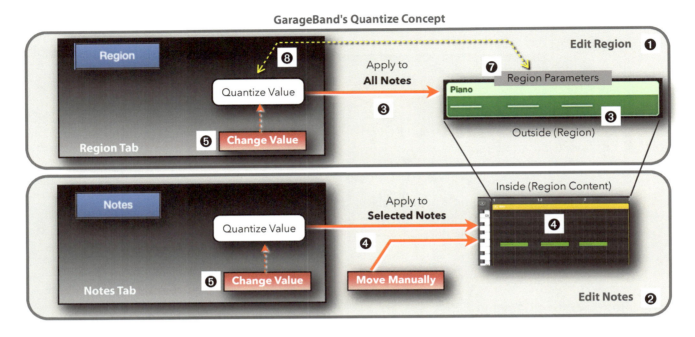

GarageBand's Quantize Concept

The two levels are the <u>Edit Regions</u> ❶ and the <u>Edit Note</u> ❷. And again, you are applying a command (Insight 2) and that command moves the MIDI Event away from its Original Position by adding an offset (Insight 1). Every time you apply a new Quantize command, the offset (how much the note gets moved) will change depending on the applied quantization value. Although this is a standard editing procedure where you update parameter values, in this case, there is a major difference:

- The update (sending a new quantize value) can be done in two places which affects different Objects: All Notes ❸ or Selected Notes ❹.
- GarageBand doesn't store the latest quantize value that was sent. Instead, it stores the "effect" which is a new position ("Playback Position") regardless of from where it was sent and with what value.

> Quantize Region applies to **All Notes**
> Quantize Notes applies to **Selected Notes**

▸ Every Quantize Command sent while in the Region View will be applied to all Notes in the Region(s) ❸. When in Notes View, only the selected Note(s) ❹ will be affected by the Quantization Command.

▸ Please note that the Quantize Command will be sent every time you change the value in the Quantize Menu ❺ in the Inspector or by using the Q-Button [Q].

▸ The Quantize value, applied in Region View ❸, is stored with the Region as its Region Parameter ❼ and is displayed ❽ in the MIDI Editor whenever you select the Region. However, if you have in the meantime quantized some Notes in the Notes View ❹, then the Region Parameter ❼ does not reflect the quantization of all Note Events inside the Region. It just tells you what value you used the last time to quantize the Region. Applying a Quantize value to the Region again will overwrite any individual Quantize value of a single note in that Region.

Insight 4: Quantize is based on the Region Timeline

Before explaining what this "Region Timeline" is, let's quickly review how GarageBand applies that Offset Position to the Original Position of a MIDI note.

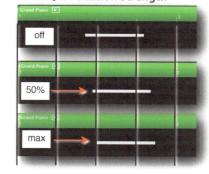
Quantization Strength

💀 Native Time Grid 960 ticks/beat

When you record MIDI notes (or any MIDI Events) in GarageBand along its timeline (x-axis), it doesn't record it at exactly the time you played it. It has an underlying Native Time Grid of 960ticks per beat. That is where it places the MIDI Events on. At a tempo of 120bpm, this grid has a resolution of 0.5ms. In other words, the smallest time division on that grid is 0.5ms. Each note you record is rounded to that grid and that becomes the "Original Position".

💀 Quantize Time Grid

When you set a quantize value, you choose a second Time Grid. When you apply that Quantize value to a note, that note will then be rounded to the nearest position on that Quantize Grid (the closest grid line) which becomes now the "Playback Position" until you apply a different Quantize Grid or remove the Grid so the note reverts back to its Original Position on the default Native Time Grid.

💀 Additional Quantize Conditions

Instead of moving a note exactly on a grid, you have the option to set a Strength value. Think about grid line magnets. If the grid has maximum magnetic strength (100), then the note will be pulled exactly onto the closest grid lines. However, you can set the strength to pull the note only a little bit towards the closest grid line. Please note that the Groove Track feature functions as an additional grid based on the Reference Track.

💀 Region Timeline

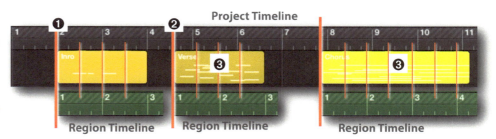

And here it comes. In case you might not have noticed, GarageBand doesn't place MIDI notes directly on the Project Timeline. What you see on the Track Lane are MIDI Regions, the containers that have the MIDI Notes embedded. That is why I make a big distinction between "Regions vs Region Content". Editing the Regions will affect all the MIDI Events inside equally. To edit individual Notes, you have to step inside into a MIDI Editor to access the Region Content.

What you see in the Workspace is the Project Timeline. You can place only Regions on that Timeline, on the Track Lane of specific Tracks. The position of those Regions (MIDI, Audio or Drummer Regions) is restricted to the same 960 ticks/beat grid resolution.

When you quantize a Region for example to 1/2 notes (now we know that you don't actually quantize Regions, you quantize the MIDI Events inside a Region), all the notes inside that Region move towards the 1/2 note grid and they line up perfectly on the beats of the Project Timeline. You think you quantized the notes to the Project Timeline - but you didn't.

Look at the following example:

The false illusion only happens if the Region starts at the beginning of a bar ❶ (which Regions usually do). If you move a Region to start somewhere in between a bar ❷ and you apply the same 1/2 quantization, then the MIDI notes WILL NOT line up to the 1/2 ❸ grid on the Project Timeline because they are quantized relative to the start of the Region. So a Region has its own "invisible Region Timeline" that the quantize command is applied to. The good news is that you don't have to worry about it as long as the MIDI Regions start at the beginning of a bar. Remember that GarageBand always rounds newly recorded MIDI Regions to the beginning of a bar.

For Audio Regions that doesn't matter because the Region Content of an Audio Region are not MIDI Events.

17 - The MIDI Editors

Piano Roll Editor

The Basic Concept

After the last chapter, we are now the MIDI edit experts, so let's start with one of the two MIDI Editors in GarageBand, the Piano Roll Editor and see how to apply those edit techniques.

Here is a recap of what you see in the Editor Window:
- Each note is represented by a horizontal bar ❶ placed on a grid.
- The vertical position on the grid represents the pitch. A vertical keyboard ❷ on the left functions as the reference for the pitch (y-axis).
- The horizontal position on the grid represents the time. The Ruler ❸ on top of the grid functions as the time reference (x-axis). Please note that the Ruler follows the selection in the Control Bar Display and displays either Musical Time 🎵 (Bars and Beats) or Absolute Time 🕐 (min:sec).
- The left edge of a note bar determines that start position of that note and its right edge determines the end of that note which, together, makes up the duration ❹ of a note.

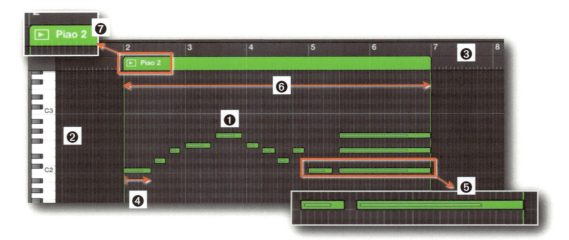

- Each note bar has a line ❺ inside. This line represents the Velocity of that note. The length of that line in relation to the length of the bar itself represents the Velocity value.

  As we have seen in the previous chapter, the **Velocity** is a parameter contained in each MIDI Note. It represents the value, how hard the MIDI keyboard has been struck when the note was recorded, ranging from 1 (soft) to 127 (hard). The Velocity usually corresponds to the loudness of a note but can also influence other parameters on a MIDI sound module that "plays" that note (filter, resonance, different samples, etc.)

- Recorded MIDI notes belong to a specific MIDI Region and the Piano Roll Editor makes that "container" visible by displaying the borders of the Region that those notes "belong" to as vertical lines ❻.
- The Ruler displays the Region Header ❼ with the Region Name and a "Solo Play" Button ▶️.

The Piano Roll Editor is one of the most common MIDI Editors in DAWs for displaying and editing MIDI notes. You might have used that interface in other DAWs before and think that you can edit the MIDI notes right away. However, this is not the case. GarageBand uses a special interface you might want to get familiar with first.

The GarageBand Concept

There are two main aspects of the Piano Roll Editor that you have to understand in GarageBand before you start editing anything. You have to know what you see and what you edit in the window.

➡ ***What do you see***

▸ The Piano Roll Editor does NOT display the content of only one single Region. It always displays a whole Track ❶ with all the Regions ❷ on that Track and the detailed view of the enclosed MIDI Notes of each Region ❸.

▸ Please pay attention to which one of the Tracks it displays.
- If no Region is selected in the Workspace, then the Editor displays the Track that is currently selected in the Tracks Area.
- If one or multiple Regions are selected in the Workspace, then the Piano Roll Editor displays the top Track that has a Region selected ❺ regardless what Track is selected ❹.

▸ The highlighted Regions in the Workspace ❺ are also highlighted in the Piano Roll Editor ❻.

➡ ***What do you edit***

Another specialty of the Piano Roll interface are the two tabs in the area on the left (the Piano Roll Inspector) of the Piano Roll Editor. They determine what the target is for the editing commands you choose in the Piano Roll Editor.

▸ **Region ❼**: When the Region tab is selected, then any command you choose in the Piano Roll Inspector is applied to ALL notes of the selected Region or Regions.

▸ **Notes ❽**: When the Notes tab is selected, then any command you choose in the Piano Roll Inspector is only applied to the SELECTED notes in the Piano Roll Editor. Please note that you can apply an edit command to selected notes of multiple Regions in the Editor at once.

Interface

Now let's go over the various elements of the interface of the Piano Roll Editor.

➡ Main Section

The Piano Roll Editor is divided into the four sections:

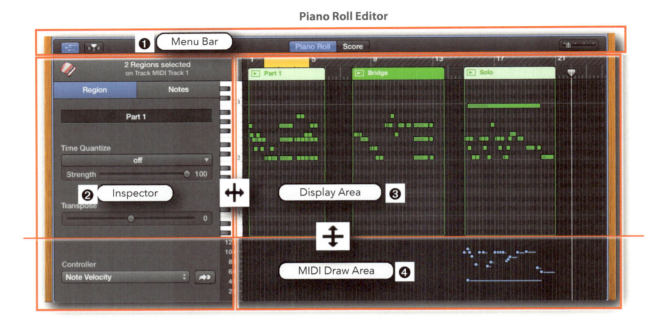

- 🔘 **Menu Bar ❶**

  The Menu Bar on top contains the following buttons:
  ▸ **MIDI Draw Button** : This toggles the visibility of the MIDI Draw Area at the bottom of the Piano Roll Editor.
  ▸ **Catch Playhead Button** : This button toggles the Autoscroll feature for the Piano Roll Editor independent from the Catch Playhead Button in the Tracks Area. If activated, the Playhead will stay fixed at the center of the Display Area which scrolls automatically underneath it.
  ▸ **Piano Roll - Score** : These two buttons switch the Editor view between the Piano Roll Editor and the Score Editor.
  ▸ **Zoom Slider** : This slider zooms the Display Area horizontally. You can also use the *Pinch* Gesture on the Track Pad or *opt+scroll* horizontally.

- 🔘 **Inspector ❷**

  The Inspector on the left contains the various displays and controls for editing the Region Content.

- 🔘 **Display Area ❸**

  The Display Area is like the Workspace in the Tracks Area just as a single Track Lane. It displays all the Regions and its contained MIDI Notes along the Timeline.

- 🔘 **MIDI Draw Area ❹**

  This section can be shown or hidden with the MIDI Draw Button in the Menu Bar. It displays additional MIDI controller data stored in the Regions.

➡ **Display Area**

The Display Area functions as a single Track Lane. Make sure you understand what you can do and what you cannot do.

> **You can edit the MIDI Notes (Region Content) - NOT the Regions**

I'll explain the specific editing commands a little later. Let me just go over the elements that you see on that Display Area.

- **Grid ❶**: The Display Area is a grid where the MIDI notes (horizontal bars) are placed on. The resolution (visible grid line) depends on how much you zoomed in or out.
- **Ruler ❷**: The Ruler is tied to the grid of the Display Area and functions as a timeline the same as in the Workspace of the Tracks Area. The units are displayed in either Musical Time 🎵 (bars and beats) or Absolute Time 🕐 (min:sec) depending on the Control Bar Display setting.
- **Cycle Area ❸**: The upper portion of the Ruler displays the yellow Cycle Area if activated 🔄 It displays the same Cycle Area as in the main Ruler of the Workspace.
- **Playhead ❹**: The lower portion of the Ruler displays the Playhead. The Catch Playhead Button 🔽 in the Menu Bar controls only this Playhead behavior, not the Playhead in the Workspace.
- **Keyboard ❺**: The vertical keyboard on the left functions as an orientation (y-axis) for the pitch.
- **Regions ❻**: All the Regions on the currently displayed Track are visible with their vertical border lines. Remember, you cannot edit the Region itself (move, resize, etc.), only the Region Content inside.
- **Region Header ❼**: Each Region displays in the lower portion of the Ruler its Region Header that is highlighted when the Region is selected. Besides the Region Name, the Header also includes the Solo Play Button ❽. When you click on it, the Cycle Area will change to the length of that Region and it plays only that Region (solo) in Cycle Mode. Stop it by clicking that button again or hit the *space bar*. The Cycle Area returns to its previous position. Please note that the Playhead, the Region Header, and the Control Bar Display turn yellow while in Solo Mode.

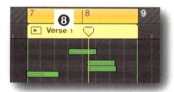

- **Notes ❾**: You can edit all the MIDI Notes (horizontal bars) in the Display Area directly with common mouse actions (move, resize, copy, delete, etc.) or by selecting them first and applying edit commands.

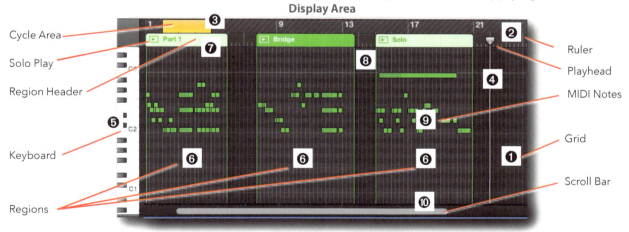

Display Area

- **Scroll**: You scroll the Display Area vertically and horizontally with the standard scroll commands. Use the Scroll Bars ❿ on the Display Area, use the *Scroll* Gestures on your Track Pad
- **Zoom**: You can only zoom the Display Area horizontally by using the Zoom Slider on the Menu Bar, the *Pinch* Gesture *opt+scroll* horizontally, or *cmd+Left/RightArrow*.. However, you can *drag* the Divider Line up to increase the space vertically.

➡ *Inspector*

Please, be aware! The Inspector has only a few controls and some even might look familiar. But that is exactly the danger. You should not go ahead and use any of the controls without first understanding how they work or how they are implemented in GarageBand. The following section might look a little bit more advanced, but it is necessary to wrap your head around it if you want to use the Piano Roll Editor to edit your music.

You have to ask yourself two questions:
- ☑ **Interface**: How does the Interface work or what do you see, why and when?
- ☑ **Controls**: What are the available controls that I can use to edit notes?

Interface

I mentioned the roll of an Inspector Window a few times already but it is worth repeating, especially in the context of the Piano Roll Editor:

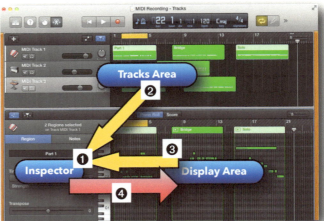

- ▸ **See**: The Inspector Window changes its content to display the data of objects that are selected in a different Window or Window Pane. In the case of the Piano Roll Editor, what is displayed in its Inspector ❶ depends on what is selected in the Tracks Area ❷ of the GarageBand Window or the Display Area ❸ of the Piano Roll Editor.
- ▸ **Affect**: Changing the setting in the Inspector Window changes the data of those objects of the currently selected window. In the case of the Piano Roll Editor, the Parameters are applied to the notes ❹ in the Display Area of the Piano Roll Editor where you can see the changes visually right away.

So before you touch any of the controls in the Inspector (**Affect**), make sure to know what is displayed (**See**). Only then you know what notes you are editing.

Display Status

The Piano Roll Inspector can have three different display statuses. Only if you aware of what the current display status is, you will know what MIDI notes you are actually editing with the available controls.

- **None**: No Regions are selected in the Tracks Area ❷ of the GarageBand Window and no Notes are selected in the Display Area ❸ of the Piano Roll Editor.
- **Region**: One or multiple Regions are selected in the Tracks Area ❷ of the GarageBand Window.
- **Notes**: One or multiple Notes are selected in the Display Area ❸ of the Piano Roll Editor.

Please note that the Display Status doesn't change the appearance or any selection in the Display Area, only what elements are displayed in the Inspector. The implementation of these three display statuses in GarageBand is a little problematic. There are only two buttons, "Region" and "Notes", that indicate the current display status. The third status "None" is hidden from the user. This makes sense when trying to simplify the user interface. However, the third status is still active and the user might accidentally affect the position of MIDI notes without knowing why this is happening. To avoid that, I will explain all three display statuses and maybe you will even find yourself using that third (advanced) display status all the time.

Here is the implementation of the three display statuses:

▸ **Notes ❶**
- How to select: *Click* the Notes Tab in the Inspector.
- Status Indication ❹: The Notes Tab is blue (active). The Inspector Header displays how many notes are selected and in what Regions. If notes are selected in multiple Regions, then it displays the number of Regions. If you select notes with the same start position, then GarageBand interprets that as a chord and displays the chord symbol.
- Available Controls ❼: Time Quantize and Velocity.
- What is affected: Only the selected Notes in the Display Area will be edited.

▸ **Region ❷**
- How to select: *Click* the Region Tab in the Inspector.
- Status Indication ❺: The Region Tab is blue (active). The Inspector Header displays the name of the selected Region or how many Regions are selected. The second line displays the Track Name and the Track Icon is also displayed.
- Available Controls ❽: Region Name, Time Quantize, Quantize Strength, Transpose.
- What is affected: All the notes of the selected Region(s) will be edited. Please note that although you can see the Region in the Piano Roll, you cannot select them there. You have to select the Region(s) in the Workspace of the Tracks Area.

▸ **None ❸**
- How to select: *Click* the Region Tab and deselect any Regions and any Notes.
- Status Indication ❻: The Region Tab is blue (active) and the Track Header displays "No Regions selected" ❿. The Inspector Header also displays a Track Icon and a Track Name, but that is only the name of the previously selected Track and has no effect.
- Available Controls ❾: Time Quantize. Strength and Transpose controls are visible but have no effect.
- What is affected: Think about it as an "automatic future quantize value". That means whenever you record a new MIDI Region, its notes will be automatically quantized with the value you set for the Time Quantize. Please note that the Quantize command is a non-destructive playback parameter. You can change it to any other value later or set it to "none" to retain the original recorded "un-quantized" note position.

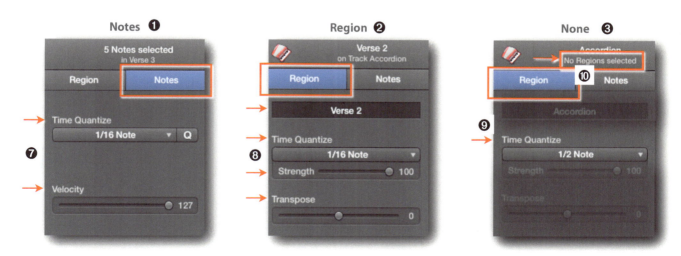

17 - The MIDI Editors

Controls

Here is a look at the Controls that are available in the Inspector. Make sure to resize the Window Pane high enough to display all the Controls.

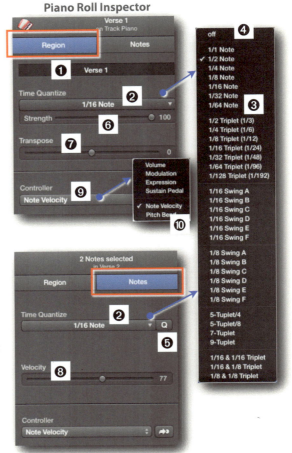

▸ **Region Name ❶** (Regions only): This field displays the currently selected Region (or the first Region of multiple selected Regions). You can **double-click** on the field to enter a new Region Name for one or multiple selected Regions. When you enter a number at the end (Part 1), then all the selected Regions will be numbered sequentially. (Part 1, Part 2, Part 3, etc.)

▸ **Time Quantize ❷**: This is a popup button that opens a menu ❸ with a variety of quantize values (33 Quantize Grids). They determine the timing grid a note will be moved to. Selecting "off" ❹ will disable the quantize value and resets the note to their original recorded time position, the Native Time Grid (960Ticks/quarter). You apply a Quantize value by selecting it from the menu. The Notes View has an additional Q Button ❺ that lets you apply the currently visible Quantize value to the selected notes.

▸ **Quantize Strength ❻** (Regions only): The slider sets the Quantize Strength. The value determines how far a note should be pulled towards the selected quantize grid. Select from 0 (no quantize) to 100 (pulled on the timing grid).

▸ **Transpose ❼** (Regions only): The slider lets you set a transposition value in semitones from -24 (two octaves down) to +24 (two octaves up). Each Region Header on the Track Lane will display any applied Transpose value next to the Region name.

▸ **Velocity ❽** (Notes only): Select a Note and the slider will display its Velocity value. Move the slider up or down to change the Velocity value for that note. If you have multiple notes selected, then the slider displays the value of the note with the highest Velocity. Moving the slider up or down changes the Velocity value for all notes proportionally.

▸ **Controller ❾**: This menu button is only visible if the MIDI Draw Area is visible (toggle its visibility with the MIDI Draw Button in the Inspector's Menu Bar). **Click** on the button to open the Controller Menu that lets you select which data to display in the MIDI Draw Area or **click** the "Next Controller" ❿ Button to display other available data. Make sure to have Region View and at least one Region selected.

➡ **MIDI Draw Area**

The MIDI Draw Area can display different types of additional MIDI data stored with the MIDI Region. These are mostly controller data that I mentioned in the previous chapter. I explain how to edit those controllers a little later.

Please note that you can resize the height of the MIDI Draw Area by dragging the Divider Line.

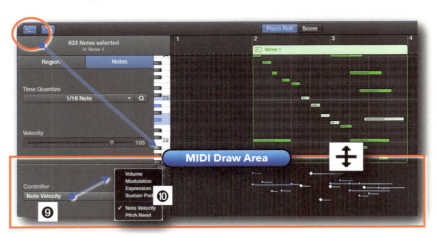

Edit Notes Directly

Using any of the controls in the Inspector window to edit the Notes in the Piano Roll requires two steps, select the Notes and then apply the command. However, you can also edit the Notes directly with the mouse by using any of the following commands.

➡ **Add Notes**

Usually, the notes displayed in the Piano Roll Editor are the ones that you recorded into GarageBand by playing your MIDI keyboard. However, you can also enter notes manually with your Mouse Pointer.

- ▸ Holding down the *command key* while moving over the Display Area of the Piano Roll changes the Pointer Tool to the Pencil Tool.
- ▸ **Pitch and Start**: *Cmd+click* anywhere on the Display Area to create a new note. The position on the matrix you click on determines the Pitch (vertically) and the start position (horizontally) of the Note.
- ▸ **Length**: The length of the newly created note depends on a few factors.
  - When you just click once, then a note with the default length of 1/4 note will be created.
  - When you *click-hold*, you can drag the note to any length before releasing the mouse.
  - This "set length while creating" action will also set the new default length for any newly created note from now on (until you create a new default length by doing "set length while creating a note")
- ▸ **Velocity**: Manually created notes will have a default Velocity value of 60.
- 💡 Assistance: The Help Tag displays the length in bar-beat-division-tick which might be a little strange to read. In this example, the length is"0bar-0beat-2division-0tick" which is 1/8 note long (1 Division is 1/16 note).

Create Note and set length

Length: 0 0 2 0

➡ **Select (deselect) Notes**

There are a wide variety of commands to select notes. Please note that you can select any note in the Display Area from different Regions.

- 🖱 *Click* on a single note
- 🖱 *Sh+click* on multiple notes in a sequence
- 🖱 *Drag* around a group of notes ("lasso around") to select all of them
- 🖱 *Sh+click* on a note to deselect one note
- 🖱 *Cmd+A* to select all notes in the Display Area
- 🖱 *Click* on the Display Area background to deselect all notes

Selected (highlighted) Notes

You can also use the vertical keyboard on the left to select notes

- 🖱 *Click* a key to select all the notes in all Regions in the Display Area with that pitch
- 🖱 *Sh+Click* individual keys on the keyboard to add the select notes with that pitch to the group
- 🖱 *Drag* along the keyboard to select a range of keys

💡 Assistance: The selected notes are highlighted and the vertical keyboard displays a blue key if there is any selected note with that pitch.

➡ Move Notes horizontally (time position)

Snap Mode is automatically active during any horizontal dragging operation, aligning the note to the visible grid lines. The more you're zoomed in, the more grid lines are visible.

- *Drag* one or multiple selected notes
- *Ctr+drag* disables Snap Mode while moving

○ Assistance: There is a wide variety of information especially in the Help Tag while dragging notes around.

- The upper line of the Help Tag displays the time position ❶ and the lower portion displays the pitch ❷
- If the note is at its original position or pitch, then that number is yellow ❸.
- If you move a note, then the number for the original position or pitch turns white and next to it appears the time deviation ❹ and the pitch offset ❺ in semitones.
- Moving notes(s) leaves a ghost note(s) ❻ behind that indicates the original note position.
- A gray bar ❼ across the Display Area shows the pitch of the note you are moving. It extends all the way to the keyboard on the left which highlights that note in blue ❽ and plays the note every time you move it up or down in pitch.
- A thin white vertical line ❾ moves with the start position of the note you are moving to act as an alignment guide.

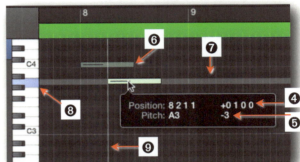

Move a Note

➡ Move Notes vertically (pitch)

You can change the pitch of a note (or group of notes) by dragging it vertically up or down.

- *Drag* one or multiple selected notes vertically
- Use the Key Command *opt+UpArrow* or *opt+DownArrow* to move the selected note(s) by a semitone.
- Use the Key Command *sh+opt+UpArrow* or *sh+opt+DownArrow* to move them by an octave

➡ Copy Notes

For copying notes, the same procedures apply as for moving Regions. Just hold down the *option* key. An additional plus ⊕ icon ❿ appears next to the Pointer Tool to indicate that you are copying the note and not just moving it.

- *Opt+drag* a note to copy it to a new position.
- Us the standard copy-paste functionality with the Key Command *cmd+C* and *cmd+V* or from the Edit Menu (*Copy*, *Paste*). The copied notes will be pasted at the current Playhead Position on the selected Track.

Copy a Note

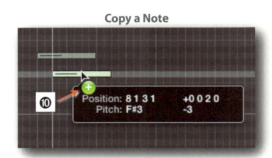

Absolute Time

When you select to display Absolute Time in the Control Bar Display, then the Help Tag will also display all the time values as absolute time.

Absolute Time

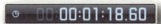

➡ **Resize**

The left and right edge of a note bar is a Click Zone. The Pointer Tool changes to the Resize Tool when you move over it. *Drag* the left or right edge of the note.

💡 Assistance:
- Dragging the left border changes the Start Position of the note without affecting the end position.
- The Help Tag displays that Position value.
- Dragging the right border changes the end position of the note without affecting the start position.
- The Help Tag displays the Length value.

Resize Multiple Notes

There is some special functionality when resizing multiple selected notes at the same time.
- 📌 **Relative Length Change**: *Drag* the end point on any of the selected notes left or right to resize all notes proportionally by the same amount.
- 📌 **Absolute Length Change**: *Sh+opt+drag* the end point on any of the selected notes left or right to resize all selected notes to the same length. You can press or release the shift key while dragging to switch between relative and absolute length change.
- 📌 **Same End Position**: *Sh+drag* the end of any of the selected notes will resize all notes to the same end position.

➡ **Split Notes, Join Notes**

The "Split Regions" and "Join Regions" command in the Edit Menu changes to "Split Notes" and "Join Notes" when the Piano Roll Editor is selected (has key focus).

➡ **Delete Note**

Select the note(s) and choose any of the common delete commands:
- 📌 Key Command *delete*
- 📌 Main Menu Command *Edit ➤ Delete*

Edit Controllers

As I showed earlier, any additional MIDI Controller data that are stored with a MIDI Region can be displayed in the MIDI Draw Area. You can edit those Controller data and also create new data with specific mouse actions.

First, you make the MIDI Draw Area visible with the MIDI Draw Button on the Menu Bar and then choose any of the six controller types from the Controller Menu or click on the "Next Controller" Button.

➡ **Velocity**

Velocity is technically not a MIDI Controller data. We learned earlier that it is part of the MIDI Note Message. Each horizontal bar ❶ in the Piano Roll Display Area representing a note, has a line ❷ inside that indicates the Velocity value for that MIDI note. The length of that line in relation to the length of the bar itself represents the Velocity value.

You can also read and write the Velocity value of a selected note with the Velocity Slider ❸ in the Inspector.

Now the MIDI Draw Display provides an alternate interface to display and edit those Velocity values for each note.

Here is how it works:

▸ Each note bar ❶ in the Display Area has a corresponding Velocity line ❹ in the MIDI Draw Area with a dot at the beginning marking the start position of this note.
▸ Selecting a note bar (highlighted) ❺ selects its Velocity line ❹ and vice versa.
▸ The length of that line ❹ matches the length of its note bar ❺.
▸ The vertical position of those lines indicate the Velocity value, referenced to the y-axis on the left ❻. The higher the line ❹, the higher the Velocity value. That means, the height of the Velocity Line in the MIDI Draw Area corresponds to the length of the Velocity Line ❷ inside the Note Bar in the Display Area and also the displayed value on the Velocity Slider ❸.
▸ **Drag** the dot up and down to change the Velocity value for that note. The movement is restricted to the vertical direction.
▸ A Help Tag displays the Velocity value ❼ while you drag the line. As you can see, the Position and Pitch value are yellow ❽ because they are not changing, only the Velocity value does

Additional Action

 Sh+drag to select a group of Velocity lines by "lasso around" them
 Opt+drag snaps to the original Velocity
 Ctr+drag lets you move the line up and down in smaller increments
 Drag multiple selected Velocity lines: The lines get squeezed at the top and bottom when moved all the way up or down but the lines retain their relationship when moved back (if you haven't released the mouse button yet). Once you release the mouse button, the values at that moment stay permanent (unless you undo the action).
 Draw a line in the MIDI Draw Area to create velocity ramps (crescendo and decrescendo)

Here is the procedure how to draw velocity lines.

Original Velocity values

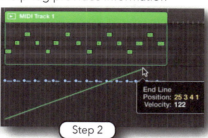

Step 1

Draw a line with the Pointer Tool. A Help Tag provides information

Step 2

Release the mouse so the Velocity values follow the line you drew

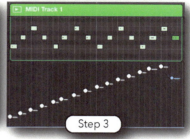

Step 3

If you are looking for a really advanced feature: Use the **cmd+draw** command to apply a line that scales the current Velocity values.

➡ Automation Curves

The other five Controller data that can be displayed in the MIDI Draw Area use a common interface known as an Automation Curve. Each value is represented by a dot (Control Point) on a graph where the x-axis represents the time (along the timeline of the Ruler) and the y-axis the value of the controller. The Control Points are automatically connected with lines to end up as the Automation Curve that describes the change of that Controller value over time.

Here are the available actions to edit the Automation Curve.

- ▸ **Cmd+click** to create a single Control Point
- ▸ **Cmd+drag** to draw a line. Multiple Control Points are created along your "drawings"
- ▸ **Click** on the line to create a new Control Point
- ▸ **Click** on a Control Point to delete that Control Point
- ▸ **Drag** a Control Point or a line up and down or left and right to reshape the curve
- ▸ **Drag** around an area to select a whole section of the curve
- ▸ **Drag** the line of a section vertically to move the curve in absolute values
- ▸ **Drag** a Control Point of a section vertically to moves the curve relative to each other. This compresses or expands the data
- ▸ Use the **delete** command to remove a whole section of the selected Automation Curve
- ▸ **Ctr+drag** for finer resolution

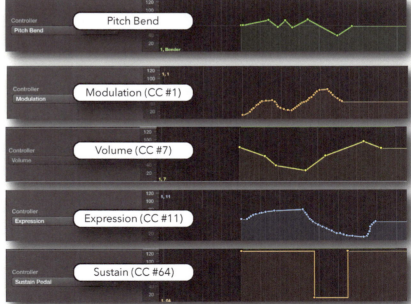

Available Controller Data in the MIDI Draw Area

Score Editor

The Score Editor is the second MIDI Editor in GarageBand. It displays the recorded MIDI notes in standard musical notation. For this chapter, I assume that you have basic knowledge about music notation itself (Notes, Rests, Staff, Clefs, etc.) in order to understand what we discuss in this chapter.

Many of the controls and actions in the Score Editor are similar to the Piano Roll Editor. After all, it is just a different user interfaces for the same thing, MIDI Notes in your MIDI Regions.

The GarageBand Concept

Again, here are the same two main aspects of the Score Editor that you have to understand.

➡ **What do you see**

▸ The Score Editor does NOT display the content of only one single Region. It always displays a whole Track ❶ with all the Regions ❷ on that Track and the view of the enclosed MIDI Notes ❸.

▸ Please pay attention to which one of the Tracks it displays.
- If no Region is selected in the Workspace, then the Editor displays the Track that is currently selected in the Tracks Area.
- If one or multiple Regions are selected in the Workspace, then the Score Editor displays the top Track that has a Region selected ❺ regardless what Track is selected ❹.

▸ The highlighted Region(s) in the Workspace ❺ is also highlighted in the Score Editor ❻.

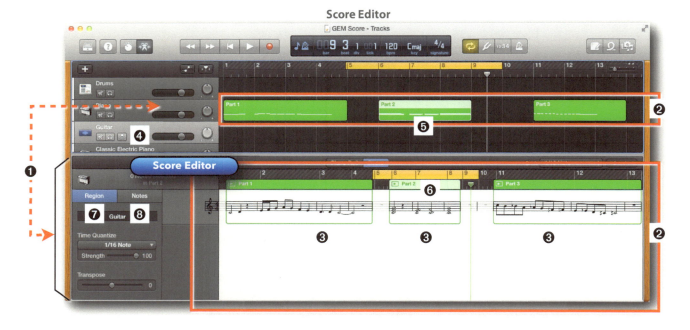

➡ **What do you edit**

The Score Editor has the same two tabs in the Inspector, "Region" and "Notes".

▸ **Region ❼**: When the Region tab is selected, then any command you choose in the Score Inspector is applied to <u>ALL</u> notes of the selected Region or Regions.

▸ **Notes ❽**: When the Notes tab is selected, then any command you choose in the Score Inspector is only applied to the <u>SELECTED</u> notes in the Score Editor. Please note that you can apply an edit command to selected notes of multiple Regions at once.

Interface

Now let's go over the various elements of the interface of the Score Editor.

➡ Main Section

The Score Editor is divided into three sections:

- 🟡 **Menu Bar ❶**

    The Menu Bar on top contains the following buttons.
    - ▸ ~~Catch Playhead~~: The Score Editor doesn't have the Catch Playhead button . The window is always in Autoscroll Mode.
    - ▸ **Piano Roll - Score** : These two buttons switch the Editor view between the Piano Roll Editor and the Score Editor.
    - ▸ **Grid**: This is a visual Quantize Grid only applied to the appearance of the notes. It has no effect on the actual playback itself.
    - ▸ **Zoom Slider** : This slider zooms the Display Area as a whole, making the score appearance bigger or smaller. You can also use the *Pinch* Gesture on the Track Pad.

- 🟡 **Inspector ❷**

    The Inspector on the left contains the various displays and controls for editing the Region Content.

- 🟡 **Display Area ❸**

    The Display Area is like the Workspace in the Tracks Area just for a single Track Lane. It displays all the Regions and its contained MIDI Notes along the Timeline as standard musical notation. Please note that the length of the time divisions in the Ruler vary depending on how many notes are in a bar.

- 🟡 ~~MIDI Draw Area~~

    The Score Editor cannot display the MIDI Draw Area to show MIDI Controllers. The Sustain Pedal is the only exception which is displayed directly in the Score.

- ▸ **Scroll**: You can scroll the Display Area only horizontally. Use the Scroll Bar ❹ on the Display Area or use the *Scroll* Gestures on your Track Pad. Also, the *end* key scrolls forward and the *home* key scrolls backwards.
- ▸ **Zoom**: You only can zoom the Display Area horizontally by using the Zoom Slider on the Menu Bar or the *Pinch* Gesture. This will make the score bigger or smaller. Use the Divider Line ❺ between the Inspector and Display Area to resize these two sections proportionally.

17 - The MIDI Editors

Score Inspector

The concept of the Inspector Window in the Score Editor is the same as in the Piano Roll Editor which I just explained.

You are editing the MIDI Notes (Region Content) - NOT the Regions

The functionality of the two tabs is also the same:

Even the controls in the Inspector window are the same with the exception of an additional control in the Notes tab.

Here is a look at the controls that are available in the Inspector. Make sure to resize the Window Pane high enough to display all the controls.

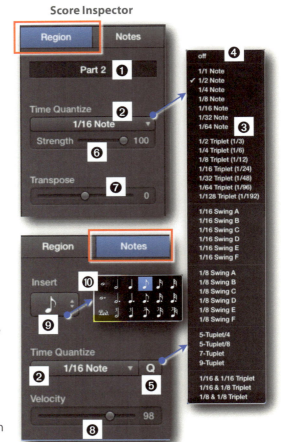

- ▶ **Region Name ❶** (Regions only): This field displays the currently selected Region (or the first Region of multiple selected Regions). *Double-click* on the field to enter a new Region Name.

- ▶ **Time Quantize ❷**: Selecting any of the 33 Quantize Grid values from this popup button will quantize the selected Notes. The Notes View has an additional Q Button ❺ that lets you apply the currently visible Quantize value to the selected notes.

- ▶ **Quantize Strength ❻** (Regions only): Set the Quantize Strength between 0 and 100.

- ▶ **Transpose ❼** (Regions only): Set the transposition value in semitones from -24 (two octaves down) to +24 (two octaves up). Each Region Header on the Track Lane displays any applied Transpose value next to the Region name.

- ▶ **Velocity ❽** (Notes only): The slider displays the Velocity value of the selected note. Move the slider to change it.

There is one Control specific to the Score Editor.

- ▶ **Insert**: Select a Note Symbol from the popup menu that represents a specific note value. This is the Note Symbol when manually adding notes in the Display Area.

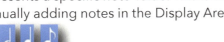

You can also add Pedal markers to the score which adds a MIDI CC#64 to the Region.

234 17 - The MIDI Editors

Display Area

Here are the various interface elements in the Display Area:

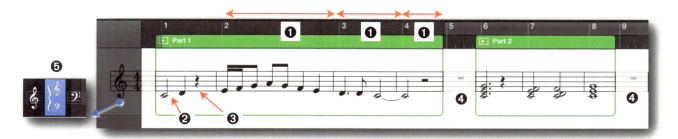

➡ **Regions**

The current Track is displayed as one long musical staff with the Regions and its notes visually overlaid on top of it. This way you can see the note symbols (the Region Content) and still identify the Regions the notes belong to.

➡ **Bars**

Unlike the Ruler in all the other Windows, the Ruler in the Score Editor displays the bars non-symmetrical. The bars are visually longer or shorter ❶ depending on how many notes have to be displayed.

➡ **Rests**

Each Note symbol ❷ represents a MID Note (a note-on MIDI Message plus a note-off MIDI Message). The Rest symbols ❸ are automatically placed in the Region where there is no MIDI note. The "empty" space between two Regions is also displayed with rest symbols ❹.

➡ **Clefs**

You can choose from three different clefs to display the Track. Click on the Clef to open a popup menu with three options ❺. Treble Clef ❻, Bass Clef ❼, Treble+Bass Clef ❽. For that piano style notation, the split point between upper and lower staff is the C3.

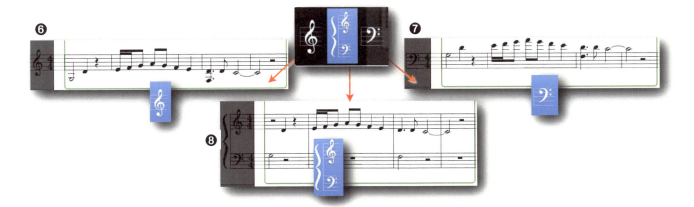

➡ **Signature (Key - Time)**

Whatever Key Signature and Time Signature you have set for your Project in the Control Bar Display ❾ will automatically be displayed at the beginning of the staff ❿.

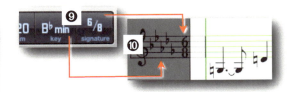

Edit Notes Directly

Here are the commands to edit Notes directly in the Display Area.

➡ Add (Insert) Notes

Holding down the **command key** while moving over the Display Area of the Score Editor also changes the Pointer Tool to the Pencil Tool. However, the process of adding the actual note is a little bit different.

- ▸ **Note Length**: In the Score Editor, you have to determine the note length first before you create the note. Select from the Insert popup menu what symbol you want to add. The different note symbols (note values) define the length of the MIDI note you add to the Region.
- ▸ **Pitch and Position**: Now, **cmd+click** on the staff to add that note value at the click position.
    - The 5 lines of the staff are your guidance for the vertical position of the added note (the pitch). Please note that you can click above or below the staff to add a note with ledger lines.
    - Although not as accurate as the matrix in the Piano Roll Editor, the existing bar lines on the staff give you the horizontal orientation to place the note at the right time position.
    - As an optional third step, you could keep pressing the mouse and keep moving the note to precisely position the note symbol or moving it in any direction on the staff, even between different Regions.
- ▸ **Velocity**: Manually created notes will have a default Velocity value of 64.

Adding a Pedal Symbol to the score adds two symbols, the Pedal-on 𝓟𝓮𝓭. and the Pedal-off ✻ sign. This creates two MIDI controller data, MIDI CC#64 value 64 (on) and 0 (off). Moving the symbol will move the MIDI Event in the MIDI Region.

💡 Assistance: The Help Tag displays three values. The position value again is in that confusing long form (bar-beat-division-tick). The pitch value is as expected and the third value, the MIDI Channel, is always set to Channel 1. Please note that all the values are yellow which makes sense because these are the original values of the note you are creating even if you move it around while positioning it.

Add a New Note

➡ Select (deselect) Notes

The commands for selecting notes are the same as with the Piano Roll Editor. The visual feedback however is different. Here, selected notes are not only highlighted, they also display a horizontal Duration Bar attached to the note. This simulates the horizontal Note Bar we know from the Piano Roll Editor. That Duration Bar is used for resizing the notes.

- **Click** on a single note
- **Sh+click** on multiple notes in a sequence
- **Drag** around a group of Notes ("lasso around") to select all of them
- **Sh+click** on a note to deselect one note
- **Cmd+A** to select all Notes in the Display Area
- **Click** on the Display Area background to deselect all notes

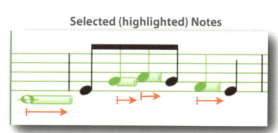

Selected (highlighted) Notes

➡ Move Notes

Move a Note

- ▸ *Drag* a Note to change just that single note.
- ▸ Select multiple notes first and then *drag* one of them (that's the info, displayed in the Help Tag) to move the whole group.
- ▸ You can *drag* the note(s) in any direction to change the pitch (vertical movement) or the time position (horizontal movement).
- ▸ Use the Key Command *opt+UpArrow* or *opt+DownArrow* to move the selected note(s) by a semitone.
- ▸ Use the Key Command *sh+opt+UpArrow* or *sh+opt+DownArrow* to move them by an octave.

🔔 Assistance: There is a wide variety of information, especially in the Help Tag, while dragging notes around.

- The upper line of the Help Tag displays the time position ❶ and the lower portion displays the pitch ❷
- Any value that is the current ("un-moved") value is displayed in yellow numbers ❸.
- If you move a note, then the number for the original time position or pitch turns white and next to it appears the time deviation ❹ and the pitch offset ❺ in semitones.
- Moving notes(s) leaves a ghost note(s) behind that indicates the original note position.

➡ Copy Notes

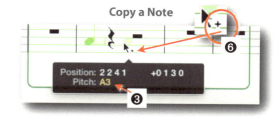
Copy a Note

For copying notes, the same procedures apply as for moving notes. Just hold down the *option* key. This time, instead of a big green plus sign, there is only a tiny little plus ❻ next to the pointer.

- 🔔 *Opt+drag* a note to copy it to a new position.
- 🔔 Use the standard copy-paste functionality with the Key Command *cmd+C* and *cmd+V* or from the Edit Menu (*Copy*, *Paste*). The copied notes will be pasted at the current Playhead Position.

➡ Resize

You have to select a Note (or multiple Notes) first when you want to resize it. The note's Duration Bar appears when it is selected. The right edge of a Duration Bar is a Click Zone. When you move the Mouse Pointer over it, it changes to the Resize Tool ❼.

🔔 Assistance:

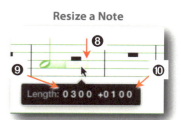
Resize a Note

- The Duration Bar moves along with the mouse movement ❽ to give you a rough indication about the end position of the note.
- The Help Tag displays the current (resized) Length ❾ and the length change ❿ from the note's original length.

➡ Delete Note

Select the note(s) and choose any of the common delete commands. Rest Symbols will be added to replace the deleted notes.

- Key Command *delete*
- Main Menu Command *Edit ➤ Delete*

Visual Grid

In addition to the quantize command in the Inspector that moves the playback position of the actual MIDI note to the selected Quantize Grid, there is a second Quantize Menu available on the right side of the MenuBar.

This moves the notes only visual to the selected Grid without changing their playback position. Use this command to "clean-up" the appearance of the score.

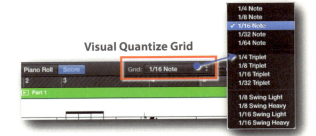

Print the Score

GarageBand also lets you print the score of your Project, however only one Track at a time.

Whenever you are in the Score Editor, the Print command in the File Menu becomes active. Select the Menu Command *Edit ➤ Print* or use the Key Command **cmd+P**. The standard Print Dialog Window will open where you can choose the print settings.

Please note that you can use the PDF command in the Print Dialog to create a pdf file from that score instead of sending it to the printer.

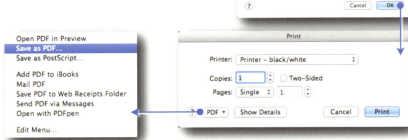

GarageBand prints the whole song for that Track and automatically includes the following elements:

- ☑ **Tempo**: This is the Project's Tempo
- ☑ **Project Name**: This is the name of the Project
- ☑ **Track Name**: This is the name of the Track (Instrument)
- ☑ **Composer Name**: This is the name that you entered in the *Preferences ➤ My Info ➤ Composer Name*

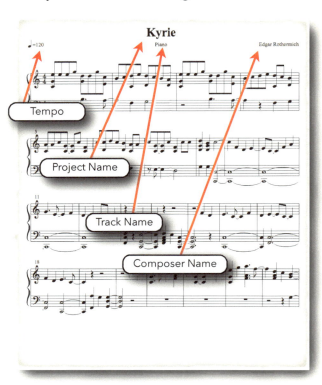

18 - Editing Audio

As we just saw, editing your MIDI recording is fairly simple. Changing the pitch or the timing of individual notes is as easy as moving a note (in the form of note bars or note symbols) vertically or horizontally.

Editing your audio recording is a completely different story. First of all, editing in general is more restricted and the tools available to do the actual edits are more complicated.

GarageBand tries to simplify the process but sometimes that could lead to confusion or frustration when you lose some of your edits due to an "over-simplified" command. On top of that, the official documentation provides very little information about the different commands.

In this chapter I will explain GarageBand's audio editing tools in more detail so you have a better understanding about the process. The material might seem a bit more advanced at times but I encourage you to hang in there to understand the cool features and amazing tools that are available to you.

Basics

You can do some basic Audio Regions editing in the Tracks Area, everything related to the Region itself. However, the Audio Editor is much better suited for any kind of editing related to the Audio Region. Similar to the MIDI Editor, the Audio Editor displays a close-up view of a single Track Lane the selected Region is on. It provides all the commands for editing not only the Region but also the Region Content itself.

➡ *A Better View*

One big advantage of the Audio Editor is the better view. The Track Lane in the Tracks Area has a fixed height for the displayed Regions. The Audio Editor, on the other hand, lets you resize the Region for a more detailed look of the waveform which is crucial for making precise edits. The Audio Editor also displays a dual waveform if the Audio File is in stereo (two channels). The Workspace displays a dual waveform only when Automation is displayed (more on that later).

What we are dealing with?

Although the Editor Window for Audio Regions looks pretty simple with just a few controls, the editing procedures might be difficult to understand without some basic background knowledge about digital audio. I already discussed the two forms of capturing music.

Music Written down as <u>instructions</u> (Score, MIDI data)	Music Recorded from a <u>performance</u> (CD, audio file)

As long as music is written down, you can change it every time you perform it. For example, if the band leader decides after the first evening to play the song xyz faster, one note higher, or without the drummer, he just changes those "instructions" and the song will sound differently the second night. If you bought the CD of that song however, it will always sound the same as it was recorded. You cannot change it.

So far, this was also true for any recording in the studio. Once you recorded the performance of a musician on tape, you couldn't alter it, only manipulate what was printed on tape with added effects. I already pointed out that this limitation doesn't exist when you record MIDI data because you record "musical instruction" that can be altered any time.

The limitation with recorded music has been lifted over the last couple of years with the advancement in digital audio technology, now that audio is recorded to a hard drive instead of tape. While still not perfect, you can treat recorded audio material now almost as if it was MIDI data.

Here are the three main parameters that describe music. This is basically the instruction you give a musician: tell them **what** to play (pitch of the notes), **when** to play it (the rhythmical sequence) and **how** to play it (loud, soft, legato, etc.).

When we now look at the various controls in the Audio Editor window, we first have to know which of the parameters you can alter and then learn what the available tools are and how they work.

➡ Audio Waveform

The main tool when editing audio in general is the waveform. This is a visual representation of the audio, "*what the sound looks like*".

The waveform is a simple graph, where the x-axis (horizontal line) represents the time and the y-axis (vertical line) represents the amplitude of the sound, in other words, how loud the music is at any specific time. It shows actually an oscillation (up and down movement) and if you paid attention in physics class, then you can read even more information out of it.

The more you work with audio waveforms, the better you will get at "reading" those waveforms. It takes practice, but over time, you can figure out how to recognize the musical content in those graphs.

What to Edit

Instead of going through the list of available editing commands, I want to group them first. Always keep in mind to what group an individual command belongs to. This has the advantage of thinking about the big picture and not getting caught up in the (sometimes confusing) details.

I already pointed out earlier the difference between a Region, the container for the data (your music), and the Region Content, the data (your music) inside that container. The Region itself (the outside) looks and behaves similar for MIDI Regions and Audio Regions. The Region Content (the inside) however is completely different. Please review the topic "MIDI Region vs Audio Region" in the Previous Knowledge chapter.

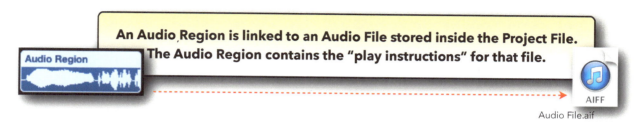

Here are the three groups for editing Audio Regions. Please note, all those edits are "non-destructive", they don't change the linked Audio File. The commands only change the play instructions.

- **Edit Region**

These are all the commands that edit the "outside" of a Region
  ▸ Move, copy, loop, trim, split, join an entire Region.

- **Edit Region Content (Pitch)**

These are all the commands that change the pitch of the audio recording, either the entire recording or sections of it.
  ▸ Follow Key: This feature transposes the Audio Region so it matches the Key Signature of your Project.
  ▸ Transpose: This is a command that lets you manually transpose the Audio Region by semitones.
  ▸ Pitch Correction: This feature automatically detects out-of-tune notes and corrects them.

- **Edit Region Content (Time)**

These are all the commands that change the timing of the audio recording, either the entire recording (play slower or faster) or sections of it.
  ▸ Follow Tempo: This feature changes the tempo according to any changes of the tempo in the Project.
  ▸ Quantize: Similar to MIDI Quantize, this feature can move sections in the waveform to a specific timing grid (like MIDI Notes).
  ▸ Time Correction: Similar to MIDI Notes that can be moved along the timeline manually, this feature lets you manually move the timing position of a section inside the waveform.

Different Audio Regions

Here is one important aspect you have to be aware of when editing Audio Regions, the different types of Regions. We learned already that GarageBand has three different types of Regions:

 MIDI Regions: These green Regions are placed on MIDI Tracks and contain the MIDI Events.

 Audio Regions: These blue Regions are placed on Audio Tracks and contain the play instructions for their linked Audio File.

 Drummer Regions: These yellow Regions are placed on a Drummer Track and contain the instructions for the Drum Pattern Generator (see next chapter).

But there is not just one type of Audio Region. GarageBand differentiates between four variations of the Audio Region.

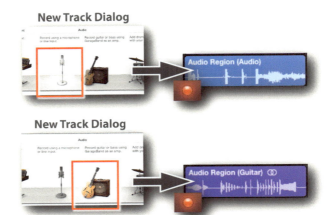

- **Audio Region: Recorded (Audio)**

If you record on an Audio Track that was created with the "Microphone icon" in the New Track Dialog, then all its Audio Regions are blue.

- **Audio Region: Recorded (Guitar)**

If you record on an Audio Track that was created with the "Guitar icon" in the New Track Dialog, then all the newly recorded Audio Regions will be purple.

- **Audio Region: Imported Apple Loop**

If you import an Audio Loop from the Loop Browser (or drag an Apple Loop from the Finder window), then the Audio Region will also be blue. This is unfortunate because you don't have a color indication if an Audio Region is linked to a newly recorded Audio File or an imported Apple Loop.

- **Audio Region: Imported Audio File**

If you import any standard Audio File from the Media Browser or directly from a Finder window, then that Audio Region will be orange. At least this is a clear color indication that this Audio Region was not recorded in the current Project.

➡ **Watch out !**

Whatever edit command you are applying to an Audio Region, you have to be aware which of the three Audio Regions you are editing because they can behave differently:
- ☑ **Recorded Audio File** (Audio or Guitar): Blue or purple Region
- ☑ **Imported Apple Loop File**: Blue Region
- ☑ **Imported Audio File**: Orange Region

Interface

Open the Audio Editor

Toggle the Audio Editor with the following commands when an Audio Region is selected. If no Region is currently selected in the Workspace, then at least an Audio Track has to be selected.

- Main Menu *View ➤ Show Editors*
- Key Command **E**
- *Click* on the Editors button in the Control Bar
- *Double-click* on an Audio Region
- *Drag* the Divider Line all the way down to close the Window Pane
- When the Editor Window is open but displaying the MIDI or Drummer Editor, then selecting an Audio Region switches the window to the Audio Editor

Menu Bar ❶

The Menu Bar on top contains the following three buttons.

- **Show/Hide Flex**: This toggles the visibility of the Flex Markers and Transient Markers. Making Flex Time visible will also enable Flex Time for that Track if it was disabled. More on that in a moment.
- **Catch Playhead**: This button toggles the Autoscroll feature for the Audio Editor independently from the Catch Playhead Button in the Tracks Area. If activated, the Playhead will stay fixed at the center of the Display Area and the waveform scrolls automatically underneath it.
- **Zoom Slider**: This slider zooms the Display Area as a whole horizontally. You can also use the *Pinch* Gesture on the Track Pad or *opt+scroll* horizontally.

Inspector ❷

The Inspector on the left contains the various displays and controls for editing the Region Content. The two tabs switch between the Track View ❸ and the Region View. ❷

Display Area ❹

The Display Area shows each Audio Region as its audio waveform. If the Region has a dual waveform, it is a stereo signal ❹ (2 channels) or a mono signal ❺ (1 channel) if it has a single waveform.

- **Scroll**: You can scroll the Display Area only horizontally. Use the Scroll Bar ❻ on the Display Area, the *Scroll* Gestures on your Track Pad or *sh+ctr+drag* the Display Area.
- **Zoom**: You can zoom the Display Area horizontally by using the Zoom Slider on the Menu Bar, the *Pinch* Gesture, the Key Command *cmd+Left/RightArrow* or *opt+scroll*. Zoom the Display Area vertically by dragging the Divider Line ❼ between the Audio Editor and the Tracks Area.

Inspector - What to Edit

Remember that I organized the available edit commands into three groups.

Edit Region **Edit Region Content (Pitch)** **Edit Region Content (Time)**

These commands are located in different areas of the Audio Editor interface depending on what is affected by the command.

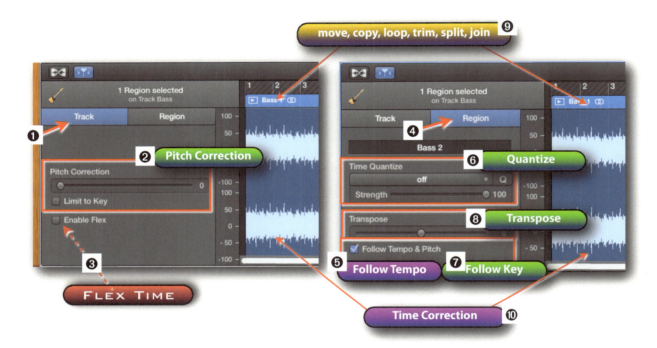

- **Inspector: Track**

    The commands in the Track View ❶ of the Inspector affect all the Regions of that Audio Track. The only command available is the Pitch Correction ❷. Please note that the "Enable Flex" ❸ checkbox is not a command. It toggles the Flex Time on and off for the whole Track. Flex Time is the powerful technology in the background that is required for other edit commands to function.

- **Inspector: Region**

    The commands in the Region View ❹ of the Inspector affect only the selected Region(s) in the Audio Editor. You can change the timing (Follow Tempo ❺, Quantize ❻) and the pitch (Follow Key ❼, Transpose ❽) of the selected Region(s).

- **Display Area - Region**

    Editing the Regions ❾ (moving, copying, trimming, etc.) can be done in the Display Area regardless of the Inspectors View, Track or Region.

- **Display Area - Waveform**

    The Time Correction ❿ (moving section inside the waveform) is performed directly on the waveform in the Display Area regardless of the Inspector View (Track or Region).

Flex Mode

So far, I just provided an overview for editing audio and the orientation of what commands are available and where they are. In this section, I will explain the technology for time-based audio editing called Flex Time. It gets again a little bit more technical, so if you don't plan to do much "surgery" with your Audio Regions, you can move on to the next section.

Concept

Back to the original discussion about the two ways to record music. This time, we will learn how to alter the timing of those recordings.

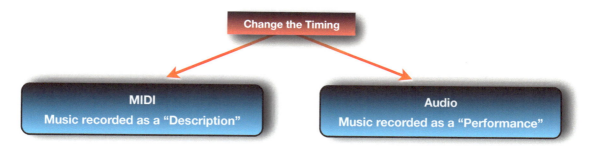

➡ **MIDI Recording**

Changing the timing in a MIDI Region is easy. You open up the Piano Roll Editor and all the individual notes are there as single events. You can drag them manually to any position you want or apply a quantize command to have them automatically moved to a specific timing grid. It is that simple.

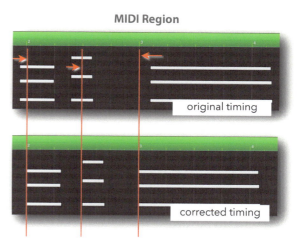

➡ **Audio Recording**

Changing the timing of an Audio Region (and therefore the audio file) was just not possible until the beginning of the era of digital audio. An Audio File is like a snapshot, a frozen event. You couldn't change the details in it. That snapshot is represented by the audio waveform where you can "see" the containing audio signal over time.

So how is it possible to change isolated notes or sections inside the waveform without affecting the rest of the audio file? This is where the Flex Time, also known as Elastic Audio, technology comes in.

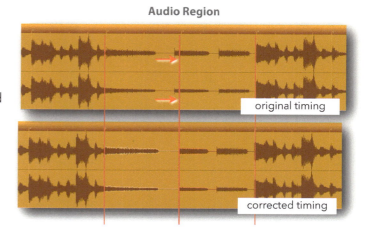

Transient Marker

If you record an audio signal, i.e. a strumming guitar, you can determine the two main parameters of that audio file:

- ☑ The **Key** the guitarist was playing: This is pitch information
- ☑ The **Tempo** the guitarist was playing: This is timing information

The problem with audio files is that these two parameters (pitch and time) are connected ❶.

- ☑ **Change the Pitch** (of an audio file): This would also change the timing. For example, raising the pitch of that guitar performance would play back the audio file faster and lowering the pitch would play back the file slower.
- ☑ **Change the Timing** (of an audio file): This would also change the pitch. For example, slowing down the tempo would lower the pitch and speeding up the playback would raise the pitch

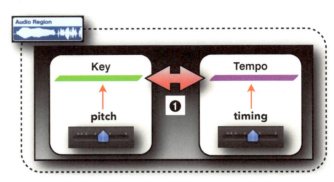

However, when you want to lower the key of your GarageBand Project because your singer can't hit the high note, then that strumming guitar you recorded earlier would play too slow if you changed the pitch of the Audio Region (and therefore the Audio File). Or, if you want to raise the Tempo of your Project by 5bpm and speed up your strumming guitar, it would play it back in a higher key. This is the main limitation when recording on tape or disk. Now, that your recording is stored as digital audio files, you can take advantage of two techniques that break the tie ❷ between pitch and time.

- ☑ **Pitch Shifting**: This technology in digital audio allows you to change the pitch of an audio file without affecting its playback speed.
- ☑ **Time Stretching**: This technology in digital audio allows you to change the playback speed of an audio file without affecting its pitch.

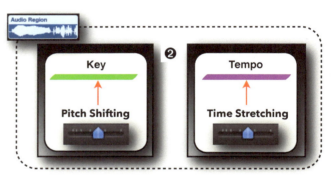

➡ Sliced Audio

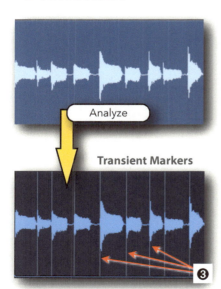

Pitch Shifting and Time Stretching use one special trick to make this work. Instead of treating an audio file as a whole, they cut it up in smaller slices and apply their digital audio processing to those individual slices in order to make the magic work. This is the process of analyzing the audio file to look for significant peaks in the waveform, so-called Transients.

Transient Markers

Instead of actually cutting the audio file at those transients, the program marks those peak positions in the audio file with Transient Markers ❸.

Flex Mode

Here is the basic concept how Pitch Shifting and Time Stretching is implemented in GarageBand.

GarageBand calls this technology "Flex". To use Flex with its Pitch Shifting and Time Stretching capabilities, you have to enable it. This is a simple checkbox.

- ▶ The "Enable Flex" checkbox ❶ toggles Flex Mode on and off.
- ▶ When you uncheck it, you don't delete any settings, it just disables Flex Mode and all the Audio Files that use features that rely on that Mode (Follow Key, Pitch, Quantize, etc.) will play back without any modification.
- ▶ Flex can be toggled on and off individually for each Audio Track ❷.
- ▶ Once Flex Mode is enabled on a Track, then the features that utilize Flex Mode (Follow Tempo, Follow Pitch, Quantize, etc.) can be enabled individually for each Audio Region. That means each one of those features can be used and configured individually for each Region ❸ on a Track.
- ▶ Any Audio Region that you record or import on a Flex enabled Track will be automatically analyzed. This is the process of finding the Transients in the Audio File and setting the Transient Markers. A progress window ❹ shows this process.

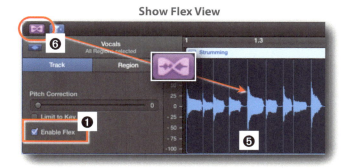

- ▶ Part of the analysis process is also to determine the best algorithm to apply Time Stretching (more on that in the next chapter).
- ▶ Once an Audio Region has been analyzed, it displays the Transient Markers ❺ on the waveform (if Flex View is on ❻).
- ▶ In Flex View, you can edit the Audio Region even more with a wide variety of commands and actions.
- ▶ The Flex View can be hidden by toggling the Flex View Button ❽ if you don't need to see all those details. Turning on Flex View will automatically enable Flex Mode if it was disabled.

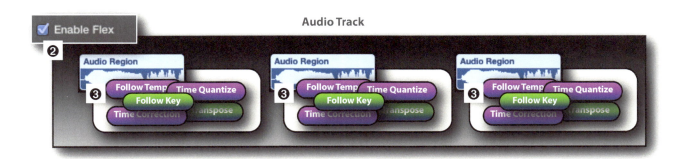

18 - Editing Audio

Flex Time - How the Magic Works

In the following screenshot, I demonstrate how Time Shifting of a single note in an Audio Region works.

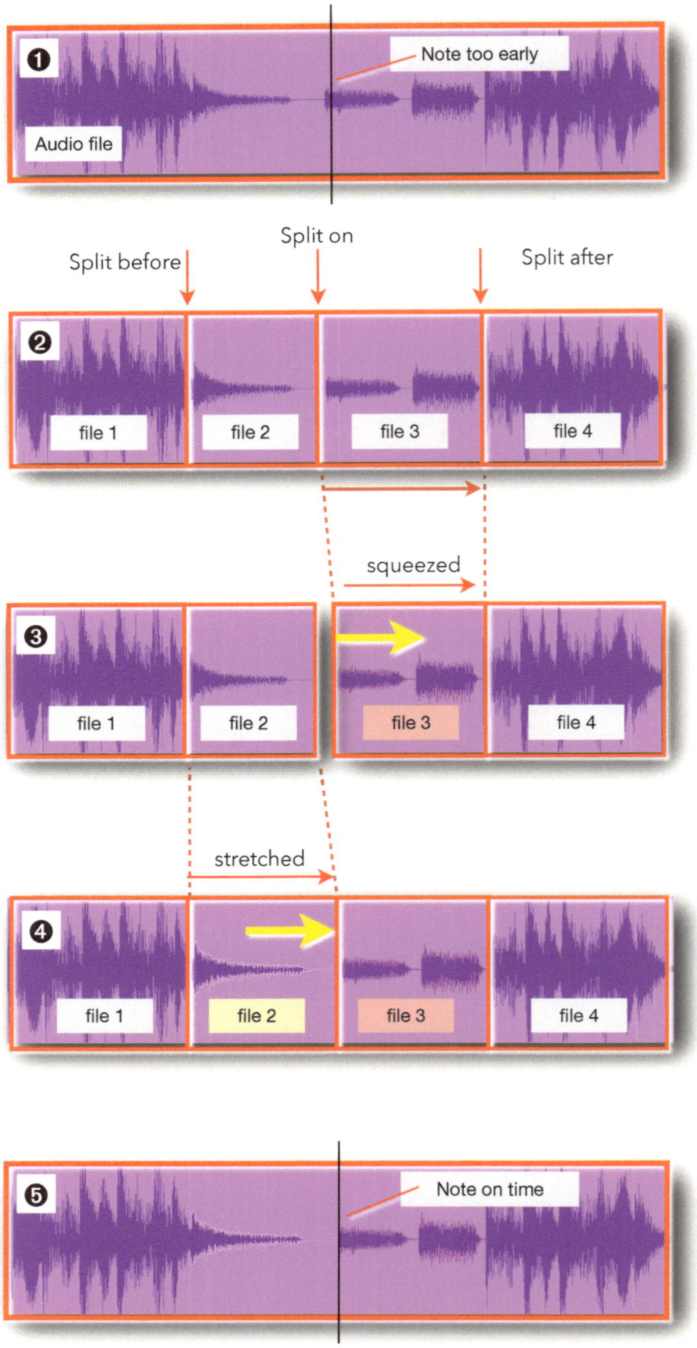

❶ The Problem

We start with an audio file that has a note with bad timing. For example, this could be the recording of a strumming guitar where the player hits one chord a little before the downbeat.

❷ The Preparation

Now imagine that we split the audio file exactly on that note, make another split on a note before and a split after that note. By making three splits on the audio file, we end up having created four files.

❸ The Operation

File 3 is the one that contains the note with the wrong timing. Let's assume the note is 10ms to early. Here is the first trick. We would squeeze (compress) that audio file 3 so it is 10ms shorter. If we keep the right border of the file locked at its position, then the left border of the file will start 10ms later. The result, the guitar chord which starts exactly at the left border of file 3 now plays 10ms later, exactly where we wanted it to be.

❹ The Clean-up

By making file 3 shorter, we left a gap of 10ms between file 2 and file 3. To fill that gap, we would take file 2 and stretch it by exactly the same amount of 10ms. This makes file 2 10ms longer. This time, we keep the left border of the file locked which means it ends 10ms later. That right border of file 2 touches now exactly the left border of file 3 and the gap is closed.

❺ The Achievement

By closing up the gap, we end up with one continuous file when we merge the 4 individual files together again. The problem note is corrected by playing exactly on time and another important aspect: If we look at the area of the former file 1 and file 2, nothing has changed there. That means the content in the audio file before and after the corrected note stayed untouched.

This was just a simplified example to demonstrate the procedure of the underlying Flex Time technology on how to do time correction inside an audio file. It uses time expansion and time compression, a common procedure in digital audio.

Please note that when it is actually happening in GarageBand, all that splitting, stretching and squeezing is done in a non-destructive way. This means that the actual audio file isn't altered at all. All the audio file manipulation is done as a playback procedure and you can modify it any time to get the best results.

248   18 - Editing Audio

Practical Use

So how is Flex Time done in GarageBand and how do we use it.

When we move an Event inside a MIDI Region in the Piano Roll Editor, we just move that Event. It is right there, an individual horizontal bar. As we have just seen in the example, in an Audio Region, we cannot grab an Event, there are no Note Bars, only one continuous waveform. Instead, in the waveform, we have to mark the position we want to move, the position where we visually identified the troubled note. In the previous example, I demonstrated that with a split. This created a separate audio file that started at that troubled note. The newly created separate file would then be moved through stretching or squeezing.

But instead of splitting up the Region, we mark that position with a marker, a so-called "Flex Marker. In addition to that, to perform a timing change at that Flex Marker, we need two additional Flex Markers, one before and one after the main Flex Marker. They mark the boundaries for the time stretching and squeezing.

Here are the elements:

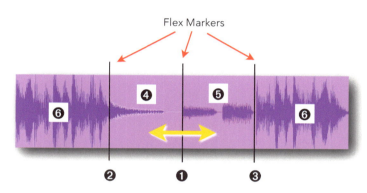

- The center Flex Marker that will be moved .
- Two Stationary Flex Markers mark the left ❷ and right ❸ boundary.
- The area of the waveform left ❹ of the center Flex Marker and right ❺ of the center Flex Marker are either extended or squeezed.

  Think of the center Flex Marker as a stick ❶ that is held in place by two rubber bands which are tied to a pole on the left ❷ and a pole on the right ❸. If you pull the stick to the right, then the rubber band shortens on the right ❺ by the same amount the left ❹ rubber band extends. If you pull the stick to the left, then the rubber band shortens on the left by the same amount the right rubber band extends.

- The two areas outside that boundary ❻ are not affected by the squeezing and stretching and stay untouched.

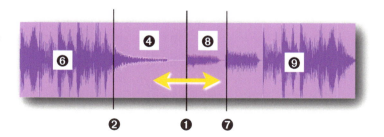

The key to a successful time correction lies in finding the best possible placements for the Flex Markers. In the example above, the right boundary marker ❸ is not a good choice. While we are moving the center Marker ❶ to the right, the right section ❺ is squeezed. If you look closely at the waveform, you will notice that there is a second event (maybe a second guitar chord) that was played correctly in time. But now, by moving the chord at the center Flex Marker, we will move that second event too. Fixing one problem, but creating a new one.

Here is a better choice how to set the Flex Marker in that case. We set the right boundary marker at that chord ❼. Now the area to the right of the center Marker ❽ includes only the problematic chord. The second chord (that shouldn't be shifted) which is at the position of the right Flex Marker ❼, lies outside the boundary ❾ and is therefore not affected wherever or how much we move the center Marker.

19 - The Audio Editor

After that dose of Flex information, let me explain how to use the edit commands in the Audio Editor. Here again is how I grouped the commands earlier.

Edit Regions

In the first category, I grouped all the commands that let you edit the Audio Region as a whole without altering anything inside, the waveform itself. Remember, most of these commands can also be applied in the Track Lane of the Workspace.

First, a few general features we already know by now.

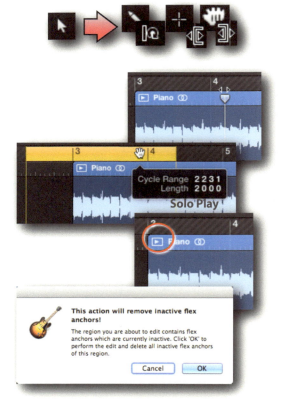

- **Click Zones**: The Click Zones play a major role when editing Audio Regions (and also the Region Content). This is the functionality that the Mouse Pointer changes from the Pointer Tool to a different Tool depending on where you move the mouse over to click on an object.

- **Playhead**: The Playhead in the Audio Editor is synced to the Playhead in the Workspace. It also works the same. *Click* on the lower part of the Ruler to move the Playhead there. *Drag* along the lower part of the Ruler to slide the Playhead across.

- **Cycle Mode**: The Cycle Mode is also tied to the Workspace. You can set the Cycle Area on the upper Part of the Ruler in the Audio Editor or the Tracks Area.

- **Solo Play**: This is a special feature of the Audio Editor (also available in the other Editor Windows). *Click* the Solo Play Button in the upper left corner of a Region to play back that Region in Solo Mode.

- **Alert Messages**: Some edits might have "consequences". In that case, watch out for Alert Windows that might pop up.

➡ Select

Many commands don't require that you select the Region first unless you want to edit multiple Regions at the same time.

- **Click** on a single Region inside the waveform, not the Region Header. Please note that you can only click on a waveform to select the Region if Flex is hidden 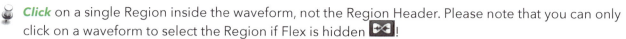!
- **Sh+click** on multiple Regions in a sequence to select them all
- **Sh+drag** across a group of Regions to select all of them
- **Sh+click** on a selected Region to deselect it
- **Cmd+A** to select all Regions in the Display Area or use the Main Menu **Edit ➤ Select All**
- **Click** on the Display Area background to deselect all Regions

➡ Name

You can rename the selected Audio Region(s) with the following commands.

- Key Command **sh+N**
- You can also **click** on the Name Field in the Inspector's Region View to rename the selected Region(s).

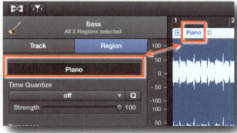

Rename Audio Region

The command highlights the name field so you can enter a new name and hit **return**.

Again, you can use the procedure for naming a sequence of multiple Regions. For example, selecting five Regions and entering "Piano 1" in the field, will name all the selected Regions in sequence "Piano 1", "Piano 2", "Piano 3", etc. You can even enter a different starting number ("Piano 25") and the Regions will be numbered through starting with that number ("Piano 25", Piano 26", etc.).

➡ Create (Pencil Tool)

Cmd+click is a command to create a new Region at the click position in the Display Area. Holding down the command key while the mouse is positioned on an empty section (not on a Region) in the Display Area, will change the Pointer Tool to the Pencil Tool. An Open Dialog pops up that lets you navigate to an Audio File. The selected Audio File will be copied into the Project File and its linked Audio Region is placed on the Display Area (and the Track Lane).

➡ Delete

You can delete a selected Region(s) with the following commands:

- Key Command **delete**
- Main Menu Command **Edit ➤ Delete** or **Edit ➤ Cut**

Please pay special attention when it comes to deleting Audio Regions.

- ▸ If there are other Audio Regions referring to the same Audio File, then only this Audio Region will be deleted but not the Audio File it is linked to.
- ▸ If the Audio Region is the last Region linked to a specific Audio File, then this action will also delete the Audio File that is stored inside the Project File.

➡ Move

Move Region procedure

The basic move command functions as expected. You **drag** the Region(s) with the Pointer Tool to the left or right. A Ghost Region(s) displaying the waveform separates from the original position and moves with the Pointer Tool along with the Help Tag. It displays the current target position, its Length, the distance from the original position plus the number of the current Track.

Please note:
- When you move a group of Regions, then the new Position in the Help Tag indicates the left Region border of the Region you are clicking on and not the first Region of the group.
- Moving a Region over an existing Region will shorten the Region "that is in the way".
- Moving a Region over an existing one and completely covering it, will delete that Region (and its linked Audio File if this was the last Region linking to it).

➡ Copy

Copy Region procedure

There are two standard commands for copying Regions:
 Opt+drag the Region(s) to the new position.
 Use the Copy-Paste command either from the Edit Menu (**Edit ➤ Copy** and **Edit ➤ Paste**) or use the Key Commands **cmd+C** and **cmd+V**. The Region(s) will be placed at the Playhead Position in the Display Area. Existing Tracks will be overwritten!

Please note:
- The Pointer Tool will have the added green plus icon ⊕ during the copy procedure.
- The difference to the move procedure is that this time, the Region that is "left behind" still displays the waveform.
- The copied Regions inherit the original Region Name followed by an incremental number (Piano, Piano.1, Piano.2, etc.)

➡ Loop

To "loop" a Region is the process of repeating a Region for a specific amount of times.

Move the Mouse Pointer over the right upper corner of the Region you want to loop. This is a Click Zone where the Mouse Pointer changes to the Loop Tool. **Dragging** the Region with the Loop Tool to the right will lengthen the looped section or shorten the section when dragging back to the left.

Loop Region Procedure

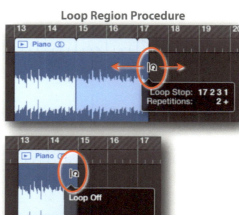

How to use the Loop Tool
- **Drag** the right border of the Region with the Loop Tool to extend the range to any position. A Help Tag displays the end point of the Region (Loop Stop) and the number of Repetitions.
- **Dragging** the right border with the Loop Tool all the way to the left will turn the Loop off (no repetitions).
- Alternatively, use the Key Command **L** to toggle the Loop function. When turning on, the Loop extends all the way to the left border of the next Region or to the end of the Project (End-of-Project Marker) if there is no other Region on that Track.

➡️ **Resize (Trim Tool)**

The Trim Tool is also part of a Click Zone. It will automatically appear when you move the Mouse Pointer over the lower left or lower right border of a Region. A Help Tag displays the start position and length when trimming the left border and the length and the length change when trimming the right border.

Please note:

- You can extend the borders of an Audio Region only as long as the Audio File is itself.

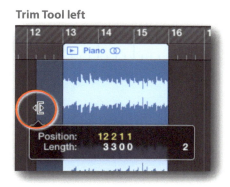

➡️ **Split**

This command splits the selected Region at the Playhead Position into two Regions. Both Regions are linked to the same Audio File. They contain different "play instructions" for the Audio File.

Splitting an existing Region is useful, when you want to move or copy only a portion of a Region or want to edit only a section of it (i.e. for individual quantize rules).

The commands are:

- Main Menu Command **Edit ➤ Split Regions at Playhead**
- Key Command **cmd+T**

➡️ **Join**

The Join command is the opposite of the Split command. It merges all the selected Regions together. Select one or multiple Regions (with or without gaps in between) and use any of the commands.

- Menu Command **Edit ➤ Join Regions**
- Key Command **cmd+J**

Joined Audio Regions = New Audio File

Please note that you cannot join Audio Regions the same way as MIDI Regions. An Audio Region contains the play instructions for its linked Audio File. When you join two or more Audio Files, GarageBand first performs a mixdown of those Audio Regions which creates a new Audio File. The new Audio Region for that Audio File will be the new "Joined Audio Region".

When you try to join two non-contiguous Audio Files, you'll get prompted with a Dialog Window with the option to Create the new Audio File.

19 - The Audio Editor

➡ **Marquee**

Draw Marquee Selection

This is a somewhat hidden editing tool. The Pointer Tool changes to the Marquee Tool ✥ when you move the Mouse Pointer over the lower half of the Display Area. It lets you draw a range on the Lane in the form of a shaded area (not restricted to the boundaries of one Region). In addition, instead of drawing a range, you can just *click* on the lower half of the Display Area to create a Marquee Line.

Click on the upper half of the Display Area (outside the Marquee Range) to deselect it.

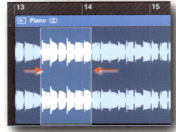
Marquee Selection

This Marquee Range can be used for the following editing commands.

- 📌 **Playback**: Playback will always start at the left border and stops at the right border of the section (priority over Cycle Mode). Use a single Marquee Line to just define a start playback position.
- 📌 **Move**: *Drag* the shaded area to cut out that section from the Region and move it to a different position. New Regions will be created linked to the same Audio File. The original Region stays untouched.

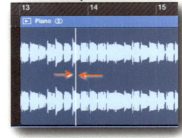
Marquee Line

- 📌 **Copy**: *Opt+drag* will only copy that section without cutting the original Region.
- 📌 **Delete**: *Delete* will only delete that range. Two separate Regions remain.
- 📌 **Split**: *Click* on the range to split the Region at the left and right border, creating three adjacent Region (linking to the same Audio File).

Assistance

Please take a moment to look at the details of those features that help you with your edits.

➡ **Snap Behavior**

Moving objects (Regions, Notes, Control Points) will snap to the time grid in the Workspace if Snap to Grid is enabled in the Edit Menu. This command is automatically enabled in the Editor Windows (and is not even visible in the Edit Menu). There are different rules depending on the settings of the Control Bar Display.

- ▸ **Musical Time** 🎵 Beats & Project : Snap to Grid is automatically enabled in the Audio Editor. But, there are three modes that affect the moving behavior.
  - *Drag*: The movement snaps to the time grid (depending on the zoom factor).
  - *Ctr+drag*: The movement does not snap to the time grid.
  - *Sh+ctr+drag*: (hold down after click): The movement snaps to the Ticks unit.
- ▸ **Absolute Time** 🕓 Time : Snap to Grid is off by default.
  - *Drag*: The movement does not snap to the time grid.
  - *Ctr+drag*: The movement snaps to the time grid in frames.
  - *Sh+ctr+drag*: (hold down after click): The movement snaps to frames.

➡ **Alignment Guides**

Usually, the Alignment Guides snap to any border of another object in the workspace. Although the Audio Editor represents only one Track Lane, you still would see the yellow Alignment Guides if enabled (*Edit ➤ Alignment Guides*). They align to other objects on the Workspace even if you can't see them in the Audio Editor's Display Area.

➡ Zoom Behavior

Zooming horizontally in and out of the waveform along the timeline is something that you have to do constantly to find the right zoom factor for the current edit you want to perform. Often, when you zoom in, the section you want to edit ❶ (for example, at bar 7) moves to the left or right out of sight ❷ and you have to scroll back to find it. This can be frustrating because you spend more time on zooming and scrolling than concentrating on the actual edit.

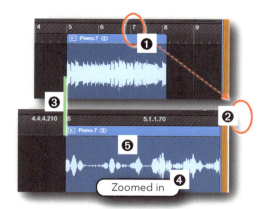

To help you with that problem, GarageBand provides some useful mechanisms when zooming in and out of the waveform. Please take a moment and get yourself familiar with those techniques. They could save you a lot of time and frustration when working in the Audio Editor.

Focus Point.

Whenever you zoom in or out of a timeline, there is one position that stays fixed. That is the point you are zooming in to, you are focusing on. The left and right side of that Focus Point "moves to the side" (and eventually out of site) while you are zooming in.

- **Problem**: When the position on the waveform you want to edit is to the left or right of that focus point ❸, then that position "disappears" ❷ when you zoom in ❹ and you have to scroll back into the viewable area. The problem is that now the waveform looks different ❺ (zoomed in ❹) and it might be difficult to find that position you wanted to edit.

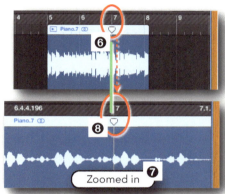

- **Solution**: You have to make sure that the position you want to zoom in to on the waveform is the focus point ❻, no matter how much you zoom in ❼ or out, so that section stays always visible ❽. To help you with that, GarageBand provides a mechanism that defines the Focus Point.

The main question is, where is the Focus Point? There are three conditions.

- ▸ Playhead is NOT visible (no Regions selected):
  In this case, the Focus Point is the left border of the visible Workspace.

- ▸ Playhead IS visible (no Regions selected):
  In this case, the Focus Point is the Playhead Position. This might be the preferred method because you can place the Playhead at the position you want to zoom in and it stays in focus without the need to scroll back and forth. Please note that no selected Regions can be visible in the Workspace!

- ▸ Region(s) is selected and visible:
  In this case, the Focus Point is the left border of the selected Region. If there are more than one selected Regions visible, then it is the left border of the first selected Region. So, any selected (and visible) Region has priority over the Playhead Position.

Edit Region Content (Pitch)

The next group of commands are the ones that change the pitch of the Audio File.

Pitch Correction

This command is available in the Track View of the Inspector. That means it will be applied to all Audio Regions of the current Track.

- ▸ Pitch Correction can be applied to any Audio Region and does not require Flex Time.
- ▸ This is an auto-tune effect that is only suitable for "monophonic" (single notes) Audio Regions not for "polyphonic" (chords) parts or drums and multiple instrument recordings.
- ▸ The effect analyzes the audio signal and adjusts the out of tune notes to correct them (pitch shift) to the chromatic scale (12 semitones).
- ▸ The slider determines the amount how much a note gets corrected towards that scale (0=no adjustment, 100= maximum adjustment).
- ▸ If the "Limit to Key" checkbox is checked, then the effect adjusts the notes not to the 12 notes of a chromatic scale but to the 7 notes of the current Key Signature of your Project

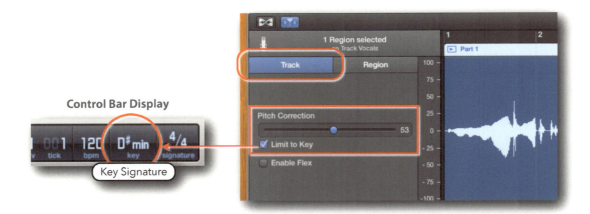

Things to consider

- The Pitch Correction in GarageBand is only a quick fix, kind of a "band aid" for tuning issues on a Track.
- It might work only on minor problems on a vocal recording or solo instruments.
- Any time you have a glissando in your recording (i.e. pitch bend on a guitar solo), the Pitch Correction would try to "correct" it. In that case, split up the Audio Region and put it on separate Tracks that have different Pitch Correction settings.
- For true Pitch Correction use a dedicated Auto-Tune plugin, or even better use a better performer.

Follow Key

The other two commands that affect the pitch of an Audio File (Follow Key and Transpose) are available in the Region View of the Inspector. That means you can set those parameters individually for each single Region.

The "Follow Tempo & Pitch" ❶ checkbox enables the "Match Key" feature. You cannot enable just Follow Key, only both Follow Key and Follow Tempo together.

Please note that the behavior is different for the different Audio Regions:

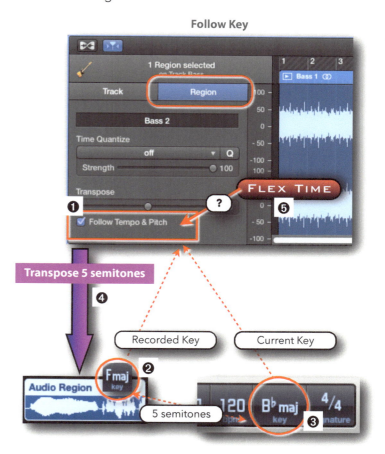

🔴 Recorded File

- When recording a new Audio File, then the checkbox will be automatically enabled for that new Audio Region.
- The Key Signature during the recording becomes the default Key ❷ for the Audio Region. Changing the Key Signature ❸ after the Audio Region has been recorded, applies the "transpose offset" ❹. For example, the Key was F ❷ during recording and changing it to Bb ❸ will transpose the Audio Region 5 semitones up ❹. Please note that GarageBand just follows the values you entered, it does not know in what key you are actually performing.
- Turning "Follow Tempo & Pitch" off will play back the Audio Region the way it was recorded ❷ regardless of the current Key Signature ❸. Be careful, this also disables any "Follow Tempo" settings.
- Another little detail to pay attention to: Turning Flex Time on will disable ❺ the Follow Key function even if the checkbox is checked!

🔵 Apple Loop File

- When importing an Apple Loop, then the checkbox is automatically enabled for that Audio Region.
- Most Apple Loops have a Key Signature value ❷ stored with the file it was recorded (i.e. F). Whenever the "Follow Tempo & Pitch" checkbox is enabled ❶, GarageBand will transpose ❹ the Region to match the current Key Signature of the Project.
- Enabling Flex Time does not disable the Follow Key function for Apple Loops as it does with Recorded File.

🟠 ~~Imported File~~

- When importing a standard Audio File (orange), the checkbox for that Audio Region is disabled and cannot be checked.
- Follow Key is not available for imported Audio Files.

Transpose

The Transpose feature ❶ lets you transpose an Audio Region. This transpose value is in addition to any transpose value applied by the Follow Key feature.

Again, this does not apply to all Audio Regions.

Recorded File
▸ You can transpose Audio Regions that you recorded in your Project.

Apple Loop File
▸ You can transpose Audio Regions based on Apple Loops that you imported to your Project.

~~Imported File~~
▸ You cannot transpose Audio Regions based on standard Audio Files you imported to your Project (orange Regions).

Please note:
- The Transpose Slider ❷ can transpose Audio Regions up/down 12 semitones (one octave) although the audio quality degrades rapidly if you transpose more than a few semitones.
- The value for the transpose amount ❸ is listed in the Region Header ❹ in the Track Lane.
- Please pay attention to the special interface: The Transpose Slider can only be moved when "Follow Tempo & Pitch" ❺ is enabled. When you turn the checkbox off, then the slider will be grayed out. However, the transpose value is still active, only the transposition based on the Follow Key is removed. To change the Transpose value, you have to enable the checkbox first to make the slider ❷ active again.

Transpose Feature

Edit Region Content (Time)

The commands in this group affect the timing of the Audio Region(s). All the Timing commands are Region based. Only Flex Time itself, that might be needed for those effects, is enabled for the entire Track.

Time Editing of Audio Files means that you can pick notes inside an audio file and move them around like individual MIDI notes. The computer compensates any time modification of the audio file so it will not be audible (hopefully). If the modification is too extreme then you will start hearing audible artifacts and the quality of the audio file will suffer. Remember, all those edits are "non-destructive", meaning that the audio file itself will not be altered.

Follow Tempo

The "Follow Tempo & Pitch" ❶ checkbox enables the "Follow Tempo" feature (plus the Follow Key feature).

- 🔴 **Recorded File**
    - ▸ When recording a new Audio File, then the checkbox will be automatically enabled for that new Audio Region.
    - ▸ The Tempo value during the recording becomes the default Tempo ❷. Changing the Tempo of your Project ❸ afterwards will change the playback speed ❹ of that Audio Region to match the new tempo. The pitch remains the same.

- 🔵 **Apple Loop File**
    - ▸ When importing an Apple Loop, then the checkbox ❶ is automatically enabled for that Audio Region.
    - ▸ The Apple Loop has its default Tempo ❷ stored with the Audio File. GarageBand looks up that info and adjusts the playback speed ❹ to match the current Project Tempo. The pitch remains the same.

- 🎵 **(Imported File)**
    - ▸ When importing a standard Audio File, the checkbox ❶ for that Audio Region is disabled and cannot be checked.
    - ▸ The only way to have an imported Audio File follow the tempo is to enable Flex Time and set the Flex Markers.

Quantize `Time Quantize`

The previous function of matching tempo affected the entire Audio Region. The whole Audio Region is played back faster or slower to match the current Tempo.

However, to "Quantize" an Audio Region is a total different story. Now you are about to manipulate the timing "inside" the Audio Region. This can affect only a small section of the Audio Region, leaving everything else untouched. I explained the details already in the previous chapter about Flex Time.

Here is just a summary of the technique how you can move a small portion of a continuous waveform and treat it as it would be a single MIDI note.

> **Manipulating Timing in an Audio File**
>
> In order to quantize an audio file, for example to correct the sloppy timing of a recorded live drummer, the audio has to be analyzed first. During that analysis, the computer tries to detect notes (just rhythmic patterns, not the pitch) by looking for peaks (transients) in the audio signal and assigns Markers (Transient Markers) to those time positions in the audio waveform. Those Transient Markers can be turned into Flex Markers (similar to dedicated MIDI events) which then can be quantized, moved to a timing grid. When those Flex Markers are moved to a timing grid, that portion of the audio waveform that is attached to the Flex Markers, gets moved too. Please note that not the entire audio file gets moved (shifted), only that little section of the audio around that Flex Marker (defined by an additional Flex Marker to the left and right). Everything else stays as it is.

➡ ***Two steps to Quantize***

 Step 1 - Analyze and Create Transient Markers

 An Audio Region has to be analyzed first before you can apply a Quantize command to it. That process creates the Transient Markers for that Audio Region which is necessary for the quantize procedure to work.

Here is a look at the different Audio Regions regarding those Transient Markers.

 Recorded File

When Flex is enabled on a Track, then GarageBand will analyze the file once you stop the recording. You can see the Progress window pop up during that process which can be very quick. If  not, then you have to enable Flex Time manually or apply a Quantize value which automatically enables Flex Time first.

 Apple Loop File

Those files have their Transient Markers already perfectly set. That's what makes them special Apple Loops (see the Apple Loops chapter for detail). GarageBand just reads them during the Analysis process.

 Imported File

Those files will be analyzed when importing them onto an Audio Track that has Flex Time enabled. Otherwise, you have to enable Flex Time manually or apply a Quantize value directly.

 Step 2 - Apply Quantize Command

Once the Audio Region has Transient Markers, you can then apply the standard quantize commands to it and treat the Audio Region as if it was a MIDI Region. GarageBand uses those Transient Markers, converts them to Flex Marker that now can be moved to the closest grid line.

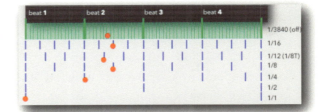

➡ Quantize Commands

The Audio Editor Inspector has three commands that let you set the quantize value for the selected Region(s). They function the same as in the Inspector for the Piano Roll Editor.

💡 Quantize Grid

The Time Quantize popup button ❶ opens a popup menu ❷ that lets you choose the timing grid you want to quantize the Flex Markers to. Selecting "off" ❸ removes the Flex Markers and the audio waveform returns to its original state, no quantization applied.

Please note:

- Selecting an item from the menu applies the quantize command right away.
- The applied quantize value is stored with the Audio Region. That means selecting a different Region will display the quantize value used for that Region.
- Be aware that you also can manually create/move Flex Markers in addition to move them via the quantize command (see next section).
- You can alter the Quantize Flex Markers with Manual Flex Markers (click on the waveform) which themselves can not be overwritten by any Quantize Flex Marker.

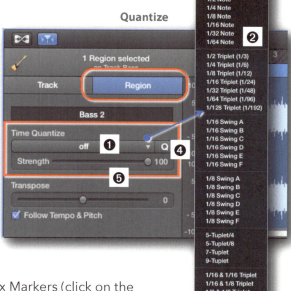

💡 Quantize Button

The Q-Button ❹ applies (or re-applies) the currently selected quantize grid.

💡 Quantize Strength

The Strength Slider ❺ determines how close the Flex Markers are moved towards the Quantize Grid (0=no quantization, 100=max quantization).

➡ About Flex Time

Here are a few things regarding Flex Time you should not be confused about when using the Quantize Command.

- ☑ Flex Time has to be enabled ❻ for the Quantize feature.
- ☑ Disabling Flex Time ❼ will only bypass (ignore) the effect. The Flex Marker positions will be recalled when enabling Flex again.
- ☑ Hide Flex Time ❽ will only visually remove the Flex Markers ❾ from the waveform. The Flex Time effect is still enabled (unless you turned it off).
- ☑ The Show/Hide Flex and Enable/Disable Flex command is applied to the entire Track. However you can still choose for each Region individually if you want to use Quantize or not (set Quantize to off).

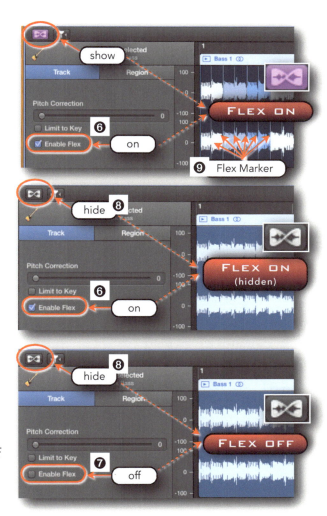

19 - The Audio Editor

Time Correction

As we have just seen, the Quantize feature will use the positions of the available Transient Markers to create Flex Marker and then move them accordingly based on the Quantize command. However, you can create Flex Markers manually at any position in the waveform. For example, correct the timing of a single note by creating a Flex Marker at the note position and move that Flex Marker along with the note to the correct time position.

In case you haven't noticed, the Flex feature is definitely a more advanced feature in GarageBand. Using it to quantize your audio recording could be as easy as turning Flex Time on and selecting a quantize value. If you are lucky, that could be all you have to know about Flex Time. However, doing manual Time Correction definitely requires that you have a deeper understanding of that technology.
So, if you are up for it, let's dive into it.

🎯 Preparation

There are three things you have to take care of up front.

- **Show Flex Time**: Flex Time should be visible so you can see and interact with the Tools. Toggle the Flex Button on at the Audio Editor Menu Bar.
- **Enable Flex Time**: Of course, in order to do that Time Correction, the Track, the Audio Region is on, has to have Flex Time enabled first.
- **Click Zones**: There are no buttons to do the manual Time Correction. Everything is done visually with mouse actions on the waveform itself. To do all that, there are multiple Click Zones, so pay attention to what Tool the Mouse Pointer changes to depending where you click.

🎯 Markers

You have to be absolutely clear about the differences between the various Markers, what they are, what they do and what they look like. There are four types of Markers with two different purposes.

Markers for Orientation

- **Transient Markers**: These are the Markers that GarageBand creates when analyzing the Audio Region the first time. This is a one time procedure and you have no influence over those Transient Markers. They function as a visual orientation where the peaks in your audio signal are.
- **Tempo Markers**: Whenever you record an Audio Region over a section in your Project that has Tempo Markers defined in the Tempo Track, then those positions are marked with separate Tempo Markers. This is a real advanced feature which you might never encounter if you stay with one Tempo in your Project.

Types of Markers

Markers for performing Time Correction

- **Quantize Flex Markers**: These are the Flex Markers that GarageBand creates when you choose a Quantize value. GarageBand re-positions these Flex Markers if you choose different Quantize values.
- **Manual Flex Markers**: These are the Flex Markers that you are in charge of to perform Time Corrections. Place them wherever you want. You even have the power to remove the Flex Markers that GarageBand places based on the Quantize command.

🎯 Time Manipulation

GarageBand colors the sections of the waveform depending on what time manipulation is performed. Needless to say, you have to know how to read this color code.

Waveform Sections Color Code

➡ Markers

Here are a few screenshots that show you the different types of Markers. Their visual difference is very subtle, so pay close attention to know what you are looking at.

Here is an Audio Region with Flex Time enabled and visible.

❶ **Transient Markers**: The thin gray lines are the Transient Markers. A Transient Marker is also placed at the beginning and end of a Region.

❷ **Tempo Markers**: The thicker blue lines are Tempo Markers

❸ **No Markers**: As you can see, the analysis process doesn't catch all peaks (the possible starting points of a note or acoustic event).

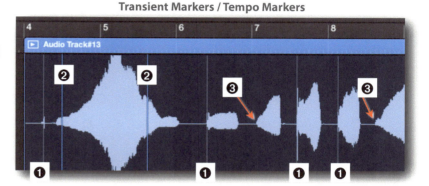

Once you apply a Quantization value, GarageBand creates the Quantize Flex Markers. Please note that GarageBand not only places the Flex Markers based on the Quantize value, it immediately moves those Flex Markers (and the waveform section attached to it) to the nearest Quantize Grid. That's why you see the colored waveform based on the performed time manipulation.

❹ **Quantize Flex Markers**: These are the thin, light blue lines, a little bit thicker than the Transient Markers.

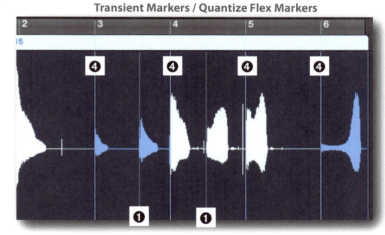

When you create your own Manual Flex Markers, you add another type of lines on the waveform. As you can see (or having difficulties to see), you really have to squint your eyes or zoom all the way in in order to visually differentiate between the different Markers.

❺ **Manual Flex Marker**: These are the little more thicker white lines.

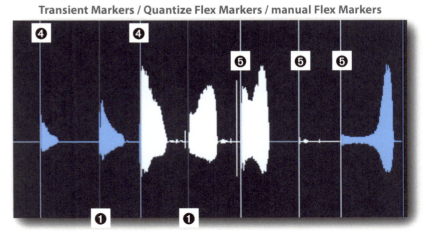

➡ **Create**

The first rule you have to know is that any time you create a Flex Marker manually, you actually create three Flex Markers.

- ☑ One Flex Marker at the click position.
- ☑ One Flex Marker at the Transient Marker (or Tempo Marker) position that is to the left of the position on the waveform you clicked.
- ☑ One Flex Marker at the Transient Marker (or Tempo Marker) position that is to the right of the position on the waveform you clicked.

You can click anywhere along the timeline on the waveform to create a Flex Marker. The Mouse Pointer however identifies two different areas and indicates that with a different Mouse Pointer.

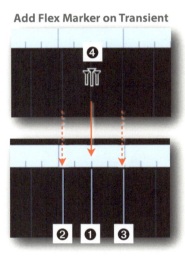

The Mouse Pointer changes to this Flex Tool ❹ when you move the mouse over an existing Transient Marker (or Tempo Marker).

Click with that Flex Tool to create a Flex Marker ❶ at that Transient Marker position. In addition, the one Flex Marker on the left ❷ and one at the right ❸ are also created.

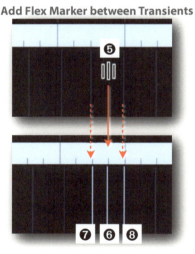

The Mouse Pointer changes to this Flex Tool ❺ when you move the mouse over any other position between Transient Markers.

Click with that Flex Tool to create a Flex Marker ❻ at that position plus the two Flex Markers on the left ❼ and right ❽ where the neighboring Transient Markers are.

➡ **Re-position**

Remember, creating a Flex Marker is like sticking a handle on that time location of the waveform. When you now move the Flex Marker, you will time shift the attached section of the waveform. However, in case you haven't set the Flex Marker precisely at the position you wanted it to be, you can move it (re-position it) without moving the waveform. You temporarily un-stick the Flex Marker from the waveform while moving.

When you move the Mouse Pointer over an existing Flex Maker and hold down the option key, it will change to this Reposition Tool.

Opt-drag a Flex Marker in the upper half of the waveform to reposition it without affecting the waveform.

➡ **Marquee**

There is another way to create those three Flex Markers by using a Marquee Selection.

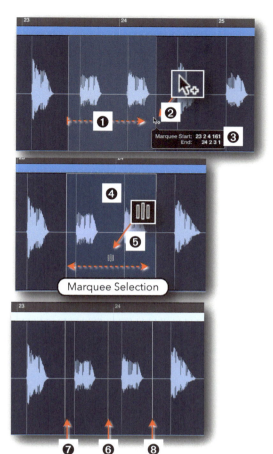

▸ **Opt+drag** on the lower portion of the waveform ❶ to draw a Marquee Selection.
- The Mouse Pointer ❷ has the added Marquee sign (+) while you're holding down the option key.
- The Help Tag ❸ displays the start and end position of the Marquee Selection.
- When you release the mouse, the shaded Marquee Selection is visible ❹ and the Mouse Pointer changes back to the Flex Tool ❺.

▸ Now when you click anywhere inside the Marquee Selection, the three Flex Markers will be created as follows:
- ☑ The center Flex Marker ❻ will be created at the click position.
- ☑ The left Flex Marker ❼ will be created on the left border of the Marquee Selection.
- ☑ The right Flex Marker ❽ will be created on the right border of the Marquee Selection.

➡ **Delete**

You can delete any Flex Marker, the one you created manually, but also the ones that were created by GarageBand via the Quantize command.

 This is the Move Tool when you move the Mouse Pointer over an existing Flex Marker. You can delete a Flex Marker with this Tool in two ways:
- *Double-click* on the Flex Marker to delete it.
- *Click* on the ⊗ on top of the Flex Marker to delete it

Please note that you only delete that one Flex Marker, not the other two Flex Markers that you created with it. Any time shifting caused by the Flex Marker will be removed. The section of the waveform resets.

Transient Marker and Tempo Marker cannot be deleted manually.

Click Action in Flex Time

The standard click action to select or drag a Region doesn't work when Flex Time is visible. A click would create a Flex Marker. However you can still use the select and move operations by using modifier keys:
- *Sh+ctr+click* on a Region to select or deselect that Region (without creating a Flex Marker).
- *Sh+ctr+drag* in the Display Area between Regions to scroll the Display Area. The mouse changes to a special Scroll Tool.

➡ Move Flex Marker and the Waveform

Now let's look at the final action, do the Time Correction. Remember, any Flex Marker on the waveform is "attached" to that position of the waveform. Moving the Flex Marker, moves that portion of the waveform. The important thing to be aware of is that not the whole waveform is moved but only the section defined by the boundaries of the next Flex Marker to the left and to the right.

Here is the process with screenshots of an imported Audio File (orange). It is the same with recorded Audio Files or Apple Loop Files.

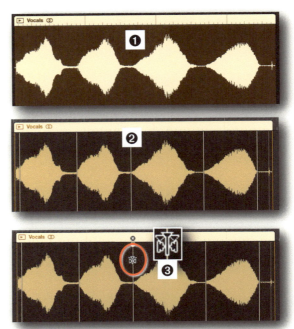

- ▸ This is how the Audio Region looks like ❶ when Flex Time is disabled and hidden .

- ▸ This is the Audio Region ❷ with Flex Time enabled and visible . I created five Flex Markers.

- ▸ **Move over the Flex Marker**

  When you move the mouse over a Flex Marker it changes to the "Create Marker Tool" ❸. On top of the Flex Marker appears an X and a marker .

- ▸ **Click on the Flex Marker**

  Now when you click on the Flex Marker, it changes to the "Move Flex Marker Tool" ❹. Also, the color of the waveform darkens while moving a Flex Marker.

- ▸ **Move the Flex Marker to the right**
  - The Region Header displays a horizontal bar ❺ that indicates how far you moved the Flex Marker away from its original position.
  - The section to the right will be squeezed ❻ (time compressed) and its color turns brighter.
  - The section to the left will be stretched ❼ (time expanded) and its color turns lighter.
  - The waveform outside the boundaries are untouched ❿.

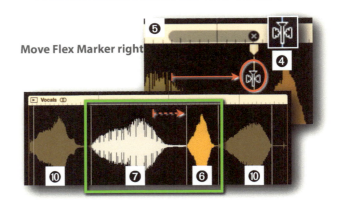

Move Flex Marker right

- ▸ **Move the Flex Marker to the left**
  - The Region Header displays a bar that indicates how far you moved the Flex Marker away from its original position.
  - The section to the left will be squeezed ❽ (time compressed) and its color turns brighter.
  - The section to the right will be stretched ❾ (time expanded) and its color turns lighter.
  - The waveform outside the boundaries are untouched ❿.

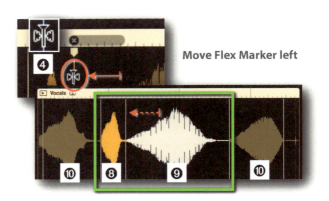

Move Flex Marker left

▶ **Move to the Extreme**

Moving the Flex Marker very close towards the boundary Flex Marker means that you squeeze that section of the audio signal very tight. That waveform section will be highly compressed. Besides the fact that this might not sound very good, it also requires more processing power to perform that high compression. GarageBand alerts you of that in two ways.

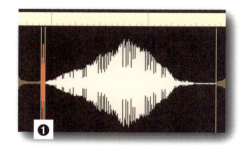

❶ The section of the waveform turns red.

❷ An Alert window pops up that lets you confirm (or cancel) that extreme compression.

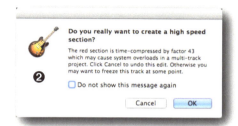

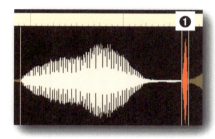

Flex Time Algorithms

Let's add one more aspect to the whole procedure in case you though Flex Time wasn't difficult enough already.

The technique of compressing one side and expanding the other side of the waveform when moving a Flex Marker is only one way to do it. There are different ways (Algorithms) and GarageBand chooses the one which it thinks is best based on the analysis of the audio signal.

Here is an example of the **Slicing Algorithm**, that GarageBand uses when the audio material is percussive ❸. When you move a note (i.e. a drum hit or a note of a single note guitar pattern) towards the right ❹ or the left ❺, then only the compression ❻ will be applied to that portion of the waveform. The expansion of the other half of the waveform as we have seen in the previous example (different Algorithm), does not happen. Instead, that portion is moved as it is ❼ or stays unchanged at its position ❽. One "side effect" is that the continuous waveform is interrupted with a small section of silence ❾. However, with percussive signals and considering that this gap might be less than a millisecond, this will (hopefully) not be noticeable.

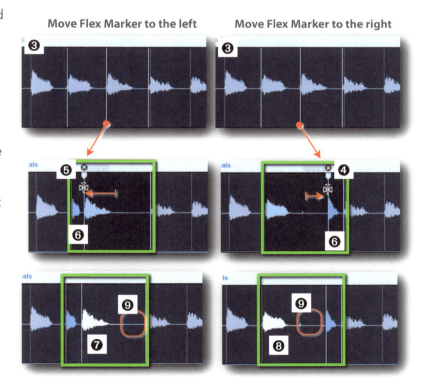

19 - The Audio Editor 267

20 - The Drummer Editor

Concept

The official explanation of the Drummer is "having different drummers like Kyle and Logan playing on your Project". This sounds amazing but behind that magic is simply the concept of a Drum Pattern Generator, although a very sophisticated one. With this new feature come new workflows that have to be understood before using them. Once you've wrapped your head around it and dived into it, the Drummer becomes an amazing tool that lets you create professional sounding live drum tracks.
And it is easy and fun to use too.

Terminology

When working with the Drummer, it is important to be aware of the main tasks that you are about to perform and the various components they belong to.

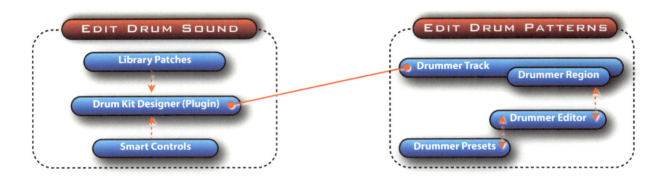

- **What is the Drummer Playing?**
    - ▸ **Drummer Track**: It all starts with this special Track, the Drummer Track.
    - ▸ **Drummer Region**: The special Drummer Track contains special Regions, the Drummer Regions. These Regions contain the drum pattern, the instructions for the Pattern Generator, what and how to play those drums. Different patterns can be loaded as **Drummer Presets**.
    - ▸ **Drummer Editor**: This is the place where you edit the individual Drummer Regions (its instructions).

- **How does the Drummer Sound?**
    - ▸ **Drum Kit Patches**: You can choose from 18 different Drum Kits available from the Library Window. They represent the 18 different Drummers (one Drummer comes free with GarageBand, the others are part of the one time in-app purchase of $4.99).
    - ▸ **Drum Kit Designer**: This is the Software Instrument Plugin that is loaded on the Drummer Track when using any of the Drum Patches. It is a sophisticated Sample Player with acoustic drum samples. Like all the other Plugins that are loaded by a Patch, it is hidden from the user and you only can change the sound via the Smart Controls Window or by loading a different Drum Kit Patch.
    - ▸ **Smart Controls**: The Smart Controls Window on a Drummer Track provides some controls to affect the sound of the drums.

The Drummer Ecosystem

Here is the Drummer concept again with the screenshots of the related window elements.

- You create a new Track, the **Drummer Track** ❶.
- The Drummer Track contains special Regions, the **Drummer Regions** ❷.
- The Regions contain the **Drum Pattern**, the instructions for the Pattern Generator what and how to play.
- Each Drummer Region (the instructions) can be edited in the **Drummer Editor** ❸.
- 18 different **Drum Kits** ❹ are available in the **Library Window** ❺.
- A Drum Kit includes style specific **Drummer Presets** ❻ that become available in the Drummer Editor ❸.
- A Drum Kit also includes all the Plugins, including the Software Instrument Plugin "Drum Kit Designer" ❼.
- The Plugins are hidden in GarageBand but their important parameters can be controlled via the Smart Controls Window ❽.

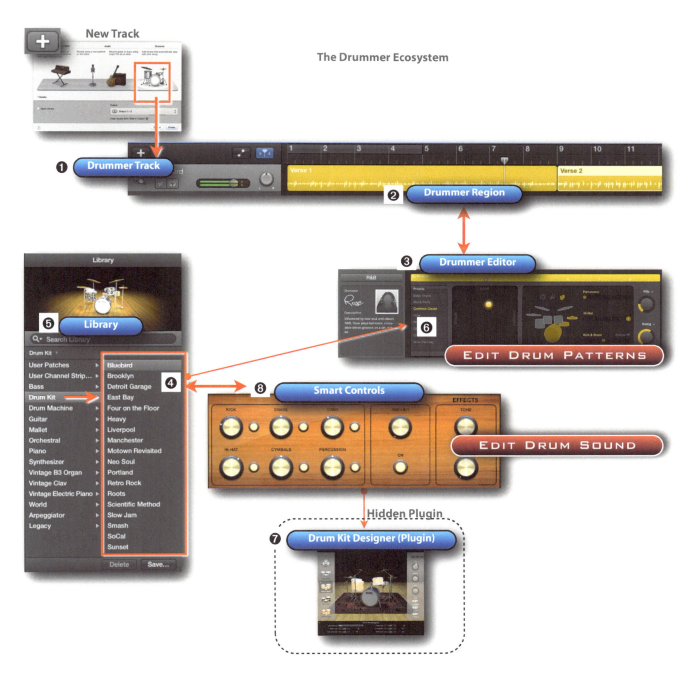

20 - The Drummer Editor

Add a Drummer

The first step of using the Drummer feature in GarageBand is to add a Drummer Track. This is like hiring a virtual Drummer (and a really good one) for your Project. Your "budget" is limited to one drummer per Project.

Click the plus button [+] on the Track List header to open the New Track Dialog.

New Track Dialog

➡ A New Drummer and much more

When creating the Drummer Track, a whole sequence of events will happen (you should be aware of).

- ☑ That special *Drummer Track* will be added to the Tracks Area.
- ☑ The Software Instrument "*Drum Kit Designer*" will be loaded.
- ☑ The Drum Kit Patch "*SoCal*" will be loaded from the Library with the (invisible) Software Instrument Plugin "Drum Kit Designer".
- ☑ Additional Effects will be loaded with a Smart Controls Layout available to control the Drum Sound.
- ☑ <u>Two 8-bar Drummer Regions</u> are created on the Drummer Track's Track Lane starting at the first bar of your Project. Both Regions represent two different Drum Patterns.
  If the Project contains Arrangement Markers, then Drummer Regions are created for each Arrangement Marker adapting their name and appropriate Drum Patterns for the sections (Intro, Verse, etc.).

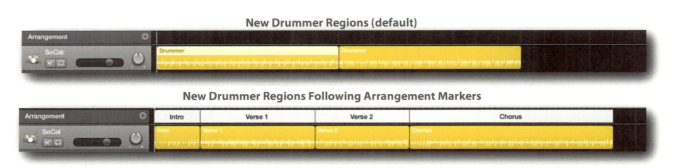

New Drummer Regions (default)

New Drummer Regions Following Arrangement Markers

➡ Add New Drummer Regions

Here is another major difference to be aware of. Instead of "recording" Regions on the Drummer Track, you just create additional Regions with a simple command. The newly created Region(s) will have a default Drum Pattern as its instructions to start with.

- ▶ **Create a Region**: *Cmd+click* on the empty Track Lane of the Drummer Track.
  - A new 8-bar Drummer Region will be created starting at the beginning of the bar you clicked in.
  - If an Arrangement Marker exists at that position, then the new Drummer Region will match the name and the length of that Arrangement Marker.

Now that you created those Regions, the question is, what are these "Drum Pattern" Regions?

Drummer Editor

Drummer Regions

A Drummer Region is a special Region. It is not a MIDI Region where you can see the individual notes that are played (and edit them). Although it sounds like the live recording of a drummer playing some grooves, the Drummer Region is also not an Audio Region where you can see and edit the audio waveform.

> **A Drummer Region contains instructions for a Drum Pattern Generator**

🟡 What is it?

So a Drummer Region contains special instructions for the Drum Pattern Generator. And guess what, the Drummer Track <u>is</u> that Drum Pattern Generator. It receives those instructions from the Drummer Regions when you play them back and the generated Pattern is then sent in real time as MIDI notes to the (hidden) Drum Kit Designer Plugin that is assigned to the Drummer Track.

🟡 How do you edit it?

If you want the Drummer to play a different Drum Pattern or change aspects of it (more of this, less of that, etc.), then you have to modify/edit the instructions. For that, you cannot use any of the existing Editors. Drummer Regions can only be edited with a special Editor, the <u>Drummer Editor.</u> It provides the interface to change the individual parameters (for each selected Region) that determine the outcome of the Drum Pattern Generator.

🟡 What do you see?

GarageBand makes those resulting Drum Patterns visible in a "musical way". If you zoom in the Drummer Region, you can see the Events on three layers. Kick, Snare and others. You can follow the groove and even spot the fills, where it gets "crowded" at the end of a Region.

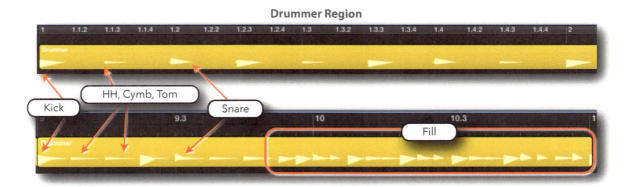

🟡 How do you convert it?

You cannot drag a Drummer Region onto a MIDI Track or Audio Track. However you can drag a MIDI Region onto a Drummer Track. The (hidden) Drum Kit Designer Plugin assigned to the Drummer Track will play those MIDI notes if they match the (General MIDI) note assignments.

Drummer Editor Interface

➡ **Open the Drummer Editor**

The Drummer Editor will be displayed in the same bottom Window Pane of the GarageBand Window as the other Editors.

Toggle the Drummer Editor with the following commands. At least one Drummer Region must be selected in the Tracks Area. If no Region is currently selected, then at least the Drummer Track has to be selected.

- Main Menu *View* ➤ *Show Editors*
- Key Command *E*
- *Click* on the Editors button in the Control Bar
- *Double-click* on a Drummer Region
- Drag the Divider Line all the way down to close the Window Pane

➡ **Interface**

The Drummer Editor has two panes:

🥁 **Track-based Editing**

The left pane is for track-based settings. That means whatever you change here will affect the whole Drummer Track and all the Regions on it.
- ▸ Select one of 18 Drummers, grouped in four Genres. Without the additional in-app purchase, you have only 1 Drummer available.

🥁 **Region-based Editing**

The pane on the right is for region-based editing. Whatever Region is selected on the Track Lane is displayed here and can be edited. Remember, you don't see MIDI Events here (not a MIDI Region) and you don't see an audio waveform (not an Audio Region). This is a pattern based Region so instead of editing MIDI events or waveforms, you use the interface elements on this window to edit the Parameters for the Drum Pattern Generator ("how to play and what to play") for each individual Drummer Region.

Track-based Editing

Select a Drummer

- ☑ **Click** on the large button ❶ on the top.
- ☑ This will open a popup menu with four Genres ❷.
- ☑ Once you've selected a Genre from the popup menu, the display changes and shows a selection of three to six Drummers ❸ available for that Genre. Move the mouse over the player's icon and a yellow Help Tag pops up to describes the Drummer's style.
- ☑ **Click** on the icon of a Drummer to choose him or her.
- ☑ You can quickly select a different Drummer from the same Genre by moving the mouse over the Drummer icon in the Drummer Editor ❻. A stacked icon ❼ will appear. **Click** on it to go back to the Drummer selection of that Genre to switch to a different Drummer.
- ☑ A Dialog Window ❺ might pop up warning you that if you change a Drummer, you will lose all the region-based settings you made. Hold down the *option* key when loading a new Drummer without changing the current Patch and Region settings.
- ☑ Once you selected a Drummer, a Character Card ❻ displays the icon and name of the Drummer plus a description of his or her playing style.

➡ ***Who (what) are these Drummers?***

On the outside, it really looks like you are loading audio files from various drummers that performed those drum patterns and the Drummer Editor now lets you tweak those performances. Why not? There is Flex Time, Flex Pitch, Melodyne and all sorts of crazy technology, maybe it is possible. Or maybe GarageBand is just using a very sophisticated Drum Pattern Generator with other sophisticated technology to make it sound that you are manipulating the performance of a live drummer.

Region-based Editing

Parameters

Before getting into the details about editing a Drummer Region, here is a comparison between a MIDI Track and a Drummer Track to demonstrate the fundamental difference of a Drummer Region.

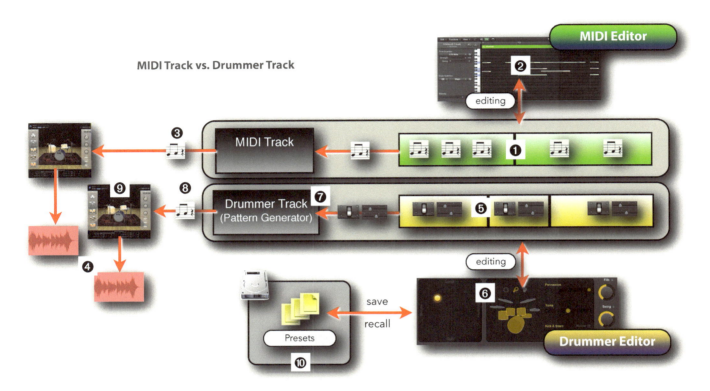

MIDI Regions

The Track Lane of a MIDI Track contains MIDI Regions. Those MIDI Regions contain musical content in the form of MIDI Events ❶. A MIDI Editor ❷ can display and edit those MIDI Events. The MIDI Events are sent to the Instrument Plugin assigned to the Track that outputs the MIDI Events as an audio signal ❹.

Drummer Regions

The Track Lane of the Drummer Track contain Drummer Regions ❺. The Drummer Regions contain the musical information (what to play) in the form of parameter values for the Drum Pattern Generator. The parameters could be: Play simple, play complex, play with toms, play a lot of fills, etc. The Drummer Editor ❻ can display and edit those Parameters. Those Parameters are the input for the Drummer Track's Pattern Generator ❼. The output of the Drum Pattern Generator are MIDI Events ❽ that represent the Drum Pattern created based on the Parameter input ❼. Those MIDI Events ❽ are sent to the Instrument Plugin (Drum Kit Designer ❾) assigned to the Drummer Track which outputs the MIDI Events as an audio signal ❹.

> **Presets**: The whole set of Parameter values that are stored in a Drummer Region and made visible in the Drummer Editor can be saved as Presets ❿, stored to disk and recalled later from disk. Actually, only Logic can save those Regions as Drummer Presets but GarageBand will display all those user Drummer Presets too that are created in Logic.

I hope it has become clear by now that when we discuss the editing of a Drummer Region it means editing of Parameter values.

Drummer Presets

So whenever you look at a Drummer Region, think of it as a parameter set, or a file with a list of instructions that tell the Drum Pattern Generator of the Drummer Track what and how to play.

➡ **Default Preset**

When you create a new Drummer Region, a default set of Parameter values is applied to that Region. Which set of Parameters, depends on the currently active Drummer.

Remember that when you load a Drummer (or create the Drummer Track in your Project), it loads also the Drummer's Presets into the Drummer Editor. One of those Presets is the Default Preset which is applied to any new Drummer Region you create on the Drummer Track's Track Lane. The Default Drummer Region is the one in the Preset Area that is marked yellow ('the chosen one') after you loaded the Drummer.

➡ **Apply a Preset**

To apply a different Preset to a Region, select the Region and *click* on a Preset in the Preset Area. You can see only 9 Presets at a time so you have to scroll up or down if there are more than 9 Presets on the list.

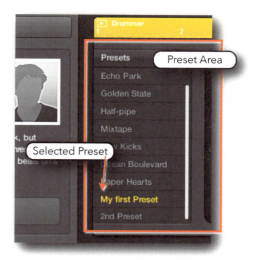

> Applying a Preset to a Drummer Region is like a starting point. It overwrites any previous settings for that Region. The currently selected Preset is yellow.

➡ **Preset Management**

The files are stored in a Preset Folder that contains subfolders for each Drummer which contains the actual Preset files with the extension .dpst.

- Factory Presets:
  /Library/Application Support/Logic/Drummer/Presets/"Name of the Drummer"/
- User Presets:
  ~/Music/Audio Music Apps/Drummer/Presets/"Name of the Drummer"/

Manual Editing - Overview

To the right of the Preset Area are the available Parameters (Performance Controls) for the Drum Pattern. You can change their values with the onscreen controls. They are grouped into three areas:

Drummer Editor (Parameters)

 Left Area ❶

On the left is the x/y Pad, a square field with a yellow puck that lets you set the Complexity and Loudness of the Drum Pattern.

 Middle Area ❷

The area in the middle provides the controls for the individual Drum Kit Pieces.

Right Area ❸

The right area provides two knobs to influence the drum fills (played at the end of a Region or a section) and the Shuffle feel of the Drum Pattern.

Parameters

Please keep in mind:

- ☑ A Drummer Region always starts with the Parameter values of the Default Preset.
- ☑ You can select a different Preset (different Parameter values) from the Preset Area.
- ☑ You can manually change the available Parameter values.
- ☑ Once you select a different Preset, you overwrite all Parameter values you set manually with the values from that newly selected Preset.

● Complexity - Loudness

This is the x/y pad with a single controller, the yellow puck. You set the value of two parameters with one controller depending where on the square you place the yellow puck. The x-axis represents the Complexity and the y-axis represents the Loudness.

▸ **Complexity**: Move the puck between left (Simple) and right (Complex). The more you place the puck to the right, the more complex the Drum Pattern gets.

▸ **Loudness**: Move the puck between low (Soft) and high (Loud) to control the intensity of the played drum pattern.

x/y Pad

Complexity

● Drum Kit Pieces

You have to pay attention to the details of the various controls in this section.

This is the place where you configure what Drum Kit Pieces (Kick, Snare, Toms, HiHat, Cymbal, Percussion) will be part of the Drum Pattern and what pattern they are playing.

- **Drum Kit Piece**: There are four Layers of Drum Kit Pieces: Percussion - "8th notes" (Cymbal, HiHat, Toms) - Snare - Kick. *Click* on their icon to turn them on (yellow) or off (gray).
- **Pattern Slider**: There are three sliders. The active (yellow) slider controls the active (yellow) Drum Kit Piece next to it. The slider has various fixed positions that produce different playing patterns. Please note that the slider "remembers" its value for its Drum Kit Piece when deactivated or switched.

Drum Kit Pieces

▸ **Percussion**: *Click* on the icons to select one of the three percussion instruments (Tambourine, Shaker, Clap) to be played in the Drum Pattern, or none. The label for the slider is "Percussion", but it remembers the individual setting for each of the three instruments when selected.

▸ **8th notes**: Usually the 8th note part (the right hand of the drummer) of a standard drum groove is played on the HiHat. Alternatively, you can choose to have it played on the Cymbals or the Toms by clicking on those icons, or select none. The label on the slider displays the name of the Drum Kit Piece that is selected.

▸ **Snare**: The Snare can be turned on or off to be included in the Drum Pattern. The value of the slider controls Snare and Kick together.

▸ **Kick**: The Kick can be turned on or off to be included in the Drum Pattern. The value of the slider controls Snare and Kick together.

🔵 Follow Rhythm

Follow Rhythm

This feature is similar to GarageBand's Groove Track feature but more flexible. With Groove Tracks you select one Track in your Project as the dedicated Reference Track and then select other Tracks that should follow that Lead Track (quantized to). With the *Follow Rhythm* feature in the Drummer Editor, you can separately choose for each Drummer Region whether or not it should follow a Lead Track. In addition, you can choose for each Region individually what Track to follow.

- ☑️ Select the "*Follow*" Checkbox. The field underneath changes to the Follow Track popup menu which lists Tracks in your Project that you can select as the rhythmical Reference Track for that Drummer Region.

🔵 Customize Fills

Adjust the Fills Knob by *dragging* it up and down to increase or decrease the number and the length of the drum fill at the end of a Region or a musical section. This is a perfect example that you are setting up instructions and not specific notes. This Fill Parameter determines what is played at the end of a Region. So you can resize the Region to 2 bars or 16 bars, and the fill is played at the end of bar 2 or bar 16. In other words, whenever you need a fill (little or over the top), you just resize (or split) the Drummer Region so it ends at that position.

The Lock 🔒 Button prevents any changes to the Fill Parameters when switching to a different Preset or Drummer. The knob itself is dimmed when Lock is activated.

🔵 Customize Swing Feel

Adjust the Swing Knob by *dragging* it up and down to increase or decrease the shuffle feel.

The Lock 🔒 Button prevents any changes to that Swing Parameter when switching to a different Preset or Drummer. The knob itself is dimmed when Lock is activated.

Drummer Regions Restrictions

Based on the knowledge we have so far, it makes sense that Drummer Regions cannot overlap. Think about it, a Drummer Region contains a list of Parameter values, so overlapping them makes no sense.

If you move a Drummer Region over another Drummer Region, it will shorten the Region you are "moving into".

Drummer Editor - Ruler

On top of the Drummer Editor is the Ruler.

- ▸ The Drummer Editor has a fixed length and can't be resized or zoomed. Therefore, the Ruler always has the same length and displays only one Region at a time (the selected Region) in that length regardless of whether it is 2 bars or 32 bars long.
- ▸ The Solo Play ❶ button lets you audition the Region in Solo Mode.
- ▸ Next to it is the name ❷ of the selected Region (sorry, read only, you can't rename the Region here).
- ▸ The Ruler units always display Musial Time in bars and beats ❸ regardless of the Display Mode of the Control Bar Display.
- ▸ The Playhead ❹ moves along the Ruler in Play Mode and can also be *dragged* manually along the Ruler.
- ▸ *Click* on the Ruler to place the Playhead at that position and *double-click* to start playback at that position. If Cycle Mode is active ⟳, then playback starts at the Left Cycle Locator (even outside the Drummer Region).

➡ Multiple Regions selection

If you've selected more than one Drummer Region in the Workspace, then the Ruler changes to a solid yellow bar without time divisions and Playhead. It only displays the text "*Multiple Regions selected*" on it.
Now, whatever Parameter you are changing, will apply to all the selected Regions.

21 - Mixing

A different Concept

GarageBand uses a different approach when it comes to mixing. There is no dedicated Mixer window like in other DAWs that simulates a traditional mixing console.

Mixer Window

Instead, you do the mixing in the GarageBand Window using the following Window Panes
- ❶ **Track Header**: Level Adjustments with Volume, Pan, Mute
- ❷ **Library**: Load different Patches (sets of Effects and Instruments) onto a Track
- ❸ **Smart Controls**: Adjust the Effects for a Track
- ❹ **AU Plugins**: Add additional Effects that can be adjusted "outside" the GarageBand Window

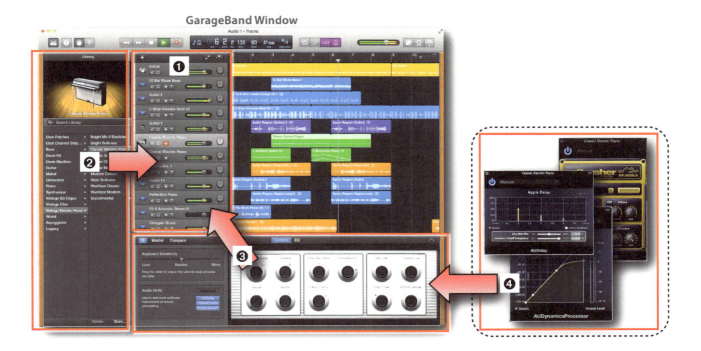
GarageBand Window

Track Header

Track List

The Track List with the individual Track Headers is as close as it gets to a Mixer Window. This is the only place in GarageBand where you can see and control all the Tracks at the same time (as long as you have a big enough screen).

This is the place where you "mix" all the Tracks together. That means you adjust their levels to set the right balance compared to the other Tracks, i.e. drums louder, less guitar, more vocals, etc. This is a direct approach, where you see the Track, you reach for the control and adjust it. There is no need to click around to open and close windows. With external hardware controllers like the Logic Remote running on an iPad, you are not only seeing the controls of multiple Tracks at the same time, you even can move multiple Faders at the same time (multi-touch Gestures).

The available controls on each Track Header are:

- **Volume Slider** : Set the level of the Track (how loud will you hear the audio signal in the mix).
- **Volume Meter**: The Meter is embedded in the Volume Slider and gives you a visual representation of the Track's signal level in the mix.
- **Pan Knob** : Set the balance of the audio signal between the left and right channel in the stereo field.
- **Mute Button** : The Mute Button also belongs to the level controls because it lets you set the level to "very very low" which is -∞dB, or in other words, silence.
- **Solo Button** : Solo is a "reverse" Mute Button that mutes all the other Tracks if you want to listen to a Track in isolation.

Library

The concept and implementation of the Library is the most important aspect of how to mix in GarageBand. Especially if you are used to the Library from earlier GarageBand versions. I explained that already in the Library chapter so here is just the summary.

- 💡 **New Rules**
    - You cannot load different Effects and Software Instrument Plugins onto a Track anymore (see exception on the next page).
    - You can only load Patches from the Library.
    - Each Patch contains a specific set of selected Effects Plugins (and one Instrument Plugin if it is a MIDI Track).
    - All these Plugins are Logic Plugins, but GarageBand doesn't reveal which ones are loaded with what Patch.
    - You cannot change, remove or add other Logic Plugins (as it was possible in earlier versions of GarageBand). If you need a Chorus Effect and the loaded Patch doesn't have that Effect, then you have to find a different Patch that has that effect.
    - You can only adjust the Parameters for the Plugins with the preconfigured Screen Controls in the Smart Controls Window.

Be Aware

▸ The open Library Window is always "connected" to the currently selected Track in the Tracks Area.
- It displays the Patch that was loaded onto that Track.
  - Be careful, if the Library has key focus (has a blue frame around it) then it is active. For example, if you use the up and down arrow keys on your keyboard, it steps through the Patches and loads that Patch onto the Track, overwriting any existing Patch and all their adjustments you did.

▸ Each Track Type (Audio, MIDI, Drummer, Master) has their own types of Patches. That means the displayed content in the Library Window (the available Patches) are different for the individual Track Types.

▸ Loading a different Patch onto a Track will overwrite all the adjustments you did with the controls in the Smart Controls window. And it will remove all the AU Plugins that you added to that Track.

Smart Controls

The new Smart Controls Window is the actual place where you mix your Project beyond the basic level settings. Here, you apply all sorts of effects to get creative with your mix.

Adjusting one Track at a Time

The Smart Controls Window displays the controls of the currently selected Track. That means you can see and control the effects ❶ only one Track at a time.

Invisible Plugins

The actual Plugins and their Parameters are not visible. The Screen Controls ❷ act as remote controls for the loaded Plugins.

Fixed Control Sets

The available Screen Controls are preconfigured. You cannot add or remove controls. The advantage of that restricted simplicity is that the user can controls complex signal processing. For example, a single Screen Control could control multiple Parameters of multiple Plugins. There is even advanced routing with Aux busses going on under the hood that the user doesn't have to worry about.

Add AU Plugins

You still have the option to load additional AU Plugins ❸.

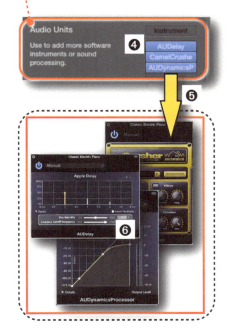

AU Plugin (Audio Units)

You can add additional AU Plugins ❹ to a Track, up to 4 Effects plus one Software Instrument if it is a MIDI Track. For those Plugins, you can open their separate Plugin Windows ❺ to have access to all the available controls ❻.

Please note that the loaded Plugins are part of the Smart Controls Window (they have to be enabled in the Preferences) and will be overwritten when you load a new Patch onto the Track.

Amp Designer & Pedalboard

I briefly introduced the Amps and Pedalboards already in the Smart Controls chapter. Here now is a closer look at this amazing tool.

Concept

As we know by now, loading a Patch from the Library ❶ onto a Track does two things.
- ☑ **Load**: It loads a set of Plugins ❷ and routing configuration on that Track.
- ☑ **Control**: It provides a Smart Controls layout ❸ that functions as a "front-end" with pre-configured Screen Controls to adjust the loaded Plugins. The Plugins can not be accessed directly ❹ (by opening their Plugin Window). You don't even know what Plugins are loaded.

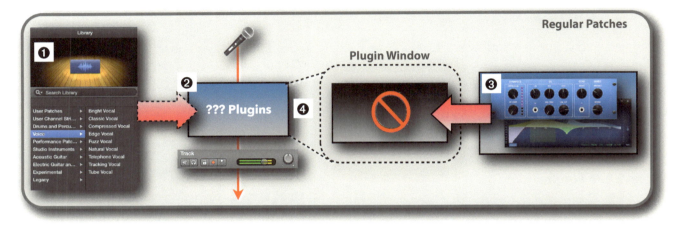

Every Patch has a specific set of Plugins and choosing different Patches is the only way (restricted way) to load different Plugins (whatever they are) to you Track. AU Plugins are the exception.

Now there is one special group of Patches that are located in the Library under the Category "Electric Guitar and Bass". ❺
- ☑ **Load**: As expected, those Patches load a set of Plugins ❻ and routing configuration on that Track. Judging by the name it will have some Plugins that are of special use for guitar sounds.
- ☑ **Control**: As expected, the Smart Controls ❼ provide a special layout for controlling those guitar-related Parameters of the loaded Plugins.
- ☑ **Plugin Window**: Now here is the difference! GarageBand allows you to open the two loaded Plugins in their own Plugin Window ❽, granting full access to all the Parameters of those two Plugins, the Amp Designer Plugin ❾ and the Pedalboard Plugin ❿.

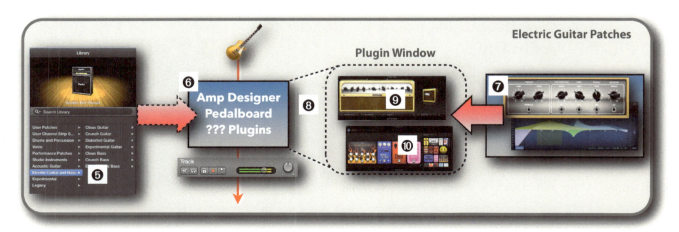

➡ Load Electric Guitar Patches

Did you ever wonder why there are two icons in the New Track Dialog to create an Audio Track, the microphone icon and the electric guitar icon? Here is the difference:

- ▶ **Microphone**: This option creates a standard Audio Track that loads a Patch with some basic Effect Plugins. After creating that Audio Track, you could just load one of those Electric Guitar Patches onto that Track and you are ready to play with the Amps and Pedalboards.
- ▶ **Guitar**: This option also creates an Audio Track. The difference is more for convenience.
    - ☑ Instead of loading a basic Patch, this option loads the Electric Guitar Patch "Brit and Clean" so you have the Amp Designer and Pedalboard Plugin pre-loaded already with the Track.
    - ☑ The only other cosmetic difference when choosing a guitar-based Audio Track is the color of the Audio Region. The Regions recorded on those Tracks are purple instead of blue.

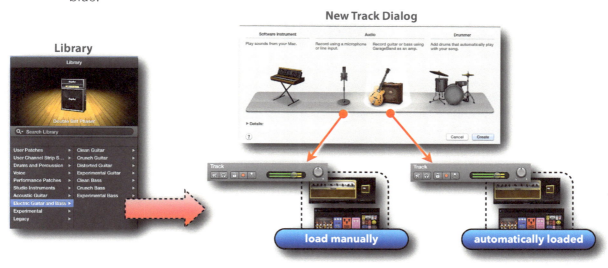

🔵 Amp Button & Pedal Button

The Smart Controls Window of an Audio Track has two buttons on the right side of its Menu Bar. They indicate if the Amp Designer 🎛 and the Pedalboard 🎚 Plugins are loaded.

- 🎛 🎚 Dimmed: The Plugins are not loaded. Most likely a non-guitar Patch.
- 🎛 🎚 Gray: The Plugins are loaded. Most likely, the current Patch is a guitar Patch. *Clicking* on the buttons will open the Plugin Windows.
- 🎛 🎚 Blue: The Plugins are loaded and the Plugin Windows are open.

Smart Controls Menu Bar

Modeling

Creating a specific guitar sound is an art form all by itself.

It starts with the choice of the guitar and its pickups. That guitar signal is then plugged into a chain of various components (stompboxes, amps, cabinets) and each one alters and shapes the sound. Even the sound engineer takes part of that sound creation by picking a specific type of microphone and placing it at the right position in front of the speaker cabinet to record the guitar signal which now is highly processed. Let's ignore all the additional sound "treatment" for now that could be added later during the mix.

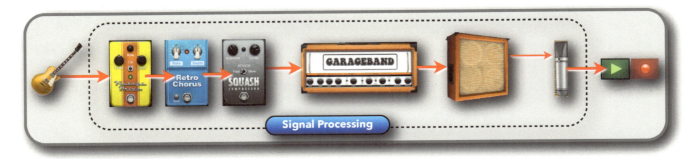

In a traditional recording session, your options are limited by the hardware that is available to you. Maybe the guitar player has only a few stompboxes, one or maybe two amps and cabinets and then, the question is what microphones are at your disposal.

This is where sound modeling comes in. Software engineers studied the characteristics of the various components used for recording electric guitars and developed Effect Plugins that simulate the sound characteristics of those components. This includes also all the individual controls on such a component (guitar amp) and how the sound changes depending on those control settings. Now, instead of plugging the guitar into different amps and speaker cabinets, you just connect the clean signal of the guitar to such a Plugin and select a Preset that is modeled after a specific amp. The user interface provides the controls that let you adjust the settings of those components (knobs and switches on an amp).

GarageBand provides two separate Plugins. The Pedalboard is an Effects Plugin that simulates famous stompboxes and the Amp Designer simulates famous guitar amps.

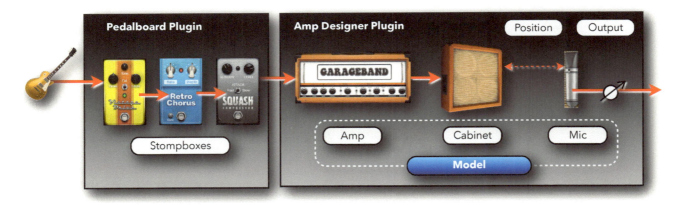

The Amp Designer Plugin provides Model Presets that lets you choose common setups of an amp its cabinet and the used mic for recording. Each Model Preset is actually a combination of three individual models, different **amp models**, different **cabinet models** and a selection of **mic models** that are available as their own Presets. This provides you with an endless variation of possible guitar sounds which of course can be saved as custom presets and then later recalled at any time.

Interface

Once you understand the concept, you have to make sure that you are not confused about the different windows and their functionality.

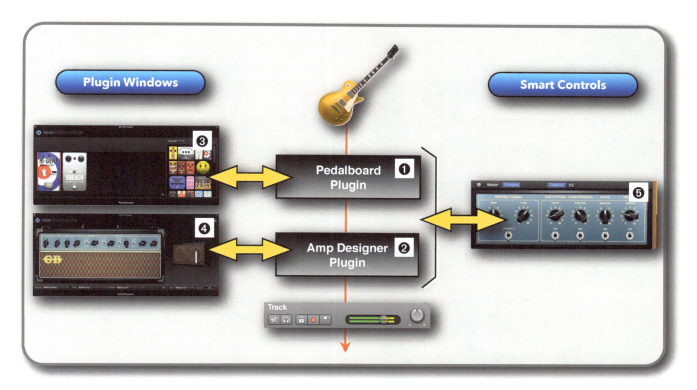

- 💡 **Plugins**

    The two Plugins (Pedalboard ❶ and Amp Designer ❷) are the two components that are loaded and placed into the signal chain of that Audio Track when you choose any of the Electric Guitar Patches from the Library.

- 💡 **Plugin Window**

    Each Plugin can be opened individually as a standard Plugin Window that contains all the controls and layouts for the specific Plugin. You open the Plugin Window by clicking on their button on the Menu Bar of the Smart Controls: Pedalboard 🔲 ❸ and the Amp Designer 🔲 ❹.

- 💡 **Smart Controls**

    Please note that the Smart Controls Window ❺ is different from the individual Plugins Windows.
    - The available Screen Controls are only a subset of all the controls for those Plugins.
    - Also, one Screen Control could affect multiple controls on the Plugins.
    - And this is very important: The single Smart Controls Window contains controls for both (!) Plugins, the Amp Designer and the Pedalboard (if loaded).

▶ If you have the Smart Controls Window and the Plugin Windows open, then you can see that adjusting the controls in one window will update the other. They are just two different interfaces for the actual Plugins.

▶ You can save the current settings you have (after creating a killer sound) as a user Patch in the Library that can be loaded later in any other Project or on a different Track of the current Project.

▶ Loading a Patch will overwrite all the changes you made to the Plugin, in either the Smart Controls Window or the individual Plugin Windows.

Amp Designer

As you can see, you have an amazing amount of control over the sound in the Amp Designer.

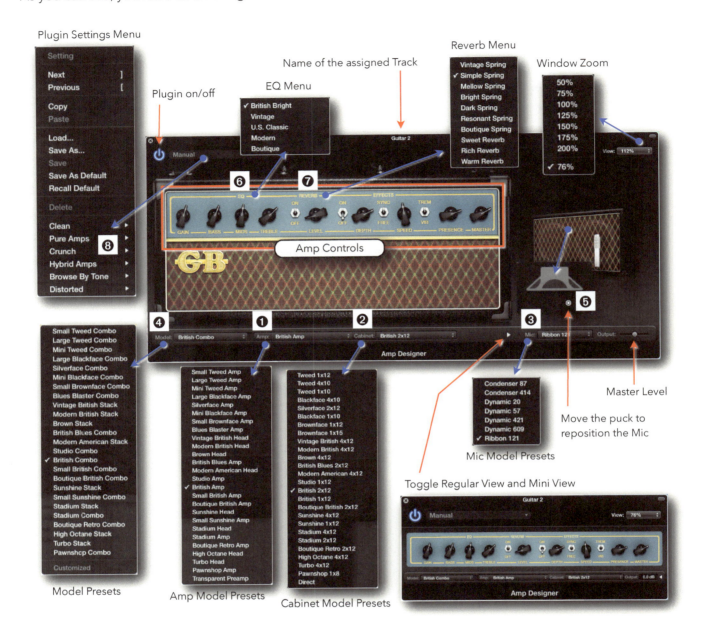

- ▸ At the bottom are all the menus to select the individual Model Presets: **Amp ❶**, **Cabinet ❷**, **Mic ❸**. The "**Model**" ❹ popup menu is like a Master Preset that includes a combination of all three individual Models.
- ▸ Move the mouse over the speaker cabinet and a square area pops up with a speaker and a puck ❺. Move the puck to indicate the position of the mic in front of the speaker.
- ▸ Click on the "EQ" label ❻ or "Reverb" label ❼ above the controls to open popup menus where you can choose from different EQ and Reverb models.

➡ *Plugin Settings Menu*

Remember that a Patch includes a wide variety of settings for the entire Track. Plugin Settings on the other hand include only the settings for the current Plugin. This Plugin Settings menu ❽ includes a list of available (factory) Plugin Settings and also lets you save your own Plug-in Settings.

Pedalboard

The Pedalboard Plugin simulates the board that many guitar players have in front of them with a lot of little so-called Stompboxes or Pedals. These are simple effect boxes with an input and output, very few controls and a button that can be "stomped" on to toggle the effect on and off. All those Pedals are usually daisy-chained together. Out to in to out to in to… The Pedalboard interface is pretty simple. It has three areas:

- **Pedal Browser ❶**

  This section contains all the available Stompboxes (35). Scroll through the list. Hide the Browser with the disclosure triangle in the left lower corner.
  - Move the mouse over a Stompbox and a Help Tag appears with a description of that effect.
  - The popup menu ❺ on top lets you restrict the displayed Pedals by category.
  - Add: *Drag* a Stompbox from the Browser to the left, over the Pedal Area.

- **Pedal Area ❷**

  The Pedal Area displays all the Pedals that are active at the moment (up to ten). Move the controllers on the Pedals to adjust their Parameter.
  - Reorder: *Drag* the Pedals left or right to change their order. The signal flows from left to right. The order is very important and can change the resulting sound dramatically.
  - Replace: *Drag* a Pedal from the Browser not between but onto an existing Pedal to replace it.
  - Remove: Select a Pedal and hit the *delete* key to remove it from the Pedal Area.

- **Routing Area ❸**

  At the bottom of the Pedal Browser are two special Utility Pedals, the **Splitter** and the **Mixer**.
  - *Drag* the Splitter ❻ to the Pedal Area between two Stompboxes and a routing diagram ❼ appears in the Routing Area on top. The Mixer Pedal ❽ will automatically be added.
  - The diagram shows the parallel/serial signal flow from box to box.
  - *Click* on a Pedal in the Routing Area ❾ to move it between the upper and lower signal chain or *click* on the dot ❿ to move the Splitter to that position
  - The Splitter and Mixer Pedal contain additional controls that further determine the signal flow.

The Pedalboard Plugin also contains many Plugin Settings ❹ with pre-configured Pedals.

Automation

Automation is a standard feature in all DAWs and virtually no mix is done without automation anymore. Instead of setting each control to a specific value and leave it throughout the song, you can change that value over time and let GarageBand perform those value changes automatically. GarageBand has a limited implementation of the Automation feature, but it is still very powerful and super easy to use.

Concept

Here is a quick look at the basic concept of Automation with a little bit of a math background.

Scenario ❶

▶ **Real Life**

You set the Fader for the vocal track on your mixing board to 0dB. You start to play the Project and throughout the 3 minutes of the song, you leave the Fader at that position without changes.

▶ **Math Representation**

You might remember from your math class that you could draw that as a graph. The x-axis represents the duration of the song (playing for 3 minutes) and the y-axis represents the position of the Fader (the value of the volume).

The Result:

> The parameter value (the Fader) stays **constant**

Scenario ❷

▶ **Real Life**

In real life, you probably find that the singer moved a little bit too close to the microphone during the song at 1min and you have to gradually lower the Volume Fader to -10dB when reaching the 2 minute mark. At that point, the singer seemed to realize that and moved away from the mic, but this time a bit too far. You compensate that by raising the Volume Fader back up, all the way to +3dB by the time the song reaches the 3 minute mark.

▶ **Math Representation**

The mathematical function is a visual representation of the movement I just did with the Fader. The parameter value starts at 0 and stays at that value up to the 1 minute mark. Now the value decreases gradually to -10 and when the graph reaches the 2 minute mark on the time axis, it gradually increases to +3 when it reaches the 3 minute mark on the time axis.

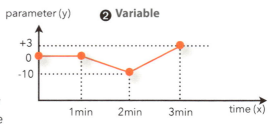

The Result:

> The parameter value (the Fader) **varies** over time

What is Automation

If we look at the graph, it is telling us one thing: "It describes the behavior of a parameter (i.e. the Fader) over time (the length of the song)". And that is exactly how you can define mix automation. Instead of doing the movement manually, you describe the movement in a graph and every time you play back your song, GarageBand performs that movement automatically:

> **Automation describes how Garageband changes the value of a Track Parameter during the song**

Let me first introduce the terminology for Automation in your GarageBand Project.

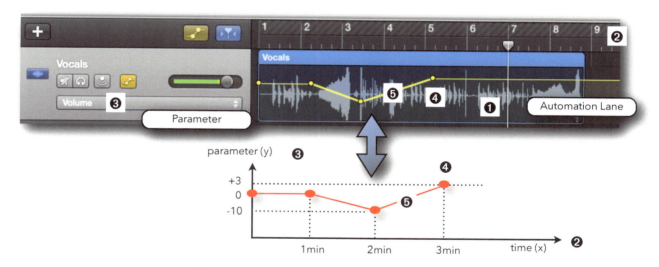

❶ Automation Lane (Graph Area)

The Track Lane changes to a mini Track Lane and leaves the rest of the space to the Automation Lane that shows the graph while still displaying the (dimmed) Region Content.

❷ Timeline (x)

The time axis of the graph is already there in GarageBand. It is the Timeline of your current Project represented by the Ruler on top of the Workspace.

❸ Parameter (y)

The Volume Fader is only one possible Parameter on a Track that you can automate. You can automate many other Parameters available on the Track. The most used ones are Volume and Pan, but any Screen Control in the Track's Smart Controls Window plus any Parameter of an assigned AU Plugin are available Parameters that can be automated.

❹ Control Points

The red dots on the math graph represent the values of the parameter at a specific time. In math class, these were called the "coordinates", but GarageBand calls them "Control Points" (other applications use the terms "nodes" or 'keyframes").

❺ Automation Curve

GarageBand connects those Control Points, resulting in the Automation Curve. This line represents the change of the Parameter value over time: Staying constant, going up or going down.

Automation Buttons

Here is the most important (potentially confusing) thing about Automation in GarageBand: There are two different Automation Buttons that look alike.

 **Show/Hide Automation**

This is a global button (rectangle shape) on top of the Track List that toggles the visibility of the automation data and the automation controls.

- ▸ This is a global button that affects all Tracks.
- ▸ You can either show ❶ or hide ❷ the Automation on all Tracks. You can also toggle the command with:
    - Main Menu *Mix* ➤ *Show Automation*
    - Key Command *A*
- ▸ Hiding the Automation doesn't affect the actual Automation data, you just won't see it.
- ▸ When Automation is shown, the following things change:
    - ☑ The Track gets higher ❸ to accommodate the additional controls on the Track Header.
    - ☑ The Track Header displays the Track Automation Button ❹.
    - ☑ The Track Header displays the Automation Parameter popup menu ❺.
    - ☑ The Track Lane splits into a dual lane. The mini Track Header on top displays the Region Header and the area underneath (still showing the visible Region Content) is now the Automation Lane displaying the Automation Curve ❻.

Track Automation

This is a Track Header button (square shape) that toggles the Automation on or off for the current Track.

- ▸ Each Track has its own Track Automation button.
- ▸ You can either enable ❼ or disable ❽ the Automation on a Track.
- ▸ Disabling the Automation on a Track just bypasses the automation data, it does not delete it.
- ▸ The Automation Curve of a Track that has the Automation disabled displays the Automation Curve in white instead of the Parameter specific color.

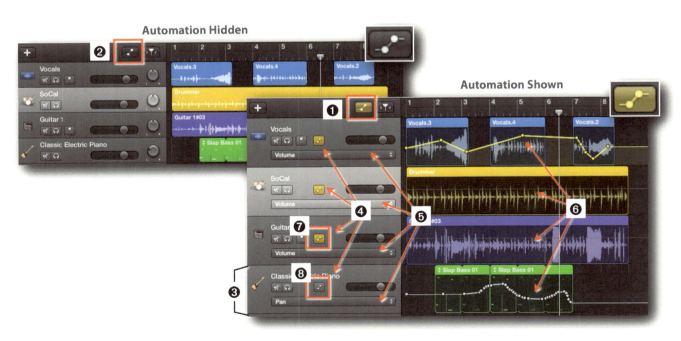

Automation Parameter Popup Menu

➡ ## What is an Automation Parameter

Think of an Automation Parameter as any control on a Track that can be automated.

The Automation Parameter popup menu is divided into sections:

❶ Volume/Pan: Volume and Pan are always available as the first two Parameters on the menu.

❷ Smart Controls: The second section lists all the Screen Controls that are available on the Smart Controls Window for that Track. Two things to pay attention to:

- Different Tracks have different Smart Controls; that means the available controls vary. The screenshot displays the popup menu for four different Track Types ❺ and their different Smart Controls. Below is a screenshot of the Smart Controls Window next to the popup menu with the identical names for the Screen Controls ❻.

- A single Screen Control may be assigned to a single control (i.e. Low Cut) or to multiple controls (i.e. Gain, Threshold, Ratio represented by the Parameter "Squeeze").

❸ AU Plugin controls: If you've loaded any AU Plugins ❼ on a Track in the Smart Controls Inspector, then those Plugins are listed by their name after the section for the Smart Controls. Individual Submenus ❽ contain all the available controls for that Plugin.

❹ Parameter with active Automation: At the bottom of the menu are all the Parameters listed that you created automation for. Remember, the Automation Parameter popup menu lets you select the Parameter to edit its Automation Curve, one at a time. However, you can automate as many Parameters as you like. They are then listed in this section.

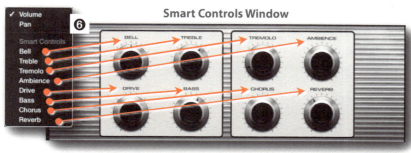

Smart Controls Window

Automation Lane

Now let's have a closer look at the Automation Lane and its different appearances.

Automation is hidden.

Automation is visible but is disabled on that Track. The wider Track displays the additional controls (Track Automation and popup menu). BTW, stereo Tracks can now show the waveform of both channels.

Automation is enabled (Automation Lane visible) but no Automation is created yet (no Automation Curve). A dimmed straight line only indicates the current value of the control, in this case the Volume Slider.

The Automation Curve has only one Control Point at the beginning of the Project, creating a straight line. You still can move the Volume Slider which updates the straight Automation Curve.

Busy Automation Curve (Volume) on the Automation Lane with many Control Points.

Same Automation Curve (Volume) active but only visible as a dimmed curve because a different Automation Parameter (Pan) is selected.

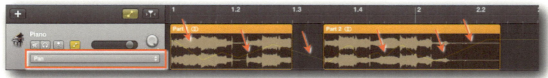

Volume is again selected as the current Automation Parameter with the Volume Automation Curve visible. Other Automation Curves are also active and can be (barely) seen as dimmed curves.

➡ "Double Lane"

The Automation Lane is actually part of a double Lane with an upper section and a lower section. You have to be very careful where to click. Each of those sections have their own Click Zones that change the Mouse Pointer to specific Tool and resulting action.

Automation Visible and Enabled

- 🟡 **Track Lane (Region Header) ❶**
    - ▸ The upper section still displays the Region Header and is not affected when switching between Track Automation enabled 🔲 and Track Automation disabled 🔲.
    - ▸ If you want to edit a Region (move, copy, trim, etc.) with the Mouse Pointer while the Automation Lane is visible, you have to point at the Region Header.
    - ▸ The mini Track Lane still displays the grid ❸ so you have the vertical time reference to the Ruler.

- 🟡 **Automation Lane (Automation Curve) ❷**
    - ▸ Below the Region Header is the actual Automation Lane.
    - ▸ It is important to understand that this is "Track-based" Automation which means the Automation Curve "belongs" to the Track and not the individual Region. It is a continuous graph along the Track's timeline.
    - ▸ Any mouse action on the Automation Lane (click, drag) does not affect the Region, only the Automation Curve. The Region content (waveform, MIDI Events) is just visible for better orientation.
    - ▸ Different Automation Parameters display the Control Points and the Automation Curve in a specific color.
    - ▸ The Track Automation Button toggles the Automation for all Automation Parameters on a Track.

Mini Track Lane + Automation Lane

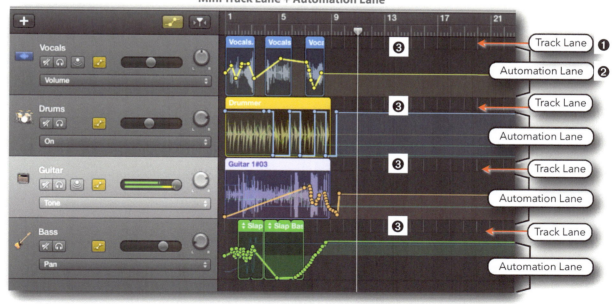

21 - Mixing

Creating an Automation Curve

Anytime you want to create automation in your Project, make sure you have the following three things checked.

➡ ***Prepare to Automate***

- ☑ Make sure the Show Automation Button ❸ in your Project is activated to see all the automation related controls.
- ☑ Make sure the Track Automation Button ❹ is activated on the Track you want to automate. This changes the appearance of the Track Lane to add the Automation Lane.
- ☑ Make sure you have selected the Automation Parameter from the popup menu ❺ you want to automate (i.e. Volume).

Please note that at this moment you made the Automation <u>visible</u>, <u>enabled</u> the Automation on the Track and <u>selected</u> the Parameter but there is still nothing automated on the Track because you haven't created any automation data yet ❻.

Now let's do it.

The Automation Curve can have three stages.

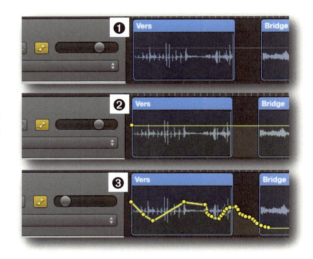

- ❶ **Default (no automation)**

    When there are no Control Points on the Automation Lane (no automation data has been created yet or they have been deleted), then a thin horizontal line indicates the current value of the selected Automation Parameter. In this example, changing the Volume Slider will move the line up or down accordingly.

- ❷ **Single Control Point**

    Click anywhere on the Automation Lane to create the first Control Point. It will be placed at the beginning of the Project at bar 1 with the current value of the Controller (in this case the Volume Slider at 0dB).

    Because you only have one Control Point defined at that moment, you can still move the Automation Curve by moving the controller of that Parameter (i.e. Volume Slider).

- ❸ **More than one Control Point**

    Now you can add more Control Points and edit them to create your Automation Curve. At this moment you could move the actual controller of the Parameter (i.e. Volume Slider) but as soon as you start the playback, the controller follows the movement of the Automation Curve (moved by invisible hands).

Now let's go over the various commands of adding and editing Control Points that make up the shape of the Automation Curve. Please note that these commands are also possible when the Automation is disabled on a Track.

Add Control Points

➡ Add individual Control Point

You can add single Control Points with the following action. The Help Tag displays the Time Position and the Parameter Value.

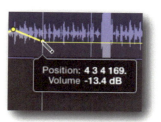

- **Click** anywhere right on the Automation Curve to add a Control Point on the Automation Curve at that position.
- **Double-click** anywhere on the Automation Lane to create a Control Point at that position. The shape of the Automation Curve updates accordingly.
- **Cmd+click** anywhere on the Automation Lane (the Mouse Pointer changes to the Pencil Tool ) to create a Control Point at that position.

➡ Draw a Curve

Instead of adding individual Control Points one at a time, you can draw the Automation Curve by **cmd+dragging**  in one movement. This draw movement still creates individual Control Points but it is much faster than creating them one by one. The slower you drag along, the more Control Points are created.

Drawing over existing Control Points will delete them.

➡ Display Control Point Values

You can display the value and exact time position of any Control Point
- **Click-hold** on a Control Point will show the Help Tag displaying the Time Position and Parameter Value of that Control Point.
- **Click-hold** on the line of the Automation Curve will display the position and value of the Control Point that is before your click position.

Editing Automation Curve

Although the Automation implementation in GarageBand is somewhat limited, it still provides many commands and procedures to edit an Automation Curve. The amount of available options might be overwhelming at first but with a little bit of practice, automating your mix becomes a simple and easy task.

➡ Select Control Points

The commands for selecting one or multiple Control Points are mostly standard
- **Click** on a single Control Point to select a single Control Point.
- **Sh+click** on multiple Control Points (even non-contiguous ones) to select a group,.
- **Sh+drag** an area ("lasso around") to select all the Control Points inside. You can do the drag without the shift key but using it avoids creating Control Points by accident.

➡ Delete Control Point(s)

There are multiple commands to delete Control Points.

- *Double-click* on a Control Point to delete that single Control Point.
- Select one or multiple Control Points first and then delete them with the *delete* key.

There are three commands to delete all Automation Curves for all Parameters on a Track.

- *Ctr+click* on the Track Header and choose from the Shortcut Menu *Delete All Automation*
- Main Menu *Mix* ➤ *Delete All Automation on Selected Track*
- Key command *sh+ctr+cmd+delete*.

Please note that a selected Region has "priority" over selected Control Points. That means when you have Control Points selected and a Region(s), then the delete command will delete the selected Region(s) instead of the Control Points.

➡ Move Control Points

Moving Control Points to a new position on the timeline will overwrite any existing Control Points. You will see the effect of how the new Automation Curve looks like while you are moving back and forth. The overwriting is executed once you release the mouse (you still can undo it).

These are the commands:

- *Drag* a single Control Point to move that one Control Point.
- *Drag* a line will move two Control Points, the beginning and end point of the line.
- *Drag* the line of a selection will move the whole selection horizontally or vertically.
- *Drag* a Control Point of a selection also can move a selection horizontally but moving it vertically has a special function. It compresses (moving down) or expands (moving up) the Curve vertically. This is useful if you have a complex movement that you want to keep but have the peaks a little lower or higher.

Move Control Points (overwrite)

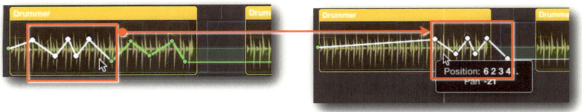

🔘 Moving Restriction

Holding down the *shift* key limits the movement to one direction. You can change the value (vertical) while keeping the original time position or changing the time position while keeping the original value. You have to hold down the shift key after you start the movement. You can release the key, change the direction and hold it down again. You have to play around with it to get used to it.

🔘 Finer Resolution

You can hold down the *control* key while moving vertically to switch to a finer resolution. You can hold or release the control key at any time to use the finer resolution when you need it during the adjustment.

➡ Copy Control Points horizontally

This is the same concept as with the moving command. Any existing Control Points at the new time position will be overwritten.

🎤 *Opt+drag* a Control Point or a selection of multiple Control Points.

➡ Move/Copy Control Points horizontally - with Regions

I mentioned earlier that the Automation feature is a "Track-based Automation" with an Automation Curve along the Track's Automation Lane regardless of the Regions on the Track Lane. However, there is one useful function that lets you "tie" the Control Points to the Regions. Think about the following scenario.

> You used a lot of Automation on the Audio Region of the guitar solo. Lots of volume movements and also some rhythmical panning. Later in the mix you decide to have that solo play again at the end during the fade out. Now when you copy the Audio Region to the end, you would have to redo or copy all the complex automation again … unless you enable the following mode.

Mix ➤ Move Automation with Regions

Please note, this is not a command, it is a mode that you enable or disable. If enabled, any Control Points that are placed over a Region are "tied" to that Region. When you move (or copy) that Region to a different time position, all its Control Points move with it. Deleting a Region also moves all the Control Points with it - to the trash.

➡ Copy Control Points - to a different Track

Here is another typical scenario during a mix session.

> You programmed some elaborate automation on one of the background vocals Tracks. The problem is that you have recorded them twice (or more often) and now have to reprogram the same Automation Curves on those Tracks … or maybe you don't.

GarageBand provides a procedure that allows you to copy the Automation Curve (or only a section of it) of the selected Automation Parameters to a different Track.

- ☑ Select the Automation Curve (or a section of it) on the Track you want to copy from
- ☑ Use the Copy command *Edit ➤ Copy* or Key Command **cmd+C**
- ☑ Select the Track you want to copy the Automation Curve to.
- ☑ Use the Paste command *Edit ➤ Paste* or Key Command **cmd+V**

Please note, copying a Track (**cmd+D**) will not copy its automation data with it.

Tempo & Transposition Tracks

I already covered the four Global Tracks briefly in the Tracks chapter. Here is a closer look at the Tempo Track and the Transposition Track. But first, a review of the Global Tracks

➡ Global Tracks

- ▸ With the exception of the Master Track that I cover in the next section, the Global Tracks are placed between the Ruler and the first visible Track in the Tracks Area ❶.
- ▸ The Master Track is placed at the bottom as the last Track in the Tracks Area ❷.
- ▸ There is only one of each Global Track in a Project.
- ▸ You can show or hide each individual Global Track with any of three types of commands:
    - Use the Main Menu *Track* ❸
    - *Ctr+click* on one of the visible Track Header to select the command from the Shortcut Menu ❹
    - Use any of the available Key Commands ❺

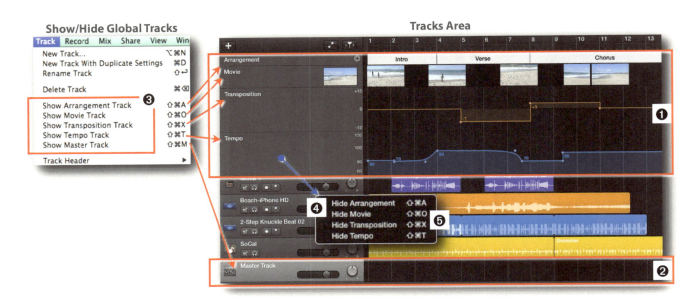

- 🔔 **Please note**
    - ▸ Global Tracks are part of each Project.
    - ▸ Global Tracks are always on.
    - ▸ You can choose to show or hide them in the Tracks Area which is just a visual command that doesn't affect the data on the Tracks.
    - ▸ These are the default values for Global Tracks.
        - **Arrangement Track**: The Track is empty. No Arrangement Markers have been created yet
        - **Movie Track**: The Track is empty. You have to manually load a movie into the Project.
        - **Transposition Track**: The Transposition value is "0" which means no additional transposition.
        - **Tempo Track**: The Track has only one value which is the Tempo displayed in the Control Bar Display.
        - **Master Track**: All controls are set to a default value.

Transposition Track

The Transposition Track lets you mark sections of your Project that you can transpose (change the pitch in semitone increments) by applying a transposition value to those sections.

➡ **Key Signature**

To understand how the Transposition Track works, you have to understand the role of the Key Signature Parameter in GarageBand first.

▸ Every Project has a specific Key Signature that has to be set as part of the Project Properties ❶ when you create a New Project ❷ in the Project Chooser.

▸ Later, you can change the Key Signature of your Project at any time in the Control Bar Display ❸.

▸ However, changing the Key Signature affects some components of your Project that you have to be aware of.

- Apple Loops ❹ (Audio Regions) transpose to the current Key Signature.
- The Score Editor displays the current Key Signature. This is only a visual affect ❺.
- The "Limit to Key" mode that affects the Pitch Correction for recorded Audio Files feature relies on the Key Signature ❻.

While the Key Signature only transposes Apple Loops (Audio), the Transpose Track can transpose other Regions too.

💡 **Regions that follow the transposition value**

- ☑ MIDI Regions ❼
- ☑ Apple Loop Regions (with a defined key signature) ❽. The transposition value will be added to the transposition value imposed by the Key Signature ❹.
- ☑ Audio Regions that are recorded in the current Project that have "Follow Tempo and Pitch" enabled ❾

💡 **Regions that ignore the transposition value**

- ☐ Imported Audio Regions
- ☐ Audio Regions that are recorded in the current Project that have "Follow Tempo and Pitch" disabled
- ☐ Apple Loop Regions that don't have a key signature assignment (drums, percussion)

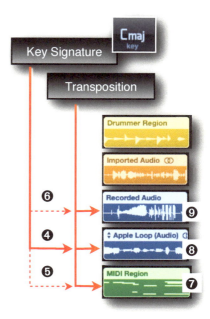

21 - Mixing

➡ Examples

Here are three examples where this feature might come in handy.
- ▸ You have almost finished your Project and want to change the key. For example, the key is too high for the singer.
- ▸ You want to transpose a section of your song for dramatic impact. For example, modulate one tone higher for the last two choruses.
- ▸ You just want to experiment and try different keys for your song or parts of it.

➡ Transpose Value

As a default, the Transposition Track contains only one value and that is set to zero ❶ with one straight line across the Transposition Track. That means the Transposition Track has no affect, nothing gets transposed by it and everything follows the set Key Signature ❷ of the Project.

Default Transposition Track

➡ Add/Edit Transposition Control Points

The handling of the Control Points is similar to what we just learned in the Automation section.
- ▸ **Add**: *Click* on the line or anywhere with *cmd+click* which changes to the Pencil Tool.
- ▸ **Select**: *Sh+drag* around the Control Point(s).
- ▸ **Move vertically ❸**: *Drag* a selected line up or down. A Help Tag displays the value change. You can set the transposition value to maximum 12 semitones up or down.
- ▸ **Move horizontally ❹**: *Drag* a selected line(s) left or right. A Help Tag displays the new position.
- ▸ **Copy horizontally**: *Opt+drag* a selected line(s) left or right.
- ▸ **Delete**: Select the Control Point(s) first and hit the *delete* key.

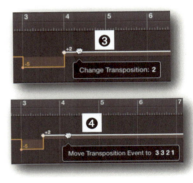

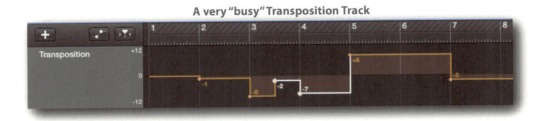

A very "busy" Transposition Track

💡 Be Aware

Although the feature seems pretty simple, there are a few things you have to pay attention to.
- ▸ Changing the Key Signature after adding Transposition values will update the Transposition values on the Tracks.
- ▸ The actual MIDI Events in the Regions are moved up or down when applying various Transposition values (as you can see in the Piano Roll Editor). Setting the value back to zero will move the MIDI Events back to their original position as long you haven't moved the Region to a different "Transposition Zone"!
- ▸ Recording a new MIDI Region over a section with a Transposition value will not apply the Transposition value to the new Region. It will only apply to an existing Region.

Tempo Track

Chances are, you have one consistent Tempo through your Project. In that case, you don't need the Tempo Track at all. However, if your Tempo needs to change during the Project, then the Tempo Track is the place where you create those Tempo changes.

➡ Default Tempo

Default Tempo Track

When you open the Tempo Track the first time, it displays one Control Point at the beginning of the Project that extends as a single horizontal blue line along the timeline. This represents the single Tempo value of your Project which is also displayed in the Control Bar Display.

➡ Tempo Display (LCD)

Before going over the commands how to program Tempo changes, let's have a look at the Tempo Display in the Control Bar Display that shows the Tempo in a bpm value ("Beats per Minutes")

You would think that this value represents the Tempo of your Project. However, when you have Tempo changes (more than one Tempo) in your Project, then the description of what this value shows has to be more precise.

> The Tempo Display shows the Tempo **at the current Playhead Position**

Here are two screenshots of a Project that has two Tempo values.

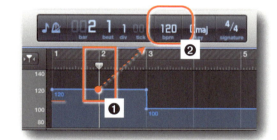

- ▸ If the Playhead ❶ is parked/moving between bar 1 and 3, then the Tempo Display ❷ shows the Tempo of 120bpm.

- ▸ If the Playhead ❸ is parked/moving after bar 3, then the Tempo Display ❹ shows the Tempo of 100bpm.

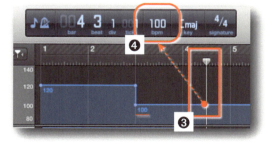

So, wherever the Playhead moves across, the Tempo Display shows the Tempo value at that position in real time. Of course, if you have only one Tempo value, then the Tempo would be the same regardless where the Playhead moves.

Please note:

Once you have more than one Tempo Event in the Tempo Track, you cannot change the Tempo in the Control Bar Display anymore. If you try to do that, you will get an error message. Now you have to change the Tempo in the Tempo Track.

➡ Tempo Scale

The height of the Tempo Track is fixed. However, the vertical scale ❶ on the right of the Tempo Track Header adjusts automatically to display all the current Tempo values on the Track. However, you can set the minimum and maximum value for that scale. The number turns blue ❷ to indicate that you set the value manually.

- *Double-click* the number ❸ for the minimum or maximum value and enter a Tempo numerically.
- *Drag* either number vertically to change it. A Help Tag ❹ indicates the value.
- *Double-click* the number again and delete the value to reset the number back to "auto adjust".

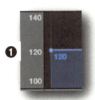 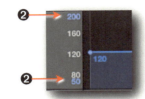  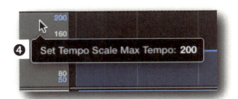

➡ Add/Edit Tempo Values

▸ **Add**: There are three ways to do that. Always watch the Help Tag for assistance.

- *Double-click* on the Tempo line
- *Cmd+click* (changes to the Pencil Tool ✏) anywhere
- *Ctr+opt+cmd+click* anywhere to enter a Tempo value numerically ❺

▸ **Select**: *Sh+drag* around the Control Point(s).

▸ **Move vertically ❸**: *Drag* a selected line up or down. A Help Tag displays the value change. *Ctr+drag* moves in finer increments to set the Tempo with 4 decimal numbers ❻.

▸ **Move horizontally ❹**: *Drag* a selected line(s) left or right or *drag* the vertical line ✥. A Help Tag displays the new position.

▸ **Copy horizontally**: *Opt+drag* a selected line(s) left or right.

▸ **Delete**: Select the Control Point(s) first and then hit the *delete* key.

Add Graphically

Add Numerically

Move Horizontally

Move Vertically

Move Vertically fine increments
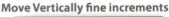
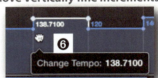

➡ Curved Tempo Line

There is a special feature to create curved Tempo lines. That means the Tempo is gradually speeding up or slowing down instead of a sudden change. First, every Tempo Event has two Control Points, a start and an end point ❼. As a default, the end point has the same time position as the start point of the next Tempo Event resulting in a vertical line.

Now, you can drag the end point towards the start point changing the sudden Tempo change ❽ to a curved Tempo change ❾ and to a diagonal Tempo change ❿ when moving the end point all the way towards the start point.

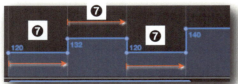 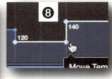 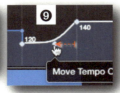 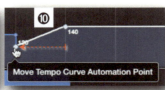

Master Track

The Master Track is placed at the bottom of the Tracks Area after the last Track in your Project. It is hidden by default and can be made visible with the two commands.

 Main Menu *Track ➤ Show/Hide Master Track*

 Key Command **sh+cmd+M**

Concept

If you look at the Track, there is not much to it.
- ▸ The entire Track Lane is empty because you can't record or place any Regions on it.
- ▸ The Track Header only contains the following components:
  - **Track Icon**
  - **Track Name**
  - **Track Lock** (doesn't seem to have any functionality)
  - **Volume Slider + Meter**
  - **Pan Knob**

● Automation Lane

The main use for the Track Lane is when you enable Track Automation and display the Automation Curve on the Automation Lane. As we have just learned in the Automation section, it adds the following two components on the Track Header.
- **Track Automation Button**
- **Automation Parameter popup menu**

➡ *Master Volume*

There is one more component that kind of belongs to the Master Track and that is the Master Volume Slider in the upper right corner of the Control Bar.

Some users might not even know about its existence because it is automatically hidden if the GarageBand Window is not big enough.

However, this is a very important control and I will go over its functionality on the next page.

21 - Mixing

Master Track Signal Flow

Here is a graph with the explanation of the basic signal flow in GarageBand.

- ▸ The signal of all Tracks ❶ in a Project are routed to the Master Track ❷.
- ▸ The Master Track has a Volume Slider ❸ that controls this (summed) output signal. It also lets you add additional processing to the output signal.
- ▸ Before the output signal reaches its final destination (Audio Device or exported file), it passes through a gain control that can add a level offset to the output signal. It is controlled by the Master Volume Slider ❹ on the Control Bar.
- ▸ Please note that the slider ❸ on the Master Track and the slider ❹ on the Control Bar are two independent volume controls.
- ▸ The Volume Automation Parameter ❺ on the Master Track controls of course the Volume Slider ❸ on the Master Track. When you have an active Automation Curve, you can see the Volume Slider ❸ moving but not the Master Volume Slider ❹ on the Control Bar.
- ▸ The signal level that is displayed in both, the slider ❸ on the Master Track and the slider ❹ on the Control Bar are measuring and displaying the same signal. It displays the final output signal ❻ that is sent to the Audio Device ❼ or exported to an audio file.

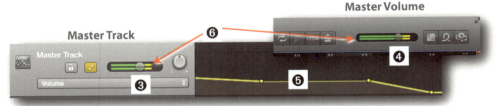

➡ **Master Track Effects**

The Master Track not only lets you adjust the overall Level, you can add Effects like with any other Tracks.

- ▸ The Master Track has its own Smart Controls ❼ that let you add signal processing to the overall signal, the final output signal. Select the Smart Controls Button 🎛 when the Master Track is selected.
- ▸ You can switch to the Smart Controls of the Master Track by using the Master Button [Master] ❽ when displaying the Smart Controls Window of any other Track.

- ▸ The Equalizer is not only handy to adjust the frequency response of the overall signal, you can use its Analyzer ❾ to check visually for any frequency response issues (too boomy, to dull, etc.).
- ▸ You can also add up to four AU Plugins ❿ to the Master Track.
- ▸ And last but not least, you can also automate all those Smart Controls by choosing them from the Automation Parameter popup menu on the Master Track.

22 - Share

Finally, when your song is ready to be shared with the world, it is time to export it. The following terms are used interchangeable to describe this process:

Export = Mix = Mixdown = Bounce = Share

The actual process involves multiple steps. Here is an overview:

- ☑ **Mix**: GarageBand creates a mix or "mixdown" of your song. Mixing means, it will play the song as it is at the current stage from a start to a stop position that you determine.

- ☑ **Offline**: The Mix is performed "offline". That means you won't hear the song while GarageBand is playing it. However, you can see the Playhead moving across very quickly. GarageBand doesn't need to actually play your Project. It just scans it and crunches the numbers of the mix, the pure data.

- ☑ **Normalize**: This optional step makes sure that your mixed audio file will have the highest possible level.

- ☑ **Export**: This is the step where GarageBand takes all that data from the mixdown and creates a new audio file. Some Share options let you determine the audio file format.

- ☑ **Share**: In this step, you determine what to do with the newly created file of your song. It depends on what Share option you chose in GarageBand. The standard procedure is that you "share" it to a location on your hard drive. However, GarageBand lets you further specify the Share destination. For example, place it in a specific Playlist in your iTunes Library, burn it on a Disk or even upload it directly to your SoundCloud account from within GarageBand.

Before you start the Share procedure, you have to take care of or at least consider a few final steps.

Final Steps

Fade Out

A Fade Out is the process of gradually lowering the volume of a Track to -∞dB. This is infinite attenuation = silence, when the Volume Fader is moved all the way down. Especially on a Master Track that controls the overall volume of your Project, it is always a good practice to fade out your song at the end to make sure that it is completely silent and nothing gets abruptly cut off like the ring out of a reverb, a delay or any other ongoing effect.

You have two options to create a Fade Out:
- ▶ **Manually**: Enable the Automation ❶ for the Master Track' and add some Control Points at the end to create a Fade Out.
- ▶ **Automatically**: GarageBand can create the Fade for you in case you skipped the section in this manual about Automation (and don't know how to do it yourself). You just use a simple Menu command *Mix ➤ Fade Out*
  - This command will add four Automation Control Points ❷ in the Master Track's Automation Lane at 10s, 7s, 4s and 0s before the end of the last Region ❸ in your Project, gradually lowering the Volume to -∞dB.
  - That means GarageBand doesn't necessarily fade out at the end of your Project at the End-of-Project Marker ❹. Keep that in mind when you bounce your Project.
  - Of course, you can open the Master Track's Automation Lane and edit those Control Points.

Export - What Tracks

Only the Tracks that are not muted are exported. If you want to make a selective export, you can do it in two ways:

- Mute all the Tracks that you don't want to be part of the export.
- Solo all the Tracks that you want to include in the export. This mutes all the Tracks that are not soloed.

Metronome

Make sure you have the Metronome turned off. The Metronome's click sound will be exported with your mix if it is enabled.

Export - What Range

One important step to do before you export your Project, is to tell GarageBand if you want to export the entire Project or only a section of it, and if so, from where to where. The exported range depends on a three part hierarchy.

🔘 Entire Project

As a default, GarageBand exports your entire Project. It starts from the left border of the first Region ❶ to the right border of your last Region ❷. This ensures that you don't export any silence in case your mix doesn't start on bar 1 and doesn't end at the End-of-Project Marker.

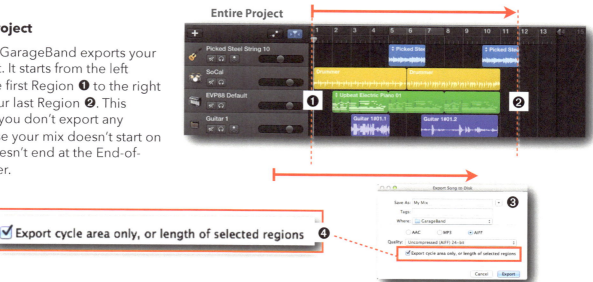

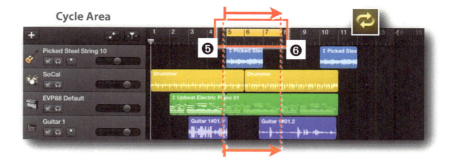

Most export options provide in their Dialog Window ❸ a checkbox ❹ that lets you override that default behavior for the export range. Please note that this checkbox is only active If you have Cycle Mode enabled or have some Regions selected. In that case, the exported range depends on two factors.

🔘 Enabled Cycle Mode

If Cycle Mode is enabled 🔁, then GarageBand exports your Project only from the left border ❺ to the right border ❻ of the yellow Cycle Area.

🔘 Selected Region(s)

If Cycle Mode is disabled 🔁, then GarageBand looks for any selected Region(s) in your Project. If you have one or multiple Regions selected when initiating the export, then GarageBand exports your Project from the left border of the first selected Region ❼ to the right border of the last selected Region ❽ in the Workspace. It doesn't matter on which Track the Regions are located, they even can be muted.

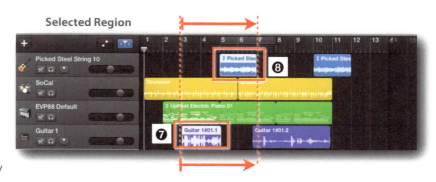

➡ Added Tail

Please note that GarageBand records about 3 seconds longer at the end of any export. This ensures that your mixed Project contains any "remaining" reverb, delay, or other effect that might ring out after you stop the playback. Unfortunately, there doesn't seem to be any option to disable that in case you want to set an exact length for your exported audio file.

Normalize

There is one optional step that you should consider when exporting your Project and that is "Normalize".

"To Normalize" is a common procedure in digital audio that ensures that a signal of an audio file hits the maximum level but doesn't go over it. You can have GarageBand take care of this procedure by enabling the checkbox in the

Preferences ➤ Advanced ➤ Auto Normalize

- ☑ While GarageBand "mixes" your Project, it measures what the highest signal level is. For example, -10dB.
- ☑ The highest possible level in digital audio without causing any clipping/distortion is 0dB (or to be precise, 0dBFS, "Full Scale").
- ☑ The difference between the highest measured level and maximum possible level is called the "Headroom". In this example, the Headroom would be 10dB. That means you could raise your mix by 10dB to reach the maximum level without going over it.
- ☑ GarageBand is doing exactly that. It automatically raises the overall signal of the mixed Project by the amount of the measured headroom to reach 0dBFS. In our example, it raises the level by 10dB.
- ☑ The "normalized mix", now with the maximum level of 0dBFS is saved as the new exported audio file.

This is a very important topic so let me show you that procedure with a few screenshots. They show you the same audio signal (same mix) with different levels.

❶ The highest (peak) level is at -20dB. Therefore, the headroom is 20dB.

❷ The peak level of this signal is -10dB. Here, the headroom is 10db.

❸ The peak level of this signal is 0dB. There is no headroom and therefore, GarageBand wouldn't raise the level of this mix.

➤ Loudness vs Level

The text in the Preferences explains that the Normalize effect "*increases the loudness*". This is technically not correct. The Normalize procedure in GarageBand "increases the overall level". For example, raising the level by 10dB makes the mix "**louder**" but doesn't increase the "**loudness**".

You can increase the loudness of your mix by using dynamic effects like a compressor and limiter. They make your mix (which is at the maximum level of 0dB ❹) "sound louder" without increasing the maximum level ❺. You can see that the same waveform is much "fuller" ❻, it has more energy if you want to express it in physics terms.

Share

Now that we did all the preparations for the final export, let's look at the different Share options that are available in GarageBand.

I mentioned already the various terms that are used for creating a mixdown of your Project. This time, I use those terms specifically to differentiate between different procedures.

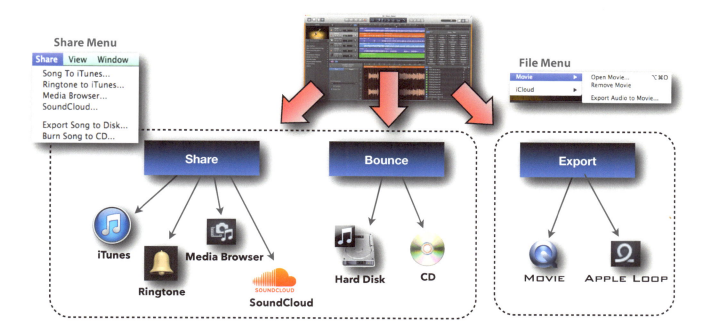

Bounce

This bounce procedure is similar to a regular save command for a document. Here, GarageBand gives you the option to save the file of your bounced mix to one of two different media, your hard drive or your CD burner.

- Export Song to Disk: Saves your song to any location on your hard drive.
- Burn Song to CD: Saves your song (burn it) directly to an Audio CD.

Share

These four options also bounce your mix but it "shares" (sends) the bounced file to a specific destination.

- Song To iTunes: Saves your song directly to your iTunes Library at a specific Playlist.
- Ringtone to iTunes: Save your song as a Ringtone to your iTunes Library.
- Media Browser: Saves your song to a special location where other OSX apps can "see" it.
- SoundCloud: Saves your song (upload) directly to SoundCloud from within GarageBand.

Export

There are two separate options that are not listed in the Share Menu. These are procedures where you export your Project or content of it for a special purpose.

- Export Audio to Movie: Saves your mix to the audio track of a copy of the QuickTime movie file that is currently loaded in your Project.
- Export as Apple Loop: We learned that procedure already in the Apple Loops chapter. It is not a command that is available in any Menu Command but I wanted to include it in that context because you export a new file out of your Project even if it is only a single Apple Loop.

Export Song to Disk...

This is not the first option in the Share Menu but arguably the most important because it gives you the freedom to save the bounced song anywhere on your drive. Here is the simple procedure:

- ☑ Select *Share* ➤ *Export Song to Disk...* ❶.
- ☑ A Save Dialog opens where you make the following selections:
    - Enter a name ❷ for the bounced file
    - Navigate to the location ❸ you want to save the file
    - Select any of the three Audio File Formats (AAC, MP3, AIFF) ❹ and choose one of the Quality Settings from the popup menu
    - Select the optional export range ❿ (Cycle/Region)
    - Click Export ❺
- ☑ GarageBand performs the export displayed by a progress bar ❻.

➡ **Audio File Formats:**

Here is a look at the available audio file formats.

▸ **AAC:** AAC (also known as mp4 format) is mainly supported by Apple. It saves an Audio File with the File Extension .m4a and has a better audio quality than mp3 but is not as widely used. The four Quality options let you choose from different Bit Rates (kBit/sec). The higher the Bit Rate the better the audio quality but also the bigger the file size. You should go for the highest Bit Rate because this is a data compressed file format so the file size is fairly small in general.

▸ **MP3:** The mp3 option also lets you choose from four Quality Settings.

▸ **AIFF:** This is an uncompressed audio file format that delivers the best audio quality, especially if you choose the 24-bit version. Only choose the 16-bit option if your songs end up later on a CD which only supports 16-bit anyway. Please note that GarageBand also saves the Tempo information of your Project with the aiff file (if your Project uses Musical Time 🎵) that can be used when importing the file in Logic Pro.

Burn Song to CD

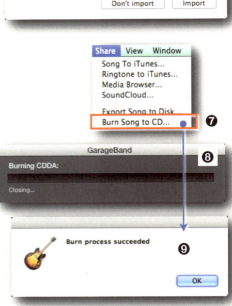

Usually, you bounce your song(s) first, create Playlists in iTunes and burn CDs from there. However, you can burn a CD directly from GarageBand with only your current song as the one Track.

- ☑ Select *Share* ➤ *Burn Song to CD...* ❼. The command will be grayed out until you have a blank CD inserted.
- ☑ Although the command has the three dots that indicate an additional Dialog Window, once you select the command, the process starts without any further interaction.
- ☑ A Progress Bar ❽ indicates the required time and when done, the CD ejects, and a window ❾ confirms the completion.

 Song To iTunes...

These are the main differences of using this command instead of the "Export Song to Disk":

- The bounced song will automatically be imported into your iTunes Library to a Playlist you choose.
- The song will have the ID3 Tags (Artist, Album, etc.) added to the file.
- You cannot choose the location for the new audio file. It will be stored in **"~/Music/iTunes/iTunes Music/Import/**
- The song will start playing in iTunes right away.

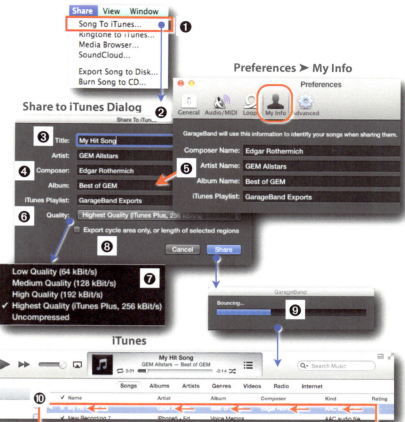

Here are the steps:

- ☑ Select **Share ➤ Song To iTunes...** ❶.
- ☑ A Dialog Window ❷ opens where you make the following selections:
  - The name of your current Project is entered automatically in the Title ❸ field, but you can change it.
  - The next three fields ❹ (Artist, Composer, Album) let you enter the ID3 tags that are stored with the bounced file.
    The fields are already filled with the information you entered in the **Preferences ➤ My Info** ❺.
  - The" iTunes Playlist" field ❻ lets you define to what Playlist the song will be assigned to.
  - The Quality popup menu ❼ provides the options for the Audio File Format (AAC or Uncompressed AIFF).
  - Select the optional export range ❽ (Cycle/Region).
  - Click the Share button to start the bounce Process.
- ☑ GarageBand performs the export and displays a Progress Bar ❾.
- ☑ The new audio file will be stored in the iTunes directory and starts to play right away in iTunes in the pre-defined Playlist. All the ID3 Tags are displayed in iTunes ❿.

Ringtone to iTunes...

This command bounces your mix as a Ringtone file with the .m4r File Extension that is saved directly into the "Tones" Library ⌐Tones⌐ in your iTunes Library.

If your Project is not exactly the required 40s long, then you get an Alert window. When you click the Adjust button, GarageBand will create a Cycle Area of 40s starting from the beginning of your Project and bounces that section.

Media Browser...

First of all, the dots in this command, which usually indicate that a Dialog Window will pop up, are misleading. Once you click the command, the bounce will be performed without any further interaction.

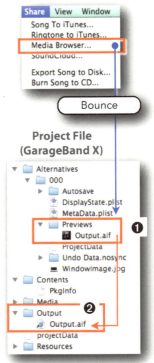

I discussed that command and the concept of the Media Browser in general in the Media Browser chapter. Saving a "Media Browser file", saves the audio file to a special location that other OSX apps (Logic, iMovie, Final Cut Pro, Pages, etc.) know about. They can access those files conveniently from their Media Browser without you, searching for them by navigating through Finder windows.

When you use the **Share ➤ Media Browser ...** . command, GarageBand will bounce your mix and save it as an uncompressed AIFF file named "Output.aif" to the current Project File, embedded inside the Package File structure **"ProjectName"/Alternatives/000/Previews/Output.aif** ❶. This file has an alias file in the Output folder ❷ where other OSX apps search for it.

Please note that that there is only one audio file in that folder. Every time you use the Media Browser command, you overwrite any existing Output.aif file that is already there.

SoundCloud...

This option lets you bounce your Project to an audio file and upload it directly to SoundCloud (a popular social network for showcasing music).
The Dialog Window contains several Parameters:

- ☑ Actually, before the dialog pops up, you will be presented with the SoundCloud Login ❸ window to log into your account.
- ☑ The Dialog Window displays the logged-in user name ❹ and the "Change" ❺ button next to it. It lets you login to a different user.
- ☑ **Source**: You can choose to upload the Bounced file from your current Project or choose an Audio File from your drive ❻.
- ☑ **Metadata**: The next four fields are the metadata for your song (Title, Artist, Composer, Album).
- ☑ **Quality**: The popup menu provides the same five encoding formats.
- ☑ **Visibility**: You can flag the audio file you are about to upload as Private or Public.
- ☑ **Permissions**: The first two checkboxes allow or deny the ability to download or to stream your song. The last checkbox lets you use the Cycle/Region to define the export range.

Please check out my own music on SoundCloud: https://soundcloud.com/edgar_rothermich/sets

Export Audio to Movie

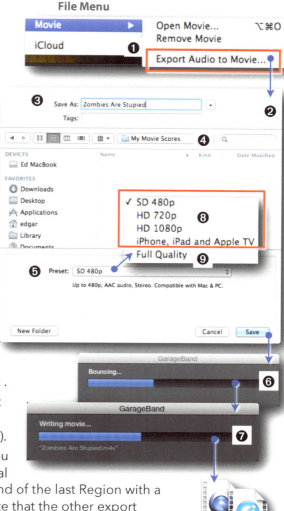

This command, which creates a new movie file, is not listed in the Share Menu, it is under **File ➤ Movie ➤ Export Audio to Movie ...** ❶

You have to have a Movie imported in your current Project. Otherwise, the command is grayed out.

- ☑ Select **File ➤ Movie ➤ Export Audio to Movie ...**
- ☑ A Save Dialog ❷ opens where you make the following selections
  - Enter a name ❸ for the new movie file
  - Navigate to the location ❹ you want to save the move file to
  - Select a movie file format from the Preset popup menu ❺
  - Click Save ❺
- ☑ GarageBand creates the new movie file in two steps
  - First, the Bouncing... Progress Bar ❻ indicates the first step where GarageBand bounces the mix of your Project.
  - After that, a second Progress Bar appears, indicating that GarageBand is creating the actual movie file ❼. You can cancel that procedure by pressing **cmd+.** (the period key).
  - GarageBand exports the length of the whole movie. If you have Regions in your Project beyond the end of the actual movie, then the new movie file will be extended to the end of the last Region with a freeze frame of the last video frame (or black). Please note that the other export criteria (Cycle Area, selected Region and End-of-Project Marker) are ignored.

➡ Movie Presets

The first four options ❽ in the Preset popup window convert the original movie file to the selected format and includes the AAC format of your bounced mixed. The "Full Quality" ❾ preset copies the original movie file (without changing its video format) and replaces its audio track with the bounced Aiff version of your mix.

Export as Apple Loop

There is no specific command in any Menu to export a file as an Apple Loop. However, I just wanted to include the option in this chapter because technically, you create a new file out of your current Project.

Whenever you *drag* a single MIDI Region or Audio Region over the open Loop Browser, you create an Apple Loop audio file that is stored in the following location **~/Library/Audio/Apple Loops/User Loops/SingleFiles/**

Please review the Apple Loops chapter for more details.

23 - Additional Features

Scoring Movies

You can use GarageBand to score your music video (or movie) or add any audio (sound effects, voice over) to a movie file directly in GarageBand. Although some of the features from GarageBand v6.0.5 were removed, you can still score your movie or do some basic post production with it.

Interface

- ▶ You can add only one movie to your Project at a time.
    - GarageBand supports a wide variety of video file formats.
- ▶ The movie is placed on GarageBand's separate Movie Track ❶.
    - It starts at the beginning of your Project.
- ▶ The Movie Track Lane displays thumbnail images ❷ of the movie.
    - You can not edit the movie in GarageBand.
- ▶ GarageBand imports the movie's audio track and places it as an orange Audio Region ❸ on a new Audio Track ❹.
    - The Audio Region is locked 🔒 and cannot be moved.
- ▶ The movie plays in sync with the Project in a separate floating window ❺ which always stays on top
    - Closing this floating window ⓧ will place a thumbnail video ❻ on the Movie Track's Track Header. *Click* on it to open the floating window again.

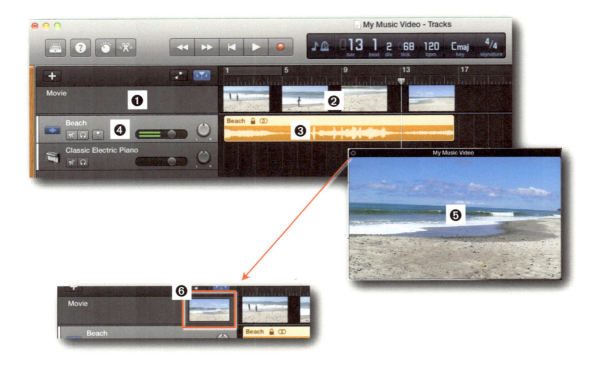

Movie Management

Here are the commands to work with the movie file

➡ Add a movie

The first step of course is to add a movie to your Project. There are many ways to do that:

- You can navigate through the standard Open Dialog Window when using any of the following commands:
    - Main Menu *File ➤ Movie ➤ Open Movie...*
    - Select *Open Movie...* from the Shortcut Menu when clicking on the label "Movie" ❶ in the Movie Track
    - Key Command *opt+cmd+O*

- You can drag a movie file directly onto your Project, onto any Track Lane but not the Movie Track
    - *Drag* a file from the Media Browser ❷ when the Movies tab is selected
    - *Drag* a file from the Finder

➡ Replace a Movie

Using any of the previous commands to add a movie to your Project will replace any existing movie.
Please note that GarageBand also replaces the Audio File of the movie's audio track with the audio track of the newly imported movie file.

➡ Remove a Movie

If you don't need the movie anymore in your Project, you can remove it with the following commands (this does not remove the movie's Audio Region):

- Main Menu *File ➤ Movie ➤ Remove Movie*
- Select *Remove Movie* from the Shortcut Menu when clicking on the label "Movie" ❶ in the Movie Track

🟡 Missing Movie

When you import a movie into your Project, GarageBand only stores the name and the location of the movie as a reference, it does not copy the file to your Project File.

- **Good**: Movie files are usually rather big, so by not storing them in the Project File doesn't inflate the file size of your Project File.
- **Bad**: However, if the movie you used in a Project is not available when you open that Project, then it can't be displayed. For example, you deleted the movie file, had it on an external drive or moved the Project to a different computer without copying the movie file too. In that case, GarageBand prompts you with a "Movie missing" error message.

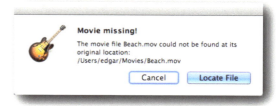

The "Locate File" button opens an Open Dialog where you can navigate to the file. GarageBand is pretty good finding the file even if you moved it to a different folder or renamed it (thanks to the OSX Spotlight search engine).

Operations

🔵 Floating Window

- ▸ The floating window displaying the movie follows the Playhead Position of your Project.
- ▸ Playing your Project will play the movie.
- ▸ Moving the Pointer Tool over the window reveals the movie's own navigation bar.
  - The handle on the timeline represents the Playhead which is linked to the Project's Playhead. You can *drag* it to position it.
  - The number on the left is the current position of the Playhead and the number on the right is the remaining time of the movie.

🔵 Thumbnails

Thumbnails are the little images that display the video as individual frames on the Movie Track.

- ▸ The number of the thumbnails depends on the zoom factor of the Workspace.
- ▸ You can change the Resolution (image quality) of those images between Low and High in the *Preferences ➤ Advanced ➤ Movie Thumbnail Resolution*.
- ▸ The left border of a thumbnail is aligned to its time position. Only the last frame is aligned to its right border so you can see the exact end of the movie.

🔵 Audio Track

The audio track of the movie file that is automatically imported as an orange Audio Region can't be moved to maintain the sync with the movie file. However, you still can use the other edit commands (trim, copy, loop)

🔵 Absolute Time

If you want to use the movie file in your Project for post-production work (sound effects, dialog, etc.), then you might want to switch the Control Bar Display to Time 🕓 to have the display and the Ruler display Absolute Time.

(You cannot set a SMPTE offset in the display to sync it to the visual timecode on a video.)

🔵 Export

The command *File ➤ Movie ➤ Export Audio to Movie ...* will copy the movie to a new movie file with the bounced Project as its audio tracks.

I explained the details already in the previous Share chapter.

Learn to Play

GarageBand provides Piano and Guitar Lessons in the form of interactive videos that are integrated into Garageband.

The Project Chooser provides two separate items in the Sidebar for those Lessons:

- **Lesson Store**

  This iTunes like interface lets you download individual lessons from Apple directly into GarageBand.

- **Learn to Play**

  This is the place that lists all the downloaded lessons and lets you play them

There are three types of lessons:
  ▸ Guitar Lessons: 20 free lessons (Basic, Rock, Blues)
  ▸ Piano Lessons: 18 free Lessons (Basic, Pop, Classical)
  ▸ Artist Lessons: 23 Lessons ($4.99 each) where artists like Sting and Norah Jones teach you how to play one of their songs.

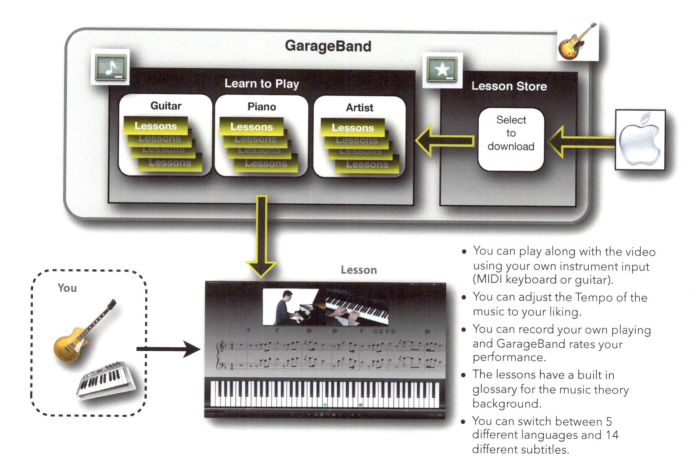

- You can play along with the video using your own instrument input (MIDI keyboard or guitar).
- You can adjust the Tempo of the music to your liking.
- You can record your own playing and GarageBand rates your performance.
- The lessons have a built in glossary for the music theory background.
- You can switch between 5 different languages and 14 different subtitles.

Logic Remote

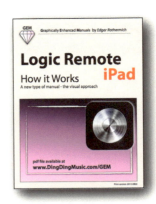

 The free iPad app "Logic Remote" is an amazing external controller that works with Logic, MainStage and also with GarageBand. This app does not only let you remote control existing functions in GarageBand over WiFi, it adds additional functionality, like a Mixer and Smart Touch Instruments.

I wrote a separate book for this app that explains all the features :
"Logic Remote - How it Works". Here is just a quick overview.

Logic Remote on the iPad recognizes any app ❶ it can connect to over WiFi and you just confirm the connection ❷ in GarageBand. It's that simple to connect the iPad to GarageBand.

 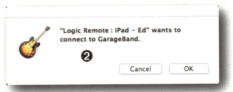

- ▸ You have a nice mixer control surface ❸ where you can move multiple controls at the same time via multi-touch Gestures plus transport controls.
- ▸ All the Key Commands can be assigned and controlled via Touch Pads ❹.
- ▸ Smart Help ❺ is a feature that you have to see. It browses the GarageBand documentation in real time based on where you move the mouse over in GarageBand.
- ▸ The Library ❻ window is a separate View on the iPad.
- ▸ The Smart Controls ❼ are also available as a separate View and can be controlled via multi-touch.
- ▸ You can even play your Software Instrument with multi-touch Gestures on the iPad using the Smart Instruments, i.e. keyboards ❽, drums ❾ and a new interface for strings and playing chord patterns.

Shortcuts

And last but not least, a tip to improve your workflow in GarageBand.

One key element of getting up to speed with GarageBand is using the available Key Commands or Keyboard Shortcuts.

The available Key Commands are listed in Apple's official GarageBand Documentation (also online http://help.apple.com/garageband/mac/10.0/)

However, there are many commands in the Main Menu that you might often use but they don't have their own Key Command. Not a problem because there is an easy fix for that.

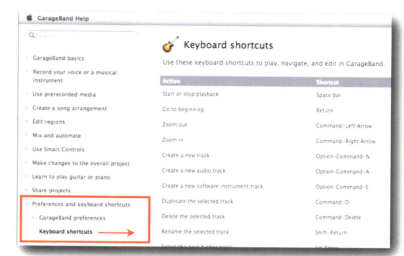

➡ OSX Keyboard Shortcuts

OSX provides a mechanism to add a Key Command to any item in the Main Menu, even if it is buried inside a submenu. These Keyboard Shortcuts can be programmed for each application individually. Here is the procedure:

- ☑ Let's say you use the Share command "Export Song to Disk…" ❶ a lot to bounce your Projects. Unfortunately, there is no Key Command for that (yet).
- ☑ Go to System Preferences (under the Apple Menu) and select the Keyboard icon ❷.
- ☑ Select the Shortcuts tab ❸ and then in the Sidebar to the left, select "App Shortcuts" ❹.
- ☑ Click the Plus ❺ button at the bottom which opens a Dialog Window.
- ☑ Select GarageBand ❻ from the Application menu, enter the Menu Title, "Export Song to Disk…" ❼, and the Keyboard Shortcut (I chose *cmd+B* ❽).
- ☑ After you click the Add button, the Shortcut will be listed in the Preferences window ❾ and shows up immediately in the GarageBand Share Menu ❿, ready to be used.

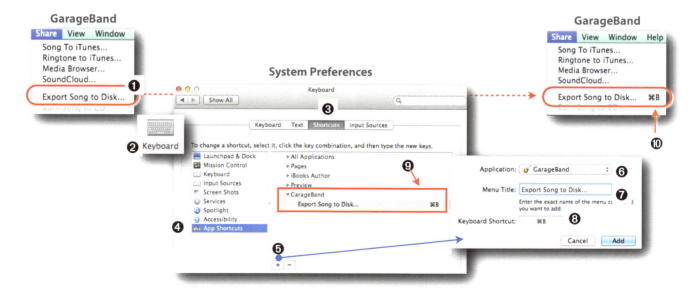

Conclusion

This concludes my manual "*GarageBand X - How it Works*".

If you find my visual approach of explaining features and concepts helpful, please recommend my books to others or maybe write a review on Amazon or the iBookstore. This will help me to continue this series.
To check out other books in my "Graphically Enhanced Manuals" series, go to my website at
www.DingDingMusic.com/Manuals

To contact me directly, email me at: GEM@DingDingMusic.com

More information about my day job as a composer and links to my social network sites are on my website:
www.DingDingMusic.com

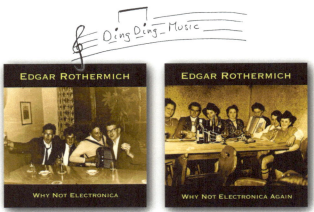
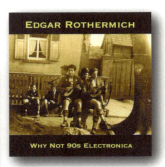

Listen to my music on SoundCloud

Thanks for your interest and your support,

Edgar Rothermich

Absolute Time, 80
Alignment Guides, 81, 201, 254
Amp Button, 283
Amp Designer, 128, 137, 282
Analyzer, 136
Apple ID, 46
Apple Loop, 45
Apple Loops Button, 85
Arpeggiator, 137
Arpeggio Button, 120, 128, 137
Arrangement Marker, 205, 270
Arrangement Track, 108, 205
Audio Editor Inspector, 261
Audio Editor, 84, 239, 250
Audio File, 147
Audio Interface, 29
Audio Region, 145, 168, 241
Audio Track, 102, 16
Audio Units (AU), 133
Automatic Level Control, 132, 166
Automation Curve, 289
Automation Lane, 292
Automation Parameter, 291
Autosave, 72
Basic Content, 47
Bit Depth, 43, 162
Bounce, 309
Catch Playhead, 68
Connectors, 37
Control Bar Display (LCD), 91
Control Bar, 53, 82
Control Points, 231, 294
Count-In, 88
Cycle Area (Cycle Strip), 81, 152
Cycle Button, 87
Cycle Mode, 86
Cycle Recording, 155
dB (Decibel), 42, 90
Device, 31
Display Modes, 56, 80, 91
Drum Kit Pieces, 276
Drummer Editor, 269, 271
Drummer Presets, 269, 274
Drummer Region, 145, 199, 242
Drummer Track, 107, 115
Editors Button, 57, 48
End-of-Project Marker, 86, 307
EQ Button, 127
Equalizer, 136
Fade Out, 306
Feedback Protection, 132
Feedback, 116
Fills, 277
Flex Markers, 263
Flex Time, 245-249
Follow Key, 257
Follow Rhythm, 277
Follow Tempo, 259
Fonts Button, 54, 85
Forward/Fast Forward Button, 82, 96
GarageBand Window, 51, 78
Global Tracks, 108, 298
Groove Track, 113
Help Tag, 201
iCloud, 68
Import, 148, 174

Input Device, 34, 106
Inspector, 16
Join Region, 204, 253
Key and Scale, 66, 186
Key Focus (Key Window), 15
Key Signature, 93. 235
Keyword Buttons, 196
Learn to Play, 317
Library Button, 53 ,83
Library, 53, 138
Lock, 115, 200
Logic Remote, 318
Loop Browser, 182
Loop Tool, 203
Loop Type, 186
Loudness, 308
Marquee, 254, 265
Master Button, 129, 304
Master Effects, 135
Master Track, 303
Master Volume, 90
Media Browser, 173
Merge (Join), 153, 155
Metronome, 88, 149, 152, 167
MIDI Controllers, 229, 231
MIDI Draw Area, 222,226
MIDI Indicator, 94
MIDI Interface, 29
MIDI Messages, 214
MIDI Region, 145, 208
MIDI Track (Software Instrument Track), 101
Monitoring Button, 106, 116
Mono-Stereo, 40
Movie Track, 181, 314
Multi-track Recording, 115, 151
Musical Time, 80
Musical Typing, 150
Mute Button, 114, 280
New Track Dialog, 55, 104
Noise Gate, 132, 165
Normalize, 308
Note Pad, 53, 85
Output Device, 35, 106
Overdub, 25
Package File, 19
Pan Control, 117, 280, 303
Patch, 139
Pedal Button, 283
Pedalboard, 137, 283
Performance Controls, 275
Piano Roll Inspector, 226
Piano Roll Menu Bar, 222
Piano Roll, 220
Pitch Correction, 256
Play Button, 95
Playhead, 81, 278
Plugins, 120, 134
Preview File, 178
Print Score, 238
Project File, 60, 70
Project Name, 61
Project Properties, 66, 93
Project, 60
Quantize Grid, 216
Quantize Strength, 234
Quantize, 215, 260

QuickHelp Button, 54
Record Button, 95, 153, 168
Record Enable, 115
Recording Level Slider, 131, 165
Regions, 145
Results List, 175, 197
Rewind/Fast Rewind Button, 82, 96
Ringtone, 311
Ruler, 74, 80, 223
Sample Rate, 159, 162
Score Editor, 232
Screen Controls, 126, 280
Scroll, 79
Scrubbing, 96
Search Field, 140, 175, 181
Share, 305
Signal Flow, 25,27
Smart Control Inspector, 130
Smart Controls Button, 83
Smart Controls, 119
Snap to Grid, 81, 201, 254
Solo Button, 117, 208
Solo Play, 250
SoundCloud, 312
Split Region, 204, 253
Stop Button, 96, 153
Swing, 277
Take Folder, 156, 170
Template, 64
Tempo Scale, 302
Tempo Track, 298
Tempo, 66, 82, 93, 108
Text Area, 85
Thumbnail, 316
Time Correction, 262
Time Signature, 66, 92
Track Automation, 118, 290
Track Header, 112
Track Icon, 113
Track Lane, 73
Track List, 74
Track Types, 100
Track, 99, 104
Tracks Area Menu Bar, 74
Tracks Area, 73
Transient Markers, 263
Transport Buttons, 95
Transpose, 234, 258
Transposition Track, 299
Tuner, 89
Velocity, 211, 217, 230
View Buttons, 82, 83
Visual Quantize Grid, 238
Volume Fader, 117
Volume Meter, 117
Waveform Display, 42, 240
Workspace, 74
X/Y Pad, 276
Zoom Slider, 81, 201, 222, 243, 255

CPSIA information can be obtained
at www.ICGtesting.com
Printed in the USA
LVHW07n1250160918
590312LV00011B/581/P